Something c

Men I Have Known

Adlai E. Stevenson

Alpha Editions

This edition published in 2023

ISBN : 9789357962117

Design and Setting By
Alpha Editions
www.alphaedis.com
Email - info@alphaedis.com

Contents

FOREWORD

To write in the spirit of candor of men he has known, and of great events in which he has himself borne no inconspicuous part, has been thought not an unworthy task for the closing years of more than one of the most eminent of our public men. It may be that the labor thus imposed has oftentimes enabled the once active participant in great affairs submissively "to entertain the lag end of his life with quiet hours."

Following the example of such at a great distance and along a humbler path, I have attempted to write something of events of which I have been a witness, and of some of the principal actors therein during the last third of a century.

My book in the main is something of men I have personally known; the occasional mention of statesmen of the past seems justified by matters at the time under discussion.

With the hope that it may not be wholly without interest to some into whose hands it may fall, I now submit this slight contribution to the political literature of these passing days.

A. E. S. BLOOMINGTON, ILLINOIS, *August 1, 1909.*

I ON THE CIRCUIT

DEVELOPMENT OF THE COUNTRY AFTER THE CIVIL
WAR—SLAVERY THE APPLE OF DISCORD BEFORE THE
WAR—LINCOLN AS A COUNTRY LAWYER—SOCIABILITY OF
THE LAWYERS OF THE PERIOD—THEIR EXCELLENCE AS
ORATORS—HENRY CLAY AS A PARTY LEADER—
EULOGIUMS ON LAWYERS—LINCOLN'S ADMIRATION FOR
GENERAL WINFIELD SCOTT—THE WRITER'S ADDRESS ON
THE LAW AND LAWYERS.

The period extending from my first election to Congress in 1874, to my retirement from the Vice-Presidency in 1897, was one of marvellous development to the country. Large enterprises were undertaken, and the sure foundation was laid for much of existing business conditions. The South had recovered from the sad effects of the Civil War, and had in a measure regained its former position in the world of trade, as well as in that pertaining to the affairs of the Government. The population of the country had almost doubled; the ratio of representation in the Lower House of Congress largely augmented; the entire electoral vote increased from 369 to 444. Eight new States had been admitted to the Union, thus increasing the number of Senators from seventy-four to ninety.

The years mentioned likewise witnessed the passing from the national stage, with few exceptions, of the men who had taken a conspicuous part in the great debates directly preceding and during the Civil War and the reconstruction period which immediately followed. By the arbitrament of war, and by constitutional amendment, old questions, for a half-century the prime cause of sectional strife, had been irrevocably settled, and passed to the domain of history. New men had come to the front, and new questions were to be discussed and determined.

To the student of history, the years immediately preceding the Civil War are of abiding interest. In some of its phases slavery was the all-absorbing subject of debate throughout the entire country. It had been the one recognized peril to the Union since the formation of the Government. Beginning with the debates in the convention that formulated the Federal Constitution, it remained for seventy years the apple of discord,—the subject of patriotic apprehension and repeated compromise. The last serious attempt to settle this question in the manner just indicated was by the adjustment known in our political history as "the compromise measures of 1850." These measures, although bitterly denounced in the South as well as in the North, received the sanction in national convention of both of the great parties that two years later presented candidates for the Presidency. It is no doubt true that a majority of the people, in both sections of the country, then believed that the question that had been so fraught with peril to national unity from the beginning was at length settled for all time. The rude awakening came two years later, when the country was aroused, as it had rarely been before, by impassioned debate in and out of Congress, over the repeal of the Missouri Compromise. It was a period of excitement such as we shall probably not see again. Slavery in all its phases was the one topic of earnest discussion, both upon the hustings and at the fireside. There was little talk now of compromise. The old-time statesmen of the Clay and Webster, Winthrop and Crittenden, school soon disappeared from the arena. Men hitherto comparatively unknown to the country at large were soon to the front.

Conspicuous among them was a country lawyer whose home was at Springfield, Illinois. With the mighty events soon to follow, his name is imperishably linked. But it is not of Lincoln the President, the emancipator, the martyr, we are now to speak. It is of Lincoln the country lawyer, as he stepped upon the arena of high debate, the unswerving antagonist of slavery extension half a century and more ago.

His home, during his entire professional life, was at the capital of the State. He was, at the time mentioned, in general practice as a lawyer and a regular attendant upon the neighboring courts. His early opportunities for education were meagre indeed. He had been a student of men, rather than of books. He was, in the most expressive sense, "of the people,"—the people as they then were. For,

"Know thou this, that men are as the time is."

His training was, in large measure, under the severe conditions to be briefly mentioned. The old-time custom of "riding the circuit" is to the present generation of lawyers only a tradition. The few who remember central Illinois as it was sixty years ago will readily recall the full meaning of the expression. The district in which Mr. Lincoln practised extended from the counties of Livingston and Woodford upon the north, almost to the Indiana line—embracing the present cities of Danville, Springfield, and Bloomington. The last named was the home of the Hon. David Davis, the presiding judge of the district. As is well known, he was the intimate friend of Mr. Lincoln, and the latter was often his guest during attendance upon the courts at Bloomington. At that early day, the term of court in few of the counties continued longer than a week, so that much of the time of the judge and the lawyers who travelled the circuit with him was spent upon horseback. When it is remembered that there were then no railroads, but few bridges, a sparse population, and that more than half the area embraced in that district was unbroken prairie, the real significance of riding the circuit will fully appear. It was of this period that the late Governor Ford, speaking of Judge Young,—whose district extended from Quincy, upon the Mississippi River to Chicago,—said: "He possesses in rare degree one of the highest requisites for a good circuit judge, —he is an excellent horseback rider."

At the period mentioned there were few law-books in the State. The monster libraries of later days had not yet arrived. The half-dozen volumes of State Reports, together with the Statutes and a few leading text-books, constituted the lawyer's library. To an Illinois lawyer upon the circuit, a pair of saddle-bags was an indispensable part of his outfit. With these, containing the few books mentioned and a change or two of linen, and supplied with the necessary horse, saddle and bridle, the lawyer of the pioneer days was duly equipped for the active duties of his calling. The lack of numerous volumes of adjudicated cases was, however, not an unmixed evil. Causes were necessarily argued upon principle. How well this conduced to the making of the real lawyer is well known. The admonition, "Beware the man who reads but one book," is of deep significance. The complaint to-day is not of scarcity, but that "of the making of many books there is no end." Professor Phelps is authority for the statement that "it is easy to find single opinions in which more authorities are cited than were mentioned by Marshall in the whole thirty years of his unexampled judicial life; and briefs that contain more cases than Webster referred to in all the arguments he ever delivered."

The lawyers of the times whereof we write were, almost without exception, politicians—in close touch with the people, easy of approach, and obliging to the last degree. Generally speaking, a lawyer's office was as open to the public as the Courthouse itself. That his surroundings were favorable to the cultivation of a high degree of sociability goes without saying. Story-telling helped often on the circuit to while away the long evenings at country taverns. At times, perchance,

"the night drave on wi' sangs and clatter."

Oratory counted for much more then than now. When an important case was on trial all other pursuits were for the time suspended, and the people for miles around were in prompt attendance. This was especially the case when it was known that one or more of the leading advocates were to speak. The litigation, too, was to a large extent different from that of to-day. The country was new, population sparse; the luxuries and many of the comforts of life yet in the future; post-offices, schools, and churches many miles away. In every cabin were to be found the powder-horn, bullet-pouch, and rifle. The restraints and amenities of modern society were in large measure unknown; and altogether much was to be, and was, "pardoned to the spirit of liberty." There were no great corporations to be chosen defendants, but much of the time of the courts was taken up by suits in ejectment, actions for assault and battery, breach of promise, and slander. One, not infrequent, was replevin, involving the ownership of hogs, when by unquestioned usage all stock was permitted to run at large. But criminal trials of all grades, and in all their details, aroused the deepest interest. To these the people came from all directions, as if summoned to a general muster. This was especially true if a murder case was upon trial. Excitement then ran high, and the arguments of counsel, from beginning to close, were listened to with breathless interest. It will readily be seen that such occasions furnished rare opportunity to the gifted advocate. In very truth the general acquaintance thus formed, and the popularity achieved, have marked the beginning of more than one successful and brilliant political career. Moreover, the thorough knowledge of the people thus acquired by actual contact—the knowledge of their condition, necessities, and wishes—resulted often in legislation of enduring benefit to the new country. The Homestead law, the law setting apart a moiety of the public domain for the maintenance of free schools, and judicious provision for the establishment of the various charities, will readily be recalled.

Politics, in the modern sense—too often merely "for what there is in it"—was unknown. As stepping-stones to local offices and even to Congress, the caucus and convention were yet to come. Aspirants to public place presented their claims directly to the people, and the personal popularity of the candidate was an important factor in achieving success. Bribery at elections was rarely heard of. The saying of the great bard,

"If money go before,
All ways do open lie,"

awaited its verification in a later and more civilized period. As late even as 1858, when Lincoln and Douglas were rival aspirants to the Senate, when every voter in the State was a partisan of one or the other candidate, and the excitement was for many months intense, there was never, from either side, an intimation of the corrupt use of a farthing to influence the result.

No period of our history has witnessed more intense devotion to great party leaders than that of which we write. Of eminent statesmen, whose names were still invoked, none had filled larger space than did Henry Clay and Andrew Jackson. The former was the early political idol of Mr. Lincoln; the latter, of Mr. Douglas. Possibly, since the foundation of the Government, no statesman has been so completely idolized by his friends and party as was Henry Clay. Words are meaningless when the attempt is made to express the idolatry of the Whigs of his own State for their great chieftain. For a lifetime he knew no rival. His wish was law to his followers. In the realm of party leadership a greater than he hath not appeared. At his last defeat for the Presidency strong men wept bitter tears. When his star set, it was felt to be the signal for the dissolution of the great party of which he was the founder. In words worthy to be recalled, "when the tidings came like wailing over the State that Harry Percy's spur was cold, the chivalrous felt somehow the world had grown commonplace."

The following incident, along the line indicated, may be considered characteristic. While Mr. Clay was a Senator, a resolution, in accordance with a sometime custom, was introduced into the Kentucky House of Representatives instructing the Senators from that State to vote in favor of a certain bill then pending in Congress. The resolution was in the act of passing without opposition, when a hitherto silent member from one of the mountain counties, springing to his feet, exclaimed: "Mr. Speaker, am I to understand that this Legislature is undertaking *to tell* Henry Clay how to vote?" The Speaker answered that such was the purport of the resolution. At which the member from the mountains, throwing up his arms, exclaimed "Great God!" and sank into his seat. It is needless to add that the resolution was immediately rejected by unanimous vote.

Two-thirds of a century ago the Hon. John P. Kennedy wrote of the lawyers of his day:

"The feelings, habits, and associations of the bar in general, have a very happy influence upon the character. And, take it altogether, there may be collected from it a greater mass of shrewd, observant, droll, playful, and generous spirits, than from any other equal numbers of society. They live in each other's presence like a set of players; congregate in courts like the former in the green room; and break their unpremeditated jests, in the intervals of business, with that sort of undress freedom that contrasts amusingly with the solemn and even tragic seriousness with which they appear in turn upon the boards. They have one face for the public, rife with the saws and learned gravity of the profession, and another for themselves, replete with broad mirth, sprightly wit, and gay thoughtlessness. The intense mental toil and fatigue of business give them a peculiar relish for the enjoyment of their hours of relaxation, and, in the same degree, incapacitate them for that frugal attention to their private concerns which their limited means usually require. They have, in consequence, a prevailing air of unthriftiness in personal matters, which, however it may operate to the prejudice of the pocket of the individual, has a mellow and kindly effect upon his disposition. In an old member of the profession, one who has grown gray in the service, there is a rich unction of originality that brings him out from the ranks of his fellowmen in strong relief. His habitual conversancy with the world in its strangest varieties and with the secret history of character, gives him a shrewd estimate of the human heart. He is quiet, and unapt to be struck with wonder at any of the actions of men. There is a deep current of observation running calmly through his thoughts, and seldom gushing out in words; the confidence which has been placed in him, in the thousand relations of his profession, renders him constitutionally cautious. His acquaintance with the vicissitudes of fortune, as they have been exemplified in the lives of individuals, and with the severe afflictions that have 'tried the reins' of many, known only to himself, makes him an indulgent and charitable apologist of the aberrations of others. He has an impregnable good humor that never falls below the level of thoughtfulness into melancholy."

A distinguished writer, two generations ago, said of the early Western bar:

"Not only was it a body distinguished for dignity and tolerance, but chivalrous courage was a marked characteristic. Personal cowardice was odious among the bar, as among the hunters who had fought the British and the Indians. Hence, insulting language, and the use of billingsgate, were too hazardous to be indulged where a personal accounting was a strong possibility. Not only did common prudence dictate courtesy among the members of the bar, but an exalted spirit of honor and well-bred politeness prevailed. The word of a counsel to his adversary was his inviolable bond. The suggestion of a lawyer as to the existence of a fact was accepted as verity by the court. To insinuate unprofessional conduct was to impute infamy."

I distinctly recall the first time I saw Mr. Lincoln. In September, 1852, two lawyers from Springfield, somewhat travel-stained with their sixty miles' journey, alighted from the stage-coach in front of the old tavern in Bloomington. The taller and younger of the two was Abraham Lincoln; the other, his personal friend and former preceptor, John T. Stuart. That evening it was my good fortune to hear Mr. Lincoln address a political meeting at the old Courthouse in advocacy of the election of General Winfield Scott to the Presidency. The speech was one of great ability, and but little that was favorable of the military record of General Pierce remained when the speech was concluded. The Mexican War was then of recent occurrence, its startling events fresh in the memory of all, and its heroes still the heroes of the hour. The more than half-century that has passed has not wholly dispelled my recollection of Mr. Lincoln's eloquent tribute to "the hero of Lundy's Lane," and his humorous description of the military career of General Franklin Pierce.

The incident now to be related occurred at the old National Hotel in Bloomington in September, 1854. Senator Douglas had been advertised to speak, and a large audience was in attendance. It was his first appearance there since the passage of the Kansas-Nebraska Bill. The writer, then a student at the Wesleyan University, with his classmate James S. Ewing and many others, had called upon Mr. Douglas at his hotel. While there the Hon. Jesse W. Fell, a prominent citizen of Bloomington and the close friend of Mr. Lincoln, also called upon Mr. Douglas, and after some conversation with him said in substance, that inasmuch as there was profound interest felt in the great question then pending, and the people were anxious to hear both sides, he thought it would be well to have a joint discussion between Judge Douglas and Mr. Lincoln. To which proposition Mr. Douglas at once demanded, "What party does Mr. Lincoln represent?" The answer of Mr. Fell was, "the Whig party, of course." Declining the proposition with much feeling Mr. Douglas said, "When I came home from Washington I was assailed in the northern part of the State by an old line abolitionist, in the central part of the State by a Whig, and in Southern Illinois by an anti-Nebraska Democrat. I cannot hold the Whig responsible for what the abolitionist says, nor the anti-Nebraska Democrat responsible for what either of the others say, and it looks like dogging a man all over the State." There was no further allusion to the subject, and Mr. Lincoln soon after called. The greeting between Judge Douglas and himself was most cordial, and their conversation, principally of incidents of their early lives, of the most agreeable and friendly character. Judge Lawrence Weldon, just then at the beginning of an honorable career, was present at the above interview, and has in a sketch of Mr. Lincoln given its incidents more in detail.

Courts of justice, and the law as a distinctive calling, are the necessary outgrowths of civilization. In his rude state, man avenged his wrongs with his own strong arm, and the dogma, "Might makes right," passed unchallenged. But as communities assumed organic form, tribunals were instituted for the administration of justice and the maintenance of public order. The progress of society, from a condition of semi-barbarism and ignorance to a state of the highest culture and refinement, may be traced by its advancement in the modes of administering justice, and in the character and learning of its tribunals. The advance steps taken from time to time in the history of jurisprudence are the milestones which stand out on the highway of civilization. All along the pathway of human progress, the courts of justice have been the sure criteria by which to judge of the intelligence and virtue of our race.

Truly it has been said: "With the coming of the lawyer came a new power in the world. The steel-clad baron and his retainers were awed by terms they had never before heard and did not understand, such as precedent, principle, and the like. The great and real pacifier of the world was the lawyer. His parchment took the place of the battle-field. The flow of his ink checked the flow of blood. His quill usurped the place of the sword. His legalism dethroned barbarism. His victories were victories of peace. He impressed on individuals and on communities that which he is now endeavoring to impress on nations, that there are many controversies that it were better to lose by arbitration than to win by war and bloodshed."

It is all-important, never more so than now, that the people should magnify the law. Whatever lessens respect for its authority bodes evil and only evil to the State. No occasion could arise more appropriate than this in which to utter solemn words of warning against an evil of greater menace to the public weal than aught to be apprehended from foreign foe. In many localities a spirit of lawlessness has asserted itself in its most hideous form. The rule of the mob has at times usurped that of the law. Outrages have been perpetrated in the name of summary justice, appalling to all thoughtful men. It need hardly be said that all this is in total disregard of individual rights, and utterly subversive of all lawful authority.

By the solemn adjudication of courts, and under the safeguards of law, the fact of guilt is to be established, and the guilty punished. The spirit of the mob is in deadly antagonism to all constituted authority. Unless curbed it will sap the foundation of civilized society. Lynching a human creature is no less murder when the act of a mob than when that of a single individual. There is no safety to society but in an aroused public sentiment that will hold each participant amenable to the law for the consequences of the crime he either perpetrates or abets. This is the land of liberty, "of the largest liberty," but let it never be forgotten that it is liberty regulated by law. Let him be accounted a public enemy who would weaken the bonds of human society, and destroy what it has cost our race the sacrifice and toil of centuries to achieve.

The sure rock of defence in the outstretched years as in the long past, will be the intelligence, the patriotism, the virtue of a law-abiding, liberty-loving people. To a degree that cannot be measured by words, the temple of justice will prove the city of refuge. "The judiciary has no guards, no palaces, no treasuries; no arms but truth and wisdom; and no splendor but justice."

II IN THE HOUSE OF REPRESENTATIVES

NOTABLE MEMBERS OF THE FORTY-FOURTH
CONGRESS—TRIAL OF GENERAL BELKNAP—THE
PRESIDENTIAL CONTEST BETWEEN HAYES AND
TILDEN—CREATION OF THE ELECTORAL COMMISSION—
THE WRITER'S SPEECH ON THAT OCCASION—
PROMINENT MEMBERS OF THE HOUSE DURING THIS
CONGRESS—ANECDOTES OF MR. BLAINE—OTHER
MEMBERS—ANECDOTES OF MR. HOAR—ELECTION OF
THE "BLIND PREACHER"—MR. LAMAR'S ERROR AT
TABLE—"BLUE JEANS WILLIAMS"—RETIREMENT OF DR.
BUTLER FROM THE CHAPLAINCY—MR. BLACKBURN'S
SPEECH AT AN EXECUTION—MR. COX'S READY WIT—
PROCTOR KNOTT'S ABILITY AS A LAWYER—HIS SPEECH
ON DULUTH—HIS REPLY TO HIS COMPETITOR FOR THE
GOVERNORSHIP.

The forty-fourth Congress—the first of which I was a member—
assembled December 6, 1875. Among its members were many gentlemen
of distinction, some of whom had known active service in the field.
Political disabilities had been in large measure removed, and the South was
now, for the first time since the war, represented in Congress by its old-
time statesmen. Of this number may be mentioned Mr. Stephens of
Georgia, Mr. Lamar of Mississippi, and Mr. Reagan of Texas. From the
membership of this House were afterwards chosen twenty-six Senators, ten
members of the Cabinet, one Justice of the Supreme Court, and from this
and the House immediately succeeding, three Vice-Presidents and two
Presidents of the United States. The proceedings of this Congress marked
an important epoch in our history. During its first session occurred the
masterful debate upon the General Amnesty Bill. The very depths of
partisan feeling were stirred, and for many days it was indeed a titanic
struggle. The speeches attracting the greatest attention were those of Blaine
and Garfield upon the one side, and Hill of Georgia and Lamar upon the
other. This great debate recalled vividly that of Webster and Hayne, in the
other wing of the Capitol, almost half a century before.

This session also witnessed the impeachment of a Cabinet officer, General
Belknap, Secretary of War. The trial occurred before the Senate, sitting as a
court of impeachment during the closing weeks of the session, and resulted
in his acquittal, less than two-thirds of the Senators voting for conviction.
General Belknap was represented by an able array of counsel, chief of

whom were Judge Black of Pennsylvania and the Hon. Matthew H. Carpenter of Wisconsin. Mr. Knott of Kentucky, Mr. Hoar of Massachusetts, and Mr. Lord of New York, conducted the prosecution in the main as managers on the part of the House of Representatives. The principal contention on the part of the counsel for the accused was that there could be no conviction, inasmuch as Belknap had resigned his office before the article of impeachment had been preferred. This view seems to have been decisive of the final vote of many Senators, and the accused stood acquitted at the bar of the Senate.

When the second session of this Congress convened, in December, 1876, the excitement throughout the country was intense over the pending Presidential contest between Hayes and Tilden. As will be remembered, the electoral vote of two States, Louisiana and Florida, was claimed by each of the candidates. These votes were decisive of the result. As the days passed and the time approached for the joint session of the Senate and the House, for the purpose of counting the electoral votes and declaring the result, the tension became greater, and partisan feeling more intense. The friends of Hayes were in the majority in the Senate; those of Tilden, in the House. With conflicting certificates, both purporting to give the correct vote from each of the States named, and no lawful authority existing to determine as to their validity, it can readily be seen that the situation was one to arouse the grave apprehension of all thoughtful men. The condition was without a precedent in our history. Twice had there been a failure to elect a President by the people, and by constitutional provision the election in each instance devolved upon the House. In the first-mentioned case, in 1801, Mr. Jefferson was chosen; and in the latter, in 1825, Mr. John Quincy Adams. In neither of the cases just mentioned had there been a question as to *how* any State had voted. It was simply that no person had received a majority of all of the electoral votes cast. The method of settlement was clearly pointed out by the Constitution. As already indicated, the case was wholly different in the Hayes-Tilden controversy. The question then was as to *how* certain States had voted. It was for the purpose of ascertaining this fact and certifying the same to the joint session of the Senate and House, that the Electoral Commission was constituted. The bill having this end in view originated in the House in January, 1877; the Commission was constituted, and the controverted questions were soon thereafter determined.

The Electoral Commission was an imperative necessity. As such it was created,—consisting of five members each from the Senate, the House of Representatives, and the Supreme Court. Its decisions were adverse to Mr. Tilden from the beginning, and resulted in the finding that all disputed votes should be counted for his opponent. This, it will be remembered, gave Hayes a majority of one on the final count, and resulted in his induction into office. Partisan feeling was at its height, and the question of the justice of the decision of the Electoral Commission was vehemently discussed.

To the end that there might be a peaceful determination of the perilous question, that of disputed succession to the Presidency, I was an earnest advocate of the bill creating the Commission. Upon the question of concurrence by the House of Representatives in the final determination of the Commission, bitter opposition was manifested upon the part of friends of Mr. Tilden, and a heated partisan debate resulted, and during this debate I spoke as follows:

"When this Congress assembled in December, it witnessed the American people from one end of the country to the other divided upon the question as to which candidate had been lawfully elected to the high office of President of the United States. The business industries of the country were paralyzed, public confidence destroyed, and the danger of civil war was imminent. That Mr. Tilden had received a majority of more than two hundred thousand of the popular vote was not disputed. That he had secured a majority of the Presidential electors in the several States, and was lawfully entitled to be inducted into the great office, was the firm belief of fully one-half of the people of this country. The hour was one of great peril to our institutions, and many were apprehensive that we were but entering into the dark night of anarchy and confusion. After many weeks of angry discussion, which resulted in still further arousing the passions of the people, a measure of adjustment was proposed. It was believed that there was still patriotism enough left in the American Congress to secure an honorable and fair settlement of this most dangerous question. We all recall how our hopes revived, and how gladly we hailed the introduction of the bill recommended by a joint committee of conference of the Senate and House of Representatives. It was welcomed as the harbinger of peace by the entire people of our country.

"I gave that bill my earnest support. It had in the House no friend more ardent in its advocacy than myself. I believed it to be a measure in the interest of peace. I believed that those who framed it, as well as those who gave it their support upon the floor, were honest in their statements, that no man could afford to take the Presidency with a clouded title, and that the object of the bill was to ascertain which of the candidates was lawfully entitled to the electoral votes of Florida and Louisiana. I never mistrusted for a moment that statesmen of high repute could in so perilous an hour, upon so grave a question, palter with words in a double sense.

"We who are the actors in this drama know, and history will record the fact, that the Conference Bill became a law, and the Electoral Commission was organized, not for the purpose of ascertaining which candidate had *prima facie* a majority of the electoral votes; not for the purpose of ascertaining that the Governor of Florida, and the *de facto* Governor of Louisiana, had given certificates to the Hayes electors. It was never dreamed that a tribunal, consisting in part of five judges of the highest court on earth, was to be constituted, whose sole duty was to report a fact known to every man in the land, that the returning-board of Louisiana had given the votes of that State to the Hayes electors. The avowed object of that bill was to ascertain which candidate had received a majority of the legal votes of those States. The avowed object of the bill was the secure the ends of justice; to see that the will of the people was executed; that the Republic suffered no harm; to see that the title to this great office was not tainted with fraud. How well the members of this tribunal have discharged the sacred trust committed to them, let them answer to history.

"The record will stand that this tribunal shut its eyes to the light of truth; refused to hear the undisputed proof that a majority of seven thousand legal votes in the State of Louisiana for Tilden was by a fraudulent returning-board changed to eight thousand majority for Hayes. The Republican Representative from Florida, Mr. Purman, has solemnly declared upon this floor that Florida had given its vote to Tilden. I am not surprised that two distinguished Republican Representatives from Massachusetts, Mr. Seelye and Mr. Pierce, have in such thrilling tones expressed their dissent from the judgment of this tribunal. By this decision fraud has become one of the legalized modes of securing the vote of a State. Can it be possible that the American people are prepared to accept the doctrine that fraud, which vitiates all contracts and agreements, which taints the judgments and decrees of courts, which will even annul the solemn covenant of marriage—fraud, which poisons wherever it enters — can be inquired into in all the relations of human life save only where a returning-board is its instrument, and the dearest rights of a sovereign people are at stake?

"But we are told that we created this tribunal and must abide by its arbitrament. I propose to do so in good faith. I have, from the beginning, opposed every movement that looked only to delay. I have voted against all dilatory motions. But the decision of this tribunal is too startling and too far-reaching in its consequences to pass unchallenged. That the returning-board of Louisiana will find no imitators in our future history is more than I dare hope. The pernicious doctrine that fraud and perjury are to be recognized auxiliaries in popular elections is one that may return to plague its inventors. The worst effect of this decision will be its lesson to the young men of our country. Hereafter old-fashioned honesty is at a discount, and villainy and fraud the legalized instruments of success. The fact may be conceded, the proof overwhelming, that the honest voice of a State has been overthrown by outrage and fraud, and yet the chosen tribunal of the people has entered of solemn record that there is no remedy.

'O Judgment, thou art fled to brutish beasts!'

"My criticism of the decision of this tribunal rests upon its finding in the cases of Louisiana and Florida; upon the Oregon case I have no criticism to offer. It is true that but two votes of that State could have been given to Hayes had the decision first adopted by the Commission been followed in the case of Oregon. However inconsistent it may be with other rulings of the Commission, standing alone it is in the main correct. The sanctity of seal of State and certificate of Governor applied only to Louisiana and Florida; the Governor of Oregon was not of the household of the faithful.

"The people of Oregon cast a majority of their votes for Hayes, and no vote or act of mine shall stand in the way of its being so recorded. Such have been my convictions from the beginning, and the great wrong done in Louisiana and Florida cannot warp my convictions at this hour.

"We have now reached the final act in this great drama, and the record here made will pass into history. Time, the great healer, will bring a balm to those who feel sick at heart because of this grievous wrong. But who can estimate, what seer can foretell, the evils that may result to us and our children from this judgment? Fortunate, indeed, will it be for this country if our people lose not faith in popular institutions; fortunate, indeed, if they abate not their confidence in the integrity of that high tribunal, for a century the bulwark of our liberties. In all times of popular commotion and peril, the Supreme Court of the United States has been looked to as the final arbiter, its decrees heeded as the voice of God. How disastrous may be the result of decisions so manifestly partisan, I will not attempt to forecast.

"Let this vote be now taken and the curtain fall upon these scenes forever. To those who believe, as I do, that a grievous wrong has been suffered, let me entreat that this arbitrament be abided in good faith, that no hindrance or delay be interposed to the execution of the law, but that by faithful adherence to its mandates, by honest efforts to revive the prostrate industries of the country, by obedience to the constituted authorities, we will show ourselves patriots rather than partisans in the hour of our country's misfortune."

Some mention will now be made of prominent members of the House during this Congress. The Hon. Michael C. Kerr of Indiana was elected Speaker of the House. The vote of the Republican minority was given to the Hon. James G. Blaine, who had been Speaker during the three Congresses immediately preceding. Mr. Kerr was a gentleman of high character and recognized ability. He had been for many years a member of the House, and was familiar with the details of its business. He was in failing health at the time of his election, and died before the close of the first session of that Congress. He was physically unable to preside during the greater part of the session, and was frequently relieved from the onerous duties of the Chair by two new members who were yet to achieve distinction in that body, Mr. Blackburn of Kentucky and Mr. Springer of Illinois.

Mr. Blaine, the leader of the minority, had been for twelve years a member of the House, having been first elected at the age of thirty-three. He was a brilliant debater, well versed in parliamentary law, and at all points fully equipped for the conflict. With the exception of Henry Clay, the House of Representatives has probably never known his equal as a party leader. That he possessed a touch of humor will appear from the following. While the discussion was at its height upon his amendment excluding Jefferson Davis from the benefit of the General Amnesty Bill, Mr. Blaine, looking across to the opposite side of the Chamber, said: "I confess to a feeling of commiseration for some gentlemen upon the other side, who represent close districts. Surrounded by their Southern associates here, and with intense Union constituencies at home, their apprehension, as they are called to vote upon this amendment, is indeed deplorable. It remind me of a Hibernian procession I once saw moving down Broadway, where the serious question was how to keep step to the music, and at the same time to dodge the omnibuses!"

My seat was just across the aisle from that of Mr. Blaine. When introduced, I handed him letters of introduction from two of his college classmates, the Hon. Robert E. Williams and the Rev. John Y. Calhoun. After reading the letters and speaking most kindly of his old Washington College classmates, he brusquely inquired, "What are John Y. Calhoun's politics?"

I answered, "He is a Democrat."

Blaine instantly replied, "Well, how strangely things do come around in this world! When we were in college together, Calhoun was the strongest kind of Presbyterian."

I intimated that his sometime classmate was still of that eminently respectable persuasion. The reply was, in manner indicating apparent surprise, "Is it possible that out in your country a man can be a Presbyterian and a Democrat at the same time?"

I was a member of the Board of Visitors to West Point in June, 1877. Mr. Blaine and Bishop Quintard of Tennessee were also members. General Hancock was with our Board for some days at the little West Point Inn, and delivered the address to the graduating class of cadets. He was then in excellent health, and as superb in appearance as he had been courageous in battle. I have never heard more brilliant conversation than that at our table, in which the chief participants were Gail Hamilton, Bishop Quintard, General Hancock, Senator Maxey, and Mr. Blaine. The last named, "upon the plain highway of talk," was unrivalled.

While the Board was in session, Mr. Blaine and I spent some hours with the Hon. Hamilton Fish, late Secretary of State, at his country home near West Point. Near by was still standing the historic Beverly Robinson House, the home of Benedict Arnold when he was in command of the Colonial forces at West Point. As we passed through the quaint old mansion, Mr. Blaine, whose knowledge of our Revolutionary history was all-embracing, described graphically the conditions existing at the time of Arnold's treason, and just where each person sat at the breakfast table in the old dining-room in which we were then standing, on the fateful morning when the courier from the British camp hurriedly announced to General Arnold the capture of Major Andre.

Mr. Blaine and I were once passing along Pennsylvania Avenue, a third of a century ago, when he remarked that the old building just to our right had once been a high-toned gambling house; that there were traditions to the effect that some well-known statesmen were not wholly unadvised as to its exact location and uses. He then told me that during his first term in Congress he was early one morning passing this building on his way to the Capitol. Just as he reached the spot where we were then standing, the Hon. Thaddeus Stevens came down the steps of the building mentioned, and, immediately after his cordial greeting to Mr. Blaine, was accosted by a negro preacher, who earnestly requested a contribution toward the building of a church for his people. Promptly taking a roll from his vest pocket, Mr. Stevens handed the negro a fifty-dollar bill, and turning to Blaine solemnly observed,

"God moves in a mysterious way
His wonders to perform!"

At the time first mentioned, Mr. Blaine was in excellent health, buoyant in spirits, aggressive to the last degree, and full of hope as to the future. The disappointments and bereavements that saddened the closing years of his life had as yet cast no shadow upon his pathway.

Next in leadership to Mr. Blaine, upon the Republican side, was the Hon. James A. Garfield. He possessed few of the qualities of brilliant leadership so eminently characteristic of Blaine, but was withal one of the ablest men I have ever known. Gifted with rare powers of oratory, with an apparently inexhaustible reservoir of information at his command, he knew no superior in debate. At one period of his life he was the recipient of public honors without a parallel in our history. While yet a Representative in Congress, he was a Senator-elect from Ohio, and the President-elect of the United States. For once, it indeed seemed that "fortune had come with both hands full." In the words of the Persian poet, "he had obtained an ear of corn from every harvest." And yet, a few months later, in the words of his great eulogist, "the stately mansion of power had become to him the wearisome hospital of pain, and he begged to be taken from its prison walls, from its oppressive, stifling air, from its homelessness and its hopelessness."

My personal acquaintance with Mr. Garfield began early in January, 1876, when we were members of the House Committee appointed by the Speaker to convey the remains of a deceased member to his late home, Norwich, Connecticut, for burial. Another member of the Committee was Representative Wheeler of New York. It was late Saturday afternoon when we were conveyed by carriages from the crossing at Jersey City to the depot where the Norwich train was in waiting. Our route lay for some distance along Broadway, through the very heart of the great metropolis. As we passed the hurrying throngs that crowded the great thoroughfare that sombre winter evening, Mr. Garfield remarked that it was a scene similar to the one we were then witnessing that suggested to Mr. Bryant one of the most stirring of his shorter poems.

At our request and in tones that linger even yet in my memory, he then repeated these lines:

"Let me move slowly through the street
Filled with an ever shifting train,
Amid the sound of steps that beat
The murmuring walks like autumn rain.

How fast the flitting figures come,
The mild, the fierce, the stony face;
Some bright with thoughtless smiles, and some
Where secret tears have left their trace!

They pass to toil, to strife, to rest,
To halls in which the feast is spread,
To chambers where the funeral guest
In silence sits beside the dead.

Each where his tasks or pleasures call
They pass, and heed each other not.
There is Who heeds, Who holds them all
In His large love, and boundless thought.

These struggling tides of life that seem
In wayward, aimless course to tend,
Are eddies of the mighty stream
That rolls to its appointed end."

Norwich, the home of the deceased member, Mr. Starkweather, and where he was laid to rest, is a beautiful city and one of much historic interest. It was here that Benedict Arnold was born, and the ruins of his early home were still to be seen. Of greater interest was a monument standing in an old Indian burying-ground near the centre of the city,—"Erected to the Memory of Uncas." It was within the memory of the oldest inhabitant that the President of the United States and his Cabinet were in attendance at the dedication of this monument, and deeply interested in the impressive ceremonies in honor of "the last of the Mohicans."

An exceedingly courteous gentleman upon the same side of the chamber was the Hon. Nathaniel P. Banks of Massachusetts. He had been a Major-general during the late war and was an ex-Governor of his State. He first achieved national distinction in the thirty-fourth Congress, when after a protracted and exciting struggle, he was elected Speaker of the House of Representatives. In the body over which he had so ably presided in ante-bellum days, he had again taken his seat. While by no means taking the highest rank as a debater, he was familiar with the complicated rules governing the House, and his opinion challenged the highest respect. He and Mr. Blaine were the only members of that House who had previously held the position of Speaker.

Near General Banks sat the Hon. William D. Kelley of Pennsylvania. He had known many years of legislative service, and was long "the father of the House." One of the features of its successive organization, as many old members will recall, was the administration of the official oath to the Speaker-elect by the member who had known the longest continuous service—"the gentleman from Pennsylvania." When in the fulness of times he passed to "the house not made with hands," his mantle fell upon Judge Holman of Indiana.

The House probably contained no member of rarer attainments in scholarship than Julius H. Seelye of Massachusetts. He stood in the front ranks of the great educators of his day, and was President of Amherst College during the latter years of his life. His political service was limited to one term in Congress. His speech near its beginning upon the General Amnesty Bill challenged the profound attention of the House, and at once gave him honored place in its membership.

The Congressional career of the Hon. George W. McCrary, of Iowa, terminated with this Congress. He was recognized as one of the ablest lawyers of the House, and was one of its most agreeable and courteous members. During the presidency of Hayes he held the position of Secretary of War, and was later a Judge of the United States Circuit Court.

The Hon. Joseph G. Cannon of Illinois, the present Speaker, was just at the beginning of his long Congressional career. For many years he has been an active leader of the House and a prominent participant in its important debates. His characteristic patience and long-suffering courtesy have no doubt at times been sorely tried by attempts to enlarge the sum total of appropriation bills reported by the Committee of which he was chairman. To the important post of "watch-dog of the Treasury," he was, *nem. con.*, the successor to the lamented Holman. In this connection a suggestive incident is recalled. One of the guides of the Capitol, when some years ago showing a visitor through the Vice-President's chamber, called attention to a little old-fashioned mirror upon its walls. The guide explained that this mirror was purchased at a cost of thirty dollars when John Adams was Vice-President, but when the bill for its payment was before the House, Mr. Holman objected. A Western member, who had just been defeated upon a proposed amendment to an appropriation bill, by reason of a fatal point of order raised by the chairman, promptly exclaimed, "I move to strike out Holman and insert Cannon."

The sagacity and untiring industry of Mr. Cannon have elevated him to the Speakership, and possibly yet higher honors await him. It is a significant fact in this connection, however, that notwithstanding the brilliant array of ambitious statesmen who have held the Speakership for more than a century, only one, Mr. Polk, has ever reached the Presidency.

The forty-fourth Congress was the last of which the Hon. William A. Wheeler of New York was a member. He was elected Vice-president in 1876, and the duties of that office have rarely been discharged by an abler or more courteous officer. He was highly esteemed by his associates during his long service in the House. His principle in action seemed ever to be, "there is nothing so kingly as kindness."

Messrs. Hale and Frye of Maine, Aldrich of Rhode Island, Money of Mississippi, Taylor of Tennessee, and Elkins of West Virginia, were members of this House; all of whom are now Senators of marked ability, and well known to the entire country.

A member of this House, who at a later date, and in the other wing of the Capitol, achieved yet greater distinction, was the Hon. George F. Hoar of Massachusetts. At the close of this Congress he was transferred to the Senate, where for more than a quarter of a century he was a prominent leader. His ability and attainments were of the highest, and he was the worthy successor of Webster in the great body of which he was so long an honored member.

In addition to more solid qualities, Mr. Hoar was gifted with a keen sense of humor, as will appear from one or two incidents to be mentioned. In the House, Mr. Springer, in order to prevent the reconsideration of resolutions and debate thereupon under the rules, had frequently cut off the possibility of such debate by the timely interposition of the words, "Not to be brought back on a motion to reconsider." Now, it so fell out that upon a certain day Mr. Springer received a telegram calling him home just as the roll-call was ordered upon an important bill. Earnestly desiring to vote— which owing to the early departure of his train was impossible if he waited until his name was regularly reached upon the roll —he moved to the front of the Speaker, and after brief explanation, asked unanimous consent to vote at once. Permission was of course granted, his name at once called, and his vote given. Grateful for the courtesy, he bowed repeatedly to each side of the Chamber, and, hurrying up the aisle, was about to take his exit, when Mr. Hoar, pointing his finger at the retreating figure, solemnly exclaimed, "Not to be *brought back* upon a motion to reconsider!"

At a much later day the Senate was "advising and consenting" over the appointment of a distinguished gentleman whose name had just been sent in for confirmation as Ambassador to an important European Court. The gentleman in question had voted for the then incumbent of the great office, but his former political affiliations had been wholly with the opposing party. The nomination was about being confirmed without objection when Mr. Hoar, arising with apparent reluctance, said:

"As this is in some measure a family affair, Mr. President, I hesitate to interfere. If our friends upon the opposite side of the Chamber are satisfied with this appointment, I certainly shall interpose no objection. The gentleman named is well qualified, and has more than once held high place at the hands of the party which he has but recently deserted, and to which he will no doubt return in due time. We have, however, in New England an old-time custom, as sacred as if part of the written law, that if a man is so unfortunate as to lose his companion he will not marry again within one year. Now sir, I have always thought this rule, as to time, might well be applied to the matter of office-seeking. Where a man has been repeatedly honored by his party as this appointee has been, but where, prompted by motives purely unselfish no doubt, he has gone over to the camp of the enemy, I think a due sense of modestly should impel him *to serve in the ranks at least one year* before being an applicant for high office at the hands of his newly found friends."

Coming over to the Democratic side of the Chamber, well to its front sat the Hon. William R. Morrison of Illinois. By virtue of his position as Chairman of the Committee on Ways and Means he was the traditional leader of the House. Possessing little of the brilliancy of the leader of the minority, Colonel Morrison was none the less one of the ablest and most useful members of that body. He had for many sessions been a member of the House, and had been a soldier in the Mexican and in the Civil War. His record was honorable, both as soldier and legislator. He was the author of the Tariff Bill which was fully debated during the first session of that Congress, and was in some measure a determining factor in the Presidential campaign that soon followed. At a later day, Colonel Morrison was a prominent candidate for nomination as President by the national convention of his party. His personal friendships and antagonisms were well known. It is related of him that during a serious illness, apprehending that the dread messenger was in near waiting, arousing himself to what appeared to be a last effort, he said in scarcely audible tones to a sorrowing colleague at his bedside: "I suppose when this is all over they will have something to say about me, as is the custom, in the House. Well, if Springer, and Cox, and Knott, and Stevenson want to talk, let them go ahead, but if old Spears tries to speak *just cough him down.*"

Never in any political gathering has there been a more effective speech, of a single sentence, than that in which Colonel Morrison presented to the Democratic caucus of the House members the name of the "Blind Preacher" for Chaplain. Three or four candidates were already in nomination when Morrison arose and said: "Mr. Chairman, I present for the office of Chaplain of the House the name of Doctor Milburn, a man who loves God, pays his debts, and votes the Democratic ticket!" Before the applause that followed had entirely died away the names of his competitors were withdrawn, and the "Blind Preacher" was nominated by acclamation.

The Hon. William M. Springer, of the same State, had just entered upon his twenty years of continuous service in the House. He came promptly to the front as a ready debater and skilful parliamentarian. He was thoroughly educated, ambitious, and withal an excellent speaker, and was the possessor in full measure of the *suaviter in modo*. His personal popularity was great, and a more obliging, agreeable, and pleasing associate it would have been difficult to find. He was optimistic to the last degree. To him every cloud had a silver lining,—the lining generally concealing the cloud. It was said of him by one of his colleagues that when the election returns were coming in, showing overwhelming defeat to his party,— even before they were fully summed up,—Mr. Springer with beaming countenance would promptly demonstrate by figures of his own how we were sure to be victorious four years later.

The Hon. Carter H. Harrison was a prominent member of the Illinois delegation. He soon took high rank as an orator, and never failed to command the attention of the House. Few speeches delivered during that session of Congress were so generally published, or more extensively quoted than were those of Mr. Harrison. At the end of four years' service in Congress he was elected Mayor of Chicago, an office he filled most acceptably for many years. His tragic death, upon the concluding day of the great Exposition, was universally deplored throughout the entire country.

The Hon. John H. Reagan, of Texas, was a Representative in Congress before the war. At its beginning he resigned his seat in the House, and cast in his fortunes with the South. He was early selected a member of the Davis Cabinet, and continued to discharge the duties of Postmaster-General until the fall of the Confederacy. He was a citizen of Texas while it was yet a Republic, and took an active part in securing its admission to the Federal Union. Judge Reagan was a gentleman of recognized ability, and of exceedingly courteous and dignified bearing.

An old-time statesman, on the same side of the Chamber, was the Hon. Fernando Wood of New York. A generation had passed since he first entered Congress. He was a Representative in the old hall of the Capitol while Webster, Calhoun, and Clay were in their prime. Erect, stately, faultless in his attire, and of bearing almost chivalric, Mr. Wood was long one of the active and picturesque personages of the House. At the time whereof we write, his sands were almost run, but, courageous to the last, he was in his accustomed seat but a little time before the final summons came, and he died, as was his wish, with the harness on. All in all, we shall hardly see his like again.

Surrounded by his colleagues near the centre of the hall sat one of the most remarkable men of his day, philosopher, jurist, statesman, orator, Lucius Q. C. Lamar of Mississippi. In his early manhood he was a member of the House, and even then was recognized as one of the most brilliant of the many brilliant men his section had sent to the national councils. During the war his services in field and council were given to the South, and something less than a decade after the return of peace, Mr. Lamar, still in his prime, again took his seat in the hall where his first laurels had been won. His great speech—one that touched all hearts—was not long delayed; the occasion was the day set apart in the House for tributes to the memory of the lamented Sumner. Many eulogies were delivered; that of Lamar still lingers in the memory of all who heard it. "The theme was worthy the orator; the orator, the theme." As a splendid tribute to a great tribune, as a plea for peace,—abiding, eternal, between all sections of a restored union,—it stands unsurpassed among the great masterpieces of ancient or modern eloquence.

Later, Mr. Lamar was a prominent participant in one of the fiercest debates the Senate has ever known. A leading Senator upon the opposite side of the chamber, in advocating the passage of the "Force bill," reflected bitterly upon Mississippi and her Senators. In replying to the personal portion of the speech, Lamar said, "the Senator has uttered upon this floor a falsehood—knowing it to be such. The language I have used, Mr. President, is severe. It was so intended. It is language, sir, that no honest man would deserve, *and that no brave man will wear!*"

Mr. Lamar was one of the most absent-minded of men. A number of years ago, by invitation of the Faculty, he delivered an address to the graduating class of Centre College, Kentucky. The day was quite warm, the exercises somewhat protracted, and, at the close of his able and eloquent address, he was very much exhausted.

An excellent collation, prepared by the ladies connected with the College, was served in the chapel near by, at the close of the exercises. Seated upon the platform, with Mr. Lamar at the head of the table, were Doctor Young, the President, Justice Harlan, Governor Knott, the Rev. Doctor Bullock, Chaplain of the Senate, Judge McCormick, and others.

At the plate of each guest a large tomato was in readiness and, excellent itself, was, moreover, the earnest of better things to come. Immediately upon being seated, Mr. Lamar "fell to" and, wholly oblivious of the surroundings, soon made way with the one viand then in visible presence. Just as its last vestige disappeared, the President of the College arose and, with a solemnity eminently befitting the occasion, called upon Doctor Bullock to offer thanks. Deeply chagrined, Mr. Lamar was an attentive listener to the impressive invocation which immediately followed. At its conclusion, with troubled countenance, he turned to Knott and said, "I am humiliated at my conduct. I should have remembered that Presbyterians always say grace before meals, but I was very hungry and exhausted, and the tomato very tempting; I have really disgraced myself." To which Knott replied, "You ought not to feel so, Mr. Justice; the blessing of Doctor Bullock's was broad and general; in large measure retrospective as well as prospective. It reminds me of a little incident that occurred on the 'Rolling Fork.' An old-time deacon down there was noted for the lengthy blessing which at his table was the unfailing prelude to every meal. His hired man, Bill Taylor, an unconverted and impatient youth, had fallen into the evil habit of commencing his meal before the blessing thereon had been fully invoked. The frown and rebuke of the good deacon were alike unavailing in effecting the desired reform. Righteously indignant thereat, the deacon, in a spirit possibly not the most devout, at length gave utterance to this petition, 'For what we are *about to* receive, and for what William Taylor *has already* received, accept our thanks, O Lord!"

In cheery tones the great orator at once replied, "Knott, you are the only man on earth who could have thought of such a story just at the opportune moment." The temporary depression vanished; Lamar was himself again, and was at once the brilliant conversationalist of the delighted assemblage.

The surviving members of that Congress will recall a little chair that daily rolled down the aisle to the front to the Speaker's desk. It contained the emaciated form of a man whose weight at his best was but ninety pounds— Alexander H. Stephens of Georgia, "whose little body lodged a mighty mind." No one who saw Mr. Stephens could ever forget him. He looked as though he had just stepped out from an old picture, or dropped down from the long-ago. There was probably as little about him "of the earth, earthy" as of any mortal this world has known. Upon his weak frame time had done its work, and, true it is, "the surest poison is time." And yet, his feeble piping voice—now scarcely heard an arm's length away—was potent in the contentions of the great hall when he was the honored associate of men whose public service reached back to the formation of the Government. In the old hall near by—now the Valhalla of the nation—he had sat with John Quincy Adams and contemporaries whose names at once recall the Revolutionary period. After serving as Vice-President of the Confederacy, whose rise and fall he had witnessed, Mr. Stephens, with the shadows falling about him, was, by unanimous voice of his people, again, in his own words, "in our father's house." His apartments in the old National Hotel, as he never failed to explain to his visitors, were those long ago occupied by his political idol, Henry Clay. His couch stood in the exact spot where Mr. Clay had died; and he no doubt thought—possibly wished— that his own end might come just where that great Commoner had breathed his last. This, however, was not to be. His last hours were spent at the capital of his native commonwealth, which had, with scarce a dissenting voice, just honored itself by electing him to its chief executive office.

The Hon. Samuel J. Randall, of Pennsylvania, was the successor of the lamented Kerr as Speaker of the House. As such he presided during the last session of the forty-fourth Congress, and during the two Congresses immediately succeeding. He had long been a member, coming in with Blaine and Garfield just before the close of the war. Able, courageous, and thoroughly skilled in parliamentary tactics, he had achieved a national reputation as the leader of the minority in the forty-third Congress. During the protracted and exciting struggle near its close, over the Force Bill—the House remaining in continuous session for fifty-six hours—Mr. Randall had displayed wonderful endurance and marvellous capacity for successful leadership. He was more than once presented by his State in Democratic national conventions for nomination to the Presidency. He was an excellent presiding officer, prompt, often aggressive, and was rarely vanquished in his many brilliant passages with the leaders of the minority. One incident is recalled, however, when the tables were turned against the Speaker, no one joining more heartily than himself in the laugh that followed. Mr. Conger, of Michigan, with great earnestness and persistency, was urging the consideration of a resolution which the Speaker had repeatedly declared out of order. By no means disconcerted by the decision, Mr. Conger, walking down the aisle, was vehement in his demand for the immediate consideration of his resolution. At which the Speaker with much indignation said, "Well, I think the Chair has a right to exercise a little common sense in this matter." To which Mr. Conger instantly responded, "Oh, if the Chair has the slightest intention of *doing anything of that kind*, I will immediately take my seat!"

The Hon. David Dudley Field, elected to fill a vacancy, was a Representative from the city of New York during the closing session of the forty-fourth Congress. He was an eminent lawyer, and, at the time, stood at the head of the American bar. His name is inseparably associated with many important reforms in legal procedure during the last half century. He had been instrumental in securing the appointment of a committee of distinguished jurists, chosen from the leading nations, to prepare the outlines of an international code. His report accompanying the plan, to the preparation of which he had given much thought and time, received the earnest commendation of leading publicists and jurists in Europe, as well as in his own country. His untiring efforts, looking to the substitution of international courts of arbitration for war, have given his name honored place among the world's benefactors.

Mr. Field was the eldest of four brothers, whose names are known wherever our language is spoken. The family was distinguished for talents of the highest order. It would indeed be difficult to find its counterpart in our history. One of the brothers, Stephen J. Field, was for a third of a century a distinguished justice of the Supreme Court of the United States. The youngest, Dr. Henry M. Field, was eminent alike as theologian and author. The name of the remaining brother, Cyrus W. Field, is, and will continue, a household word in two hemispheres. After repeated failures, to the verge even of extremity, "the trier of spirits," the dream of his life became a reality. The Atlantic cable was laid, and, in the words of John Bright, Mr. Field had "moored the New World alongside the Old."

The Hon. Henry Watterson, of Kentucky, was a representative during the closing session of Congress. As the editor of a great journal, Mr. Watterson was already well known to the country. His talents were of a high order. In his chosen field he had no superior. For many years he was a recognized leader of his party, and one of the chief managers in all its national conventions. His contributions to the literature of three decades of political campaigns were almost unparalleled. As a forcible, trenchant writer he is to be mentioned with Greeley, Raymond, Prentice, and Dana. His career, too, as a public lecturer, has been both successful and brilliant. The Congressional service of Mr. Watterson terminated with the session just mentioned. His speech, near its close, upon the bill creating an electoral commission to determine the Tilden-Hayes Presidential controversy was listened to with earnest attention, and at once gave him high place among the great debaters of that eventful Congress.

While a passenger on a train to Washington, to be present at the opening of Congress, my attention was directed to a man of venerable appearance, who entered the sleeping-car at a station not many miles out from Cincinnati. He was dressed in "Kentucky jeans" and had the appearance of a well-to-do farmer. Standing in the aisle near me, he was soon engaged in earnest conversation with the porter, endeavoring to secure a berth. The porter repeatedly assured him that this was impossible, as every berth was taken. He told the porter that he was quite ill, and must get on his journey. I then proposed that he share my berth for the night. He gladly did so until other accommodations were provided.

On the Monday following, when the House was in the process of organization, the name of James D. Williams of Indiana being called, my sleeping-car acquaintance, still attired in blue jeans, stepped forward with his colleagues to the Speaker's desk and was duly sworn in as a member of Congress. This was his first term, but he soon became quite well known to the country. As chairman of the Committee of Accounts, having to do with small expenditures, he closely scrutinized every claim presented, and scaled to the lowest many pet measures. His determination to economize, as well as his peculiarity of dress and appearance, soon made him an especial object of amusement to newspaper correspondents. He was the butt of many cheap jokes; one being his alleged complaint that hundreds of towels were being daily used by members at the Capitol, at the public expense, while at his home, on his farm, one towel would last a week, with eleven in the family. Despite, however, all jokes and gibes, he soon became the most popular man in his State. "Blue Jeans Williams" became a name to conjure with; and in the celebrated campaign of 1876, after an exciting contest, he was elected Governor, defeating an able and popular leader, who, twelve years later, was himself elected President of the United States.

No sketch of "the American Commons" during the last fifty years would be in any measure complete that failed to make mention of the man who was nineteen times elected a Representative, the Hon. William S. Holman, of Indiana. Whatever the ups and downs of party supremacy, despite all attempts by gerrymandering to relegate him to the shades of private life, Judge Holman, with unruffled front, "a mien at once kindly, persuasive, and patient," held sturdily on his way. Amid political upheavals that overwhelmed all his associates upon the ticket, his name, like that of Abou Ben Adhem, led all the rest. From Pierce to McKinley—whatever the issues, and howsoever determined—at each successive organization of the House "the gentleman from Indiana" was an unfailing respondent to the opening roll-call. An old English stanza comes to mind:

"And this is law, that I'll maintain
Until my dying day, sir,
That whatsoever King shall reign,
Still I'll be vicar of Bray, sir."

His integrity was unquestioned; his knowledge of public business, phenomenal. With no brilliancy, little in the way of oratory, Judge Holman was nevertheless one of the most valuable members ever known to the House of Representatives. The Lobby regarded him as its mortal foe. He was for years the recognized "watch-dog of the Treasury." Personal appeals to his courtesy, to permit the present consideration of private bills, had, in the main, as well have been made to a marble statue. His well known and long to be remembered, "I object, Mr. Speaker," sounded the knell of many a well devised raid upon the Treasury. It may be that he sometimes prevented the early consideration of meritorious measures, but with occasional exceptions his objections were wholesome. He kept in close touch with the popular pulse, and knew, as if by instinct, which would be the safe and which the dangerous side of the pending measure. It sometimes seemed that he could even "look into the seeds of time and tell which grain will grow and which will not."

It has been said that even great men have at times their little weaknesses. An incident to be related will show that possibly Judge Holman was no exception to that rule. The consideration of sundry bills for the erection of post-office buildings in a number of districts having "gone over" by reason of his objection, the members having the bills in charge joined forces and lumped the several measures into an "omnibus bill" which was duly presented. The members especially interested in its passage, to "make assurance doubly sure," had quietly inserted a provision for the erection of a Government building in one of the cities of Holman's district. When the bill was read, Judge Holman, as he sat busily writing at his desk, was, without solicitation upon his part, the closely observed of every member. Apparently oblivious, however, to all that was occurring, he continued to write. No objection being made, the bill was in the very act of passing when an exceedingly bright member from Wisconsin, "being moved and instigated by the devil," no doubt, rushed to the front and exclaimed, "Mr. Speaker, I desire to call the attention of the gentleman from the fourth district of Indiana to the fact that the Treasury is being robbed!" Unmoved by the appeal, the Judge continued to write, and, as one of his colleagues afterwards remarked, "was chewing his tobacco very fine." After a moment of suspense, and amid applause in which even the galleries took part, the member from Wisconsin, in tragic tones, exclaimed, "Ah, Mr. Speaker, our watch-dog of the Treasury, like all other good watch-dogs, *never barks when his friends are around!*"

Mr. Blackburn, of Kentucky, began his long and eventful legislative career as a member of this Congress. As the representative of the Ashland District, he was the successor of Clay, Crittenden, Marshall, Breckenridge, Beck—illustrious names in the history of the State and of the nation. He was worthy of the succession, and, at the close of ten years' service in the House, was elected to the Senate. He came within a few votes of being chosen as the candidate of his party for Speaker at the opening of the forty-sixth Congress. He was a born orator. It was as natural for him to speak as to breathe. Wake him up at any hour of the night, and he would be ready upon the instant for an eloquent speech of any length, upon any subject. Thoroughly familiar with all that pertained to our political history, with a voice easily heard above the storm, he was ever in the forefront of the hurly-burly of heated partisan debate. There was little that was conciliatory about him. He neither gave nor asked quarter. A born fighter, he had rather

"Follow his enemy through a fiery gulf,
Than flatter him in a bower."

Possessing neither the keen wit of his colleague, McKenzie, nor the profound humor of Knott, he was nevertheless the hero of more interesting narratives than any member who ever crossed the Blue Ridge Mountains.

The incident to be related may have suggested the witty reply of Senator Proctor to the Vice-President when invited by the latter to come into the devotional exercises: "Excuse me, I am *paired* with Blackburn on prayers." This equals his reply when asked by Senator Hale what he thought of Senator Chandler: "I *like* him, but it is an acquired taste."

Upon the occasion of the retirement of the Rev. Dr. Butler from the Chaplaincy of the Senate—a position he had filled most acceptably for many years—many of the Senators spoke regretfully of his retirement. The speech of Mr. Blackburn, for beauty of expression and pathetic eloquence, was unrivalled. He spoke most tenderly of the faithfulness of the venerable man of God; how for long years he had gone in and out before us; of his daily walk and conversation; how, like the Blessed Master, his only thought was of doing good; of how he had often invoked the Divine blessing upon us and our loved ones, and lifted us as it were in his arms up to the very throne of grace. The orator seemed inspired, as though his lips were indeed touched with a live coal from the altar. The counterpart of the scene that followed his closing words had never been witnessed in legislative assembly. All were in tears. It was even said that venerable Senators, who had never shed a tear since the ratification of the treaty of Ghent, actually sobbed aloud, and refused to be comforted. At length, amid silence that could be felt, an adjournment was effected, and the Senators passed sadly out to their homes. As he passed the Chair, Senator Vest, in undertone, remarked to the Vice-President, *"Jo never saw him!"*

The next day, in the absence of his successor, "the blind chaplain," Dr. Butler again, and for the last time, officiated, simply repeating in manner most solemn and impressive, the Lord's Prayer. At its conclusion, Senator Blackburn, who had been a most attentive listener, came forward to the desk and remarked to Vice-President Stevenson: "I tell you, sir, I like that new chaplain of ours. What a splendid prayer! There is something *original* about that man!"

Thirty years and more ago, when first a candidate for Congress, Mr. Blackburn attended a public execution—in common parlance "a hanging"—in one of the counties in his district. Being a gentleman of great distinction, and a candidate for Congress, he was appropriately invited by the sheriff to occupy a seat with the prisoner and his spiritual adviser upon the gallows. At the near approach of the fatal hour, the sheriff, with watch in hand, amid the sea of upturned faces, stated to the prisoner that he had yet five minutes to live, and it was his privilege if he so desired to address the audience. The prisoner meekly replied that he did not wish to speak. Whereupon Mr. Blackburn, stepping promptly to the front of the scaffold, said: "As the gentleman does not wish to speak, if he will kindly yield me his time, I will take this occasion to remark that I am a candidate for Congress, regularly nominated by the Democratic Convention," etc. This incident being told in the presence of Mr. Marshall, the opposing candidate, the latter remarked that he remembered it well, and could vouch for its truth. He then added that when Mr. Blackburn proposed to speak out the prisoner's time, the latter turned to the Sheriff and inquired who that was. To which the officer replied, "Captain Blackburn." At this the prisoner, who had amid all the exciting scenes of his arrest and trial, and even up to the present moment, with his open coffin beside him, displayed marvellous fortitude, suddenly exhibiting deep emotion, piteously exclaimed, "Please hang me first, *and let him speak afterwards!"*

When, in the tide of time, will the House of Representatives witness the like of "Sunset" Cox? Beginning a Congressional career, which was to terminate only with his death, when scarcely of the constitutional age, he was in close succession a representative from two great States,—in his early manhood from the Capital district of Ohio, and in his maturer years, even down to old age, the most prominent of the delegation from the great State of New York. Mr. Cox was gifted as few men have been in this world. His literary attainments were of a high order, and some of the books of which he was the author will no doubt furnish instructive and entertaining reading for many generations to come. He was an indefatigable student, and seemed, as did Lord Bacon, to have "taken all knowledge for his province." His accurate knowledge of the history of all countries and times was a marvel, and, all at his instant command, placed him upon rare vantage ground in the many forensic struggles in which he took part. Woe betide the unfortunate antagonist whose record was other than faultless. He was a born debater, full of resources, and aggressive to the last degree. He never waited for opportunities, but sought them. In great emergencies he was often put forward by his political associates for the fierce encounter with the great leaders upon the opposite side of the Chamber. He was withal one of the most kindly of men. He was the soul of personal and official honor. His integrity could know no temptation. It may truly be said of him that—

"Whatever record leaps to light,
He never can be shamed."

His sympathies were deeply enlisted for the safety of those "who go down to the sea in ships." For years he was the earnest advocate of a thorough life-saving system. Much of the present efficiency of this humane branch of the public service is due to his untiring efforts. He had travelled to all countries, and even to the islands of the sea. He was of sunny disposition, and believed that "whatever places the eye of Heaven visits are to the wise man ports and happy havens."

Mr. Cox was one of the most genial and delightful of associates. With him and Vance, Knott, and Randolph Tucker as companions for the social hour, the night would flee away like a shadow. His wit was of the rarest order. He would have been on terms of recognized kinship with Sydney Smith and Charles Lamb. He once said of a vinegar-visaged member that the only regret he had on earth was that there were no more commandments to keep; what few there were he kept so easily. As illustrating his readiness and elasticity, whatever the emergency, two instances, out of the many that crowd upon memory, will be given. During an all-night session of the House, amid great confusion, the roll-call was ordered. The first name, "Mr. Archer," was called, and the response "Aye" was given. The clerk, failing to hear the response, immediately repeated,

"Mr. Archer," to which the latter, in tones heard above the din of many voices, again answered "Aye." Instantly Mr. Cox exclaimed: "Insatiate Archer, would not one suffice?"

A new member from a district far to the westward entered the House. His advoirdupois was in keeping with the vast territorial area he represented. As a wit, he was without a rival in his section. The admiration of his constituents over the marvellous attainments of the new member, scarcely exceeded his own. Only the opportunity was wanting when the star of the gentleman from New York should go down and his own be in the ascendant. The opportunity at length came. Mr. Cox was the victim of the hour; the recipient of many compliments much more fervid than kind. The seven vials of wrath were opened upon him. A vast storehouse of wit, ancient and modern, was literally exhausted for the occasion. Even the diminutive size of the New York member was mentioned in terms of disparagement. The speech caused much merriment in the House during its delivery, and its author with an air of self-satisfaction rarely witnessed even in that body, resumed his seat. Mr. Cox at once took the floor. No attempt will be made to do justice to his speech. The manner, the tone of voice, which caused an uproar upon the floor and in the galleries, can never find their way into print. Referring to the ill-mannered allusion to his size, he said "that his constituents preferred a representative with brains, rather than one whose only claims to distinction consisted in an abnormal abdominal development." In tragic tones he then pronounced a funeral eulogy over his assailant, and suggested, as a fitting inscription for his tombstone, the pathetic words of Byron,

"'T is Greece, but living Greece no more!"

Soon after the nomination of Tilden for President, Mr. Cox was invited to attend a political meeting at the State capital, and address the Democracy of Vermont. When the scarcity of Democrats in the Green Mountain State is taken into account, the significance of Mr. Cox's reply will readily appear. His telegram was to the effect that pressing engagements prevented his attending, but "if the Democracy of Vermont *will drop into my library* any afternoon, about four o'clock, I will address them with great pleasure."

In attempting to write something of a member so long and so favorably known to the House as the Hon. J. Proctor Knott of Kentucky, I am reminded of the opening sentences of the touching tribute of Judge Baldwin to an honored associate:

"I nib my pen and impart to it a fine hair stroke in order that I may give the more delicate touch which can alone show forth the character of this distinguished gentleman. If I hold the pen in hand in idle reverie, it is because my mind rests lovingly upon a picture I feel incapable of transcribing with fidelity to the original; and therefore I pause a moment to look once more at the original, before it is obscured by the rude counterpart."

It was worth while to have known Proctor Knott, to have been his cotemporary in public life, the sharer of his confidence, the guest at his hearthstone. In the highest sense of the expression, he was a gentleman of the old school. To him there was rare meaning in the words, "Old wood to burn! Old wine to drink! Old friends to trust!"

He was as familiar with the Bible, with Shakespeare, and Burns, as though he had written them. His quotations, whether in private conversation, or in public speech, were always timely. There was little in the way of the best literature, ancient or modern, that he had not read. As was truly said of the gifted Prentiss:

"His imagination was colored and imbued with the light of the shadowy past. He lingered spell-bound among the scenes of mediaeval chivalry. His spirit had dwelt until almost naturalized in the mystic dreamland of the Paladins, Crusaders, and Knights Templars; with Monmouth and Percy, with Bois-Guilbert and Ivanhoe and the bold McGregor; with the Cavaliers of Rupert, and the iron enthusiasts of Fairfax."

He was the inveterate hater of shams of all kinds, and of mere pretenders of every description. He ever avoided the short cuts, and kept steadily along in the old way. His heroes, like those of Dickens, were taken from the common walk; the men he had met in the road and at the hustings, at whose firesides he had passed many hours. Whatever concerned them, whatever involved in any manner their welfare, was of deep interest to him. If he had chosen his own epitaph it might have read:

"In common ways, with common men,
I served my race and time."

He was both an artist and a poet. He loved flowers, and there was to his ears no music so sweet as the merry laughter of children. And, whether in private life, or in his great executive office as "the arbiter of human fate," the tale of woe never failed to touch a sympathetic cord. He had in very deed,

"A tear for pity, and a hand open as day to melting charity."

He was welcome at every hearthstone, as one "who cometh unto you with a tale which holdeth children from play, and old men from the chimney corner."

Soon after his admission to the bar, Mr. Knott removed to Missouri, where he was almost immediately elected to the responsible position of Attorney-

General of the State. In due time he returned to his native State, and was for six terms a representative in Congress. Yet later, and as the shadows were beginning to fall to the eastward, he was, almost by common acclaim, called to the chief executive office of the commonwealth. It may truly be said of him that "with clear head, and with clean hands, he faithfully discharged every public trust."

Mr. Knott entered Congress just at the close of the great Civil War. It was a period of excitement throughout the entire country, and of intense foreboding to the section he represented. In the debates of that stormy period he bore no mean part. He was counted a foeman worthy the steel of the ablest who entered the lists. A thorough student from the beginning, of all that pertained to Magna Charta, the Bill of Rights, and the Federal Constitution, he was equipped as few men have been, for forensic contests that have left their deep impress upon history. The evidence of his ability as a lawyer is to be found in the satisfactory manner in which for three Congresses he discharged the duties of the trying position of Chairman of the Judiciary Committee of the House of Representatives. The ablest lawyers of both political parties constituted this great committee, and its chairman, if possessing only mediocre talents or attainments, would have been sadly out of place.

But with his heavy armor laid aside, the genius of Knott was made manifest along more pleasing lines. Few speeches ever delivered in Congress have been so generally read, or so thoroughly imbedded into current literature, as one he delivered soon after his first admission to the House. Duluth awoke the morning after its delivery to find itself famous. As, "the zenith city of the unsalted seas," it has been known and read of all men. As such, it will probably continue to be known for ages to come. The speech hopelessly defeated a bill making a land grant to a proposed railroad, of which Duluth was to be the terminus. His mirthful prediction, however, as to its marvellous future has been fulfilled. How true it is that "jesters do oft prove prophets!" Bearing in mind that the great city of to-day then had no place even upon the map, the words quoted from the speech will be appreciated:

"Duluth, Duluth! The word fell upon my ear with peculiar and indescribable charm, like the gentle murmur of a brook stealing forth in the midst of roses, or the soft sweet accent of an angel's whisper in the bright joyous dream of sleeping innocence. Duluth! 'T was the name for which my soul had panted for years, as the hart panteth for the water brooks. I was convinced that the greatest calamity that ever befell the benighted nations of the ancient world was their having passed away without a knowledge of the actual existence of Duluth; that their fabled Atlantis, never seen save by the hallowed vision of inspired poesy, was in fact but another name for Duluth; that the golden orchard of the Hesperides was but a poetical synonym for the beer-gardens in the vicinity of Duluth. As that name first fell upon my ear, a resplendent scene of ineffable glory opened before me, such as I imagine burst upon the enraptured visions of the wandering Peri through the opening gates of Paradise."

Mr. Knott was often the sad and silent man. His real intimacies were few, and to strangers he was reserved. But to those who came within the circle of his personal friendship he was one of the most delightful of companions. No man was ever given less to a parade either of his friendships or of his animosities. His enemies —and it would have been strange if, passing through the eventful scenes he did, he had had none—knew just where to find him. He was, in very truth,

"Lofty and sour to them that loved him not;
But, to those men that sought him, sweet as summer."

The cause often of mirth in others, he was at times far from being joyous himself. Few men have been the possessors in so rare degree of the gift of humor, the sure indication of the humane and sympathetic in our nature; that "which blends the pathetic with the ludicrous, and by the same stroke moves to laughter and to tears." As Emerson says, "Both an ornament and a safeguard—genius itself." The line of separation between wit and humor is shadowy, not easily defined. There may be in the same individual, in some measure, a blending of the two. As has been said: "While wit is a purely intellectual thing, into every act of the humorous mind there is an influx of the moral nature. Humor springs up exuberantly, as from a fountain, and runs on, its perpetual game to look with considerate good-nature at every object in existence, and dismiss it with a benison." While wit, the purely intellectual quality, sparkles and stings, humor, "touched with a feeling of our infirmity," would "gently scan thy brother man," remembering ever that

"What's done we partly may compute,
But know not what's resisted."

It is not strange, then, that he who in large degree possesses or is possessed by this subtle quality should be subject to moods, it may be melancholy— "the effect of that humor that sometime hath his hour with every man." That Governor Knott was deeply endowed with humor in its best sense, no one who knew him could doubt. In relating incidents that convulsed his listeners, he gave no sign; his own features remained as solemn as if he were attending the obsequies of his dearest friend. There is something that is suggestive in the lines of Thomas Hood,

"There's not a string attuned to mirth
But has its chord in melancholy."

While Governor of Kentucky, he sent to the Hon. Stoddart Johnson a certificate, officially signed and bearing the impress of the great seal of State, duly commissioning him as "Mister," a distinctive and honorable title that no Kentuckian had previously borne. This recalls the witty remark of Max O'Rell: "The only thing that Mr. Ingersoll appears to hold in common with his countrymen *is the title of Colonel.*"

Many years ago McCullough, the tragedian, was giving his splendid impersonations of the two masterpieces of Shakespeare at the national Capital. The morning following one of these, Mr. Knott and I, passing along the avenue on our way to the House, were stopped by an exceedingly solemn-visaged individual who, addressing the former, said: "Mr. Knott, I would like to have your judgment as to which is the best play, *Hamlet* or *Macbeth.*"

Gazing earnestly at his inquisitor, and in a tone at once deprecatory and inimitable, Knott replied: "My friend, don't ask me that question. I am a politician, and a candidate for re-election to Congress; my district is about equally divided; Hamlet has his friends down there, and Macbeth his, and I am unwilling *to take any part between them!*"

When in joint canvass with his competitor for the Governorship of the State, Mr. Knott, having, by appointment, at one of the county seats in "the Purchase," made the opening speech, was seated near by to listen to that of the opposing candidate. The latter, a gentleman having a high sense of propriety, and a dignity of bearing that would have done no discredit to an assembly of divines, had been exceedingly annoyed by Knott's speech, which had in very truth kept the audience in an uproar during its entire delivery. Beginning his reply, he said:

"Fellow-citizens, I will endeavor to indicate to you the kind of a man who, in my judgment, should be elected to the position of Governor of this grand old commonwealth. In the first place, that exalted position would never be filled by one who, for lack of serious argument, constantly appeals to the risibilities of his audience; never by a wit, a mere joker, a story-teller; in other words—if you will pardon me, my fellow-citizens—by a mere buffoon. On the contrary, the incumbent of the exalted position of chief executive of this grand old commonwealth should be a gentleman of character, of ability, the worthy successor of Shelby, of Morehead, of Crittenden; he should be a gentleman of scholastic attainments and of dignified bearing, well versed in classic lore and a thorough student of the higher order of state-craft. In a word, fellow-citizens, you should elect as your Governor a gentleman of lofty character, of ripe scholarship, of commanding dignity, of exalted statesmanship, of ——"

At this point, Knott, interrupting, said, in manner and tone the exact counterpart of that of the speaker, "Pardon me, Colonel Smith, but I am too modest a man to listen longer to the beautiful and truthful description *you have just given of me!"*

Whereupon, amidst the wildest applause, he retired from the hall, as did the audience, and the speaking for the day, and the joint discussion for the campaign, were closed.

III AGAIN IN CONGRESS

CHANGES IN THE PERSONNEL OF THE HOUSE CONTRASTED
WITH THOSE IN THE
BRITISH HOUSE OF COMMONS—LEVI P. MORTON—MR.
COVERT AND MR. SHELLEY
—GEN. JOSEPH E. JOHNSTON—TWO NOTABLE SPEECHES BY
JAMES A. McKENZIE
—JOHN E. KENNA—BENJAMIN BUTTERWORTH—MR. KEIFER
OF OHIO—MR.
CARLISLE OF KENTUCKY—SPEAKER REED—PRESIDENT
McKINLEY—THE WRITER'S
SPEECH AT THE PEACE JUBILEE BANQUET, 1898.

After an absence of two years I was returned to the forty-sixth Congress. Circumstances over which I had no control had prevented my taking a seat in the intervening Congress, my successful competitor being the Hon. Thomas F. Tipton. In politics, however, as in other things, "the whirligig of time brings in his revenges," and I was in turn the successful competitor of my late opponent in his candidacy for re-election.

Meanwhile, many changes had occurred in the personnel of the House. Many familiar names had been dropped from its roll. Of these, nine had been transferred to that of the Senate, a former member was now in the Cabinet, and Mr. Wheeler of New York was Vice-President. A significant fact in this connection, and one illustrating the uncertainty of the tenure by which place is held in that body, was that more than one-third of those with whom I had so recently served were now in private life. Possibly no feature of our governmental system causes more astonishment to intelligent foreigners than the many changes biennially occurring in the membership of the House of Representatives. There is marked difference between the British House of Commons, and the popular branch of the American Congress. A seat lost in the latter—it may be by a single unfortunate utterance, or unpopular vote—is usually a seat lost forever; while in the former, membership may continue for an almost indefinite period, and until an "appeal to the country" by the Ministry upon a new and vital issue. If defeated by one constituency, the member of Parliament may soon be returned by another, the question of residence having no significance. In fact if possessing superior talents, the member is liable to be chosen by two or more constituencies at the same election, the choice then resting with himself as to which he will represent. Such has been the experience of the most eminent of British statesmen. The names of Burke, Peel, Gladstone, and Balfour, quite recently, will readily be recalled in this connection. In the little island the aspirant to legislative honors has several hundred constituencies from which to choose, or be chosen, while in the larger America his political fortunes are usually bound up in his own residence district.

Upon the roll of the House in the new Congress, called in special session in March, 1879, in addition to some heretofore mentioned, were names well known to the country. Of these none is more worthy of honorable mention than that of the Hon. Levi P. Morton of New York. In the business world his name was a synonym for integrity. The head of a great banking house, he was almost as well known in the principal cities of Europe as in the great city of his residence. At the time of his first election to Congress Mr. Morton was, by appointment of the President, an honorary commissioner to the Paris Exposition. At the close of his legislative career he held successively the honored positions of Ambassador to France, Vice-President of the United States, and Governor of New York. In Congress, Mr. Morton was the able representative of a great constituency; as chief executive of his State his name is worthy of mention with the most eminent of those who have been called to that exalted station; as ambassador to a foreign court the honor of his country was ever in safe keeping; as Vice-President, he was the model presiding officer over the greatest deliberative body known to men.

One of the brightest members of the New York delegation was the Hon. James W. Covert of Flushing. Altogether he served ten years in the House, and became in time one of its leading members. He was an excellent lawyer, a delightful associate, and an able and ready debater. That he was gifted with a touch of the humorous will appear from the following. The House was passing through the agony of an all-night session. Confusion reigned supreme. During it all, Mr. Shelley, from one of the Gulf States, stood at his desk and repeatedly made the point of order upon Covert, Springer, Kenna, McKenzie, and others, as they successively addressed the Chair, that "The gentleman is not speaking from his desk." The point of order was as repeatedly sustained by the Speaker, the rules requiring members to address the Chair only from their respective desks. The confusion at length became so great that many members, in their eagerness to be heard, pressed to the front. The voice of Mr. Shelley, however, was heard above the din still calling for the enforcement of the rule; to which the Speaker, his patience exhausted, now turned a deaf ear. Desperate beyond measure, Mr. Shelley at length *left his own desk*, and taking his position immediately in front of the clerk's desk fiercely demanded, "Mr. Speaker, I call for the enforcement of the rule." At which Covert immediately exclaimed, "Mr. Speaker, I call for the enforcement of *the rule in Shelley's case!*"

Almost directly in front of the Speaker's desk sat a gentleman, small in stature, and of quiet dignified bearing, "The silent man," "whose voice was in his sword," General Joseph E. Johnston of Virginia. Until this, his first election to Congress from the Capital District of the Old Dominion, he had known none other than military public service. He was a born soldier. No one who saw him could mistake his calling. Napoleon did not more truly look the soldier than did General Johnston. A graduate of West Point, his first service was in the Black Hawk War, and later in Mexico. For gallant conduct at the battle of Cerro Gordo, he was brevetted colonel in the regular army. His last service was when, as Lieutenant-General of the Confederate Army, he surrendered to Sherman, thus ending the great Civil War. He had already reached the allotted threescore years and ten when he entered Congress, and its ordinary details apparently interested him but little. He earnestly desired the return of the era of good feeling between the North and South, and upon his motion the House duly adjourned in honor of the day set apart for the decoration of the graves of Union soldiers.

No member of this House attracted more attention than did the Hon. James A. McKenzie of Kentucky, the representative from what in local parlance was known as "the pennyryle district." He was the youngest member of the body, tall, erect, and handsome. Mr. McKenzie rendered a valuable service to his constituents and the country during this Congress, by securing the passage of a bill placing quinine upon the free list. His district was seriously afflicted with the old-time fever and ague, and the reduction by his bill to a nominal cost of the sure and only specific placed his name high upon the list of benefactors.

Two of his kinsmen, one from Illinois, the other from Florida, occupied seats immediately in his front. Addressing them one day, he said: "It seems strange, indeed, that we three cousins—one from Illinois, one from Florida, and one from Kentucky—are all here together in Congress"; and then added, with apparent gravity, "and *ours not an office-seeking family either!*"

As the session drew near its close, he made repeated efforts to obtain unanimous consent for the consideration of a bill for the erection of a Government building in the principal city of his district. The interposition of the stereotyped "I object" had, however, in each instance, proved fatal. During a night session, near the close of the Congress, requests for recognition came to the Speaker from all parts of the chamber. In the midst of the tumult Mr. McKenzie arose and, addressing the Chair, stated with great solemnity of manner that he arose to a question of personal privilege. This at once arrested the attention of the Speaker, and he requested the gentleman from Kentucky to state his question of privilege. "I rise, Mr. Speaker," said McKenzie, "to a question of the *highest* privilege, one pertaining to the right of a member to a seat upon this floor—*in the next*

Congress. If I don't get that post-office bill through now, my seat will be imperilled. I beg the House for unanimous consent for its immediate consideration." The House was convulsed; no objection was interposed, the bill was considered and passed, and McKenzie's seat was safe for many years to come.

Has there ever been a more feeling two-minutes' speech, than that of McKenzie in the National Convention of 1892, when he arose to second the nomination of Cleveland? After a night of intense excitement, the convention was still in session at three o'clock in the morning. A storm was raging without, while within, thousands in the great hall were impatiently and loudly demanding an immediate vote. More than one of the chief orators of the party,—men well known to the country—had in vain attempted to be heard. Chaos seemed to have come again at the crucial moment that McKenzie, standing upon his chair in the centre of the vast enclosure, began: "If I speak longer than two minutes, I hope that some honest half-drowned Democrat will suspend my carcass from one of the cross-beams of this highly artistic, but terribly leaky auditorium. Cleveland needs no nomination from this convention. He has already been nominated by the people all along the line—all the way from Hell Gate to Yuba Dam!"

The bedlam that now broke loose exceeded all that had gone before. The uproar drowned the voice of the orator within, and even, for the time, called a halt upon the raging elements without. The speech was never concluded. What might have been the closing words of McKenzie's speech, with such a beginning, can never be known. The effect of his opening, however, was instantaneous. It was the immediate prelude to the overwhelming nomination of his candidate.

The Hon. John E. Kenna, of West Virginia, was just at the beginning of a remarkably brilliant career. He was under thirty years of age when he first entered Congress. At the close of his third term in the House, he was elected to the United States Senate, and held his seat in that body by successive elections until his death at the early age of forty-four. He possessed rare gifts as a speaker, and was an active participant in many of the important debates during that eventful period. Senator Kenna was the beloved of his State, and his early death brought sorrow to many hearts.

His manners were pleasing, and he was companionable to the last degree. He often related an amusing incident that occurred in the convention that first nominated him for Congress. His name was presented by a delegate from the Crossroads in one of the mountain counties, in substantially the following speech: "Mr. President, I rise to present to this convention, as a candidate for Congress, the name of John E. Kenna—the peer, sir, *of no man* in the State of West Virginia."

Among the new members elected to this Congress was the Hon. Benjamin Butterworth of Ohio. His ability as a lawyer and his readiness in debate soon gave him prominence, while his abundant good-nature and inexhaustible fund of anecdotes made him a general favorite in the House. One of his stories was of a Western member whose daily walk and conversation at the national Capital was by no means up to the orthodox home standard. The better element of his constituents at length became disgusted, as reports derogatory to their member from time to time reached them. A bolt in the approaching Congressional convention was even threatened, and altogether serious trouble was brewing. The demand was imperative upon the part of his closest friends that he at once come home and face his accusers. Homeward he at length turned his footsteps, and was met at the depot by a large concourse of his friends and constituents. Hurriedly alighting from the train and stepping upon the platform, with beaming countenance and heart made glad by such an enthusiastic reception, he thus began:

"Fellow-citizens, my heart is deeply touched as my eyes behold this splendid assemblage of my constituents and friends gathered here before and around me. During my absence in Congress my friends have spoken in my vindication. I am here now to speak for myself. Vile slanders have been put in circulation against me. I have been accused of being a defaulter; I have been accused of being a drunkard; I have been accused of being a gambler; but, thank God, fellow-citizens, *no man has ever dared to assail my good moral character!*"

One incident is related by Butterworth of a judge in his State who, becoming thoroughly disgusted with the ease with which naturalization papers were obtained, determined upon a radical reform. That the pathway of the reformer—along this as other lines—was by no means one of flowers will appear from the sequel. Immediately upon taking his seat, the judge, with great earnestness of manner, announced from the bench that thereafter no applicant could receive from that court his final papers, entitling him to the exercise of the high privilege of citizenship, unless he was able to read the Constitution of the United States. A few mornings later, Michael O'Connor, a well-known partisan of the Seventh Ward, appeared in court accompanied by a diminutive-looking countryman, Dennis Flynn by name. Mr. O'Connor stated to the judge that his friend Dennis Flynn had already taken out his first papers, and the legal time had passed, and he now wanted His Honor to grant him his final papers. With much solemnity of manner the judge inquired whether Mr. Flynn had ever read the Constitution of the United States. Somewhat abashed by the unusual interrogatory, Mr. O'Connor looked inquiringly at Mr. Flynn, at which the latter, wholly unconscious of the purport of the inquiry, looked appealingly to Mr. O'Connor. The latter then replied that he presumed he had not, at which the judge, handing the applicant a copy of the revised statutes containing the Constitution, admonished him to read it carefully. Mr. Flynn, carrying the volume in his arms, and followed by his patron, sadly left the court-room. Just eight minutes elapsed, the door suddenly opened and both reappeared, Mr. O'Connor in front, bearing the book aloft, and exclaiming, "Dinnie couldn't rade it, Your Honor, but I rid it over to him, *and he is parefictly deloighted wid it!"*

Three gentlemen, each of whom at a later day reached the Speakership, had served but a single term in the House at the opening of the forty-sixth Congress: Mr. Keifer of Ohio, Mr. Carlisle of Kentucky, and Mr. Reed of Maine. Mr. Keifer was a gentleman of ability and of exceedingly courteous manners. He took a prominent part in debate, and was the immediate successor of Mr. Randall in the chair. After an absence of twenty years he has again been returned to his seat in the House.

Few abler men than Mr. Carlisle have been in the public service. He was a recognized leader of his party from his first appearance in the House, and an authority upon all questions pertaining to tariff or finance. During his long service as Speaker he established an enduring reputation as an able presiding officer; as possessing in the highest degree "the cold neutrality of the impartial Judge." While a Senator, he was appointed by President Cleveland to the important position of Secretary of the Treasury. The duties of that great office have never been discharged with more signal ability.

Mr. Reed stood alone. He was unlike other men, a fact which probably caused him little regret. Self-reliant, aggressive, of will indomitable, he was a political storm centre during his entire public career. His friends were devoted to him, and he was never forgotten by his enemies. Whoever was brought into close contact with him, usually carried away an impression by which to remember him. Upon one occasion, in the House, when in sharp debate with Mr. Springer, the latter quoted the familiar saying of Henry Clay, "Sir, I would rather be right than be President." Mr. Reed, in a tone far from reassuring, retorted, "The gentleman from Illinois *will never be either!"*

The retort courteous, however, was not always from the lips of the Speaker. Mr. Springer, having at one time repeatedly attempted, but in vain, to secure the floor, at length demanded by what right he was denied recognition. The Speaker intimated that such ruling was in accord with the high prerogative of the Chair. To which Springer replied:

"Oh, it is excellent
To have a giant strength; but 't is tyrannous
To use it like a giant."

Of immense physical proportions, towering above his fellows, with voice by no means melodious, a manner far from conciliatory, a capacity for sarcastic utterance that vividly recalled the days of John Randolph and Tristram Burgess, and, withal, one of the ablest men of his generation, Mr. Reed was in very truth a picturesque figure in the House of Representatives. He apparently acted upon the supposition of the philosopher Hobbes that war is the natural state of man. The kindly admonition,

"Mend your ways a little
Lest they may mar your fortunes,"

if ever given him, was unheeded. In very truth,

"He stood,
As if a man were author of himself,
And knew no other kin."

No man in his day was more talked of or written about. At one time his star was in the ascendent, and he seemed to be on the highroad to the Presidency. His great ambition, however, was thwarted by those of his own political household. At the close of a turbulent session, while he was in the Chair, the usual resolution of thanks to the Speaker "for the able, fair, and courteous manner in which he had presided" was bitterly antagonized, and finally adopted only by a strictly party vote. It was an event with a single antecedent in our history, that of seventy-odd years ago, when the Whig minority in the House opposed the usual vote of thanks to Speaker Polk upon his retirement from the Chair. In the latter case, the cry of persecution that was instantly raised had much to do with Mr. Polk's almost immediate election to the Governorship of his State, and his subsequent elevation to the Presidency. The parallel incident in Mr. Reed's career, however, failed to prove "the prologue to the swelling act."

The Hon. William McKinley, of Ohio, was a member of this Congress. He was one of the most pleasing and delightful of associates, and my acquaintance with him was of the most agreeable character. One of his earliest official acts as President was my appointment as a member of the Bimetallic Commission to Europe.

Mr. McKinley was in very truth one of Fortune's favorites: five times elected a member of the House of Representatives, three times Governor of his State, and twice elevated to the Presidency. He was the third of our Presidents to fall by the hand of an assassin. His tragic death is yet fresh in our memories.

The last time I met President McKinley was at the Peace Jubilee Banquet at the Auditorium in Chicago, on the evening of October 19, 1898. On this occasion, following the toast to the President of the United States, I spoke as follows:

"The incumbent of this great office holds with unchallenged title the most exalted station known to men. Monarchs rule by hereditary right, or hold high place only by force of arms. The elevation of a citizen to the Presidency of the United States is the deliberate act, under the forms of law, of a sovereign people. As an aspirant, he may have been the choice only of a political party; as the incumbent of the great office, he is the representative of all the people—the President of all the people. It augurs well for the future of the Republic when the American people magnify this office; when the honor, as now, the President who has so ably upheld its dignity, so worthily met its solemn responsibilities, so patriotically discharged its exacting and imperative duties.

"The office of President of a self-governing people is unique. It had no place in ancient or mediaeval schemes of government, whether despotic, federative, or in name republican. It has in reality none amongst the nations of modern Europe. The Presidency of the United States, in the highest degree, represents the majesty of the law. It stands for the unified authority and power of seventy-five millions of free men. It typifies what is most sacred to our race: stability in government and protection to liberty and life. The President is the great officer to whom the founders of the government entrusted the delicate and responsible function of treating with foreign States; in whom was vested in time of peace and of war, chief command of the army and of the navy.

"An eminent writer has well said: 'The ancient monarchs of France reigned and governed; the Queen of England reigns but does not govern; the President of France neither reigns nor governs; the President of the United States does not reign, but governs!'

"Experience has demonstrated the more than human wisdom of the framers of the great federal compact which for more than a century, in peace and amid the stress of war, has held States and people in indissoluble bond of union. In no part of their matchless handiwork has it been more clearly manifested than in the creation of a responsible executive. To secure in the largest measure the great ends of government, responsibility must attach to the executive office; and of necessity, with responsibility, *power*. The sooner France learns from the American Republic this important lesson, the sooner will government attain with her the stability to which it is now a stranger. Her statesmen might well recall the words of Lord Bacon: 'What men will not alter for the better, Time, the great innovator, will alter for the worse.'

"The splendid commonwealth in which we are assembled contains a population a million greater than did the entire country at the first inauguration of President Washington. The one hundred and nine years which have passed since that masterful hour in history have witnessed the addition of thirty-two States to our federal Union, and of seventy millions to our population. And yet, with but few amendments, our great organic law as fully meets the requirements of a self-governing people to-day as when it came from the hands of its framers. The builders of the Constitution wisely ordained the Presidential office a co-ordinate department of the Government. Moving in its own clearly defined orbit, without usurpation or lessening of prerogative, the great executive office, at the close as at the beginning of the century, is the recognized constitutional symbol of authority and of power. The delegated functions and prerogatives that pertained in our infancy and weakness have proved ample in the days of our strength and greatness as a nation.

"It is well that to the people was entrusted the sovereign power of choosing their chief magistrate. It is our glory, in the retrospect of more than a century, that none other than patriots —statesmen well equipped for the discharge of its timeless duties —have ever been chosen to the Presidency. May we not believe that the past is the earnest of the future, and that during the rolling years and centuries the incumbents of the great office—the chosen successors of Washington and of Lincoln—in the near and in the remote future, will prove the guardians and defenders of the Constitution, the guardians and defenders of the rights of all the people?

"Luminous will be the pages of history that tell to the ages the story of our recent conflict, of its causes and of its results. In brilliancy of achievement, the one hundred days war with Spain is the marvel of the closing century. It was not a war of our seeking. It was the earnest prayer of all, from the President to the humblest in private life, that the horrors of war might be averted. Had our ears remained deaf to the cry of the stricken and starving at our doors, we would not have been guiltless in the high court of conscience, and before the dread judgment seat of history. The plea 'Am I my brother's keeper?'—whether interposed by individual or by nation— cannot be heard before the august tribunal of the Almighty.

"Justified then, as we solemnly believe, in the sight of God for our interposition, we rejoice over the termination of a struggle in which our arms knew no defeat. The dead hand of Spain has been removed forever from the throats of her helpless victims. Emphasizing our solemn declaration as a nation, that this was a war for humanity, not for self-aggrandizement, we demand no money indemnity from the defeated and impoverished foe.

"The sacrifice of treasure and of blood has not been in vain. However it may have been in the past, the United States emerges from the conflict with Spain a united people. Sectional lines are forever obliterated. Henceforth, for all time, we present to foreign foe and unbroken front. In the words of Webster: 'Our politics go no farther than the water's edge.'

"No less important is the fact, that the United States of America to-day, as never before, commands the respect and admiration of the world. No foreign coalition, however formidable, can excite our serious apprehension or alarm. For all this, all honor to our brave soldiers and sailors; all honor to the helpful hands and sympathetic hearts of America's patriotic women.

"As in the early morning and in the noon of the nineteenth century, America gave to the world its best lessons in liberty and in law, so in its closing hours, it has given to all the nations a never-to-be-forgotten lesson in the dread art of war. In quick response to the splendid achievements of American valor comes from across the sea the startling proposal of despotic Russia for the disarmament of continental Europe—and in the end universal peace.

"Thankful to God for all he has vouchsafed to us in the past, and with the prayer that henceforth peace may be the priceless boon of all nations, we await the dawn of the new century, and turn our faces hopefully to the future."

IV THE VICE-PRESIDENCY

ELECTION, POWERS, AND DUTIES OF THE VICE-
PRESIDENT—NAMES AND DATES OF ALL THE VICE-
PRESIDENTS—FOUR WHO BECAME PRESIDENTS BY
ELECTION —FIVE WHO SUCCEEDED UPON THE DEATH
OF THE PRESIDENT—ATTEMPTS TO SECURE THE
IMPEACHMENTS OF PRESIDENTS—THE TWELFTH
AMENDMENT TO THE CONSTITUTION—REMARKS ON
SOME OF THE VICE-PRESIDENTS—THE WRITER'S
FAREWELL ADDRESS TO THE SENATE.

By the provisions of the Federal Constitution, a Vice-President of the United States is elected at the same time, for the same term, and in like manner as the President—by electors chosen in each of the States. A majority of the votes cast in the several electoral colleges is necessary to an election. The Vice-President is the President of the Senate, and in the event of an equal division in that body, he gives the deciding vote. Under no other contingency has he a vote. The powers and duties of the office of President devolve upon the Vice-President in case of the death, resignation, or removal from office of the President. The Vice-President is included in the list of public officers liable to removal from office on impeachment, on conviction for treason, bribery, or other high crimes and misdemeanors. By the twelfth amendment to the Constitution no person constitutionally ineligible to the office of President can be elected to that of Vice-President. In the event of a vacancy occurring in the office of Vice-President, the Senate is presided over by a member of that body. In such contingency the death of the President would, under existing law, devolve the office of President upon the Secretary of State.

Twenty-seven persons have held the office of Vice-President; the dates of their respective elections are as follows: John Adams of Massachusetts, in 1788, re-elected in 1792; Thomas Jefferson of Virginia, in 1796; Aaron Burr of New York, in 1800; George Clinton of New York, in 1804, re-elected in 1808; Elbridge Gerry of Massachusetts, in 1812; Daniel D. Tompkins of New York, in 1816, re-elected in 1820; John C. Calhoun of South Carolina, in 1824, re-elected in 1828; Martin Van Buren of New York, in 1832; Richard M. Johnson of Kentucky, in 1836; John Tyler of Virginia, in 1840; George M. Dallas of Pennsylvania, in 1844; Millard Fillmore of New York, in 1848; William R. King of Alabama, in 1852; John C. Breckenridge of Kentucky, in 1856; Hannibal Hamlin of Maine, in 1860; Andrew Johnson of Tennessee, in 1864; Schuyler Colfax of Indiana, in 1868; Henry Wilson of Massachusetts, in 1872; William A. Wheeler of New York, in 1876; Chester A. Arthur of New York, in 1880; Thomas A. Hendricks of Indiana, in 1884; Levi P. Morton of New York, in 1888; Adlai E. Stevenson of Illinois, in 1892; Garrett A. Hobart of New Jersey, in 1896; Theodore Roosevelt of New York, in 1900; Charles W. Fairbanks of Indiana, in 1904; James S. Sherman of New York, in 1908.

Four Vice-Presidents were subsequently elected Presidents, namely: John Adams in 1796; Thomas Jefferson in 1800 and 1804; Martin Van Buren in 1836; and Theodore Roosevelt in 1904. The dates given have reference to the election by vote of the electors in the several States by whom the President and Vice-President were subsequently chosen. Six Vice-Presidents died in office: namely, Clinton, Gerry, King, Wilson, Hendricks, and Hobart. In the Presidential contest of 1836, Martin Van Buren received a majority of the electoral votes for President, but no candidate received a majority for Vice-President. By Constitutional requirement the duty of electing a Vice-President then devolved upon the Senate, the candidates from whom such choice was to be made being restricted to the two who had received the highest number of electoral votes. One of these, Richard W. Johnson of Kentucky, was duly elected by the Senate. The only Vice-President who resigned the office was John C. Calhoun. This occurred in 1832, and Mr. Calhoun soon thereafter took his seat in the Senate, to which body he had been elected by the Legislature of South Carolina.

Five Vice-Presidents have, upon the death of the President, succeeded to the Presidency. The first President to die during his incumbency of the great office, was William Henry Harrison. His death occurred April 4, 1841, just one month after his inauguration. The Vice-President John Tyler, then at his country home in Virginia, was officially notified of the event, and upon reaching the seat of Government at once took the oath of office as President. There was much discussion for a time in and out of Congress as to his proper title, whether "Vice-President of the United States acting as President," or "President." The language of the Constitution however, is clear, and it is no longer controverted that upon the death of the President the Vice-President becomes, in name as in fact, President. Upon the death of President Zachary Taylor, July 9, 1850, Vice-President Millard Fillmore succeeded to the Presidency, and was at a later date an unsuccessful candidate for election to that office. The third Vice-President who reached the Presidency by succession was Andrew Johnson; this occurred April 15, 1865, the day following the assassination of President Lincoln. President Garfield was shot July 2, 1881, and died in September of that year, when he was succeeded by Vice-President Chester A. Arthur. Vice-President Roosevelt was the successor of President McKinley, who died by the hand of an assassin in September, 1901.

Two attempts have been made to secure the impeachment of Presidents, the incumbent in each instance having been elected Vice-President and succeeded to the higher office upon the death of the President. A resolution looking to the impeachment of President Tyler was introduced into the House of Representatives in January, 1843, but was defeated, and no further steps were taken. Articles of impeachment, for "high crimes and misdemeanors," were presented by the House of Representatives against President Johnson in 1868. By constitutional provision the trial was by the Senate, the Chief Justice of the United States presiding. Less than two-thirds of the Senators voting for conviction, he was acquitted.

Until the adoption of the twelfth amendment, no Constitutional provision existed for separate votes in the electoral colleges for President and Vice-President; the candidate receiving the highest number of votes (if a majority of all) became President, and the one receiving the second highest, Vice-President. In 1801, Jefferson and Burr each received seventy-three electoral votes, and by constitutional requirement the election at once devolved upon the House of Representatives, voting by States. On the thirty-sixth ballot a majority of the States voting for Jefferson, he became President, and Burr, Vice-President. The Constitutional amendment above indicated, by which separate ballots were required in the electoral colleges for each office, was the result of the intense excitement throughout the country engendered by this contest. The earnest opposition of Alexander Hamilton to Aaron Burr in the above-mentioned contest, was the prime cause of the duel by which Hamilton lost his life at the hands of Burr in 1804.

George Clinton, the fourth Vice-President, had as a member of the Continental Congress voted for the Declaration of Independence, and held the rank of Brigadier-General during the War of the Revolution. The fifth Vice-President, Elbridge Gerry, had been a prominent member of the Constitutional Convention of 1787. William R. King, elected in 1852, by reason of ill health never entered upon the discharge of the duties of his office. By special act of Congress, the oath of office was administered to him in Cuba and his death occurred soon thereafter. Of the twenty-seven Vice-Presidents thus far elected, ten have been from the State of New York. Adams and Jefferson, the first and second Vice-Presidents, rendered valuable service to the young Republic at foreign courts; each by election was elevated to the Presidency; and their deaths occurred upon the same historic Fourth of July, just fifty years from the day they had signed the Declaration of Independence.

A marble bust of each of the Vice-Presidents has been placed in the gallery of the Senate Chamber. The office of Vice-President is one of great dignity. He is the presiding officer of the most august legislative assembly known to men. In the event of an equal division in the Senate, he gives the deciding vote. This vote, many times in our history, has been one of deep significance. It will readily be seen that the contingency may often occur when the Vice-President becomes an important factor in matters of legislation.

On the occasion of the writer's retirement from office, March 4, 1897, he delivered the following farewell address before the Senate:

"Senators: The hour has arrived which marks the close of the fifty-fourth Congress, and terminates my official relation to this body.

"Before laying down the gavel for the last time, I may be pardoned for detaining you for a moment, in the attempt to give expression to my gratitude for the uniform courtesy extended me, for the many kindnesses shown me, during the time it has been my good fortune to preside over your deliberations. My appreciation of the Resolution of the Senate personal to myself, can find no adequate expression in words. Intentionally, I have at no time given offence; and I carry from this presence no shadow of feeling of unkindness toward any Senator, no memory of any grievance.

"Chief among the favors political fortune has bestowed upon me, I count that of having been the associate—and known something of the friendship—of the men with whom I have so long held official relation in this chamber. To have been the presiding officer of this august body is an honor of which even the most illustrious citizen might be proud. I am persuaded that no occupant of this Chair, during the one hundred and eight years of our Constitutional history, ever entered upon the discharge of the duties pertaining to this office more deeply impressed with a sense of the responsibilities imposed, or with a higher appreciation of the character and dignity of the great Legislative Assembly.

"During the term just closing, questions of deep import to political parties and to the country have here found earnest and at times passionate discussion. This Chamber has indeed been the arena of great debate. The record of four years of parliamentary struggles, of masterful debates, of important legislation, is closed, and passes now to the domain of history.

"I think I can truly say, in the words of a distinguished predecessor, 'In the discharge of my official duties, I have known no cause, no party, no friend.' It has been my earnest endeavor justly to interpret, and faithfully to execute, the rules of the Senate. At times the temptation may be strong to compass partisan ends by a disregard or a perversion of the rules. Yet, I think it safe to say, the result, however salutary, will be dearly purchased by a departure from the method prescribed by the Senate for its own guidance. A single instance, as indicated, might prove the forerunner of untold evils.

"'T will be recorded for a precedent,
And many an error by the same example
Will rush into the State.'

"It must not be forgotten that the rules governing this body are founded deep in human experience; that they are the result of centuries of tireless effort in legislative hall, to conserve, to render stable and secure, the rights and liberties which have been achieved by conflict. By its rules, the Senate wisely fixes the limits to its own power. Of those who clamor against the Senate and its mode of procedure it may be truly said, 'They know not what they do.' In this Chamber alone are preserved, without restraint, two essentials of wise legislation and of good government—the right of amendment and of debate. Great evils often result from hasty legislation, rarely from the delay which follows full discussion and deliberation. In my humble judgment, the historic Senate, preserving the unrestricted right of amendment and of debate, maintaining intact the time-honored parliamentary methods and amenities which unfailingly secure action after deliberation, possesses in our scheme of government a value which can not be measured by words. The Senate is a perpetual body. In the terse words of an eminent Senator now present: 'The men who framed the Constitution had studied thoroughly all former attempts at Republican government. History was strewn with the wrecks of unsuccessful democracies. Sometimes the usurpation of the executive power, sometimes the fickleness and unbridled license of the people, had brought popular governments to destruction. To guard against these dangers, they placed their chief hope in the Senate. The Senate which was organized in 1789, at the inauguration of the Government, abides and will continue to abide, one and the same body, until the Republic itself shall be overthrown, or time shall be no more.'

"Twenty-four Senators who have occupied seats in this Chamber during my term of office are no longer members of this body. Five of that number— Stanford, Colquitt, Vance, Stockbridge, and Wilson— 'shattered with the contentions of the Great Hall,' full of years and of honors have passed from earthly scenes. The fall of the gavel will conclude the long and honorable terms of service of other Senators, who will be borne in kind remembrance by their associates who remain.

"I would do violence to my feelings if I failed to express my thanks to the officers of this body for the fidelity with which they have discharged their important duties, and for the kindly assistance and unfailing courtesy of which I have been the recipient.

"For the able and distinguished gentleman who succeeds me as your presiding officer, I earnestly invoke the same co-operation and courtesy which you have so generously accorded me.

"Senators, my parting words have been spoken, and I now discharge my last official duty, that of declaring the Senate adjourned without day."

V THE SENATE OF THE UNITED STATES

DIFFICULTY OF FORMULATING A FEDERAL CONSTITUTION—THE CONVENTION OF 1787 SEES THE NECESSITY FOR A GENERAL GOVERNMENT WITH PLENARY POWERS—JEALOUSY OF THE SMALLER TOWARD THE LARGER STATES— BRITISH PARLIAMENT TAKEN, WITH QUALIFICATIONS, AS THE MODEL FOR THE HOUSES OF CONGRESS—EQUAL STATE REPRESENTATION IN THE SENATE— NON-EXISTENCE OF ANY METHOD FOR TERMINATING DEBATES IN THE SENATE— POTENCY OF THE PRESIDENT'S VETO—ABUSE OF THE *CLOTURE* IN THE HOUSE—PROCEDURE IN THE EVENT OF THE FAILURE OF THE PEOPLE TO ELECT A PRESIDENT OR A VICE-PRESIDENT—THE HAYES-TILDEN CONTEST—DANGER OF USURPATION OF POWER BY THE EXECUTIVE—THE SENATE AS A HIGH COURT OF IMPEACHMENT—TRIAL OF CHASE OF MARYLAND—TRIAL OF BELKNAP, SECRETARY OF WAR—TRIAL OF PRESIDENT JOHNSON.

It is a well-known fact in our political history that the convention which formulated our Federal Constitution greatly exceeded the powers delegated to its members by their respective States. It was the supreme moment, and upon the action of the historic assemblage depended events of far-reaching consequence. The Constitution of the United States is the enduring monument to the courage, the forecast, the wisdom of the members of the Convention of 1787. It was theirs to cut the Gordian knot, to break with the past, and, regardless of the jealousies and antagonisms of individual States, to establish the more perfect union, which has been declared by an eminent British statesman "the greatest work ever struck off at a given time from the brain and purpose of man."

The oft-quoted expression of Gladstone is, however, more rhetorical than accurate. The Constitution of the United States was not "struck off at a given time," but as declared by Bancroft, "the materials for its building were the gifts of the ages." In the words of Lieber, "What the ancients said of the avenging gods, that they were shod with wool, is true of great ideas in government. They approach slowly. Great truths dwell a long time with small minorities."

The period following the treaty of peace with Great Britain in 1783, which terminated the War of the Revolution, has been not inaptly designated "the critical period of American history." The Revolutionary Government, under which Washington had been chosen to the chief command of the colonial forces, the early battles fought, and the Declaration of Independence promulgated, had been superseded in 1781 by a Government created under the Articles of Confederation. The latter Government, while in a vital sense a mere rope of sand, was a long step in the right direction; the earnest of the more perfect union yet to follow.

Under the Government, more shadowy than real, thus created, the closing battles of the Revolution were fought, independence achieved, a treaty of peace concluded, and our recognition as a sovereign Republic obtained from our late antagonist and other European nations.

The Articles of Confederation, submitted for ratification by the Colonial Congress to the individual States while the country was yet in the throes of a doubtful struggle, fell far short of establishing what in even crude form could properly be designated a Government. The Confederation was wholly lacking in one essential of all Governments: the power to execute its own decrees. Its avowed purpose was to establish "a firm league of friendship," or, as the name indicates, a mere confederation of the colonies. The parties to this league were independent political communities, and by express terms, each State was to retain all rights, sovereignty, and jurisdiction not expressly delegated to the Confederation. In a Congress consisting of a single House were vested the powers thus grudgingly conferred. Its members were to be chosen by the States as such; upon every question the vote was given by States, each, regardless of population, having but a single vote. The revenues and the regulation of foreign commerce were to remain under the control of the respective States, and no provision was made for borrowing money for the necessary maintenance of the general Government. In a word, in so far as a Government at all, it was in the main one of independent States, and in no sense that with which we are familiar, a Government of the entire people. Whatever existed of executive power was in a committee of the Congress; the only provision for meeting the expenses of the late war and the interest upon the public debt was by requisition upon the States, with no shadow of power for its enforcement.

Under the conditions briefly mentioned, with the United States of America a byword among the nations, the now historic Convention of 1787 assembled in Philadelphia, in the room where eleven years earlier had been promulgated the Declaration of Independence. It consisted of fifty-five members; and without a dissenting voice, Washington, a delegate from Virginia, was elected its President. Not the least of his public services was now to be rendered in the work of safeguarding the fruits of successful revolution by a stable Government. Chief among the associates with whom he was daily in earnest, anxious counsel in the great assemblage, were men whose names live with his in history. If Franklin, Wilson, Sherman, King, Randolph, Rutledge, Mason, Pinckney, Hamilton, Madison, and their associates had rendered no public service other than as builders of the Constitution, that alone would entitle them to the measureless gratitude of all future generations of their countrymen.

When they were assembled, the startling fact was at once apparent that, under the Confederation, with its constituent States at times in almost open hostility to one another, the country was gradually drifting into a condition of anarchy.

It is our glory to-day, and will be that of countless on-coming generations, that the men of '87 were equal to the stupendous emergency. Regardless of instructions, expressed or implied, the master spirits of the Convention, looking beyond local prejudices and State environment, and appealing to time for vindication, with a ken that now seems more than human, discerned the safety, the well-being, the glory of their countrymen, bound up in a general Government of plenary powers, a Government "without a seam in its garment, to foreign nations."

To this end the proposition submitted by Paterson of New Jersey, in the early sittings of the Convention, for a mere enlargement of the powers of the Confederation, was decisively rejected. With the light that could be gleaned from the pages of Montesquieu, the suggestive lessons to be drawn from the fate of the short-lived republics whose wrecks lay along the pathway of history, and from the unwritten Constitution of the mother country, as their only guides, the leaders of the Convention were at once in the difficult role of constructive statesmen. The Herculean task to which with unwearied effort they now addressed themselves was that of "builders" of the Constitution; the establishers, for the ages, of the fundamental law for a free people.

One of the perils which early beset the Convention, and whose spectre haunted its deliberations till the close, was the hostility engendered by the dread and jealousy of the smaller toward the larger States. This fact will in some measure explain what in later years have been denominated the anomalies of the Constitution. To a correct understanding of the motives of the builders, and an appreciation of their marvellous accomplishment, it must not be forgotten that "The foundations of the Constitution were laid in compromise." The men of '87 had but recently emerged from the bloody conflict through which they had escaped the domination of kingly power. With the tyranny of George the Third yet burning in their memories, it is not to be wondered that the Revolutionary patriots of the less populous States were loath to surrender rights, deemed, by them, secure under their local governments; that they dreaded the establishment of what they apprehended might prove an overshadowing—possibly unlimited—central authority.

The creation of a general Government, with its three separate and measurably independent departments, happily concluded, with the delegated powers of each distinctly enumerated, the salient question as to the basis of representation in the Congress at once pressed for determination. Upon the question of provision for a chief executive, and his investment with the powers necessarily incident to the great office, there was after much debate a practical consensus of opinion. And practical unanimity in the end prevailed regarding the judicial department, with its great court without a prototype at its creation, and even yet without a counterpart in foreign Governments.

The rock upon which the Convention barely escaped early dissolution, was the basis of representation in the Congress created under the great co-ordinate legislative department. The model for our Senate and House of Representatives was unquestionably the British Parliament. This statement is to be taken with weighty qualifications; for hereditary or ecclesiastical representation, as in the House of Lords, is wholly unknown in our system of government. The significant resemblance is that of our Lower House to the British Commons. In these respective chambers, the people, as such, have representation.

The earnest, at times violent, contention of the smaller States, in our historic Convention, was for equal representation in both branches of the proposed national legislature. This was strenuously resisted by the larger States under the powerful leadership of Madison of Virginia, and Wilson of Pennsylvania. Their equally earnest, and by no means illogical contention was for popular representation in each House, as outlined in the Virginia plan which had been taken as the framework of the proposed Constitution. The opposing views appeared wholly irreconcilable, and for a time the parting of the ways seemed to have been reached. Threats of dissolution were not uncommon in the Chamber, and for many days the spirit of despair brooded over the Convention. A delegate from Maryland vehemently declared: "The Convention is on the verge of dissolution, scarcely held together by the strength of a hair." Well has it been said: "In even the contemplation of the fearful consequence of such a calamity, the imagination stands aghast."

At the crucial moment mentioned, Sherman and Ellsworth presented upon behalf of Connecticut the first and most far-reaching of the great compromises of the Constitution. The Connecticut plan was in brief to the effect that in fixing the ratio of representation there should be recognition alike of the federal and of the national feature in government, in a word, that in the Lower House the national, and in the upper the federal principle should have full recognition. This was a departure from the Virginia plan to the extent that it in effect proposed the establishment of a federal republic,—in the concrete, that the House should be composed of representatives chosen directly by the people from districts of equal population; while representation in the Senate should be that of the States, each, regardless of population, to have two members, to be chosen at stated periods by their respective legislatures.

After heated debate, this compromise was carried by a bare majority, and the provision for popular representation in the House, and equal State representation in the Senate, became engrafted upon our Federal Constitution. This feature, an eminent foreign writer has declared, "is the chief American contribution to the common treasures of political civilization." The eminent writer, De Tocqueville, has well said: "The principle of the independence of the States triumphed in the formation of the Senate, and that of the sovereignty of the nation in the composition of the House of Representatives."

The success of the Connecticut plan made possible that of other essential compromises which followed; and the result was, as the sublime consummation of wise deliberation and patriotic concession, the establishment of the Government of the United States.

It is the proud boast of the Briton, that "the British Constitution has no single date from which its duration is to be reckoned, and that the origin of English law is as undiscoverable as that of the Nile." Our Government, buttressed upon a written Constitution of enumerated and logically implied powers, had its historic beginning upon that masterful day, April 30, 1789, when Washington took solemn oath of office as our first President.

The Senate of the United States has been truly declared "the greatest deliberative body known to men." By Constitutional provision it consists of two members from each State, chosen by the Legislature thereof, for the term of six years. No person has the legal qualification for Senator "unless he shall have attained the age of thirty years, be an inhabitant of the State for which he is chosen, and have been nine years a citizen of the United States." No State, without its consent, can ever be deprived, even by Constitutional amendment, of its equal representation in the Senate. Nevada with a population of less than forty thousand has her equal voice with New York with a population exceeding seven million. This anomaly was occasioned by concession by the larger to the smaller States in the Convention of 1787, a concession which made possible the establishment of the federal Union.

One essential difference between the House of Representatives and the Senate is that to the latter "the previous question" is unknown; no method existing for terminating debate, other than by unanimous consent. Here, unlimited discussion and amendment can have their perfect work. Within the last three or four decades many fruitless attempts have been made to introduce a modified "previous question" or *cloture*, by which the Senate could be brought to an immediate vote. At first blush such change might seem desirable, but experience has demonstrated the wisdom of the method to which there has been such steady adherence. It secures time for consideration and full discussion upon every question. In the end the vote will be taken. Debate is rarely prolonged beyond reasonable limit. Not infrequently the public welfare is imperilled by too much, rather than too little, legislation. It was the belief of Jefferson that government should touch the citizen at the fewest possible points. The quaint lines of the old English poet have lost nothing of their significance:

"How small, of all that human hearts endure,
That part which laws or kings can cause or cure!"

The House of Representatives has in large degree ceased to be a deliberative body. Under the iron rule of the "previous question" measures of importance are hurriedly passed without the possibility of discussion or amendment. The rights of the minority are at times but as the dust in the balance.

Unlike the House of Lords, the Senate is in reality an important factor in legislation. As is well known in recent years, government in Great Britain is virtually that of the House of Commons, in large measure through a cabinet practically of its own appointment. The King is little more than a ceremonial figure-head, and the House of Lords is almost in a death struggle for existence. The end would probably come by serious attempt upon its part to thwart the popular will as expressed through the House of Commons. The power of Edward the Seventh is but a shadow of that exercised almost without let or hindrance by the predecessors of Queen Victoria. The veto power, so potent an instrumentality in the hands of the American President, is to all intents a dead letter in the mythical British Constitution. For a century and a half it has remained in practical abeyance. It is believed that its attempted exercise at this day would produce revolution; possibly endanger the existence of the throne.

By means of what is known as a suspension of the rules, under the operation of the "previous question," much important legislation is enacted in our House of Representatives, without the minority having the privilege of debate, or amendment, or even the necessary time to a full understanding of the pending measure. The constantly recurring "River and

Harbor Bill," with its enormous sum total of appropriations, is a striking object lesson of the vicious character of such methods.

In the light of what has been suggested, the wisdom displayed in the establishment of the bicameral, or two-chamber system, in our legislative scheme, is strikingly apparent. At the time of its creation, it had no counterpart in any of the Governments of continental Europe. Its only prototype, in so far as it was such, was the British House of Lords as already indicated.

Save only in the right to originate revenue bills, the power of the Senate is concurrent with that of the House in all matters of legislation; and these are wisely subject to amendment by the Senate. The presiding officer of the Senate is the Vice-President of the United States, and in his absence a Senator chosen as President *pro tempore.*

In the event of a failure on the part of the people to elect a President or a Vice-President of the United States, through electors duly appointed at the stated time, the duty of such election devolves upon the House and the Senate acting independently of each other. The choice of President is limited to the three candidates who have received the highest number of votes in the several electoral colleges. The determination is by the House of Representatives, the vote being by States. In such event the vote of Nevada would again count equally with that of New York. In the contingency mentioned, of a failure to elect a Vice-President, the election devolves upon the Senate, each Senator having a personal vote; and the person chosen must by Constitutional requirement be one of the two receiving the highest number of electoral votes. In 1836, Mr. Van Buren of New York received a majority of the electoral votes for President; but no person receiving a majority for the second office, Colonel Richard M. Johnson, of Kentucky, one of the two persons eligible, was chosen by the Senate. No similar instance has occurred in our history.

In the Presidential election of 1800, and in that of 1824, the ultimate determination was by the House of Representatives. In the former, Jefferson and Burr each received seventy-three electoral votes, without specification as to whether intended for the first or second office. The protracted struggle which followed resulted in the choice of Jefferson for the higher office. This fortunate termination was in large measure through the influence of Alexander Hamilton, and was the initial step in the bitter personal strife which eventuated in his early death at the hands of Burr. In the light of events, we may well believe that not the least of the public services of Hamilton was his unselfish interposition at the critical moment mentioned. The possibility of similar complication again arising in the election of the President was soon thereafter obviated by the Twelfth Amendment to the Constitution.

Seldom in Presidential contests has there been such an array of great names presented as in that of 1824. The era of good feeling which characterized the administration of Monroe found sudden termination in the rival candidacy of two members of his cabinet, for the succession—Mr. Adams, Secretary of State, and Mr. Crawford, of the Treasury. The other aspirants were Clay, the brilliant Speaker of the House of Representatives, and Jackson, with laurels yet fresh from the battlefield of New Orleans. Mr. Clay receiving the smallest number of electoral votes, and no candidate the majority thereof, the selection again devolved upon the House, resulting eventually in the choice of John Quincy Adams.

In the two Presidential contests last mentioned, the Senate had no part in the final adjustment. An occasion, however, arose nearly a half-century later, involving the succession to the Presidency, in which the Senate, equally with the House, was an important factor in the final determination. The country has known few periods of profounder anxiety to thoughtful men, or of greater peril to stable government, than the feverish hours immediately succeeding the Presidential contest of 1876. The shadow cast by the Hayes-Tilden contest even yet, in a measure, lingers. As a Representative in Congress at the time, I was deeply impressed with the gravity of the situation. In the instances first mentioned it was the mere question of the failure of any candidate to receive a majority of the electoral votes. The framers of the Constitution had wisely provided for such contingency by action of the House in manner indicated. The far more serious question now confronting was, For whom had the disputed States of Florida and Louisiana cast their votes? The settlement of this question virtually determined which candidate should be inaugurated President. Conflicting certificates from the States named had been forwarded to the seat of government, and were in keeping of the officer designated by law as the custodian of the electoral returns from the several States. The contingency which had now arisen was one for which there was no provision. The sole function of the joint session of the Senate and the House was "to open all the certificates and count the votes." This was "the be all and end all" of its authority. Upon the arising of any question demanding a vote, or even deliberation, the members of the joint session could only return to their separate chambers. They could act only in their separate capacities. In a word, the perilous exigency presented was, the friends of one candidate having a majority in the Senate, and of the other in control of the House; conflicting certificates presented, upon which hinged the result, and the tension throughout the entire country assuming alarming proportions. Coupled with the question of peaceable succession to the great office was that of the durability of popular government. Tremendous issues, upon which depended unfathomable consequences, pressed for settlement; and no tribunal was in existence for their determination.

The sober second thought of those upon whom was then cast the responsibility asserted itself at the opportune moment, and a commission consisting of an equal number of Senators, Representatives, and Judges of the Great Court was created. This commission— extra-Constitutional, as was believed by many—decided as to the validity of the conflicting certificates, and in effect determined as to the Presidential succession.

The justification of the act creating the commission might well rest upon the fact that an overshadowing emergency had arisen, where necessity becomes the paramount law. "The pendulum of history swings in centuries," and a single term of the great office weighed little in view of the perils that surely awaited a failure to secure peaceful adjustment.

I may be pardoned for adding that in the retrospect of a life, no longer a short one, I have no regrets that my humble voice and vote were given for peaceable and lawful adjustment of a perilous controversy, that cast its dark shadow across our national pathway —such a one, as, please God, our country may never witness again.

Unquestionably the least satisfactory of the devices of our Federal Constitution is that for the election of President and Vice-President through the instrumentality of colleges of electors chosen by the several States. Upon this subject notes of warning have been many times sounded by eminent statesmen of the past. In view of the hazardous complications through which we have happily passed, and of those which may possibly beset our future pathway as a nation, it would indeed be the part of wisdom, if by Constitutional amendment a less complicated and cumbrous instrumentality could be devised for ascertaining and making effective the popular will in the selection of President and Vice-President of the United States.

One of the apprehensions of the framers of the Constitution was that of executive usurpation of functions lawfully pertaining to the co-ordinate department of the Government. This was measurably guarded against by the provision requiring appointment to high office to be by and with the advice and consent of the Senate. While the President by the exercise of the veto power possesses a negative upon legislation, the Senate by virtue of the provision quoted has an equally effective negative upon executive appointments to important office.

To the President is confided primarily the treaty-making power. Treaties are the law of the land, and their observance in spirit as well as letter touches the national honor. Upon this often depends the issue of peace or war. Before becoming effective their ratification by a two-thirds vote of the Senate is indispensable. From these and other safeguards strikingly appear what are known as "the checks and balances" of the Constitution.

An important function of the Senate yet to be mentioned is that of sitting as a high court of impeachment. The President, Vice-President, and other high officials are amenable to its jurisdiction. The initial step, however, in such procedure is by the House of Representatives, as the grand inquest of the nation, presenting articles of impeachment, the Senate possessing the sole power of trial. Six times only in our history has the Senate been resolved into a Court of Impeachment, and only twice—in the case of district judges—has there been a conviction. The earliest trial, more than a century ago, was that of a supreme justice, Chase of Maryland. Apart from the high official position of the accused, and the august tribunal before which he was arraigned, this trial is of historic interest from the fact that it involved the once famous Alien and Sedition Laws; that John Randolph was chief of the managers on the part of the House; Pinckney, Martin, and William Wirt of counsel for the defence; and Vice-President Aaron Burr, the presiding officer of the court.

The trial of Belknap, Secretary of War, is still within the memory of many. As a member of the House, I attended it from the beginning. It appearing from the evidence that Belknap had resigned his office before the presentation of the articles of impeachment, he was acquitted. The fate of General Belknap was indeed a sad one, that of a hitherto honorable career suddenly terminated under a cloud. Morally guiltless himself, his chivalric assumption of responsibility for the act of one near to him, and his patiently abiding the consequence, has invested with something of pathos, and even romance, the memory of his trial.

An impeachment that has left its deep impress upon history, and before which all others pale into insignificance, was that of President Johnson, charged by the House of Representatives with the commission of "high crimes and misdemeanors." He had been elected to the second place upon the ticket with Mr. Lincoln in 1864, and upon the death of the latter, succeeded to the Presidency. Radical differences with the majority in the Congress, upon questions vital and far-reaching, ultimately culminated in the presentation of articles of impeachment. Partisan feeling was at its height, and the excitement throughout the country intense. The trial was protracted for many weeks without jot or tittle of abatement in the public interest. The chief managers on the part of the House were Benjamin F. Butler and Thaddeus Stevens. The array of counsel for the accused included the names of Benjamin R. Curtis, Henry Stanberry, and William M. Evarts. The Senate, in its high character of a court, was presided over for the first and only time by the Chief Justice of the United States. The trial was conducted with marked decorum; every phase of questions touching the exercise of executive authority, or lawful discretion, was fully discussed, the very springs of legislative power, and its limitation under Constitutional government, were laid bare—all with an eloquence unparalleled save only in the wondrous efforts of Sheridan, Fox, and Burke in the historic impeachment of Warren Hastings before the British House of Lords. The spectacle presented was one that challenged the attention and wonder of the nations; that of the chief magistrate of a great republic at the bar of justice, calmly awaiting judgment without popular disturbance or attempted revolt, under the safeguards of law and its appointments. The highest test of the virtue of our system of representative government, and of the unfaltering devotion of our people to its prescribed methods, is to be found in the fact, that during the protracted trial the various departments proceeded with wonted regularity; the verdict of the Senate was acquiesced in without manifestation of hostility; partisan passion soon abated and the great impeachment peaceably relegated to the domain of history.

The House of Representatives has an official life of short duration. Its reorganization is biennial. The Senate is enduring. Always organized, it is the continuing body of our national legislature. Its members change, but the Senate continues the same now, as in the first hour of the Republic.

In his last great speech in the Senate, Mr. Webster said:

"It is fortunate that there is a Senate of the United States; a body not yet moved from its propriety, not lost to a full sense of its own dignity and its own high responsibilities, and a body to which the country looks with confidence for wise, moderate, patriotic, and healing counsels."

Upon the first assembling of the Senate in its present magnificent chamber nearly half a century ago, the Vice-President closed his eloquent dedicatory address with the words:

"Though these marble walls moulder into ruins, the Senate in another age may bear into a new and larger chamber the Constitution vigorous and inviolate, and the last generation of posterity shall witness the deliberations of the representatives of American States still united, prosperous, and free."

VI A TRIBUTE TO LINCOLN

THE WRITER'S SPEECH AT THE LINCOLN CENTENNIAL
CELEBRATION, 1909 —PATRIOTIC CHARACTER OF THE
MEETING—LEADING HISTORICAL EVENTS BETWEEN 1809
AND 1909—BIRTH OF LINCOLN—TERRITORIAL
ORGANIZATION OF ILLINOIS—BIRTH OF DARWIN AND
GLADSTONE—CAREER OF NAPOLEON—WAR OF 1812—
THE SLAVERY QUESTION—SEIZURE AND SURRENDER OF
MASON AND SLIDELL—EMANCIPATION OF SLAVES.

February 12, 1909, will long be remembered as the day of the celebration of the hundredth anniversary of the birth of Abraham Lincoln. For on that day was the culmination of a celebration which, in various parts of the country, had begun at least a week before. Rarely has there been an occasion of so much decoration, so many addresses, or so much patriotism. The largest celebration occurred in New York City, but that of Chicago, if not so large, was at least as interesting and impressive, for in it and surrounding parts of Illinois some of the most memorable events in the life of Lincoln took place. Yet these manifestations were not a whit more patriotic than those of many small towns and villages.

Every hamlet, every town, and every city of the United States seemed to be imbued with a desire to do honor to the memory of the man Lincoln. Every newspaper and every magazine of whatever name or order was filled with pictures, anecdotes, and sketches of the life of "Honest Abe." Books galore were published emphasizing every phase of his life, character, work, and influence; and they sold well.

My contribution to this occasion was the following speech delivered at Bloomington, Illinois, February 12:

"We have assembled to commemorate one of the epoch-making events in history. In the humblest of homes in the wilds of a new and sparsely settled State, Abraham Lincoln was born one hundred years ago, this day.

"The twelfth day of February, like the twenty-second day of the same month, is one of the sacred days in the American calendar. It is well that this day be set apart from ordinary uses, the headlong rush in the crowded mart suspended, the voice of fierce contention in legislative halls be hushed, and that the American people—whether at home, in foreign lands, or upon the deep—honor themselves by honoring the memory of the man of whose birth this day is the first centennial.

"This coming together is no idle ceremony, no unmeaning observance. To this man, more than to any other, are we indebted for the supreme fact that ninety millions of people are at this hour, in the loftiest sense of the expression, fellow-citizens of a common country. Some of us, through the mists of half a century, distinctly recall the earnest tones in which Mr. Lincoln in public speech uttered the words, 'My fellow-citizens.' Truly the magical words 'fellow-citizens' never fail to touch a responsive chord in the patriotic heart. Was it the gifted Prentiss who at a critical moment of our history exclaimed:

"'For whether upon the Sabine or the St. John's; standing in the shadow of Bunker Hill or amid the ruins of Jamestown; near the great northern lakes or within the sound of the Father of Waters flowing unvexed to the sea; in the crowded mart of the great metropolis or upon the western verge of the continent, where the restless tide of emigration is stayed only by the ocean—everywhere upon this broad domain, thank God, I can still say "fellow-citizens"!'

"Let us pause for a moment and briefly note some of the marvellous results wrought out by the toil, strife, and sacrifice of the century whose close we commemorate. The Year of Our Lord 1809 was one of large place in history. The author of the Declaration of Independence was upon the eve of final retirement from public place, and the Presidential term of James Madison just beginning, when in a log cabin near the western verge of civilization the eyes of Abraham Lincoln first opened upon the world. The vast area stretching from the Rocky Mountains to the Pacific Ocean was under the dominion of Spain. Two decades only had passed since the establishment of the United States Government under the Federal Constitution, and the inauguration of Washington as its first President. Lewis and Clark had but recently returned from the now historic expedition to the Columbia and the Oregon,—an expedition fraught with momentous consequences to the oncoming generations of the Republic. Only five years had passed since President Jefferson had purchased, for fifteen millions of dollars from Napoleon Bonaparte, the Louisiana country, extending from the Gulf of Mexico to the frozen lakes, out of which were to be carved sixteen magnificent States to become enduring parts of the American Republic. From the early Colonial settlements that fringed the Atlantic, a tide of hardy emigration was setting in to the westward, and, regardless of privation or danger, laying the sure foundation of future commonwealths. Four States only had been admitted into the Federal Union, and the population of the entire country was less than that of the State of New York to-day. This same year witnessed the first organization of Illinois into a distinct political community and its creation, by act of Congress, as the Territory of Illinois, with a white population less than one-twentieth of that of this good county to-day. The United States having barely escaped a war with France,—our ally in securing our independence,—was earnestly struggling for distinct place among the nations.

"No less significant, and fraught with deep consequences, were events occurring in the Old Worlds. The year 1809 witnessed the birth of Darwin and Gladstone. The despotism of the Dark Ages still brooded over Continental Europe, and whatever savored of popular public rule—even in its mildest form—was yet in the distant future. Alexander the First was on the throne of Russia,— and her millions of serfs were oppressed as by the iron hand of the Caesars. The splendid German Empire of to-day had no place on the map of the world; its present powerful constituencies were antagonistic provinces and warring independent cities. Napoleon Bonaparte—'calling Fate into the lists'—by a succession of victories unparalleled in history had overturned thrones, compelled kings upon bended knee to sue for peace, and substituted those of his own household for dynasties that reached back the entire length of human history. With his star still in the ascendant, disturbed by no forecast of the horrid nightmare of the retreat from Moscow, 'with legions scattered by the artillery of the snows and the cavalry of the winds,' tortured by no dream of Leipsic, of Elba, of Waterloo, of St. Helena, he was still the 'man of destiny,' — relentlessly pursuing the *ignis fatuus* of universal empire.

"The year that witnessed the birth of Abraham Lincoln witnessed the gathering of the disturbing elements that were to precipitate the second war with the mother country. England—with George the Third still upon the throne—by insulting and cruel search of American vessels upon the high seas, was rendering inevitable the declaration of war by Congress,—a war of humiliation upon our part by the disgraceful surrender of Hull at Detroit and the wanton burning of our Capitol, but crowned with honor by the naval victories of Lawrence, Decatur, and Perry, and eventually terminated by the capture of the British army at New Orleans. As an object lesson of the marvels of the closing century, an event of such momentous consequence to the world as the formulation of the Treaty of Ghent, by which peace was restored between England and America, would to-day be known at every fireside a few hours after its occurrence. And yet, within the now closing century, the battle of New Orleans was fought twenty-three days after the Treaty of Ghent, coming by slow-sailing vessels across the Atlantic, had received the signature of our commissioners; all unsettled accounts squared eternally between America and Great Britain; and the United States, by valor no less than by diplomacy, exalted to honored and enduring place among the nations.

"The fifty-six years that compassed the life of Abraham Lincoln were years of transcendent significance to our country. While he was yet in his rude cradle the African slave trade had just terminated by constitutional inhibition. While Lincoln was still in attendance upon the old field school, Henry Clay—yet to be known as the 'great pacificator'—was pressing the admission of Missouri into the Union under the first compromise upon the question of slavery since the adoption of the Federal Constitution. From the establishment of the Government the question of human slavery was the one perilous question,—the one constant menace to national unity, until its final extinction amid the flames of war. Marvellous to man are the purposes of the Almighty. What seer could have foretold that, from this humblest of homes upon the frontier, was to spring the man who at the crucial moment should cut the Gordian knot, liberate a race, and give to the ages enlarged and grander conception of the deathless principles of the declaration of human rights?

"'Often do the spirits of great events
Stride on before the events,
And in to-day already walks to-morrow.'

"The first inauguration of President Lincoln noted the hour of breaking with the past. It was a period of gloom, when the very foundations were shaken, when no man could foretell the happening of the morrow, when strong men trembled at the possibility of the destruction of our Government.

"Pause a moment, and recall the man who, under the conditions mentioned, on the fourth of March, 1861, entered upon the duties of the great office to which he had been chosen. He came from the common walks of life—from what, in other countries, would be called the great middle class. His early home was one of the humblest, where he was a stranger to the luxuries and to many of the ordinary comforts of life. His opportunities for education were only such as were common in the remote habitations of our Western country one century ago.

"Under such conditions, began a career which in grandeur and achievement has but a single counterpart in our history. And what a splendid commentary this upon our free institutions,—upon the sublime underlying principle of popular government! How inspiring to the youth of high aims every incident of the pathway that led from the frontier cabin to the Executive Mansion,—from the humblest position to the most exalted yet attained by man! In no other country than ours could such attainment have been possible for the boy whose hands were inured to toil, whose bread was eaten under the hard conditions that poverty imposes, whose only heritage was brain, integrity, lofty ambition, and indomitable purpose. Let it never be forgotten that the man of whom I speak possessed an integrity that could know no temptation, a purity of life that was never questioned, a patriotism that no sectional lines could limit, and a fixedness of purpose that knew no shadow of turning.

"The decade extending from our first treaty of peace with Great Britain to the inauguration of Washington has been truly denominated the critical period of our history. The eloquence of Adams and Henry had precipitated revolution; the unfaltering courage of Washington and his comrades had secured independence; but the more difficult task of garnering up the fruits of victory by stable government was yet to be achieved. The hour for the constructive statesman had arrived, and James Madison and his associates, equal to the great emergency, formulated the Federal Constitution.

"No less critical was the period that bounded the active life of the man whose memory we honor to-day. One perilous question to national unity which for nearly three-quarters of a century had been the subject of repeated compromise by patriotic statesmen; the apple of discord producing sectional antagonism, whose shadow had darkened our national pathway from the beginning,—was now for weal or woe to find determination. Angry debate in the Senate and upon the forum was now hushed, and the supreme question that took hold of national life was to find enduring arbitrament in the dread tribunal of war.

"It was well that in such an hour, with such tremendous issues in the balance, a steady hand was at the helm; that a conservative statesman—one whose mission was to save, not to destroy—was in the high place of responsibility and power. It booted little then that he was untaught of schools, unskilled in the ways of courts, but it was of supreme moment that he could touch responsive chords in the great American heart, all-important that his very soul yearned for the preservation of the Government established through the toil and sacrifice of the generation that had gone. How hopeless the Republic in that dark hour, had its destiny hung upon the statecraft of Talleyrand, the eloquence of Mirabeau, or the genius of Napoleon! It was fortunate indeed that the ark of our covenant was then borne by the plain, brave man of conciliatory spirit and kind words, whose heart, as Emerson has said, 'was as large as the world, but nowhere had room for the memory of a wrong.'

"Nobler words have never fallen from human lips than the closing sentences of his first inaugural uttered on one of the pivotal days of human history, immediately after taking the oath to preserve, protect, and defend his country:

"'I am loath to close. We are not enemies, but friends. Though passion may have strained, it must not break our bonds of affection. The mystic chords of memory, stretching from every battlefield and patriot's grave to every heart and hearthstone of this broad land, will yet swell the chorus of the Union when touched as they will be by the better angels of our nature.'

"In the light of what we now know so well, nothing is hazarded in saying that the death of no man has been to his country so irreparable a loss, or one so grievous to be borne, as that of Abraham Lincoln. When Washington died his work was done, his life well rounded out. Save one, the years allotted had been passed. Not so with Lincoln. To him a grander task was yet in waiting, one no other could so well perform. The assassin's pistol proved the veritable Pandora's box from which sprung evils untold,—whose consequences have never been measured.—to one-third of the States of our Union. But for his untimely death how the current of history might have been changed,—and many a sad chapter remained unwritten! How earnestly he desired a restored Union, and that the blessings of peace and of concord should be the common heritage of every section, is known to all.

"When in the loom of time have such words been heard above the din of fierce conflict as his sublime utterances but a brief time before his tragic death—

"'With malice toward none; with charity for all; with firmness in the right, as God gives us to see the right, let us strive on to finish the work we are in, to bind up the nation's wounds; to care for him who shall have borne the battle, and for his widow and his orphan, to do all which may achieve a lasting peace among ourselves, and with all nations.'

"No fitter occasion than this can ever arise in which to refer to two historical events that at crucial moments tested to the utmost the safe and far-seeing statesmanship of President Lincoln. The first was the seizure upon the high seas of Mason and Slidell, the accredited representatives from the Southern Confederacy to the courts of England and France, respectively. The seizure was in November, 1861, by Captain Wilkes of our navy; and the envoys named were taken by him from the *Trent*, a mail-carrying steamer of the British Government. The act of Captain Wilkes met with enthusiastic commendation throughout the entire country; he was voted the thanks of Congress, and his act publicly approved by the Secretary of the Navy.

"The demand by the British government for reparation upon the part of the United States was prompt and explicit. The perils that then environed us were such as rarely shadow the pathway of nations. Save Russia alone, our Government had no friend among the crowned heads of Europe. Menaced by the peril of the recognition of the Southern Confederacy by England and France, with the very stars apparently warring against us in their courses, the position of the President was in the last degree trying. To surrender the

Confederate envoys was in a measure humiliating and in opposition to the popular impulse; their retention, the signal for the probable recognition of the Southern Confederacy by the European powers, and the certain and immediate declaration of war by England.

"The good genius of President Lincoln—rather his wise, just, far-seeing statesmanship—stood him well in hand at the critical moment. Had a rash and impulsive man then held the executive office, what a sea of troubles might have overwhelmed us! How the entire current of our history might have been changed!

"The calm, wise President, in his council chamber, aided by his closest official adviser, Secretary Seward, discerned clearly the path of national safety and of honor. None the less was the act of the President one of justice, one that will abide the sure test of time. Upon the real ground that the seizure of the envoys was in violation of the Law of Nations, they were eventually surrendered, and war with England, as well as the immediate danger of recognition of the Confederacy, averted. Let it not be forgotten that this very act of President Lincoln was a triumphant vindication of our Government in its second war with Great Britain—a war waged as a protest on our part against British seizure and impressment of American citizens upon the high seas.

"The other incident, to which I briefly refer, was the proclamation of emancipation. As a war measure of stupendous significance in the national defence, as well as of justice to the enslaved, such proclamation, immediate in time and radical in terms, had to greater or less degree been urged upon the President from the outbreak of the Rebellion. That slavery was to perish amid the great upheaval became in time the solemn conviction of all thoughtful men. Meanwhile there were divided counsels among the earnest supporters of the President as to the time the masterful act 'that could know no backward steps' should be taken. Unmoved amid divided counsels, and at times fierce dissensions, the calm, far-seeing executive, upon whom was cast the tremendous responsibility, patiently bided his time. Events that are now the masterful theme of history crowded in rapid succession, the opportune moment arrived, the hour struck, the proclamation that has no counterpart fell upon the ears of the startled world, and, as by the interposition of a mightier hand, a race was lifted out of the depths of bondage.

"To the one man at the helm it seemed to have been given to know the day and the hour. At the crucial moment, in one of the exalted days of human history,

"'He sounded forth the trumpet that has never called retreat.'

"The men who knew Abraham Lincoln, who saw him face to face, who heard his voice in public assemblage, have with few exceptions passed to the grave. Another generation is upon the busy stage. The book has forever closed upon the dreadful pageant of civil strife. Sectional animosities, thank God, belong now only to the past. The mantle of Peace is over our entire land, and prosperity within our borders.

"'The war-drum throbs no longer,
And the battle flags are furled
In the parliament of men,
The federation of the world.'

"Through the instrumentality, in no small measure, of the man whose memory we now honor, the Government established by our fathers, untouched by the finger of Time, has descended to us. The responsibility of its preservation and transmission rests upon the successive generations as they come and go. To-day, at this auspicious hour sacred to the memory of Lincoln, let us, his countrymen, inspired by the sublime lessons of his wondrous life, and grateful to God for all He has vouchsafed to our fathers and to us in the past, take courage and turn our faces resolutely, hopefully, trustingly to the future. I know of no words more fitting with which to close this humble tribute to the memory of Abraham Lincoln, than those inscribed upon the monument of Moliere:

"'Nothing was wanting to his glory; he was wanting to ours.'"

VII STEPHEN A. DOUGLAS

DOUGLAS'S HARDSHIPS IN YOUTH—HE IS ADMITTED TO
THE BAR—JACKSON'S TRIUMPH OVER ADAMS IN 1828—
DOUGLAS ENTERS THE ARENA OF DEBATE AT THE AGE
OF 22—BECOMES ATTORNEY-GENERAL—CHOSEN TO
THE TENTH GENERAL ASSEMBLY OF ILLINOIS—
BECOMES SECRETARY OF STATE IN ILLINOIS —DEFENDS
JACKSON'S DECLARATION OF MARTIAL LAW AT NEW
ORLEANS— TAKES PART IN THE OREGON BOUNDARY
DEBATE—ADVOCATES THE ANNEXATION OF TEXAS—IS
ELECTED TO THE SENATE—ADVOCATES THE ADMISSION
OF CALIFORNIA AS A FREE STATE—HE PROCURES A LAND
GRANT TO THE ILLINOIS CENTRAL RAILROAD
COMPANY—IN DEBATING THE KANSAS-NEBRASKA BILL
HE CONTENDS FOR POPULAR SOVEREIGNTY—ORIGIN OF
THE REPUBLICAN PARTY —DOUGLAS LOSES THE
FRIENDSHIP OF THE SOUTH—DEBATES BETWEEN
DOUGLAS AND LINCOLN—LINCOLN'S EARLY HISTORY—
DOUGLAS'S REASONS FOR ADVOCATING POPULAR
SOVEREIGNTY—LINCOLN'S REPLY—THE SLAVERY
QUESTION —THE DEMOCRATIC PARTY RENT ASUNDER—
CONSEQUENT FAILURE OF DOUGLAS TO WIN THE
PRESIDENCY—HIS DEATH.

History has been defined, "the sum of the biographies of a few strong men." Much that is of profound and abiding interest in American history during the two decades immediately preceding our Civil War is bound up in the biography of the strong man of whom I write. Chief among the actors, his place was near the middle of the stage during that eventful and epoch-making period.

Stephen A. Douglas was born in Brandon, Vermont, April 23, 1813, and died in Chicago, Illinois, June 3, 1861. Between the dates given lie the years that up a crowded, eventful life. Left penniless by the death of his father, he was at a tender age dependent upon his own exertions for maintenance and education. At the age of fifteen he apprenticed himself to a cabinet-maker in the town of Middlebury in his native State. Naturally of delicate organization, he was unable long to endure the physical strain of this calling, and at the close of two years' service he returned to his early home. Entering an academy in Brandon, he there for a time pursued with reasonable diligence the studies preparatory to a higher course.

Supplementing the education thus acquired, by a brief course of study in an academy at Canandaigua, New York, at the age of twenty he turned his footsteps westward.

One of his biographers says:

"It is doubtful if among all the thousands who in those early days were constantly faring westward from New England, Virginia, and the Carolinas, there ever was a youth more resolutely and boldly addressed to opportunity than he. Penniless, broken in health, almost diminutive in physical stature, and unknown, he made his way successively to Cincinnati, Louisville, and St. Louis, in search of employment, literally of bread."

By a sudden turn in fortune's wheel his lot was cast in Central Illinois, where his first vocation was that of teacher of a village school. Yet later— after laborious application—admitted to the bar, he courageously entered upon his marvellous career.

His home was Jacksonville, and to the hardy pioneers of Morgan and neighboring counties, it was soon revealed that notwithstanding his slight stature and boyish appearance the youthful Douglas was at once to be taken fully into the account. Self-reliant to the very verge, he unhesitatingly entered the arena of active professional and political strife with foemen worthy the steel of veterans at the bar, and upon the hustings.

The issues were sharply drawn between the two political parties then struggling for ascendancy, and Central Illinois was the home of as brilliant an array of gifted leaders as the Whig party at any time in its palmiest days had known. Hardin, Stuart, Browning, Logan, Baker, Lincoln were just then upon the threshold of careers that have given their names honored and enduring place upon the pages of our history. Into the safe keeping of the leaders just named, were entrusted in large degree the advocacy of the principles of the now historic party, and the political fortunes of its great chieftain, Henry Clay.

As is well known, the principal antagonist of the renowned Whig chieftain was Andrew Jackson. Earlier in their political careers, both had been earnest supporters of the administration of President Monroe, but at its close the leaders last named, with Adams and Crawford, were aspirants to the great office. No candidate receiving a majority of the electoral votes and the selection by Constitutional requirement devolving upon the House of Representatives, Mr. Adams was eventually chosen. His election over his principal competitor, General Jackson, was largely through the influence of Mr. Clay; and the subsequent acceptance by the latter of the office of Secretary of State gave rise to the unfounded but vehement cry of "Bargain and corruption," which followed the Kentucky statesman through two presidential struggles of later periods, and died wholly away only when the clods had fallen upon his grave.

Triumphant in his candidacy over Adams in 1828, President Jackson, four years later, encountered as his formidable competitor his colossal antagonist—the one man for whom he had no forgiveness, even when the shadows were gathering about his own couch.

"The early and better days of the Republic" is by no means an unusual expression in the political literature of our day. Possibly all the generations of men have realized the significance of the words of the great bard:

"Past and to come seem best;
Things present worst.
We are time's subjects."

And yet, barring the closing months of the administration of the elder Adams, this country has known no period of more intense party passion, or of more deadly feuds among political leaders, than was manifested during the presidential contest of 1832. The Whig party, with Henry Clay as its candidate and its idol, was for the first time in the field. Catching something of the spirit of its imperious leader, its campaign was recklessly aggressive. The scabbard was thrown away, and all the lines of retreat cut off from the beginning. No act of the party in power escaped the lime-light; no delinquency, real or imaginary, of Jackson—its candidate for re-election— but was ruthlessly drawn into the open day. Even the domestic hearthstone was invaded and antagonisms engendered that knew no surcease until the last of the chief participants in the eventful struggle had descended to the tomb.

The defeat of Clay but intensified his hostility toward his successful rival, and with a following that in personal devotion to its leader has scarcely known a parallel, he was at once the peerless front of a powerful opposition to the Jackson administration.

Such were the existing political conditions throughout the country when Stephen A. Douglas, at the age of twenty-two, first entered the arena of debate. It would not be strange if such environment left its deep impress, and measurably gave direction to his political career. The period of probation and training so essential to ordinary men was unneeded by him. Fully equipped—and with a self-confidence that has rarely had a counterpart—he was from the beginning the earnest defender of the salient measures of the Democratic administration, and the aggressive champion of President Jackson. Absolutely fearless, he took no reckoning of the opposing forces, and regardless of the prowess or ripe experience of adversaries, he at all times, in and out of season, gladly welcomed the encounter. To this end, he did not await opportunities, but eagerly sought them.

His first contest for public office was with John J. Hardin, by no means the least gifted of the brilliant Whig leaders already mentioned. Defeated by Douglas in his candidacy for re-election to the office of Attorney General, Colonel Hardin at a later day achieved distinction as a Representative in Congress, and at the early age of thirty-seven fell while gallantly leading his regiment upon the bloody field of Buena Vista. In the catalogue of men worthy of remembrance, there is to be found the name of no braver, manlier man, than that of John J. Hardin.

With well-earned laurels as public prosecutor, Douglas resigned, after two years' incumbency of that office, to accept that of Representative in the State Legislature. The Tenth General Assembly —to which he was chosen—was the most notable in Illinois history. Upon the roll of members of the House—in the old Capitol at Vandalia —are names inseparably associated with the history of the State and the nation. From its list were yet to be chosen two Governors of the commonwealth, one member of the Cabinet, three Justices of the Supreme Court of the State, eight Representatives in Congress, six Senators, and one President of the United States. That would indeed be a notable assemblage of law-makers in any country or time, that included in its membership McClernand, Edwards, Ewing, Semple, Logan, Hardin, Browning, Shields, Baker, Stuart, Douglas, and Lincoln.

In this assembly, Douglas encountered in impassioned debate, possibly for the first time, two men against whom in succession he was soon to be opposed upon the hustings as candidate for Congress; and later as an aspirant to yet more exalted stations, another, with whose name—now "given to the ages"—his own is linked inseparably for all time.

The most brilliant and exciting contest for the national House of Representatives the State has known—excepting possibly that of Cook and McLean a decade and a half earlier—was that of 1838 between John T. Stuart and Stephen A. Douglas. They were the recognized champions of their respective parties. The district embraced two-thirds of the area of the State, extending from the counties immediately south of Sangamon and Morgan, northward to Lake Michigan and the Wisconsin line. Together on horseback, often across unbridged streams, and through pathless forest and prairie, they journeyed, holding joint debates in all the county seats of the district—including the then villages of Jacksonville, Springfield, Peoria, Pekin, Bloomington, Quincy, Joliet, Galena, and Chicago. That the candidates were well matched in ability and eloquence readily appears from the fact that after an active canvass of several months, Major Stuart was elected by a majority of but eight votes. By re-elections he served six years in the House of Representatives and was one of its ablest and most valuable members. In Congress, he was the political friend and associate of Crittenden, Winthrop, Clay, and Webster. Major Stuart lives in my memory as a splendid type of the Whig statesman of the Golden Age. Courteous and kindly, he was at all times a Kentucky gentleman of the old school if ever one trod this blessed earth.

Returning to the bar after his defeat for Congress, Douglas was, in quick succession, Secretary of State by appointment of the Governor, and Judge of the Circuit and Supreme Courts by election by the Legislature. The courts he held as *nisi prius* judge were in the Quincy circuit, and the last-named city for a time his home. His associates upon the Supreme Bench were Justices Treat, Caton, Ford, Wilson, Scates, and Lockwood. His opinions, twenty-one in number, will be found in Scammon's Reports. There was little in any of the causes submitted to test fully his capacity as lawyer or logician. Enough, however, appears from his clear and concise statements and arguments to justify the belief that had his life been unreservedly given to the profession of the law, his talents concentrated upon the mastery of its eternal principles, he would in the end have been amply rewarded "by that mistress who is at the same time so jealous and so just." This, however, was not to be, and to a field more alluring his footsteps were now turned. Abandoning the bench to men less ambitious, he was soon embarked upon the uncertain and delusive sea of politics.

His unsuccessful opponent for Congress in 1842 was the Hon. Orville H. Browning, with whom, in the State Legislature, he had measured swords over a partisan resolution sustaining the financial policy of President Jackson. "The whirligig of time brings in his revenges," and it so fell out that near two decades later it was the fortune of Mr. Browning to occupy a seat in the Senate as the successor of Douglas—"touched by the finger of death." At a later day, Mr. Browning, as a member of the Cabinet of President Johnson, acquitted himself with honor in the discharge of the exacting duties of Secretary of the Interior. So long as men of high aims, patriotic hearts, and noble achievements are held in grateful remembrance, his name will have honored place in our country's annals.

The career upon which Douglas now entered was the one for which he was pre-eminently fitted, and to which he had aspired from the beginning. It was a career in which national fame was to be achieved, and—by re-elections to the House, and later to the Senate —to continue without interruption to the last hour of his life. He took his seat in the House of Representatives, December 5, 1843, and among his colleagues were Semple and Breese of the Senate, and Hardin, McClernand, Ficklin, and Wentworth of the House. Mr. Stephens of Georgia,—with whom it was my good fortune to serve in the forty-fourth and forty-sixth Congresses—told me that he entered the House the same day with Douglas, and that he distinctly recalled the delicate and youthful appearance of the latter as he advanced to the Speaker's desk to receive the oath of office. Conspicuous among the leaders of the House in the twenty-eighth Congress were Hamilton Fish, Washington Hunt, Henry A. Wise, Howell Cobb, Joshua R. Giddings, Linn Boyd, John Slidell, Barnwell Rhett, Robert C. Winthrop, the Speaker, Hannibal Hamlin, elected Vice-President upon the ticket with Mr. Lincoln in 1860, Andrew Johnson, the successor of the lamented President in 1865, and John Quincy Adams, whose brilliant career as Ambassador, Senator, Secretary of State, and President, was rounded out by nearly two decades of faithful service as a Representative in Congress.

The period that witnessed the entrance of Douglas into the great Commons was an eventful one in our political history. John Tyler, upon the death of President Harrison, had succeeded to the great office, and was in irreconcilable hostility to the leaders of his party upon the vital issues upon which the Whig victory of 1840 had been achieved. Henry Clay—then at the zenith of his marvellous powers—merciless in his arraignment of the Tyler administration, was unwittingly breeding the party dissentions that eventually compassed his own defeat in his last struggle for the Presidency. Daniel Webster, regardless of the criticism of party associates, and after the retirement of his Whig colleagues from the Tyler cabinet, still remained at the head of the State Department. His vindication, if needed, abundantly appears in the treaty by which our northeastern boundary was definitely adjusted, and war with England happily averted.

In the rush of events, party antagonisms, in the main, soon fade from remembrance. One, however, that did not pass with the occasion, but lingered even to the shades of the Hermitage, was unrelenting hostility to President Jackson. For his declaration of martial law in New Orleans just prior to the battle—with which his own name is associated for all time—General Jackson had been subjected to a heavy fine by a judge of that city. Repeated attempts in Congress looking to his vindication and reimbursement, had been unavailing. Securing the floor for the first time, Douglas—upon the anniversary of the great victory—delivered an impassioned speech in vindication of Jackson which at once challenged the attention of the country, and gave him high place among the great debaters of that memorable Congress. In reply to the demand of an opponent for a precedent for the proposed legislation, Douglas quickly responded:

"Possibly, sir, no case can be found on any page of American history where the commanding officer has been fined for an act absolutely necessary to the salvation of his country. As to precedents, let us make one now that will challenge the admiration of the world and stand the test of all the ages."

After a graphic description of conditions existing in New Orleans at the time of Jackson's declaration of martial law, "the city filled with traitors, anxious to surrender; spies transmitting information to the camp of the enemy, British regulars—four-fold the number of the American defenders—advancing to the attack—in this terrible emergency, necessity became the paramount law, the responsibility was taken, martial law declared, and a victory achieved unparalleled in the annals of war; a victory that avenged the infamy of the wanton burning of our nation's Capitol, fully, and for all time."

The speech was unanswered, the bill passed, and probably Douglas knew no prouder moment than when, a few months later, upon a visit to the Hermitage, he received the earnest thanks of the venerable commander for his masterly vindication.

Two of the salient and far-reaching questions confronting the statesmen of that eventful Congress pertained to the settlement of the Oregon boundary question, and to the annexation of the republic of Texas. The first-named question—left unsettled by the treaty of Ghent—had been for two generations the apple of discord between the American and British governments. That it at a critical moment came near involving the two nations in a war is a well-known fact in history. The platform upon which Mr. Polk had, in 1844, been elected to the Presidency, asserted unequivocally the right of the United States to the whole of the Oregon Territory. The boundary line of "fifty-four-forty" was in many of the States the decisive party watchword in that masterful contest.

Douglas, in full accord with his party upon this question, ably canvassed Illinois in earnest advocacy of Mr. Polk's election. When, at a later day, it was determined by the President and his official advisers to abandon the party platform demand of "fifty-four degrees and forty minutes" as the only settlement of the disputed boundary, and accept that of the parallel of forty-nine degrees—reluctantly proposed by Great Britain as a peaceable final settlement—Mr. Douglas earnestly antagonizing any concession, was at once in opposition to the administration he had assisted to bring into power. Whether the part of wisdom was a strict adherence to the platform dicta of "the whole of Oregon," or a reasonable concession in the interest of peaceable adjustment of a dangerous question, was long a matter of vehement discussion. It suffices that the treaty with Great Britain establishing our northwestern boundary upon the parallel last named was promptly ratified by the Senate, and the once famous Oregon question peaceably relegated to the realm of history.

A question—sixty odd years ago—equal in importance with that of the Oregon boundary was the annexation of Texas. The "Lone Star State" had been virtually an independent republic since the decisive victory of General Houston over Santa Ana in 1837 at San Jacinto, and its independence as such had been acknowledged by our own and European governments. The hardy settlers of this new Commonwealth were in the main emigrants from the United States, and earnestly solicitous of admission into the Federal Union. The question of annexation entered largely into the Presidential canvass of 1844, and the "lone star" upon Democratic banners was an important factor in securing the triumph of Mr. Polk in that bitterly contested election. In the closing hours of the Tyler administration, annexation was at length effected by joint resolution of Congress, and Texas passed at once from an independent republic to a State of the American Union. This action of Congress, however, gave deep offence to the Mexican government, and was the initial in a series of stirring events soon to follow. The Mexican invasion, the brilliant victories won by American valor, and the treaty of peace —by which our domain was extended westward to the Pacific— constitute a thrilling chapter in the annals of war. Brief in duration, the Mexican War was the training school for men whose military achievements were yet to make resplendent the pages of history. Under the victorious banners of the great commanders, Taylor and Scott, were Thomas and Beauregard, Shields and Hill, Johnston and Sherman, McClellan and Longstreet, Hancock and Stonewall Jackson, Lee and Grant. In the list of heroes were eight future candidates for the Presidency, three of whom—Taylor, Pierce, and Grant—were triumphantly elected.

Meanwhile, at the nation's Capitol was held high debate over questions second in importance to none that have engaged the profound consideration of statesmen—that literally took hold of the issues of war, conquest, diplomacy, peace, empire. From its inception, Douglas was an unfaltering advocate of the project of annexation, and as chairman of the Committee on Territories, bore prominent part in the protracted and exciting debates consequent upon the passage of that measure in the House of Representatives. In his celebrated colloquy with Mr. Adams he contended that the joint resolution he advocated was in reality only for the re-annexation of territory originally ours under the Louisiana Purchase of 1803. That something akin to the spirit of "manifest destiny" brooded over the discussion may be gathered from the closing sentences of his speech:

"Our Federal system is admirably adapted to the whole continent; and while I would not violate the laws of national or treaty stipulations, or in any manner tarnish the national honor, I would exert all legal and honorable means to drive Great Britain and the last vestige of royal authority from the continent of North America, and extend the limits of the republic from ocean to ocean."

Elected to the Senate at the age of thirty-four, Douglas took his seat in that august body in December, 1847. On the same day Abraham Lincoln took the oath of office as a member from Illinois in the House of Representatives. The Senate was presided over by the able and accomplished Vice-President, George M. Dallas. Seldom has there been a more imposing list of great names than that which now included the young Senator from Illinois. Conspicuous among the Senators of the thirty States represented, were Dix of New York, Dayton of New Jersey, Hale of New Hampshire, Clayton of Delaware, Reverdy Johnson of Maryland, Mason of Virginia, King of Alabama, Davis of Mississippi, Bell of Tennessee, Corwin of Ohio, Crittenden of Kentucky, Breese of Illinois, Benton of Missouri, Houston of Texas, Calhoun of South Carolina, and Webster of Massachusetts. It need hardly be said that the debates of that and the immediately succeeding Congress have possibly never been surpassed in ability and eloquence by any deliberative assembly.

The one vital and portentous question—in some one of its many phases—was that of human slavery. This institution—until its final extinction amid the flames of war—cast its ominous shadow over our nation's pathway from the beginning. From the establishment of the Government under the Federal Constitution to the period mentioned, it had been the constant subject of compromise and concession.

Henry Clay was first known as "the great pacificator" by his tireless efforts in the exciting struggle of 1820, over the admission of Missouri—with its Constitution recognizing slavery—into the Federal Union. Bowed with the weight of years, the Kentucky statesman, from the retirement he had sought, in recognition of the general desire of his countrymen, again returned to the theatre of his early struggles and triumphs. The fires of ambition had burned low by age and bereavement, but with earnest longing that he might again pour oil upon the troubled waters, he presented to the Senate, as terms of final peaceable adjustment of the slavery question, the once famous compromise measures of 1850.

The sectional agitation then at its height was measurably the result of the proposed disposition of territory acquired by the then recent treaty with Mexico. The advocates and opponents of slavery extension were at once in bitter antagonism, and the intensity of feeling such as the country had rarely known.

The compromise measures—proposed by Mr. Clay in a general bill — embraced the establishment of Territorial Governments for Utah and New Mexico, the settlement of the Texas boundary, an amendment to the Fugitive Slave Law, and the admission of California as a free State. In entire accord with each proposition, Douglas had—by direction of the Committee on Territories, of which he was the chairman—reported a bill providing for the immediate admission of California under its recently adopted free State Constitution. Separate measures embracing the other propositions of the general bill were likewise duly reported. These measures were advocated by the Illinois Senator in a speech that at once won him recognized place among the great debaters of that illustrious assemblage. After many weeks of earnest, at times vehement, debate, the bills in the form last mentioned were passed, and received the approval of the President. Apart from the significance of these measures as a peace offering to the country, their passage closed a memorable era in our history. During their discussion Clay, Calhoun, and Webster —"the illustrious triumvirate"—were heard for the last time in the Senate. Greatest of the second generation of our statesmen, associated in the advocacy of measures that in the early day of the Republic had given us exalted place among the nations, within brief time of each other, "shattered by the contentions of the Great Hall, they passed to the chamber of reconciliation and of silence."

Chief in importance of his public services to his State was that of Senator Douglas in procuring from Congress a land grant to aid in the construction of the Illinois Central Railroad. It is but justice to the memory of his early colleague, Senator Breese, to say that he had been the earnest advocate of a similar measure in a former Congress. The bill, however, which after persistent opposition finally became a law, was introduced and warmly advocated by Senator Douglas. This act ceded to the State of Illinois—subject to the disposal of the Legislature thereof—"for the purpose of aiding in the construction of a railroad from the southern terminus of the Illinois and Michigan Canal to a point at or near the junction of the Ohio and Mississippi Rivers, with a branch of the same to Chicago, and another to Dubuque, Iowa, every alternate section of land designated by even numbers for six sections in width on each side of said road, and its branches." It is difficult at this day to realize the importance of this measure to the then sparsely settled State. The grant in aggregate was near three million acres, and was directly to the State. After appropriate action by the State Legislature, the Illinois Central Railroad Company was duly organized—and the road eventually constructed.

A recent historian has truly said:

"For this, if for no other public service to his State, the name of Douglas was justly entitled to preservation by the erection of that splendid monumental column which, overlooking the blue waters of Lake Michigan, also overlooks for long distance that iron highway which was in no small degree the triumph of his legislative forecast and genius."

The measure now to be mentioned aroused deeper attention—more anxious concern—throughout the entire country than any with which the name of Douglas had yet been closely associated. It pertained directly to slavery, the "bone of contention" between the North and the South, the one dangerous quantity in our national politics from the establishment of the Government. Beginning with its recognition—though not in direct terms—in the Federal Constitution, it had through two generations, in the interest of peace, been the subject of repeated compromise.

As chairman of the Senate Committee on Territories, Douglas in the early days of 1854 reported a bill providing for the organization of the Territories of Nebraska and Kansas. This measure, which so suddenly arrested public attention, is known in our political history as the "Kansas-Nebraska Bill." Among its provisions was one repealing the Missouri Compromise or restriction of 1820. The end sought by the repeal was, as stated by Douglas, to leave the people of said Territories respectively to determine the question of the introduction or exclusion of slavery for themselves; in other words, "to regulate their domestic institutions in their own way, subject only to the Constitution of the United States." The principle strenuously contended for was that of "popular sovereignty" or non-intervention by Congress, in the affairs of the Territories. In closing the protracted and exciting debate just prior to the passage of the bill in the Senate, he said:

"There is another reason why I desire to see this principle recognized as a rule of action in all time to come. It will have the effect to destroy all sectional parties and sectional agitation. If you withdraw the slavery question from the halls of Congress and the political arena, and commit it to the arbitrament of those who are immediately interested in and alone responsible for its consequences, there is nothing left out of which sectional parties can be organized. When the people of the North shall all be rallied under one banner, and the whole South marshalled under another banner, and each section excited to frenzy and madness by hostility to the institutions of the other, then the patriot may well tremble for the perpetuity of the Union. Withdraw the slavery question from the political arena and remove it to the States and Territories, each to decide for itself, and such a catastrophe can never happen."

These utterances of little more than half a century ago, fall strangely upon our ears at this day. In the light of all that has occurred in the long reach of years, how significant the words, "No man is wiser than events"! Likewise, "The actions of men are to be judged by the light surrounding them at the time—not by the knowledge that comes after the fact." The immediate effect of the passage of the Kansas-Nebraska Bill was directly the reverse of that so confidently predicted by Douglas. The era of concord between the North and the South did not return. The slavery question—instead of being relegated to the recently organized Territories for final settlement—at once assumed the dimensions of a great national issue. The country at large—instead of a single Territory—became the theatre of excited discussion. The final determination was to be not that of a Territory, but of the entire people.

One significant effect of the passage of the bill was the immediate disruption of the Whig party. As a great national organization —of which Clay and Webster had been eminent leaders, and Harrison and Taylor successful candidates for the Presidency—it now passes into history. Upon its ruins, the Republican party at once came into being. Under the leadership of Fremont as its candidate, and opposition by Congressional intervention to slavery extension as its chief issue, it was a formidable antagonist to the Democratic party, in the Presidential contest of 1856. Mr. Buchanan had defeated Douglas in the nominating convention of his party that year. His absence from the country as Minister to England, during the exciting events just mentioned, it was thought would make him a safer candidate than his chief competitor, Douglas. He had been in no manner identified with the Kansas-Nebraska Bill, or the stormy events which immediately followed its passage. In his letter of acceptance, however, Mr. Buchanan had given his unqualified approval of his party platform, which recognized and adopted "the principle contained in the organic law establishing the Territories of Nebraska and Kansas as embodying the only sound and safe solution of the slavery question." Upon the principle here declared, issue was joined by his political opponents, and the battle fought to the bitter end.

Although Douglas had met personal defeat in his aspiration to the Presidency, the principle of non-intervention by Congress in the affairs of the Territories, for which he had so earnestly contended, had been triumphant both in the convention of the party, and at the polls. This principle, in its application to Kansas, was soon to be put to the test. From its organization, that Territory had been a continuous scene of disorder, often of violence. In rapid succession three Governors appointed by the President had resigned and departed the Territory, each confessing his inability to maintain public order. The struggle for mastery between the Free State advocates and their adversaries arrested the attention of the entire country. It vividly recalled the bloody forays read of in the old chronicles of hostile clans upon the Scottish border.

The parting of the ways between Senator Douglas and President Buchanan was now reached. The latter had received the cordial support of Douglas in the election which elevated him to the Presidency. His determined opposition to the re-election of Douglas became apparent as the Senatorial canvass progressed. The incidents now to be related will explain this hostility, as well as bring to the front one of the distinctive questions upon which much stress was laid in the subsequent debates between Douglas and Lincoln.

A statesman of national reputation, the Hon. Robert J. Walker, was at length appointed Governor of Kansas. During his brief administration a convention assembled without his co-operation at Lecompton, and formulated a Constitution under which application was soon made for the admission of Kansas into the Union. This convention was in part composed of non-residents, and in no sense reflected the wishes of the majority of the *bona fide* residents of the Territory. The salient feature of the Constitution was that establishing slavery. The Constitution was not submitted to the convention to popular vote, but in due time forwarded to the President, and by him laid before Congress, accompanied by a recommendation for its approval, and the early admission of the new State into the Union.

When the Lecompton Constitution came before the Senate, it at once encountered the formidable opposition of Senator Douglas. In unmeasured terms he denounced it as fraudulent, as antagonistic to the wishes of the people of Kansas, and subversive of the basic principle upon which the Territory had been organized. In the attitude just assumed, Douglas at once found himself in line with the Republicans, and in opposition to the administration he had helped place in power. The breach thus created was destined to remain unhealed. Moreover, his declaration of hostility to the Lecompton Constitution was the beginning of the end of years of close political affiliation with Southern Democratic statesmen. From that moment Douglas lost prestige as a national leader of his party. In more than one-half of the Democratic States he ceased to be regarded as a probable or even possible candidate for the Presidential succession. The hostility thus engendered followed him to the Charleston convention of 1860, and throughout the exciting Presidential contest which followed. But the humiliation of defeat —brought about, as he believed, by personal hostility to himself— was yet in the future. In the attempted admission of Kansas under the Lecompton Constitution, Douglas was triumphant over the administration and his former political associates from the South. Under what was known as the "English Amendment," the obnoxious Constitution was referred to the people of Kansas, and by them overwhelmingly rejected.

The close of this controversy in the early months of 1858 left Douglas in a position of much embarrassment. He had incurred the active hostility of the President, and in large measure of his adherents, without gaining the future aid of his late associates in the defeat of the Lecompton Constitution. His Senatorial term was nearing its close, and his political life depended upon his re-election. With a united and aggressive enemy, ably led, in his front; his own party hopelessly divided—one faction seeking his defeat—it can readily be seen that his political pathway was by no means one of peace. Such, in brief outline, were the political conditions when, upon the adjournment of Congress, Douglas returned to Illinois in July, 1858, and made public announcement of his candidacy for re-election.

In his speech at Springfield, June 17, accepting the nomination of his party for the Senate, Mr. Lincoln had uttered the words which have since become historic. They are quoted at length, as they soon furnished the text for his severe arraignment by Douglas in debate. The words are:

"We are now far into this fifth year since a policy was initiated with the avowed object and confident promise of putting an end to slavery agitation. Under the operation of that policy, that agitation has not only not ceased, but has constantly augmented. In my opinion, it will not cease until a crisis shall have been reached and passed. 'A house divided against itself cannot stand.' I believe this country cannot endure permanently half slave and half free. I do not expect the Union to be dissolved—I do not expect the house to fall—but I do expect it will cease to be divided. It will become all one thing or all the other. Either the opponents of slavery will arrest the further spread of it and place it where the public mind shall rest in the belief that it is in the course of ultimate extinction, or its advocates will push it forward until it shall become alike lawful in all the States, old as well as new, North as well as South."

This, at the time, was a bold utterance, and, it was believed by many, would imperil Mr. Lincoln's chances for election. Mr. Blaine in his "Twenty Years of Congress," says:

"Mr. Lincoln had been warned by intimate friends to whom he had communicated the contents of his speech in advance of its delivery, that he was treading on dangerous ground, that he would be misinterpreted as a disunionist, and that he might fatally damage the Republican party by making its existence synonymous with a destruction of the Government."

The opening speech of Senator Douglas at Chicago a few days later—sounding the keynote of his campaign—was in the main an arraignment of his opponent for an attempt to precipitate an internecine conflict, and array in deadly hostility the North against the South. He said:

"In other words, Mr. Lincoln advocates boldly and clearly a war of sections, a war of the North against the South, of the free States against the slave States—a war of extermination—to be continued relentlessly until the one or the other shall be subdued, and all the States shall either become free or become slave."

The two speeches, followed by others of like tenor, aroused public interest in the State as it had never been before. The desire to hear the candidates from the same platform became general. The proposal for a joint debate came from Mr. Lincoln on July 24 and was soon thereafter accepted. Seven joint meetings were agreed upon, the first to be at Ottawa, August 21, and the last at Alton, October 15. The meetings were held in the open, and at each place immense crowds were in attendance. The friends of Mr. Lincoln largely preponderated in the northern portion of the State, those of Douglas in the southern, while in the centre the partisans of the respective candidates were apparently equal in numbers. The interest never flagged for a moment from the beginning to the close. The debate was upon a high plane; each candidate enthusiastically applauded by his friends, and respectfully heard by his opponents. The speakers were men of dignified presence, their bearing such as to challenge respect in any assemblage. There was nothing of the "grotesque" about the one, nothing of the "political juggler" about the other. Both were deeply impressed with the gravity of the questions at issue, and of what might prove their far-reaching consequence to the country.

Kindly reference by each speaker to the other characterized the debates from the beginning. "My friend Lincoln," and "My friend the Judge," were expressions of constant occurrence during the debate. While each mercilessly attacked the political utterances of the other, good feeling in the main prevailed. Something being pardoned to the spirit of debate, the amenities were well observed. They had been personally well known to each other for many years; had served together in the Legislature when the State Capitol was at Vandalia, and at a later date, Lincoln had appeared before the Supreme Court when Douglas was one of the judges. The amusing allusions to each other were taken in good part. Mr. Lincoln's profound humor is now a proverb. It never appeared to better advantage than during these debates. In criticising Mr. Lincoln's attack upon Chief Justice Taney and his associates for the Dred Scott decision, Douglas declared it to be an attempt to secure a reversal of the high tribunal by an appeal to a town meeting. It reminded him of the saying of Colonel Strode that the judicial system of Illinois was perfect, except that "there should be an appeal allowed from the Supreme Court to two justices of the peace." Lincoln replied, "That was when you were on the bench, Judge." Referring to Douglas's allusion to him as a kind, amiable, and intelligent gentleman, he said:

"Then as the Judge has complimented me with these pleasant titles, I was a little taken, for it came from a great man. I was not very much accustomed to flattery and it came the sweeter to me. I was like the Hoosier with the gingerbread, when he said he reckoned he loved it better and got less of it than any other man."

In opening the debate at Ottawa, Douglas said:

"In the remarks I have made on the platform and the position of Mr. Lincoln, I mean nothing personally disrespectful or unkind to that gentleman. I have known him for twenty-five years. There were many points of sympathy between us when we first got acquainted. We were both comparatively boys, and both struggling with poverty in a strange land. I was a school-teacher in the town of Winchester, and he a flourishing grocery-keeper in the town of Salem. He was more successful in his occupation than I was in mine, and hence more fortunate in this world's goods. Lincoln is one of those peculiar men who perform with admirable skill everything which they undertake. I made as good a school-teacher as I could, and when a cabinet-maker I made a good bedstead and table, although my old boss said I succeeded better with bureaus and secretaries than anything else. I met him in the Legislature and had a sympathy with him because of the up-hill struggle we both had in life. He was then just as good at telling an anecdote as now. He could beat any of the boys wrestling or running a foot-race, in pitching quoits or tossing a copper, and the dignity and impartiality with which he presided at a horse-race or a fist-fight, excited the admiration and won the praise of everybody. I sympathized with him because he was struggling with difficulties, and so was I."

To which Lincoln replied:

"The Judge is woefully at fault about his friend Lincoln being a grocery-keeper. I don't know as it would be a sin if I had been; but he is mistaken. Lincoln never kept a grocery anywhere in the world. It is true that Lincoln did work the latter part of one Winter in a little still house up at the head of a hollow."

The serious phases of the debates will now be considered. The opening speech was by Mr. Douglas. That he possessed rare power as a debater, all who heard him can bear witness. Mr. Blaine in his history says:

"His mind was fertile in resources. He was master of logic. In that peculiar style of debate which in its intensity resembles a physical combat, he had no equal. He spoke with extraordinary readiness. He used good English, terse, pointed, vigorous. He disregarded the adornments of rhetoric. He never cited historic precedents except from the domain of American politics. Inside that field, his knowledge was comprehensive, minute, critical. He could lead a crowd almost irresistibly to his own conclusions."

Douglas was, in very truth, imbued with little of mere sentiment. He gave little time to discussions belonging solely to the realm of the speculative or the abstract. He was in no sense a dreamer. What Coleridge has defined wisdom—"common sense, in an uncommon degree"—was his. In phrase the simplest and most telling, he struck at once at the very core of the controversy. Possibly no man was ever less inclined "to darken counsel with words without knowledge." Positive, and aggressive to the last degree, he never sought "by indirections to find directions out." In statesmanship— in all that pertained to human affairs—he was intensely practical. With him, in the words of Macaulay, "one acre in Middlesex is worth a principality in Utopia."

It is a pleasure to recall—after the lapse of half a century—the two men as they shook hands upon the speaker's stand, just before the opening of the debates that were to mark an epoch in American history. Stephen A. Douglas! Abraham Lincoln! As they stood side by side and looked out upon "the sea of upturned faces"—it was indeed a picture to live in the memory of all who witnessed it. The one stood for the old ordering of things, in an emphatic sense for the Government as established by the fathers—with all its compromises. The other, recognizing equally with his opponent the binding force of Constitutional obligation, yet looking, away from present surroundings, "felt the inspiration of the coming of the grander day." As has been well said, "The one faced the past; the other, the future."

The name of Lincoln is now a household word. But little can be written of him that is not already known to the world. Nothing that can be uttered or withheld can add to, or detract from, his imperishable fame. But it must be remembered that his great opportunity and fame came after the stirring events separated from us by the passing of fifty years. It is not the Lincoln of history, but Lincoln the country lawyer, the debater, the candidate of his party for political office, with whom we have now to do. Born in Kentucky, much of his early life was spent in Indiana, and all his professional and public life up to his election to the Presidency, in Illinois. His early opportunities for study, like those of Douglas, were meagre indeed. Neither had had the advantage of the thorough training of the schools. Of both it might truly have been said, "They knew men rather than books." From his log-cabin home upon the Sangamon, Mr. Lincoln had in his early manhood volunteered, and was made captain of his company, in what was so well known to the early settlers of Illinois as the Black Hawk War. Later on, he was surveyor of his county, and three times a member of the State Legislature. At the time of the debates with Senator Douglas, Mr. Lincoln had for many years been a resident of Springfield, and a recognized leader of the bar. As an advocate, he had probably no superior in the State. During the days of the Whig party he was an earnest exponent of its principles, and an able champion of its candidates. As such, he had in successive contests eloquently presented the claims of Harrison, Clay, Taylor, and Scott to the Presidency. In 1846, he was elected a Representative in Congress, and upon his retirement he resumed the active practice of his profession. Upon the dissolution of the Whig party, he cast in his fortunes with the new political organization, and was in very truth one of the builders of the Republican party. At its first national convention, in 1856, he received a large vote for nomination to the Vice-Presidency, and during the memorable campaign of that year canvassed the State in advocacy of the election of Fremont and Dayton, the candidates of the Philadelphia convention.

In the year 1858—that of the great debates—Douglas was the better known of the opposing candidates in the country at large. In a speech then recently delivered in Springfield, Mr. Lincoln said:

"There is still another disadvantage under which we labor and to which I will ask your attention. It arises out of the relative positions of the two persons who stand before the State as candidates for the Senate. Senator Douglas is of world-wide renown. All the anxious politicians of his party have been looking upon him as certainly at no distant day to be the President of the United States. They have seen in his ruddy, jolly, fruitful face, postoffices, land-offices, marshalships, and cabinet appointments, and foreign missions, bursting and sprouting out in wonderful exuberance, ready to be laid hold of by their greedy hands. On the contrary, nobody has ever seen in my poor lank face that any cabbages were sprouting out."

Both, however, were personally well known in Illinois. Each was by unanimous nomination the candidate of his party. Douglas had known sixteen years of continuous service in one or the other House of Congress. In the Senate, he had held high debate with Seward, Sumner, and Chase from the North, and during the last session—since he had assumed a position of antagonism to the Buchanan administration—had repeatedly measured swords with Tombs, Benjamin, and Jefferson Davis, chief among the great debaters of the South.

Mr. Lincoln's services in Congress had been limited to a single term in the lower house, and his great fame was yet to be achieved, not as a legislator, but as Chief Executive during the most critical years of our history.

Such, in brief, were the opposing candidates as they entered the lists of debate at Ottawa, on the twenty-first day of August, 1858. Both were in the prime of manhood, thoroughly equipped for the conflict, and surrounded by throngs of devoted friends. Both were gifted with remarkable forensic powers and alike hopeful as to the result. Each recognizing fully the strength of his opponent, his own powers were constantly at their tension.

"the blood more stirs
To rouse a lion than to start a hare."

In opening, Senator Douglas made brief reference to the political condition of the country prior to the year 1854. He said:

"The Whig and the Democratic were the two great parties then in existence; both national and patriotic, advocating principles that were universal in their application; while these parties differed in regard to banks, tariff, and sub-treasury, they agreed on the slavery question which now agitates the Union. They had adopted the compromise measures of 1850 as the basis of a full solution of the slavery question in all its forms; that these measures had received the endorsement of both parties in their National Conventions of 1852, thus affirming the right of the people of each State and Territory to decide as to their domestic institutions for themselves; that this principle was embodied in the bill reported by me in 1854 for the organization of the Territories of Kansas and Nebraska; in order that there might be no misunderstanding, these words were inserted in that bill: 'It is the true intent and meaning of this act, not to legislate slavery into any State or Territory, or to exclude it therefrom, but to leave the people thereof perfectly free to form and regulate their domestic institutions in their own way, subject only to the Federal Constitution.'"

Turning to his opponent, he said:

"I desire to know whether Mr. Lincoln to-day stands as he did in 1854 in favor of the unconditional repeal of the Fugitive Slave Law; whether he stands pledged to-day as he did in 1854 against the admission of any more slave States into the Union, even if the people want them; whether he stands pledged against the admission of a new State into the Union with such a Constitution as the people of that State may see fit to make. I want to know whether he stands to-day pledged to the abolition of slavery in the District of Columbia; I desire to know whether he stands pledged to prohibit slavery in all the Territories of the United States north as well as south of the Missouri Compromise line. I desire him to answer whether he is opposed to acquisition of any more territory unless slavery is prohibited therein. I want his answer to these questions."

Douglas then addressed himself to the already quoted words of Mr. Lincoln's Springfield speech commencing: "A house divided against itself cannot stand." He declared the Government had existed for seventy years divided into free and slave States as our fathers made it; that at the time the Constitution was framed there were thirteen States, twelve of which were slave-holding, and one a free State; that if the doctrine preached by Mr. Lincoln that all should be free or all slave had prevailed, the twelve would have overruled the one, and slavery would have been established by the

- 90 -

Constitution on every inch of the Republic, instead of being left, as our fathers wisely left it, for each State to decide for itself. He then declared that:

"Uniformity in the local laws and institutions of the different States is neither possible nor desirable; that if uniformity had been adopted when the Government was established it must inevitably have been the uniformity of slavery everywhere, or the uniformity of negro citizenship and negro equality everywhere. I hold that humanity and Christianity both require that the negro shall have and enjoy every right and every privilege and every immunity consistent with the safety of the society in which he lives. The question then arises, What rights and privileges are consistent with the public good? This is a question which each State and each Territory must decide for itself. Illinois has decided it for herself."

He then said:

"Now, my friends, if we will only act conscientiously upon this great principle of popular sovereignty, it guarantees to each State and Territory the right to do as it pleases on all things local and domestic; instead of Congress interfering, we will continue at peace one with another. This doctrine of Mr. Lincoln of uniformity among the institutions of the different States is a new doctrine never dreamed of by Washington, Madison, or the framers of the Government. Mr. Lincoln and his party set themselves up as wiser than the founders of the Government, which has flourished for seventy years under the principle of popular sovereignty, recognizing the right of each State to do as it pleased. Under that principle, we have grown from a nation of three or four millions to one of thirty millions of people. We have crossed the mountains and filled up the whole Northwest, turning the prairies into a garden, and building up churches and schools, thus spreading civilization and Christianity where before there was nothing but barbarism. Under that principle we have become from a feeble nation the most powerful upon the face of the earth, and if we only adhere to that principle we can go forward increasing in territory, in power, in strength, and in glory, until the Republic of America shall be the North Star that shall guide the friends of freedom throughout the civilized world. I believe that his new doctrine preached by Mr. Lincoln will dissolve the Union if it succeeds; trying to array all the Northern States in one body against the Southern; to excite a sectional war between the free States and the slave States in order that one or the other may be driven to the wall."

Mr. Lincoln said in reply:

"I think and will try to show, that the repeal of the Missouri Compromise is wrong—wrong in its direct effect, letting slavery into Kansas and Nebraska; wrong in its prospective principle, allowing it to spread to every other part of the wide world where men can be found inclined to take it. This declared indifference, but as I must think covert zeal for the spread of slavery, I cannot but hate. I hate it because of the monstrous injustice of slavery itself. I hate it because it deprives our Republic of an example of its just influence in the world—enables the enemies of free institutions with plausibility to taunt us as hypocrites. I have no prejudices against the Southern people; they are just what we would be in their situation. If slavery did now exist amongst us we would not instantly give it up. This I believe of the masses North and South. When the Southern people tell us they are no more responsible for the origin of slavery than we, I acknowledge the fact. When it is said that the institution exists, and that it is very difficult to get rid of in any satisfactory way, I can understand and appreciate the same. I surely will not blame them for what I should not know how to do myself. If all earthly powers were given me, I should not know what to do as to the existing institution."

Declaring that he did not advocate freeing the negroes, and making them our political and social equals, but suggesting that gradual systems of emancipation might be adopted by the States, he added, "But for their tardiness in this, I will not undertake to judge our brethren of the South. But all this to my judgment furnishes no more excuse for permitting slavery to go into our free territory than it would for reviving the African slave trade by law."

He then added:

"I have no purpose directly or indirectly to interfere with the institution of slavery in the States where it exists. I believe I have no lawful right to do so, and I have no inclination to do so. I have no purpose to introduce political and social equality between the white and black races. But I hold that notwithstanding all this there is no reason in the world why the negro is not entitled to all the natural rights enumerated in the Declaration of Independence, the right to life, liberty, and the pursuit of happiness. I hold that he is as much entitled to these as the white man. I agree with Judge Douglas he is not my equal in many respects—certainly not in color, perhaps not in moral and intellectual endowment. But in the right to eat the bread, without the leave of anybody else, which his own hand earns, he is my equal, and the equal of Judge Douglas, and the equal of every living man."

Referring to the quotation from his Springfield speech of the words, "A house divided against itself cannot stand," he said:

"Does the Judge say it can stand? If he does, then there is a question of veracity, not between him and me, but between the Judge and an authority of somewhat higher character. I leave it to you to say whether, in the history of our Government, the institution of slavery has not only failed to be a bond of union, but on the contrary been an apple of discord and an element of division in the house. If so, then I have a right to say that in regard to this question the Union is a house divided against itself; and when the Judge reminds me that I have often said to him that the institution of slavery has existed for eighty years in some States and yet it does not exist in some others, I agree to that fact, and I account for it by looking at the position in which our fathers originally placed it—restricting it from the new Territories where it had not gone, and legislating to cut off its source by abrogation of the slave trade, thus putting the seal of legislation against its spread, the public mind did rest in the belief that it was in the course of ultimate extinction. Now, I believe if we could arrest its spread and place it where Washington and Jefferson and Madison placed it, it would be in the course of ultimate extinction, and the public mind would—as for eighty years past —believe that it was in the course of ultimate extinction."

Referring further to his Springfield speech, he declared that he had no thought of doing anything to bring about a war between the free and slave States; that he had no thought in the world that he was doing anything to bring about social and political equality of the black and white races.

Pursuing this line of argument, he insisted that the first step in the conspiracy, the passage of the Kansas-Nebraska Bill, followed soon by the Dred Scott Decision—the latter fitting perfectly into the niche left by the former—"in such a case, we feel it impossible not to believe that Stephen and Franklin, Roger and James, all understood one another from the beginning, and all worked upon a common plan or draft drawn before the first blow was struck."

In closing, Douglas, after indignant denial of the charge of conspiracy, said:

"I have lived twenty-five years in Illinois; I have served you with all the fidelity and ability which I possess, and Mr. Lincoln is at liberty to attack my public action, my votes, and my conduct, but when he dares to attack my moral integrity by a charge of conspiracy between myself, Chief Justice Taney, and the Supreme Court and two Presidents of the United States, I will repel it."

At Freeport, Mr. Lincoln, in opening the discussion, at once declared his readiness to answer the interrogatories propounded. He said:

"I do not now, nor ever did, stand in favor of the unconditional repeal of the Fugitive Slave Law; I do not now, nor ever did, stand pledged against the admission of any more slave States into the Union; I do not stand pledged against the admission of a new State into the Union with such a Constitution as the people of that State may see fit to make; I do not stand to-day pledged to the abolition of slavery in the District of Columbia; I do not stand pledged to the prohibition of the slave trade between the different States; I am impliedly, if not expressly, pledged to a belief in the right and duty of Congress to prohibit slavery in all the United States Territories."

Waiving the form of the interrogatory, as to being pledged, he said:

"As to the first one in regard to the Fugitive Slave Law, I have never hesitated to say, and I do not now hesitate to say, that I think under the Constitution of the United States the people of the Southern States are entitled to a Congressional Fugitive Slave Law. Having said that, I have had nothing to say in regard to the existing Fugitive Slave Law further than that I think it should have been framed so as to be free from some of the objections that pertain to it without lessening its efficiency. In regard to whether I am pledged to the admission of any more slave States into the Union, I would be exceedingly glad to know that there would never be another slave State admitted into the Union; but I must add that if slavery shall be kept out of the Territories during the Territorial existence of any one given Territory, and then the people shall, having a fair chance and a clear field when they come to adopt the Constitution, do such an extraordinary thing as to adopt a slavery Constitution uninfluenced by the actual presence of the institution among them, I see no alternative, if we own the country, but to admit them into the Union. I should be exceedingly glad to see slavery abolished in the District of Columbia. I believe that Congress possesses Constitutional power to abolish it. Yet, as a member of Congress, I should not be in favor of endeavoring to abolish slavery in the District of Columbia unless it would be upon these conditions: First, that the abolition should be gradual; second, that it should be on a vote of the majority of qualified voters in the district; third, that compensation should be made unwilling owners. With these conditions, I confess I should be exceedingly glad to see Congress abolish slavery in the District of Columbia, and in the language of Henry Clay, 'Sweep from our Capital that foul blot upon our nation.'"

These carefully prepared answers will never cease to be of profound interest to the student of human affairs. They indicate unmistakably the conservative tendency of Mr. Lincoln, and his position at the time as to the legal status of the institution of slavery. But "courage mounteth with occasion." Five years later, and from the hand that penned the answers given came the great proclamation emancipating a race. The hour had struck—and slavery perished. The compromises upon which it rested were, in the mighty upheaval, but as the stubble before the flame.

Recurring to the Freeport debates, Mr. Lincoln propounded to his opponent four interrogatories as follows:

"First, if the people of Kansas shall by means entirely unobjectionable in all other respects adopt a State Constitution and ask admission into the Union under it before they have the requisite number of inhabitants according to the bill—some ninety-three thousand— will you vote to admit them? Second, can the people of a United States Territory in any lawful way, against the wish of any citizen of the United States, exclude slavery from its limits prior to the formation of a State Constitution? Third, if the Supreme Court of the United States shall decide that States cannot exclude slavery from their limits, are you in favor of acquiescing in, adopting, and following such decision as a rule of political action? Fourth, are you in favor of acquiring additional territory in disregard of how such acquisition may affect the nation on the slavery question?"

The questions propounded reached the marrow of the controversy, and were yet to have a much wider field for discussion. This was especially true of the second of the series. Upon this widely divergent—irreconcilable— views were entertained by Northern and Southern Democrats. The evidence of this is to be found in the respective national platforms upon which Douglas and Mr. Breckenridge were two years later rival candidates of a divided party. The second interrogatory of Mr. Lincoln clearly emphasized this conflict of opinion as it existed at the time of the debates. It is but just, however, to Douglas—of whom little that is kindly has in late years been spoken—to say that there was nothing in the question to cause him surprise or embarrassment. It would be passing strange if during the protracted debates with Senators representing extreme and antagonistic views, a matter so vital as the interpretation of the Kansas-Nebraska Act— as indicated by the interrogatory—had never been under discussion. Conclusive evidence on this point is to be found in the speech delivered by Senator Douglas at Bloomington, July 16, forty-two days before the Freeport debate, in which he said:

"I tell you, my friends, it is impossible under our institutions to force slavery on an unwilling people. If this principle of popular sovereignty, asserted in the Nebraska Bill, be fairly carried out by letting the people decide the question for themselves by a fair vote, at a fair election, and with honest returns, slavery will never exist one day or one hour in any Territory against the unfriendly legislation of an unfriendly people. Hence if the people of a Territory want slavery they will encourage it by passing affirmatory laws, and the necessary police regulations; if they do not want it, they will withhold that legislation, and by withholding it slavery is as dead as if it were prohibited by a Constitutional prohibition. They could pass such local laws and police regulations as would drive slavery out in one day or one hour if they were opposed to it, and therefore, so far as the question of slavery in the Territories is concerned in its practical operation, it matters not how the Dred Scott case may be decided with reference to the Territories. My own opinion on that point is well known. It is shown by my vote and speeches in Congress."

Recurring again to the Freeport debate, in reply to the first interrogatory, Douglas declared that in reference to Kansas it was his opinion that if it had population enough to constitute a slave State, it had people enough for a free State; that he would not make Kansas an exceptional case to the other States of the Union; that he held it to be a sound rule of universal application to require a Territory to contain the requisite population for a member of Congress before its admission as a State into the Union; that it having been decided that Kansas has people enough for a slave State, "I hold it has enough for a free State."

As to the third interrogatory, he said that only one man in the United States, an editor of a paper in Washington, had held such view, and that he, Douglas, had at the time denounced it on the floor of the Senate; that Mr. Lincoln cast an imputation upon the Supreme Court by supposing that it would violate the Constitution; that it would be an act of moral treason that no man on the bench could ever descend to. To the fourth—which he said was very "ingeniously and cunningly put"—he answered that, whenever it became necessary in our growth and progress to acquire more territory he was in favor of it without reference to the question of slavery, and when we had acquired it, he would leave the people to do as they pleased, either to make it free, or slave territory as they preferred.

The answer to the second interrogatory—of which much has been written—was given without hesitation. Language could hardly be more clear or effective. He said:

"To the next question propounded to me I answer emphatically, as Mr. Lincoln has heard me answer a hundred times, that in my opinion the people of a Territory can by lawful means exclude slavery from their limits prior to the formation of a State Constitution. It matters not what way the Supreme Court may hereafter decide as to the abstract question whether slavery may or may not go into a Territory under the Constitution, the people have the lawful means to introduce it or exclude it, as they please, for the reason that slavery cannot exist a day, or an hour anywhere, unless it is supported by local police regulations. These police regulations can only be established by the local Legislature, and if the people are opposed to slavery they will elect representatives to that body who will by unfriendly legislation effectually prevent the introduction of it into their midst. If, on the contrary, they are for it, their Legislature will favor its extension. Hence, no matter what the decision of the Supreme Court may be on that abstract question, still the right of the people to make a slave Territory or a free Territory is perfect and complete under the Nebraska Bill."

The trend of thought, the unmeasured achievement of activities looking to human amelioration, during the fifty intervening years, must be taken into the account before uncharitable judgment upon what has been declared the indifference of Douglas to the question of abstract right involved in the memorable discussion. It must be remembered that the world has moved apace, and that a mighty gulf separates us from that eventful period, in which practical statesmen were compelled to deal with institutions as then existing. And not to be forgotten are the words of the great interpreter of the human heart,

"But know thou this, that men are as the time is."

The great debates between Douglas and Lincoln—the like of which we shall not hear again—had ended and passed to the domain of history. To the inquiry, "Which of the participants was the victor?" there can be no absolute answer. Judged by the immediate result, the former; by consequence more remote and far-reaching, the latter. Within three years from the first meeting at Ottawa, Mr. Lincoln —having been elected and inaugurated President—was upon the threshold of mighty events which are now the masterful theme of history; and his great antagonist in the now historic debates had passed from earthly scenes.

It has been said that Douglas was ambitious.

  "If it were so, it was a grievous fault,
  And grievously hath he answered it."

We may well believe that, with like honorable ambition to the two great popular leaders of different periods—Clay and Blaine —his goal was the Presidency.

In the last three national conventions of his party preceding his death, he was presented by the Illinois delegation to be named for the great office. The last of these—the Charleston convention of 1860—is now historic. It assembled amid intense party passion, and after a turbulent session that seemed the omen of its approaching doom, adjourned to a later day to Baltimore. Senator Douglas there received the almost solid vote of the Northern, and a portion of that of the Border States, but the hostility of the extreme Southern leaders to his candidacy was implacable to the end. What had seemed inevitable from the beginning at length occurred, and the great historical party—which had administered the Government with brief intermissions from the inauguration of Jefferson—was hopelessly rent asunder. This startling event—and what it might portend— gave pause to thoughtful men of all parties. It was not a mere incident, but an epoch in history. Mr. Blaine, in his "Twenty Years of Congress," says:

"The situation was the cause of solicitude and even grief with thousands to whom the old party was peculiarly endeared. The traditions of Jefferson, of Madison, of Jackson, were devoutly treasured; and the splendid achievements of the American Democracy were recounted with the pride which attaches to an honorable family inheritance. The fact was recalled that the Republic had grown to its imperial dimensions under Democratic statesmanship. It was remembered that Louisiana had been acquired from France, Florida from Spain, the independent Republic of Texas annexed, and California, with its vast dependencies, and its myriad millions of treasure, ceded by Mexico, all under Democratic administrations, and in spite of the resistance of their opponents. That a party whose history was inwoven with the glory of the Republic should now come to its end in a quarrel over the status of the negro in a country where his labor was not wanted, was to many of its members as incomprehensible as it was sorrowful and exasperating. They might have restored the party to harmony, but at the very height of the factional contest, the representatives of both sections were hurried forward to the National Convention of 1860, with principle subordinated to passion, with judgment displaced by a desire for revenge."

The withdrawal from the Baltimore Convention of a large majority of the Southern delegates and a small following, led by Caleb Cushing and Benjamin F. Butler from the North, resulted in the immediate nomination by the requisite two-thirds vote of Senator Douglas as the Presidential candidate. The platform upon the question of slavery was in substance that contended for by the candidate in the debates with Lincoln. The Democratic party divided —Breckenridge receiving the support of the South—Douglas's candidacy was hopeless from the beginning. But his iron will, and courage, that knew no faltering, never appeared to better advantage than during that eventful canvass. Deserted by former political associates, he visited distant States and addressed immense audiences in defence of the platform upon which he had been nominated, and in advocacy of his own election. His speeches in Southern States were of the stormy incidents of a struggle that has scarcely known a parallel. Interrogated by a prominent citizen at Norfolk, Virginia, "If Lincoln be elected President, would the Southern States be justified in seceding from the Union?" Douglas replied, "I emphatically answer, No. The election of a man to the Presidency in conformity with the Constitution of the United States would not justify an attempt to dissolve the Union."

Defeated in his great ambition, broken in health, the sad witness of the unmistakable portents of the coming sectional strife—the few remaining months of his mortal life were enveloped in gloom. Partisan feeling vanished—his deep concern was now only for his country. Standing by the side of his successful rival—whose wondrous career was only opening, as his own was nearing its close —he bowed profound assent to the imperishable utterances of the inaugural address: "I am loath to close. We are not enemies but friends. We must not be enemies. Though passion may have strained, it must not break our bonds of affection."

Yet later—immediately upon the firing of the fatal shot at Sumter that suddenly summoned millions from peaceful pursuits to arms— by invitation of the Illinois Legislature Douglas addressed his countrymen for the last time.

Broken with the storms of state, the fires of ambition forever extinguished, standing upon the threshold of the grave, his soul burdened with the calamities that had befallen his country, in tones of deepest pathos he declared:

"If war must come—if the bayonet must be used to maintain the Constitution—I can say before God, my conscience is clear. I have struggled long for a peaceful solution of the trouble. I deprecate war, but if it must come, I am with my country, and for my country, in every contingency, and under all circumstances. At all hazards our Government must be maintained, and the shortest pathway to peace is through the most stupendous preparation for war."

Who that heard the last public utterance that fell from his lips can forget his solemn invocation to all who had followed his political fortunes, until the banner had fallen from his hand,— to know only their country in its hour of peril?

The ordinary limit of human life unreached; his intellectual strength unabated; his loftiest aspirations unrealized; at the critical moment of his country's sorest need—he passed to the grave. What reflections and regrets may have been his in that hour of awful mystery, we may not know. In the words of another: "What blight and anguish met his agonized eyes, whose lips may tell? what brilliant broken plans, what bitter rending of sweet household ties, what sundering of strong manhood's friendships?"

In the light of what has been discussed, may we not believe that with his days prolonged, he would during the perilous years have been the safe counsellor—the rock—of the great President, in preserving the nation's life, and later in "binding up the nation's wounds."

Worthy of honored and enduring place in history, Stephen A. Douglas — statesman and patriot—lies buried within the great city whose stupendous development is so largely the result of his own wise forecast and endeavor,—by the majestic lake whose waves break near the base of his stately monument and chant his eternal requiem.

VIII THE FIRST POLITICAL TELEGRAM

SENATOR SILAS WRIGHT NOMINATED FOR VICE-PRESIDENT—WORD OF HIS NOMINATION SENT HIM BY THE MORSE TELEGRAPH—MORSE'S FIRST CONCEPTION OF AN ELECTRO-MAGNETIC TELEGRAPH—OBSTACLES TO THE CARRYING OUT OF HIS INVENTION—A BILL APPROPRIATING $30,000 TO TEST THE VALUE OF HIS TELEGRAPH—EARLIER FORMS OF TELEGRAPHIC INTERCOURSE—A EULOGY ON THE INVENTOR BY MR. GARFIELD—ANOTHER, BY MR. COX—THE FIRST MESSAGE THAT EVER PASSED OVER THE WIRE—DR. PRIME'S PRAISE OF MORSE AFTER HIS DEATH.

By all odds, the most venerable in appearance of the Representatives in the forty-sixth Congress, was Hendrick B. Wright of Pennsylvania. After a retirement of a third of a century, he had been returned to the seat he had honored while many of his present associates were in the cradle. Of massive build, stately bearing, lofty courtesy; neatly appareled in blue broadcloth, with brass buttons appropriately in evidence, he appeared indeed to belong to a past generation of statesmen.

"And thus he bore without abuse
The grand old name of gentleman."

In one of the many conversations I held with him, he told me that he was the president of the Democratic National Convention which met in Baltimore in 1844. As will be remembered, a majority of the delegates to that convention were favorable to the renomination of Mr. Van Buren, but his recently published letter opposing the annexation of Texas had rendered him extremely obnoxious to a powerful minority of his own party. After a protracted struggle, Mr. Van Buren, under the operation of the "two-thirds rule," was defeated, and Mr. Polk nominated. The convention, anxious to placate the friends of the defeated candidate, then tendered the nomination for Vice-President to Senator Silas Wright, the close friend of Mr. Van Buren.

At the time the convention was in session, Samuel F. B. Morse was conducting in a room in the Capitol the electrical experiments which have since "given his name to the ages." Under an appropriation by Congress, a telegraph line had been recently constructed from Washington to Baltimore.

Immediately upon the nomination of Senator Wright, as mentioned, the president of the convention sent him by the Morse telegraph a brief message, the first of a political character that ever passed over the wire, advising him of his nomination, and requesting his acceptance. Two hours later he read to the convention a message from Senator Wright, then in Washington, peremptorily declining the nomination.

Upon the reading of this message to the convention, it was openly declared to be a hoax, not one member in twenty believing that a message could possibly have been received. The convention adjourned till the next day, first instructing its president to communicate with Senator Wright by letter. A special messenger, by hard riding and frequent change of horse, bore the letter of the convention to Wright in Washington, and returned with his reply by the time the convention had reassembled. As will be remembered, Wright persisting in his declination, George M. Dallas was nominated and duly elected.

Later, in conversation with the Hon. Alexander H. Stephens of Georgia, he told me that he was in the room of the Capitol set apart for the experiments which Mr. Morse wished to make, and distinctly remembered the fact of the transmission of the message to and from Senator Wright, as stated.

The incident mentioned recalls something of the obstacles encountered by Morse in the marvellous work with which his name is inseparably associated. He first conceived the idea of an electro-magnetic telegraph on shipboard on a homeward-bound voyage from Europe in 1832. Before landing from his long voyage, his plans for a series of experiments had been clearly thought out. Having constructed his first recording apparatus, his caveat for a patent was filed five years later; and in 1838, he applied to Congress for an appropriation to enable him to construct an experimental line from Washington to Baltimore in order to demonstrate the practicability of his invention. His proposal was at first treated with ridicule —even with contempt; and for more than three years no favorable action was taken by Congress. With abiding faith, however, in the merits of his invention, his zeal knew no abatement during years of poverty and discouragement. At length in the Twenty-seventh Congress, Representative Kennedy of Maryland—at a later day Secretary of the Navy—introduced a bill appropriating thirty thousand dollars "to test the value of Morse's Electro-Magnetic Telegraph," to be expended under the direction of the Secretary of the Treasury.

By the untiring efforts of Mr. Kennedy and other Representatives, the bill was finally brought before the House for consideration near the close of the session. In the light of events, the discussion that immediately preceded the vote is of interest, and in no small degree amusing, to this generation. On

February twenty-first, 1843, Mr. Johnson of Tennessee wished to say a word upon the bill. As the present Congress had done much to encourage science, he did not wish to see the science of Mesmerism neglected and overlooked. He therefore proposed that one-half of the appropriation be given to Mr. Fisk to enable him to carry on experiments as well as Professor Morse. Mr. Houston thought that Millerism should also be included in the benefits of the appropriation. Mr. Stanley said he should have no objection to the appropriation for Mesmeric experiments provided the gentleman from Tennessee was the subject. Mr. Johnson said he should have no objection provided Mr. Stanley was the operator. Several gentlemen now called for the reading of the amendment, and it was read by the clerk as follows: "Provided that one-half of the said sum shall be appropriated for trying Mesmeric experiments under the direction of the Secretary of the Treasury."

Mr. Mason arose to a question of order. He maintained that the amendment was not *bona fide,* and that such amendments were calculated to injure the character of the House. He appealed to the Chair, the House being then in committee of the whole, to rule the amendment out of order.

The Chairman said that it was not for him to judge of the motives of members who offered amendments, and that he could not therefore undertake to pronounce the amendment not *bona fide.* Objection might be raised to it on the ground that it was not sufficiently analogous in character to the bill under consideration; but, in the opinion of the Chair, it would require a scientific analysis to determine how far the magnetism of mesmerism was analogous to that employed in telegraphs. He therefore ruled the amendment in order.

The amendment was rejected. The bill was subsequently reported favorably to the House, and two days later passed by the close vote of eighty-nine to eighty-three.

The bill then went to the Senate, and was placed upon the calendar. A large number of bills were ahead of it, and Mr. Morse was assured by a kindly Senator that there was no possible chance for its consideration. All hope seemed to forsake the great inventor, as, from his seat in the gallery, he was a gloomy witness of the waning hours of the session. Unable longer to endure the strain, he sought his humble dwelling an hour before final adjournment. On arising the next morning, a little girl, the daughter of a faithful friend, ran up to him with a message from her father, to the effect that in the hurry and confusion of the midnight hour, and just before the close of the session, the Senate had passed his bill, which immediately received the signature of the President.

With the sum thus appropriated at his command, Morse now earnestly resumed the experiments, which a few months later resulted so successfully. Referring to the homeward voyage from Europe, in 1832, his biographer says:

"One day Dr. Charles S. Jackson of Boston, a fellow passenger, described an experiment recently made in Paris by means of which electricity had been instantaneously transmitted through a great length of wire; to which Morse replied, 'If that be so, I see no reason why messages may not instantaneously be transmitted by electricity.'"

The key-note was struck, and before his ship reached New York the invention of the telegraph was virtually made, and even the essential features of the electro-magnetic transmitting and recording apparatus were sketched on paper. Of necessity, in reaching this result, Morse made use of the ideas and discoveries of many other minds. As stated by his biographer:

"Various forms of telegraphic intercourse had been devised before; electro-magnetism had been studied by *savants* for many years; Franklin even had experimented with the transmission of electricity through great lengths of wire. It was reserved for Morse to combine the results of many fragmentary and unsuccessful attempts, and put them, after many years of trial, to a practical use; and though his claims to the invention have been many times attacked in the press and in the courts, they have been triumphantly vindicated alike by the law and the verdict of the people, both at home and abroad. The Chief Justice of the United States in delivering the opinion of the Supreme Court in one of the Morse cases, said: 'It can make no difference whether the inventor derived his information from books or from conversation with men skilled in the science; and the fact that Morse sought and obtained the necessary information and counsel from the best sources and acted upon it, neither impairs his right as an inventor, nor detracts from his merits.'"

It will be remembered that soon after his first successful experiment, Morse was harassed by protracted litigation, and that many attempts were made to deprive him of the just rewards of his great invention. True, he had been preceded along the same lines by great discoveries. This fact no man recognized more unreservedly than himself. He was the inventor, his work, that of gathering up and applying the marvellous discoveries of others to the practical purposes of human life. As stated by Mr. Garfield:

"His to interpret to the world that subtle and mysterious element with which the thinkers of the human race had so long been occupied. As Franklin had exhibited the relation between lightning and the electric fluid, so Oersted exhibited the relation between magnetism and electricity. From 1820 to 1825, his discovery was further developed by Davy and Sturgeon of

England, and Arago and Ampere of France. The electro-magnetic telegraph is the embodiment, I might say the incarnation, of many centuries of thought, of many generations of effort to elicit from Nature one of her deepest mysteries. No one man, no one century, could have achieved it. It is the child of the human race, the heir of all ages. How wonderful are the steps that led to its creation! The very name of this telegraphic instrument bears record of its history—Electric, Magnetic.

"The first, named from the bit of yellow amber whose qualities of attraction and repulsion were discovered by a Grecian philosopher twenty-four centuries ago, and the second, from Magnesia, the village of Asia Minor where first was found the lodestone, whose touch turned the needle forever toward the north. These were the earliest forms in which that subtle, all-pervading force revealed itself to men. In the childhood of the race men stood dumb in the presence of its more terrible manifestations. When it gleamed in the purple aurora, or shot dusky-red from the clouds, it was the eye-flash of an angry God before whom mortals quailed in helpless fear."

More than three centuries ago, Shakespeare put into the mouth of one of his creations the words,

"I'll put a girdle round about the earth
In forty minutes."

The words spoken in jest were in the nature of a prophecy. After the passing of many generations, in a country unknown to the great bard, Morse, in the words of Mr. Cox, one of the most eloquent of his eulogists—

"Gave to the universal people the means of speedy and accurate intelligence, and so stormed at once the castles of the terrible Giant Doubt and Giant Despair. He has saved time, shortened the hours of toil, accumulated and intensified thought by the rapidity and terseness of electric messages. He has celebrated treaties. Go to the uttermost parts of the earth; go beneath the deep sea; to the land where snows are eternal, or to the tropical realms where the orange blooms in the air of mid-winter, and you will find this clicking, persistent, sleepless instrument ready to give its tireless wing to your purpose."

It was my good fortune to serve in the House of Representatives with Mr. Stephens of Georgia, and Mr. Wood of New York, both of whom more than a third of a century before had given their votes in favor of the appropriation that made it possible for Morse to prosecute experiments fraught with such stupendous blessing to our race. The member who reported back the bill from the Committee on Commerce, with favorable recommendations, and then supported it by an eloquent speech upon the floor of the House, was Robert C. Winthrop of Massachusetts. No public man I have ever known impressed me more favorably than did Mr. Winthrop. He had been the close friend of Everett, Choate, Webster, and Clay. He was the last survivor of as brilliant a coterie of party leaders and statesmen as our country has ever known. On a visit he made to the House of Representatives, of which he had many years before been the Speaker, business was at once suspended, and the members from all parts of the Great Hall gathered about him. In a letter to the Morse Memorial meeting in Boston, Mr. Winthrop stated that he was present in the Capitol while the first formal messages were passing along the magic cords between Washington and Baltimore. He referred to the declination read by Senator Wright in his presence, of the nomination to the Vice-Presidency tendered him, and added:

"All this gave us the most vivid impression, not only that a new kind of *wire-pulling* had entered into politics, but that a mysterious and marvellous power of the air had at length been subdued and trained to the service of mankind."

It is an interesting fact in this connection, to note that the little girl, Miss Ellsworth, who brought to Mr. Morse the joyful tidings of the passage of the bill on that early May morning in 1843, was rewarded by being requested by the great inventor to write the first message that ever passed over the wire. When she selected,

"What hath God wrought,"

words to find utterance by all tongues—she builded better than she knew, for in the words of Speaker Blaine:

"The little thread of wire placed as a timid experiment between the national capital and a neighboring city grew, and lengthened, and multiplied with almost the rapidity of the electric current that darted along its iron nerves, until, within his own lifetime, continent was bound to continent, hemisphere answered through ocean's depths to hemisphere, and an encircled globe dashed forth his eulogy in the unmatched eloquence of a grand achievement."

Words of praise, spoke by Dr. Prime, of the great inventor just after he had passed from the world, to which he left such a heritage, can never lose their interest:

"Morse in his coffin is a recollection never to fade. He lay like an ancient prophet or sage such as the old masters painted for Abraham, or Isaiah. His finely chiselled features, classical in their mould and majestic in repose, and heavy flowing beard; the death calm upon the brow that for eighty years had concealed a teeming brain, and that placid beauty that lingers upon the face of the righteous dead, as if the freed spirit had left a smile upon its forsaken home—these are the memories that remain of the most illustrious and honored private citizen that the New World has yet given to mankind."

IX ALONG THE BYPATHS OF HISTORY

THE WIDOW OF GEN. GAINES CLAIMS PROPERTY AT NEW ORLEANS WORTH $30,000,000—HER SUCCESS AFTER MUCH LITIGATION—THE WIDOW OF JOHN H. EATON, SECRETARY OF WAR—A CLOUD ON HER REPUTATION— HER HUSBAND A FRIEND OF GEN. JACKSON—A DUEL BETWEEN RANDOLPH AND CLAY—HOSTILITY OF THE LEADERS OF WASHINGTON SOCIETY TO MRS. EATON— SECRETARY EATON DISLIKED BY HIS COLLEAGUES— CONSEQUENT DISRUPTION OF JACKSON'S CABINET— MRS. EATON'S POVERTY IN HER OLD AGE.

Nearly a third of a century ago, as the guest in a Washington house, I had the opportunity of meeting Mrs. Gaines, the widow of General Edmund P. Gaines, a distinguished officer of the War of 1812, and Mrs. Eaton, the widow of the Hon. John H. Eaton of Tennessee, for a number of years a Senator from that State, and later Secretary of War during the administration of President Jackson. Their names suggested interesting events in our history, I gladly availed myself of the invitation to meet them.

I found Mrs. Gaines an old lady of small stature, with a profusion of curls, and gifted with rare powers of conversation. She spoke freely of her great lawsuits, one of which was then pending in the Supreme Court of the United States. As I listened, I thought of the wonderful career of the little woman before me. Few names, a half-century ago, were more familiar to the reading public than that of Myra Clark Gaines. She was born in New Orleans in the early days of the century; was the daughter of Daniel Clark, who died in 1813, the owner of a large portion of the land upon which the city of New Orleans was afterwards built. She was his only heir, and soon after attaining her majority, instituted a suit, or series of suits, for the recovery of her property. After years of litigation, the seriously controverted fact of her being the lawful heir of Daniel Clark was established, and the contest, which was to wear out two generations of lawyers, began in dead earnest. The value of the property involved in the litigation then exceeded thirty millions of dollars. At the time I saw her, she had just arrived from her home in New Orleans to be present at the argument of one of her suits in the Supreme Court. She had already received nearly six millions of dollars by successful litigation, and she assured me that she intended to live one hundred years longer, if necessary, to obtain her rights, and that she expected to recover every dollar to which she was rightfully entitled. The air of confidence with which she spoke, and the pluck manifested in her every word and motion, convinced me at once that the only possible question as to her ultimate success was that of time. And so indeed it proved, for,

"When like a clock worn out with eating time,
The wheels of weary life at last stood still,"

numerous suits, in which she had been successful in the lower courts, were still pending in the higher.

She told me with apparent satisfaction, during the interview, that she could name over fifty lawyers who had been against her since the beginning of her contest, all of whom were now in their graves. Her litigation was the one absorbing thought of her life, her one topic of conversation.

General Gaines had died many years before, and her legal battles,— extending through several decades and against a host of adversaries, —she had, with courage unfaltering and patience that knew no shadow of weariness, prosecuted single-handed and alone.

In view of the enormous sums involved, the length of time consumed in the litigation, the number and ability of counsel engaged, and the antagonisms engendered, the records of our American courts will be searched in vain for a parallel to the once famous suit of Myra Clark Gaines against the city of New Orleans.

At the close of this interview, I was soon in conversation with the older of the two ladies. Mrs. Eaton was then near the close of an eventful life, one indeed without an approximate parallel in our history. Four score years ago, there were few persons in the village of Washington to whom "Peggy O'Neal" was a stranger. Her father was the proprietor of a well-known, old-style tavern on Pennsylvania Avenue, which, during the sessions of Congress, included among its guests many of the leading statesmen of that day. Of this number were Benton, Randolph, Eaton, Grundy, and others equally well known. The daughter, a girl of rare beauty, on account of her vivacity and grace soon became a great favorite with all. She was without question one of the belles of Washington.

It was difficult for me to realize that the care-worn face before me was that of the charming Peggy O'Neal of early Washington days. Distress, poverty, slander possibly, had measurably wrought the sad change, but after all,

"the surest poison is Time."

Traces of her former self still lingered, however, and her erect form and dignified mien would have challenged respect in any assembly.

While yet in her teens, she had married a purser in the Navy, who soon after died by his own hand, while on a cruise in the Mediterranean. A year or two after his death, with reputation somewhat clouded, she married the Honorable John H. Eaton, then a Senator from Tennessee. He was many years her senior, was one of the leading statesmen of the day, and had rendered brilliant service in the campaign which terminated so triumphantly at New Orleans. He was the devoted personal and political friend of General Jackson, his earliest biographer, and later his earnest advocate for the Presidency. Indeed, the movement having in view the election of "Old Hickory" was inaugurated by Major Eaton assisted by Amos Kendall and Francis P. Blair.

This was in 1824, before the days of national conventions. Eaton visited several of the States in the interest of his old commander, and secured the hearty co-operation of many of the most influential men. It was in large degree through his personal efforts that the Legislatures of Pennsylvania and Tennessee proposed the name of Andrew Jackson for the great office.

The Presidential contest of that year marked an epoch in our political history. It was at the close of the Monroe administration, "the era of good feeling." The struggle for supremacy which immediately followed was the precursor of an era of political strife which left its deep and lasting impress upon the country. Of the four candidates in the field, two were members of the outgoing Cabinet of President Monroe: John Quincy Adams, Secretary of State, and William H. Crawford, Secretary of the Treasury. The remaining candidates were Henry Clay, the eloquent and accomplished Speaker of the House of Representatives, and Andrew Jackson, "the hero of New Orleans." The candidates were all of the same party, that founded by Jefferson; the sun of the once powerful Federalists had set, and the Whig party was yet in the future.

No one of the candidates receiving a majority of the electoral vote, the election devolved upon the House of Representatives. Mr. Clay being the lowest upon the list, the choice by constitutional requirement was to be made from his three competitors. The influence of the Kentucky statesman was thrown to Mr. Adams, who was duly elected, receiving the votes of a bare majority of the States. The determining vote was given by the sole representative from Illinois, the able and brilliant Daniel P. Cook, a friend of Mr. Clay. The sad sequel was the defeat of Cook at the next Congressional election, his immediate retirement from public life, and early and lamented death.

Not less sad was the effect of the vote just given upon the political fortunes of Henry Clay. His high character and distinguished public services were scant protection against the clamor that immediately followed his acceptance of the office of Secretary of State tendered him by President Adams. "Bargain and Corruption" was the terrible slogan of his enemies in his later struggles for the Presidency and its echo scarcely died out with that generation.

In this connection, the bitter words spoken in the Senate by John Randolph will be recalled: "the coalition between the Puritan and the blackleg." The duel which followed, now historic, stands alone in the fierce conflicts of men. Whatever the faults of Randolph, let it be remembered to his eternal honor, that after receiving at short range the fire of Mr. Clay, he promptly discharged his own pistol in the air. Even after the lapse of eighty years how pleasing these words: "At which Mr. Clay, throwing down his own pistol, advanced with extended hand to Mr. Randolph, who taking his hand quietly remarked, 'You owe me a coat, Mr. Clay,' to which the latter exclaimed, 'Thank God the obligation is no greater!'"

Immediately upon the defeat of Jackson, his friends began the agitation which resulted in his overwhelming triumph over Adams, in 1828. Chief among his supporters in this, as in his former contest, was Major Eaton. The untiring devotion of Jackson to his friends is well known. It rarely found more striking illustration than in the selection of Eaton as Secretary of War, and in the zeal with which he sustained him through good and evil report alike, during later years.

When it became known that Senator Eaton was to hold a seat in the Cabinet of the new administration, the fashionable circles of the capital were deeply agitated, and protests earnest and vehement assailed the ears of the devoted President. The objections urged were not against Major Eaton, but against his beautiful and accomplished wife. Rumors of an exceedingly uncomplimentary character, that had measurably died out with time, were suddenly revived against Mrs. Eaton, and gathered force and volume with each passing day. It is hardly necessary to say that this hostility was, in the main, from her own sex. To all remonstrances and appeals, however, President Jackson turned a deaf ear. The kindness shown by the mother of Mrs. Eaton to the wife of the President during a former residence, and while he was a Senator, in Washington, had never been forgotten. It will be remembered that during the late Presidential contest not only had Jackson himself been the object of merciless attack, but even his invalid wife did not escape. Divorced from her first husband because of his cruel treatment, she had married Jackson, when he was a young lawyer in Nashville, many years before. As the result of the aspersions cast upon her, the once famous duel was evolved in which Charles Dickinson fell by the hand of Jackson in 1806.

After his election, but before his inauguration, Mrs. Jackson died, the victim of calumny as her husband always believed. A few days after he had turned away from that new-made grave, he was in the turmoil of politics at the national capital. With the past fresh in his memory, it is not strange that he espoused the cause of his faithful friend, and the daughter of the woman who had befriended one dearer to him than his own life. Thoroughly convinced of the innocence of Mrs. Eaton, he made her cause his own, and to the end he knew no variableness or shadow of turning.

The new administration was not far upon its tempestuous voyage before the trouble began. The relentless hostility of the leaders of Washington society against Mrs. Eaton was manifested in every possible way. Their doors were firmly closed against her. This, of itself, would have been of comparatively little moment, but serious consequences were to grow out of it. From private parlors and drawing-rooms the controversy soon reached the little coterie that constituted the official family of President Jackson. While this is almost forgotten history now, one chapter of Jackson's biography published soon after the events mentioned, was headed, "Mr. Van Buren calls upon Mrs. Eaton." As is well known, the creed in action of the most suave of our presidents was,

"The statues of our stately fortunes
Are sculptured with the chisel, not the axe."

Mr. Van Buren was Secretary of State, and one of the most agreeable and politic of statesmen. He was in line of succession to the great office, and understood well the importance of maintaining his hold upon President Jackson. A widower himself, the call upon which so much stress was laid at the time subjected the Secretary of State to no embarrassment at home. Not so, however, with three of his colleagues in the Cabinet: Mr. Ingham, Secretary of the Treasury, Mr. Branch of the Navy, and Mr. Berrien the Attorney-General. The wife of each of these gentlemen refused to return Mrs. Eaton's call, or to recognize her in any possible manner. No remonstrance on the part of the President could avail to secure even a formal exchange of courtesies on the part of these ladies. All this only intensified the determination on the part of the President to secure to the wife of the Secretary of War the social recognition to which he considered her justly entitled, but it would not avail; the purpose of the most resolute man on earth was powerless against a determination equal to his own. Never was more forcibly exemplified the truth of the old couplet:

"When a woman will, she will, you may depend on't,
And when she won't, she won't, and there's an end on't."

As to how Mrs. Eaton meanwhile appeared to others, something may be gleaned from the statement of a distinguished gentleman who called at the home of the Secretary of War:

"I went to the house in the evening, and found assembled there a large company of gentlemen who paid assiduous court to the lady. Mrs. Eaton was not then the celebrated character she was destined ere long to be made. To me she seemed a strikingly beautiful and fascinating woman, all graciousness and vivacity—the life of the company."

That the discordant status of the households of the official advisers of the President was the topic of discussion among leading statesmen, may be inferred from the following extract from a letter written at the time by Daniel Webster:

"Mr. Van Buren has evidently, at this moment, quite the lead in influence and importance. He controls all the pages on the back stairs, and flatters what seems to be, at present, the Aaron's serpent among the President's desires, a settled purpose of making out of the lady of whom so much has been said, a person of reputation."

Of curious interest even now, is the closing sentence in Mr. Webster's letter, in which with prophetic ken he forecasts the effect of the Eaton controversy upon national politics: "It is odd enough, but too evident to be doubted, that the consequence of this dispute in the social and fashionable world is producing great political effects, and *may very probably determine who shall be successor to the present chief magistrate.*"

As explanatory of the above quotation, it will be remembered that next to President Jackson, the two most prominent leaders of the dominant party were Vice-President Calhoun and Secretary of State Van Buren. The political forces were even then gathering around one or the other of these great leaders, and there was little question in official circles that the successor to Jackson would be either Van Buren or Calhoun. It was equally certain that the successful aspirant would be the one who had the good fortune to secure the powerful influence of Jackson. Chief among the friends of Calhoun were the Cabinet officers Ingham, Branch, and Berrien. The incumbent of the office of Postmaster-General—now for the first time a Cabinet office—was William T. Barry of Kentucky. He was the friend of Van Buren, and in the social controversy mentioned, he sided with the President and the Secretary of State as a champion of Mrs. Eaton. As to the views of the Vice-President upon the all-absorbing question, we have no information. Not being one of the official advisers of the President, he probably kept entirely aloof from a controversy no doubt in every way distasteful to him.

Meanwhile the relations between Secretary Eaton and his colleagues of the Treasury, Navy, and Department of Justice, became more and more unfriendly, until all communication other than of the most formal official character ceased. The soul of the President was vexed beyond endurance; and as under existing conditions harmony in his official family was impossible, he determined upon a reorganization of his Cabinet. To this end, the resignations of Van Buren, Eaton, and Barry were voluntarily tendered, and promptly accepted. A formal request from the President to Messrs. Ingham, Branch, and Berrien secured the resignation of these three official advisers; and thus was brought about what is known in our political history as "the disruption of Jackson's Cabinet."

The three gentlemen whose resignations had been voluntarily tendered, were, in modern political parlance, at once "taken care of." Mr. Van Buren was appointed minister to St. James, Barry to Madrid, and Eaton to the governorship of Florida Territory. No such good fortune, however, was in store for either Ingham, Branch, or Berrien. Each was, henceforth, *persona non grata* with President Jackson.

The end, however, was not yet. A publication by the retiring Secretary of the Treasury contained an uncomplimentary allusion to Mrs. Eaton, which resulted first in his receiving a challenge from her husband, and later in a street altercation.

The almost forgotten incidents just mentioned were rapidly leading up to matters of deep consequence. The true significance of the words of Webster last quoted will now appear. A rupture, never yet fully explained, now occurred between President Jackson and Mr. Calhoun. The intention of the former to secure to Mr. Van Buren the succession to the presidency was no longer a matter of doubt.

Van Buren, "the favorite," was meanwhile reposing upon no bed of roses. He was, in very truth, "in the thick of events." His confirmation as Minister was defeated by the casting vote of Vice-President Calhoun, after the formal presentation of his credentials to the Court to which he had been accredited. It was believed that this rejection would prove the death knell to Van Buren's Presidential hopes. But it was not so to be. His rejection aroused deep sympathy, secured his nomination upon the ticket with Jackson in 1832, and for four years he presided over the great body which had so lately rejected his nomination, and as is well known, four years later he was chosen to succeed Jackson as President. Unfortunately for Calhoun, one of the ablest and purest of statesmen, he had incurred the hostility of Jackson, and never attained the goal of his ambition.

During my interview with Mrs. Eaton I said to her, "Madam, you must have known General Jackson when he was President?" "Known General

Jackson," she replied, "known General Jackson?" "Oh, yes," I said, "your husband was a member of his Cabinet and of course you must have known him. I would like to know what kind of a man General Jackson really was?" "What kind of a man," replied Mrs. Eaton in a manner and tone not easily forgotten. "What kind of *a man*—a god, sir, a god." The spirit of the past seemed over her, as with trembling voice and deep emotion she spoke of the man whose powerful and unfaltering friendship had been her stay and bulwark during the terrible ordeal through which she had passed.

Accompanying her that evening to the humble home provided for her by a distant relative, she remarked, "I have seen the time, sir, when I could have invited you to an elegant home." She then said that when Major Eaton died, he left for her an ample fortune but that some years later she unfortunately married a man younger than herself, who succeeded in getting her property into his hands and then cruelly deserted her.

Fiction indeed seems commonplace when contrasted with the story of real life such as this now penniless and forgotten woman had known. Once surrounded by all that wealth could give, herself one of the most beautiful and accomplished of women, her husband the incumbent of exalted official position,—now, wealth, beauty, and position vanished; the grave hiding all she loved; sitting in silence and desolation, the memories of the long past almost her sole companions. When in the tide of time has there been truer realization of the words of the great bard—

"The web of our life is of a mingled yarn,
Good and ill together?"

X THE CODE OF HONOR

The very name "Bladensburg" is suggestive of pistol and bullet, savors indeed of human blood. It is associated with tragic events that during successive generations stirred emotions of indignation and horror that have not yet wholly died out from the memories of men. As the words "Baden-Baden" and "Monte Carlo" bring before us the gambler "steeped in the colors of his trade," so the mere mention of Bladensburg calls to mind the duellist, pistol in hand, standing in front of his slain antagonist.

Personal difficulties are now rarely if ever in this country adjusted by an appeal to "the code." The custom, now universally condemned as barbarous, was at an early day practically upheld by an almost omnipotent public opinion. As is well known, in many localities to have declined an invitation to "the field of honor" from one entitled to the designation of a "gentleman" would have entailed not only loss of social position, but to a public man would have been a bar to future political advancement. Thanks to a higher civilization, and possibly a more exalted estimate of the sacredness of human life, the code in all our American States is a thing of the past.

And yet, revolting as the custom now appears, it held its place as a recognized method for the settlement of personal controversies among "gentlemen," to a time within the memories of men still living. The code, a heritage from barbaric times, lingered till it had caused more than one bloody chapter to be written, until it had taken from the walks of life more than one of our most gifted American statesmen.

Truer words were never written than those of Franklin at the time when the code was appealed to for the settlement of every dispute pertaining to personal honor: "A duel decides nothing; the man appealing to it, makes himself judge in his own cause, condemns the offender without a jury, and undertakes himself to be the executioner." And yet, the startling record remains that in the State of New Jersey, one of the ablest and most brilliant of statesmen met death at the hands of an antagonist scarcely less gifted, who was at the time Vice-President of the United States. The survivor of an encounter equally tragic, occurring near the banks of the Cumberland in 1806, was a little more than a score of years later elevated to the Presidency. The valuable life of the Secretary of State during the administration of the younger Adams was saved only by his antagonist magnanimously refusing to return the fire which came within an ace of ending his own life. Thirteen years after the Clay and Randolph duel, a member of Congress from Maine perished in an encounter at Bladensburg with a representative from Kentucky. Sixty-six years ago, a challenge to mortal combat was accepted by one who in later years was twice elected to the Presidency. One of the signers of the Declaration of Independence fell in a duel with an officer of the Colonial army, soon after that great event. There are many yet living who read the startling telegram from the Pacific coast that a Senator from California had fallen in a duel with the Chief Justice of that State, and sad as it is, this dreadful recital might be much farther extended.

While a member of Congress many years ago, in company with Representatives Knott and McKenzie of Kentucky I spent some hours upon the historic duelling ground at Bladensburg, a Maryland village of a few hundred inhabitants, six miles from the city of Washington. Governor Knott pointed out the exact spot where Barron and Decatur stood in the memorable duel in 1820, in which the latter was killed. It is impossible to read the account of this fatal meeting even after the lapse of more than four score years, without a feeling of profound regret for the sad fate of one of the most gallant of all the brave officers the American Navy has known. It was truly said of Decatur: "He was one of the most chivalric men of any age or country." He was one of the little band of naval commanders who by heroic exploits at sea did so much to redeem the American name from the humiliation and disgrace caused by incompetent generalship upon land, in our second war with Great Britain. His encounters with the enemy were of frequent occurrence, and in each instance added new laurels to our little navy. If Commodore Decatur had rendered no other service to his country, that of the destruction of the Algerine pirates would alone entitle him to a place among its benefactors. His skill and daring when in command of our little fleet upon the Mediterranean destroyed forever the power of "the common enemy of mankind," avenged the insult to our flag, and secured for the American name an honored place among the nations of the world.

The tragic death of Decatur—recalling so much of gallant service— has cast a spell about his name. It belongs in the list of immortals, with the names of Sir Walter Raleigh, Captain Lawrence, Lord Nelson, and Oliver Hazard Perry. Cities and counties without number throughout our entire country have been given the honored name of Decatur.

Commodore Barron, too, had known much active service. For an alleged official delinquency, he had been court-martialed near the close of the War of 1812, and sentenced to a suspension of five years from his command. Smarting under this humiliation, he was bitter in his denunciation of all who were in any way concerned in what he regarded an act of flagrant injustice to himself. Chief among the officers who had incurred his displeasure was Commodore Decatur. A protracted and at length hostile correspondence ensued between the two, and this correspondence resulted at length in a challenge from Barron, accepted by Decatur. The latter had repeatedly declared that he bore no personal hostility toward Barron. Before going to the fatal field he told his friend William Wirt—then the Attorney-General of the United States—that he did not wish to meet Barron, and that the duel was forced upon him. When he received the challenge, he assured a brother officer that nothing could induce him to take the life of Barron. In connection with this sad affair, Mr. Wirt—who was untiring in his efforts to effect a reconciliation—has left the record of a conversation with Decatur in which the latter declared his hostility to the practice of duelling, but that he was "controlled by the omnipotence of public sentiment." "Fighting," said he, "is my profession, and it would be impossible for me to keep my station and preserve my respectability without showing myself ready at all times to answer the call of any one who bore the name of gentleman."

The hostile meeting between Barron and Decatur occurred at the place already mentioned, March 22, 1820. The distance was eight paces, the weapons, pistols. Decatur's second was Captain Bainbridge, at a later day a distinguished admiral in our navy. As they took their places at the deadly range, Barron said, "I hope on meeting in another world we will be better friends than in this." To which Decatur replied, "I have never been your enemy, sir." At the word both pistols were discharged, making but a single report. Both combatants fell. Decatur was supported a short distance, and sank down near his antagonist, who was severely—and as it was then supposed, mortally—wounded. Mr. Wirt says:

"What then occurred reminded me of the closing scenes of the tragedy between Hamlet and Laertes. Barron proposed that they should make friends before they met in another world. Decatur said he had never been his enemy, that he freely forgave him his death, but he could not forgive those who had stimulated him to seek his life. Barron then said: 'Would to God you had said that much yesterday.'"

Thus they parted in peace. Decatur knew he was to die, and his only regret was that he had not died in the service of his country.

The last duel fought at Bladensburg was in 1838, between Jonathan Cilley and William J. Graves. The former was at the time a Representative in Congress from Maine, and the latter from Kentucky. In its main features, this duel is without a parallel. It was fought upon a pure technicality. The parties to it never exchanged an unkind word, and were in fact, almost up to the day of the fatal meeting, comparative strangers to each other.

Briefly related, the fatal meeting between Cilley and Graves came about in this wise. In a speech in the House, Mr. Cilley in replying to an editorial in *The New York Courier and Inquirer,* criticised severely the conduct of its proprietor, James Watson Webb, a noted Whig editor of that day. At this, the latter, being deeply offended and failing to obtain a retraction by Cilley of the offensive words, challenged him to mortal combat. The bearer of this challenge was William J. Graves, a prominent Whig member of the House. Mr. Cilley in his letter to Mr. Graves, in which he declined to receive the challenge of Webb, said: "I decline to receive it because I choose to be drawn into no controversy with him. I neither affirm nor deny anything in regard to his character, but I now repeat what I have said to you, that I intended by the refusal no disrespect to you."

This letter was considered unsatisfactory by Graves, and he immediately sent by his colleague Mr. Menifee, a note to Cilley then in his seat in the House, saying: "In declining to receive Colonel Webb's communication, you do not disclaim any exception to him personally as a gentleman. I have, therefore, to inquire whether you declined to receive his communication on the ground of any personal exception to him as a gentleman or a man of honor." Mr. Cilley declining to give the categorical answer demanded, was immediately challenged by Graves. The challenge was borne by Mr. Wise, a Representative from Virginia. On the same evening, Mr. Jones—then a delegate and later a Senator from Iowa—as the second of Cilley, handed the note of acceptance of the latter to Graves. Bladensburg was designated as the place of meeting, rifles the weapons, the distance eight yards, the rifles to be held horizontally at arm's length down, to be cocked and triggers set, the words to be, "Gentlemen, are you ready?" Some delay was occasioned by the difficulty in procuring a suitable rifle for Mr. Graves. This was at length obviated, as will appear from the following note of Mr. Jones to Mr. Wise: "I have the honor to inform you that I have in my possession an excellent rifle, in good order, which is at the service of Mr. Graves." With every courtesy proper to the occasion rigidly observed, the rifle mentioned, "through the politeness of Dr. Duncan," was sent to Mr. Graves, and the hostile meeting occurred at the designated time, February 24, 1838.

From the report of a special committee of the House of Representatives at a later day appointed to investigate this affair, it appears that Mr. Graves was accompanied to the ground by his second, Mr. Wise, Mr. Crittenden, and Mr. Menifee, two of his colleagues, and Dr. Foltz his surgeon. The attendants of Mr. Cilley were his second, Mr. Jones, Representative Bynum of North Carolina, and Colonel Schoenberg, and Dr. Duncan as his surgeon. The Committee's report then continues in these words:

"Shortly after three o'clock P. M. the parties exchanged shots according to the terms of meeting. Mr. Cilley fired first before he had fully elevated his piece, and Mr. Graves one or two seconds afterwards. Both missed. It is to the credit of both the seconds and to the other gentlemen in attendance, than an earnest desire was then manifested to have the affair terminated, as will appear from the report already mentioned."

Mr. Jones now inquired of Mr. Wise whether Mr. Graves was satisfied, to which Mr. Wise replied: "These gentlemen have come here without animosity toward each other; they are fighting merely upon a point of honor. Cannot Mr. Cilley assign some reason for not receiving at Mr. Graves's hands Colonel Webb's communication, or make some disclaimer which will relive Mr. Graves from his position?" Mr. Jones replied: "While the challenge is impending, Mr. Cilley can make no explanation." Mr. Wise said: "The exchange of shots suspends the challenge, and the challenge is suspended for explanation." Mr. Jones thereupon went to Mr. Cilley, and after returning said:

"I am authorized by my friend Mr. Cilley to say, that in declining to receive the note from Mr. Graves purporting to come from Colonel Webb, he meant no disrespect to Mr. Graves because he entertained for him then as he does now, the highest respect and the most kind feeling; but that he declined to receive the note because he chose not to be drawn into any controversy with Colonel Webb."

The above not being satisfactory to Mr. Graves, and Mr. Cilley declining to make further concession, the challenge was renewed and the parties resumed their positions and again exchanged shots. Mr. Graves fired first, before he had fully elevated his piece; Mr. Cilley about two seconds afterwards. They both missed, although the witnesses then thought from the motions and appearance of Mr. Graves that he was hit. The latter immediately and peremptorily demanded another shot.

The challenge was here again, for the time, withdrawn and another unsuccessful attempt made by the seconds to effect an adjustment. In the light of what was so soon to follow, it is painful to read that all this came about and continued to the bloody end, because Mr. Cilley in substance refused to disclaim that his declination of Webb's challenge was for the reason that he did not consider him a gentleman. His repeated assurance that in doing so, he intended no disrespect to the bearer of the challenge, for whom he entertained the most kindly feelings, strangely enough to us was deemed insufficient.

The challenge being renewed, the parties, after due observance of the formalities as before, confronted each other for the third and last time. And now closes the official report: "the rifles being loaded, the parties resumed their stations, and fired the third time very near together. Mr. Cilley was shot through the body. He dropped his rifle, beckoned to some one near him, and said, 'I am shot,' put both his hands to his wound, fell, and in two or three minutes expired."

What a commentary all this upon "the code of honor"! Upon what appears the shadow of a technicality even, two young men of recognized ability, chosen representatives of the people, confronted each other in continued combat, until death closed the scene, and neither had the slightest feeling of hostility toward the other! This duel, so utterly groundless in its inception and bloody in its termination, was the last fought in Bladensburg. Intense excitement followed the death of the lamented Cilley and public sentiment was deeply aroused against the horrible custom of duelling. But the public sentiment that existed at the time must be taken into account before a too ready condemnation of one of the actors in this fearful tragedy. In announcing the death of Mr. Cilley to the Senate, Mr. Williams of Maine said: "In accepting the call, he did nothing more than he believed indispensable to avoid disgrace to himself, his family, and his constituents."

While the presiding officer of the Senate, a gentleman of small stature and advanced age called upon me and introduced himself as George W. Jones, former Senator from Iowa. I have rarely met a more interesting man. He was then ninety-two years of age, apparently in perfect health, and as active as if, for his exclusive benefit, the hands had been turned back three decades upon the dial. He had been a delegate from the Territory embracing the present States of Iowa and Wisconsin, in the twenty-fifth Congress, when the sessions of the House were held in the Old Hall. Upon the admission of Iowa as a State, he was chosen a Senator, a position he held by successive elections for many years. As delegate, he had been the associate of John Quincy Adams, and as a Senator the contemporary of Benton, Wright, Douglas, Cass, Seward, Preston, Clay, Calhoun, and Webster. He had personally known some of the men whose public life reached back to the establishment of the Government. He had taken part in the discussion of great questions that have left a deep impress upon history. As I listened to his description of the men I have named, and of the momentous events with which their names are associated, he seemed indeed the sole connecting link between the present and the long past.

But what interested me most deeply in the almost forgotten old man before me, was the fact that he was the second of the unfortunate Cilley upon the ill-fated day at Bladensburg. The conversation at length turned to that event, and strangely enough, he manifested no suggestion of embarrassment at its mention. He spoke in the highest terms of Mr. Cilley, as a gentleman of lofty character, of unfaltering courage, of rare gifts, and of splendid promise. It was evident that the passing years had not dimmed his memory of the tragic event, nor lessened his regret at the sad ending of an affair with which his own name is inseparably associated.

The first duel between men of prominence in this country, was that of Gwinett and McIntosh. The fact that one of the parties, Button Gwinett, was a signer of the Declaration of Independence gives it historic interest. He was one of the three delegates from Georgia in the second Continental Congress, and an earnest champion of independence. Six years before, he had emigrated from England, purchased a large tract of land, and devoted himself to agricultural pursuits. Less is known of him, probably, than of any of the signers of the Declaration.

In 1777, he became involved in a bitter personal quarrel with General McIntosh, an officer of the Revolution. Deeply offended at his conduct, Gwinett challenged him to mortal combat. They fought with pistols at a distance of twelve feet, and Gwinett was killed. He is buried at Augusta, Georgia, with his two colleagues in the Continental Congress.

It is now an almost forgotten fact that, but for the wise counsel of his superior officer, Nathaniel Greene, next to Washington the ablest of the American generals, would have been a party to a duel at a time when his services were so greatly in demand. Soon after his transfer to the southern army, Greene was challenged by a captain of his command. Fearing that a declination upon his part would be misunderstood by his brother officers, Greene wrote General Washington a full account of the transaction, concluding: "If I thought my honor or reputation would suffer in the opinion of the world, and more especially with the military gentlemen, I value life too little to hesitate a moment to accept the challenge." The answer of one of the wisest of men possibly saved to our little army one whose loss would have been disastrous to his country at that critical moment. Said Washington:

"I give it as my decided opinion, that your honor and reputation will stand not only perfectly acquitted for the non-acceptance of his challenge, but that your prudence and judgment would have been condemned by accepting it; because if a commanding officer is amenable to private calls for the discharge of his public duty, he has a dagger always at his heart, and can turn neither to the right nor to the left without meeting its point."

The timely words of Washington had the desired effect, and very probably saved General Greene to a brilliant career of usefulness and glory.

One of the most interesting incidents of our Revolutionary history, is what is known as "The Conway Cabal," the attempt to displace Washington from the supreme command and substitute General Horatio Gates in his stead. The latter was then in high favor as the hero of Saratoga and the capturer of the invading army of Burgoyne. In this connection, the prophetic words of the deeply embittered General Charles Lee will be recalled. On his way to take command of the southern army to which he had just been assigned, Gates called upon Lee, then in disgrace and retirement at his home. Both were Englishmen, had known service together in the British army, and were at the time owners of neighboring plantations in what is now Jefferson County, West Virginia. When parting, Lee significantly remarked to this old comrade, "Gates, your Northern laurels will soon be turned into Southern willows." The disastrous defeat at Camden soon thereafter terminated the military career of Gates no less effectually than the timely "curse" of Washington had terminated that of Lee upon his disgraceful retreat at the battle of Monmouth.

The result of the "Cabal" above mentioned was a challenge from Colonel Cadwallader to General Conway, whose name has come down to us associated with the conspiracy to supersede Washington by Gates. In an encounter which immediately followed, Conway was seriously wounded. Believing his wound to be mortal, he called for pen and paper and did much to retrieve his reputation by writing the following letter to Washington:

"SIR: I find myself just able to hold my pen during a few moments and take this opportunity of expressing my sincere grief for having written, said, or done anything disagreeable to Your Excellency. My career will soon be over, therefore justice and truth prompt me to declare my last sentiments. You are in my eyes the great and good man. May you long enjoy the love, esteem, and veneration of these States whose liberties you have asserted by your virtues."

Conway eventually recovered, entered the army of France, and died in its service.

General Charles Lee was indeed a soldier of fortune. A native of England, he held a commission in the British army, and later in that of the King of Italy. As the result of a duel in which he slew an Italian officer, he fled to America, and tendered his services to the Continental Congress just at the beginning of the struggle for independence. He was placed second in command to Washington and was not without supporters for the coveted position of Commander-in-chief. He was from the beginning the enemy of Washington, and deeply resented the fact that his position was subordinate to that of the younger and less experienced officer, for whose ability he expressed great contempt. He was a friend of Gates and one of the chief conspirators in the Conway Cabal. His military career closed at the battle of Monmouth, and from letters that have come to light there is little doubt that he was then in treasonable correspondence with the enemy.

After being deprived of his command at Monmouth, he was challenged by Colonel John Laurens, one of the aides of the Commander-in-chief, because of his denunciation of Washington. The challenge was accepted, and the parties fought with pistols in a retired spot near Philadelphia. Additional interest attaches to this duel from the fact that Colonel Alexander Hamilton of Washington's staff, was the second for Laurens.

At the first fire Lee was wounded, and then, through the interposition of Hamilton the affair terminated. The gratifying narrative has come down to us that, "upon the whole, we think it a piece of justice to the two gentlemen to declare that, after they met, their conduct was strongly marked with all the politeness, generosity, coolness, and firmness, that ought to characterize a transaction of this nature."

The last years of Lee's life were spent at his Virginia plantation. He died in an obscure boarding-house in Philadelphia, in 1782. Upon a visit I made to his Virginia home some years ago, I was shown a certified copy of his will, which contained this remarkable provision:

"It is my will, that I shall not be buried within one mile of any churchyard, or of any Presbyterian or Anabaptist church, for the reason that *as I have kept a great deal of bad company in this world, I do not wish to do so in the next.*"

This country has known few abler or more eminent men than DeWitt Clinton. He was successively Mayor of the city of New York, Governor of that State, a Senator in Congress, and in 1812 an unsuccessful candidate for the Presidency against Mr. Madison. Distinguished as a lawyer and statesman, he is even better known as "the Father of the Erie Canal." His biographer says:

"After undergoing constant, unremitting, and factious resistance, he had the felicity of being borne, in October, 1825, in a barge on the artificial river— which he seemed to all to have constructed —from Lake Erie to the Bay of New York, while bells were rung, and cannon saluted him at every stage of that imposing progress."

In 1803, while in the Senate, Clinton accepted a challenge from General Dayton, a Senator from New Jersey. The ground of the challenge was words spoken by the former in debate. Before the hostile meeting, however, through the interposition of friends a satisfactory explanation upon the part of Clinton resulted in a peaceable adjustment, and the restoration of friendly relations between the two Senators.

An "affair of honor" in which Clinton was engaged one year earlier, was not quite so easily adjusted. This was with a noted politician of that day, John Swartout of New York. The latter was the friend of Aaron Burr, the political and personal enemy of Clinton. Swartout was the challenging party, and the hostile meeting occurred near the city of New York. On the ground, after the parties had been placed in position, Clinton is said to have expressed regret that Burr—the real principal in the controversy—was not before him. History might have run in a different channel had such been the fact.

Three pistol shots were exchanged without effect, at the end of each the second of Clinton demanding of Swartout, "Are you satisfied, sir?" to which the answer was, "I am not." To this, at the third exchange, was added, "neither shall I be until that apology is made which I have demanded of Mr. Clinton." Mr. Clinton declined to sign a paper presented, but declared that he had no animosity against Mr. Swartout, and would willingly shake hands and agree to meet on the score of former friendship. This being unsatisfactory, the fourth shot was promptly exchanged. Fortune, heretofore reluctant to decide between her favorites, now leaned toward the challenged party—Mr. Swartout being struck just below the knee. In reply to the inquiry, "Are you satisfied, sir?" standing erect while the surgeon kneeling beside him removed the ball, he answered, "I am not; *proceed.*" The fifth shot being exchanged, Mr. Swartout's other leg was the recipient of his antagonist's bullet. The voice of the wounded man being still for war, Mr. Clinton here threw down his pistol, declaring he would fight no longer, and immediately retired from the ground. The second of the remaining belligerent now advised his principal to retire also and have his wounds dressed, which certainly seemed reasonable under all the circumstances.

An answer to a challenge that might well stand for a model for all time, was that given during the administration of the older Adams by Mr. Thatcher of Massachusetts, to Blount of North Carolina. The challenge grew out of a heated debate in the House. In reply, Thatcher said in substance, that being a husband and father, his family had an interest in his life, and that he could not think of accepting the invitation without the consent of his wife, that he would immediately consult her, and *if successful in obtaining her permission,* he would meet Mr. Blount with pleasure. Whereupon Fisher Ames, one of the great men of the day, wittily remarked to a bachelor colleague, "Behold now the advantage of having a wife— God preserve us all from gunpowder!"

The reply of Thatcher was read in the House, causing much merriment and leaving his adversary—

"Sacred to ridicule his whole life long,
And the sad burden of some merry song."

It is hardly necessary to add that at last accounts the consent of Mrs. Thatcher had not been obtained.

It is scarcely remembered that Lord Byron, angered by a bitter criticism, once challenged the poet Southey. Accepting the challenge conditionally, Southey added:

"In affairs of this kind, the participants ought to meet on equal terms. But to establish the equality between you and me there are two things that ought to be done, and a third may also be necessary before I meet you on the field. First, you must marry and have four children—all girls. Second, you must prove that the greater part of the provision which you make for them depends upon you life, and you must be under bond for four thousand pounds not to be hanged, commit suicide, nor be killed in a duel, which are the conditions upon which I have insured my life for the benefit of my wife and daughters. Third, you must convert me to infidelity. We can then meet on equal terms, *and your challenge will be cheerfully accepted.*"

Since the writing of the letters of Junius, nothing probably has appeared equal in invective to the correspondence seventy years ago between Daniel O'Connell and Benjamin Disraeli. The former was at the time a distinguished member of Parliament, and an orator without a peer. Disraeli, at first a supporter of the policy of the great Liberator, had joined the ranks of his enemies, and was unsparing in his denunciation of O'Connell and his party. In his reply O'Connell, after charging his assailant with ingratitude and treachery, concluded as follows:

"I cannot divest my mind of the belief that if your genealogy were traced, it would be found that you are the lineal descendant and true heir-at-law of the impenitent thief who atoned for his crimes upon the cross."

The challenge from Disraeli, which immediately followed, was treated by O'Connell with supreme contempt.

The duel between Hamilton and Burr is of perennial interest to the American people. Both were men of great distinction and splendid talents. Both had been soldiers during the Revolutionary War, and Hamilton was the confidential friend and for a time chief-of-staff of Washington. Burr had been a Senator from New York, and was at the time of the duel Vice-President of the United States. He was one of the recognized leaders of the dominant party, and by many considered the probable successor of Jefferson in the great office. Whatever hopes he might have had for the Presidency were destroyed by his alleged attempt to defeat Jefferson and secure his own elevation by the House of Representatives in 1801. His hostility to Hamilton had its beginning in the opposition of the latter to Burr's aspirations to the Presidency. Differing widely, as Hamilton did, with Jefferson upon important questions then pending, he nevertheless preferred the latter to Burr, and his influence eventually turned the scales—after a protracted struggle —in favor of Jefferson.

The valuable service just mentioned was one of the many rendered by Hamilton. He was the earnest advocate of the adoption of the Federal Constitution, and his papers during that pivotal struggle have justly given him high place in the list of American statesmen. He was the first Secretary of the Treasury, and possibly no man possessed in larger degree the confidence of Washington.

Aaron Burr was the grandson of the great New England minister, Jonathan Edwards, whose only daughter, Edith, was the wife of the Reverend Aaron Burr, an eminent Presbyterian clergyman and President of Princeton College. From all that is known of this gentleman, there can be no doubt that his ability and piety were unquestioned. Edith, his wife, was a woman of rare gifts and one of the loveliest of her sex. The pathetic reference to her in the funeral sermon over Hamilton will be remembered: "If there be tears in Heaven, a pious mother looks down upon this scene and weeps."

Hamilton and Burr were both citizens of New York, the latter, of Albany, the former, of New York City. At the time of the challenge Hamilton held no public office, but was engaged in a lucrative practice of the law. Burr was near the expiration of his term as Vice-President, and was a prospective candidate for Governor of New York. This candidacy was the immediate cause of the correspondence which resulted in the fatal encounter. Four letters passed between Burr and Hamilton prior to the formal challenge. The first was from Burr, and bears date June 18, 1804. In it attention is directed to a published letter of Dr. Cooper containing the words, "General Hamilton and Judge Kent have declared in substance that they look upon Mr. Burr to be a dangerous man, and one who ought not to be trusted with the reins of government. And I could detail to you a still more deplorable opinion which General Hamilton has expressed of Mr. Burr."

It was to the last sentence that the attention of Hamilton was especially directed by Mr. Van Ness, the bearer of the letter, which closed with the demand upon the part of Burr of "a prompt and unqualified acknowledgment or denial, of the use of any expression which would warrant the assertion of Dr. Cooper."

In his reply the next day Hamilton said:

"I cannot reconcile it with propriety to make the acknowledgment or denial you desire. I will add that I deem it inadmissable on principle to consent to be interrogated as to the justness of the inferences which may be drawn from others, from whatever I may have said of a political opponent in the course of fifteen years' competition. I stand ready to avow, or disavow promptly and explicitly, any precise or definite opinion which I may be charged with having declared of any gentleman. More than this cannot be fitly expected from me; and especially it cannot be reasonably expected that I shall enter into an explanation upon a basis so vague as that which you have adopted. I trust on more reflection, you will see the matter in the same light with me. If not, I can only regret the circumstance, and must abide the consequences."

The immediate response of Burr to the above, after repeating his former demand, contained the following:

"Political opposition can never absolve gentlemen from the necessity of a rigid adherence to the laws of honor and the rules of decorum. I neither claim such privilege, nor indulge it in others."

Hamilton's reply being unsatisfactory, the formal challenge of Burr was soon thereafter handed to him by W. P. Van Ness. The last named was the second of Burr, and Nathaniel Pendleton was the friend of Hamilton.

Some days elapsed after the formal acceptance of the challenge before the fatal meeting. That Hamilton was anxious to avoid the conflict, clearly appears from a perusal of the many publications that immediately followed. A paper he prepared explanatory in character, the second of Burr declined to receive, on the ground that he considered the correspondence closed by the acceptance of the challenge.

It touches our sympathies deeply even after the lapse of a century to read the letter written by Hamilton to his wife to be delivered in the event of his death, in which he states that he has endeavored by all honorable means to avoid the duel which probably he would not survive. He begs her forgiveness for the pain his death would cause her, and entreats her to bear her sorrows as one who has placed a firm reliance on a kind Providence.

A few days before his death, he and Burr were guests at a dimmer given by the Cincinnati Society, of which both were members. Few persons were aware of what was pending, but it was observed that Hamilton "entered with glee into all the gayety of a convivial party, and even sang an old military song." Burr, upon the contrary, was "silent, gloomy, and remained apart."

In his will, written July 9, Hamilton expressed deep regret that his death will prevent the full payment of his debts. He expresses the hope that his children will, in time, make up to his creditors all that may be due them. After tenderly committing to his children the care of their mother, he says, "in all situations you are charged to bear in mind, that she has been to you the most devoted and best of mothers."

The last paper that came from his pen was evidently intended as his vindication to posterity, his appeal to time. In this he says:

"I was certainly desirous of avoiding this interview, for the most cogent reasons. My religious and moral principles are strongly opposed to duelling, and it would give me pain to be obliged to shed the blood of a fellow-creature in a private combat forbidden by the laws. My wife and children are extremely dear to me, and my life is of the utmost importance to them. I am conscious of no ill-will to Colonel Burr distinct from political opposition, which I trust has proceeded from pure and upright motives. Lastly, I shall hazard much and shall possibly gain nothing by the issue of the interview. But it was impossible for me to avoid it."

He candidly admits that his criticisms of Colonel Burr have been severe. He says:

"And on different occasions, I—in common with many others—have made very unfavorable criticisms of the private character of this gentleman. It is not my design to fix any odium on the conduct of Colonel Burr in this case. He may have supposed himself under the necessity of acting as he has done. I hope the grounds of his proceeding have been such as to satisfy his own conscience. I trust, at the same time, that the world will do me the justice to believe that I have not censured him on light grounds, nor from unworthy inducements."

How strangely in the light of history sounds the following: "It is my ardent wish that he, by his future conduct, may show himself worthy of all confidence and esteem, and prove an ornament and blessing to the country."

That some lingering apprehension existed in the mind of General Hamilton that his criticisms of Colonel Burr might not have been altogether generous, appears from the following:

"As well because it is possible that I may have injured Colonel Burr, however convinced myself that my opinions and declarations have been well-founded, as from my general principles and temper in relation to similar affairs, I have resolved, if our interview is conducted in the usual manner, and it please God to give me the opportunity, to reserve and throw away my first fire; and I have thought even of reserving my second fire, and thus giving to Colonel Burr a double opportunity to pause and to reflect."

And then, before laying down his pen for the last time, he struck the keynote to the conduct of many brave men who, like himself, reluctantly accepted a call to "the field of honor." These are his closing words:

"To those who with me, abhorring the practice of duelling, may think that I ought under no account to have added to the number of bad examples, I answer, that my relative situation as well in public as in private enforcing all the considerations which constitute what men of the world denominate honor imposed on me a peculiar necessity not to decline the call. The ability to be in future useful, whether in arresting mischief or effecting good in this crisis of our public affairs which seemed likely to happen, would probably be inseparable from a conformity with public prejudice in this particular."

At seven o'clock in the morning of July 11, 1804, at Weehawken, New Jersey, the fatal meeting took place. After the usual formal salutation, the parties were placed in position by their seconds, ten paces apart, the pistols placed in their hands, and the word being given both fired. General Hamilton instantly fell. The statement subsequently given out by the seconds is as follows:

"Colonel Burr then advanced toward General Hamilton with a manner and gesture that appeared to be expressive of regret, but without speaking turned about and withdrew, being urged from the field by his friends. No further communication took place between the principals, and the barge that carried Colonel Burr immediately returned to the city. We conceive it proper to add that the conduct of the parties in this interview was perfectly proper as suited the occasion."

The surgeon in attendance states that after Hamilton was borne to the barge he observed, "Pendleton knows that I did not intend to fire at him." As they approached the shore he said, "Let Mrs. Hamilton be immediately sent for; let the event be gradually broken to her, but give her hopes." His physician adds:

"During the night his mind retained its usual strength and composure. The great source of his anxiety seemed to be in his sympathy with his half-distracted wife and children. 'My beloved wife and children' was his often used expression, but his fortitude triumphed over his situation, dreadful as it was. Once, indeed, at the sight of his children, seven in number, brought to his bedside together, his utterance forsook him. To his wife he said in a firm voice but with a pathetic and impressive manner, 'Remember, my Eliza, that you are a Christian.' His words and the tone in which they were uttered, will never be effaced from my memory."

After indescribable agony, death came at two o'clock of the day succeeding the duel. Thus, at the age of forty-seven, perished Alexander Hamilton, a great man in any country or time. Cities and counties bear his name in almost every American State. The story of his wondrous life and tragic death will never lose its pathetic interest. His unswerving devotion to the country of his adoption, his untiring efforts in the establishment of the national Government, and his friendship for Washington, which knew no abatement, have given Hamilton honored and enduring place in American history.

As to Burr, the proverb found instant verification that "in duels the victor is always the victim." Had he, instead of Hamilton, fallen on that ill-fated July morning, how changed their possible places in history. A halo has gathered about the name of Hamilton. Monuments have been erected to his memory, his statue has been given high place in the Capitol. The hour of his fall was that of his exaltation.

The self-same hour witnessed the ruin of his antagonist. From the fatal field, unharmed in body, he turned away, henceforth to the followed by the execrations of his countrymen. Past services were forgotten, brilliant talents availed nothing. His desperate attempt to found a rival government by the partial dismemberment of the one he had helped to establish was thwarted, and after years of poverty and misfortune abroad, he returned to die in neglect and obscurity in his own country. As was truly said: "He was the last of his race; there was no kindred hand to smooth his couch, or wipe the death-damp from his brow. No banners drooped over his bier; no melancholy music floated upon the reluctant air."

The Hon. Hamilton Spencer, one of the ablest of lawyers, gave me an interesting account of an interview he had with Colonel Burr in Albany not long before his death. Notwithstanding his advanced age, broken health, and ruined fortunes, he deeply impressed Mr. Spencer as a gentleman of most courteous manners, dignified bearing, and commanding presence such as he had rarely seen.

The one object of his love was his daughter, the beautiful Theodosia. Her devotion to her father increased with his accumulating misfortunes. The ship in which she sailed from her home in Charleston, South Carolina, to meet him in New York, never reached its destination. In all history, there are few pictures more pathetic than that of the gray-haired, friendless man, with faded cloak drawn closely about him, day after day wandering alone by the seaside, anxiously awaiting the coming of the one being who loved him, the idolized daughter whose requiem was even then being chanted by the waves.

One of the men I occasionally met in Washington was Joseph C. McKibben, a former representative in Congress from the Pacific coast. He was thoroughly familiar with the history of California from its cession to the United States at the close of the Mexican War. He had been an active participant in many of the stirring events occurring soon after the admission of the State into the Union.

"Men, except in bad novels, are not all good, or all evil."

Colonel McKibben was the second of David C. Broderick in his duel with Judge Terry. At the time of the duel, Broderick was a Senator of the United States, and Terry the Chief Justice of California. The challenge given by Terry was promptly accepted. As will be remembered, in the encounter which immediately followed, Terry escaped unhurt and Broderick was killed.

I recall vividly the description given me of the meeting between these men in that early Spring morning in 1859. Both possessed unquestioned courage. Their demeanor upon the field, as in deadly attitude they confronted each other a few paces apart, was that of absolute fearlessness. "Each had set his life upon a cast, and was ready to stand the hazard of the die."

Rarely have truer words been uttered than those of the gifted Baker over the dead body of Broderick:

"The code of honor is a delusion and a snare; it palters with the hope of true courage, and binds it at the feet of crafty and cruel skill. It surrounds its victim with the pomp and grace of the procession, but leaves him bleeding on the altar. It substitutes cold and deliberate preparedness for courage and manly impulse, and arms the one to disarm the other. It makes the mere trick of the weapon superior to the noblest cause and the truest courage. Its pretence of equality is a lie; it is equal in all the form, it is unjust in all the substance. The habitude of arms, the early training, the frontier life, the border war, the sectional custom, the life of leisure, all these are advantages which no negotiations can neutralize, and which no courage can overcome. Code of honor! It is a prostitution of the name, is an evasion of the substance, and is a shield blazoned with the name of chivalry to cover the malignity of murder."

The tragic ending of the eventful career of Judge Terry, which occurred within the last decade, will be readily recalled. Immediately following his assault upon Justice Field at the railway station in Lathrop, California, he was slain by a deputy United States marshal. The wife of Terry was at his side, and the scene that followed beggars description.

The name of Terry at once recalls the "Vigilance Committee" of early San Francisco days. The committee was composed largely of leading men of the "law-and-order" element of the city. Robberies and murders were of nightly occurrence, and gamblers and criminals in many instances were the incumbents of the public offices. The organization mentioned became an imperative necessity for the protection of life and property. The work of the committee constitutes one of the bloodiest chapters of early Californian history.

Nearly a third of a century ago, Colonel Thornton, a prominent lawyer of San Francisco, related to me an incident which he had witnessed during the time the famous Vigilance Committee was in complete control. A young lawyer, recently located in San Francisco, was arrested for stabbing a well-known citizen who was at the time one of the most active members of the Vigilance Committee. The name of the lawyer was David S. Terry, at a later day Chief Justice of the State. The dread tribunal was presided over by one of the most courageous and best known citizens of the Pacific coast. At a later day, his name was presented by his State to the National Convention of his party for nomination for the Vice-Presidency.

When brought before the Vigilance Committee, the demeanor of Terry was that of absolute fearlessness. Standing erect and perfectly self-possessed, he listened to the ominous words of the president: "Mr. Terry, you are charged with attempted murder; what have you to say?" Advancing a step nearer the committee "organized to convict," and in a tone that at once challenged the respect of all, Terry replied, "If your Honor please, I recognize the jurisdiction of this court, and am ready for trial." He then clearly established the fact that his assault was in self-defence, and after a masterly speech, delivered with as much self-possession as if a life other than his own trembled in the balance, was duly acquitted.

Another California with whom I was personally acquainted, was William M. Gwin. He had long passed the allotted three score and ten when I first met him at the home of the late Senator Sharon. Few men have known so eventful a career. He had been the private secretary of Andrew Jackson. He knew well the public men of that day, and related many interesting incidents of the stormy period of the latter years of Jackson's Presidency. In his early manhood Gwin was a member of Congress from Alabama. At the close of the Mexican War he removed to California, and upon the admission of that State he and John C. Fremont were chosen its first Senators in Congress.

During a ride with him, he pointed out to me the spot where he had fought a duel in early California days. He was then a Senator, and his antagonist the Hon. J. W. McCorkle, a member of Congress. A card signed by their respective seconds appeared the day following, to the effect that after the exchange of three ineffectual shots between the Hon. William M. Gwin and the Hon. J. W. McCorkle, the friends of the respective parties, having discovered that *their principals were fighting under a misapprehension of facts,* mutually explained to their respective principals how the misapprehension had arisen. As a result, Senator Gwin promptly denied the cause of provocation and Mr. McCorkle withdrew his offensive language uttered at the race-course, and expressed regret at having used it.

To a layman in these "piping times of peace" it would appear the more reasonable course to have avoided "a misapprehension of facts" before even three ineffectual shots.

At the beginning of the great civil conflict, the fortunes of Senator Gwin were cast with the South, and at its close he became a citizen of Mexico. Maximilian was then Emperor, and one of his last official acts was the creation of a Mexican Duke out of the sometime American Senator. The glittering empire set up by Napoleon the Third and upheld for a time by French bayonets, was even then, however, tottering to its fall.

When receiving the Ducal coronet from the Imperial hand the self-expatriated American statesman might well have inquired,

"But shall we wear these glories for a day,
Or shall they last, and we rejoice in them?"

A few months later, at the behest of our Government, the French arms were withdrawn, the bubble of Mexican Empire vanished, and the ill-fated

Maximilian had bravely met his tragic end. Thenceforth, a resident but no longer a citizen of the land that had given him birth, William M. Gwin, to the end of his life, bore the high sounding but empty title of "Duke of Sonora."

Frequent as have been the instances in our own country where death has resulted from duelling, it is believed that in but one has the survivor incurred the extreme penalty of the law. That one case occurred in 1820 in Illinois. What was intended merely as a "mock duel" by their respective friends, was fought with rifles by William Bennett and Alphonso Stewart in Belleville. It was privately agreed by the seconds of each that the rifles should be loaded with blank cartridges. This arrangement was faithfully carried out so far as the seconds were concerned; but Bennett, the challenging party, managed to get a bullet into his own gun. The result was the immediate death of Stewart, and the flight of his antagonist. Upon his return to Belleville a year or two later, Bennett was immediately arrested, placed upon trial, convicted, and executed.

In more than one instance, at a later day, while well-known Illinoisans have been parties to actual or prospective duels, no instance has occurred of a hostile meeting of that character within the limits of the State. A late auditor of public account, but recently deceased, killed his antagonist in a duel with rifles nearly half a century ago in California.

William I. Ferguson, one of the most brilliant orators Illinois has known, in early professional life the associate of men who have since achieved national distinction, fell in a duel while a member of the State Senate in California.

During the sitting of the Illinois Constitutional Convention of 1847, two of its prominent members, Campbell and Pratt, delegates from the northern tier of counties, became involved in a bitter personal controversy which resulted in a challenge by Pratt to mortal combat. The challenge was accepted and the principals with their seconds repaired to the famous "Bloody Island" in the Mississippi, when by the interposition of friends a peaceable settlement was effected. The sequel to this happily averted duel was the incorporation in the Constitution, then in process of formulation, of a provision prohibiting duelling in the State, and attaching severe penalties to sending or accepting a challenge.

The earliest hostile meeting of Illinoisans was upon the island last mentioned before State organization had been effected. The principals were young men of well-known courage and ability—one of whom, Shadrack Bond, upon the admission of Illinois was elected its Governor. His adversary, John Rice Jones, was the first lawyer to locate in the Illinois country, and was the brother of the second of the unfortunate Cilley in the tragic encounter already related. The late Governor Bissell of Illinois was once challenged by Jefferson Davis. Both were at the time members of Congress, and the *casus belli* was language reflecting upon the conduct of some of the participants in the then recently fought battle of Buena Vista. After the acceptance of the challenge, mutual friends of Davis and Bissell effected a reconciliation, just before the hour set for the hostile meeting.

So far as Illinois combatants are concerned, the historic island mentioned above has little claim to its bloody designation, inasmuch as the "affairs" mentioned, and one much more famous, yet to be noted, were all honorably adjusted without physical harm to any of the participants.

The "affair of honor," the mention of which will close this chapter, owes its chief importance to the prominence attained at a later day by its principals. The challenger, James Shields, was at that time, 1842, a State officer of Illinois, and later a general in two wars and a Senator from three States. The name of his adversary has since "been given to the ages." Mr. Lincoln was, at the time he accepted Mr. Shields's challenge, a young lawyer, unmarried, residing at the State capital. He was the recognized leader of the Whig party, and an active participant in the fierce political conflicts of the day. Some criticism in which he had indulged, touching the administration of the office of which Shields was the incumbent, was the immediate cause of the challenge.

That Mr. Lincoln was upon principle opposed to duelling would be readily inferred from his characteristic kindness. That "we are time's subjects," however, and that the public opinion of sixty-odd years ago is not that of to-day will readily appear from the published statement of his friend Dr. Merryman:

"I told Mr. Lincoln what was brewing, and asked him what course he proposed to himself. He said that he was wholly opposed to duelling and would do anything to avoid it that might not degrade him in the estimation of himself and friends; but if such a degradation, or a fight, were the only alternatives, he would fight."

It is stated by one of the biographers of Mr. Lincoln that he was ever after averse to any allusion to the Shields affair. From the terms of his acceptance, it is evident that he intended neither to injure his adversary seriously nor to receive injury at his hands. In his lengthy letter of instruction to his second, he closed by saying:

"If nothing like this is done, the preliminaries of the fight are to be, first, weapons: cavalry broadswords of the largest size, precisely equal in all respects. Second, position: a plank ten feet long and from nine to twelve inches broad, to be firmly fixed on edge on the ground as the line between us which neither is to pass his foot over upon forfeit of his life. Next, a line drawn on the ground on either side of said plank and parallel with it, each at the distance of the whole length of the sword, and three feet additional from the plank; the passing of his own line by either party during the fight shall be deemed a surrender of the contest. Third, time: on Thursday evening at five o'clock within three miles of Alton on the opposite side of the river, the particular spot to be agreed on by you. Any preliminary details coming within the above rules you are at liberty to make at your discretion, but you are in no case to swerve from these rules or to pass beyond their limits."

The keen sense of the humorous, with which Mr. Lincoln was so abundantly gifted, seems not to have wholly deserted him even in the serious moments when penning an acceptance to mortal combat. The terms of meeting indicated—which he as the challenged party had the right to dictate—lend color to the opinion that he regarded the affair in the light of a mere farce. His superior height and length of arm remembered, and the position of the less favored Shields, with broadsword in hand, at the opposite side of the board, and not permitted "upon forfeit of his life" to advance an inch —the picture is indeed a ludicrous one.

Out of the lengthy statements of the respective seconds—the publication of which came near involving themselves in personal altercation—it appears that all parties actually reached the appointed rendezvous on time.

But it was not written in the book of fate that this duel was to take place. Something of mightier moment was awaiting one of the actors in this drama. Two level-headed men, R. W. English and John J. Hardin, the friends respectively of Shields and Lincoln, crossing the Mississippi in a canoe close in the wake of the belligerents, reached the field just before the appointed hour. These gentlemen, acting in concert with the seconds, Whiteside and Merryman, soon effected a reconciliation deemed honorable to all, and the Shields-Lincoln duel passed to the domain of history. That the reconciliation thus brought about was sincere was evidenced by the fact that one of the earliest acts of President Lincoln was the appointment of General Shields to an important military command.

How strangely "the whirligig of time brings in his revenges!" A few paces apart in the old Hall at the Capitol at Washington, stand two statues, the contribution of Illinois for enduring place in the "Temple of the Immortals." One is the statue of Lincoln, the other that of Shields.

XI A PRINCELY GIFT

DESCENT OF JAMES SMITHSON, FOUNDER OF THE SMITHSONIAN INSTITUTION— HIS EDUCATION AND HIS WRITINGS—HIS WILL—THE UNITED STATES HIS RESIDUARY LEGATEE—SUCCESSFUL PROSECUTION OF THE CLAIM OF THE UNITED STATES TO THE LEGACY— PLANS SUGGESTED FOR THE DISPOSAL OF THE FUND — PROF. JOSEPH HENRY APPOINTED SECRETARY— BENEFICENT WORK OF THE INSTITUTION.

Although a third of a century has passed since I met Professor Joseph Henry, I distinctly recall his kindly greeting and the courteous manner in which he gave me the information I requested for the use of one of the Committees of the House.

The frosts of many winters were then on his brow, and he was near the close of an honorable career, one of measureless benefit to mankind. He was the first secretary of the Smithsonian Institution, and the originator of the plan by which was carried into practical effect the splendid bequest for "the increase and diffusion of knowledge among men."

As Vice-President of the United States, a regent *ex-officio* of the Smithsonian Institution, I had rare opportunity to learn much of its history and something of its marvellous accomplishment. As is well known, it bears the name of James Smithson. He was an Englishman, related to the historic family of Percy, and a lineal descendent of Henry the Seventh, his maternal ancestor being the ill-fated Lady Jane Grey, cousin to Queen Elizabeth.

Mr. Langley, the late secretary of the institution, said:

"Smithson always seems to have regarded the circumstances of his birth as doing him a peculiar injustice, and it was apparently this sense that he had been deprived of honors properly his which made him look for other sources of fame than those which birth had denied him, and constituted the motive of the most important action of his life, the creation of the Smithsonian Institution."

The deep resentment of Smithson against the great families who had virtually disowned him, finds vent in a letter yet extant, of which the following is a part: "The best blood of England flows in my veins; on my father's side I am a Northumberland, on my mother's I am related to kings; but this avails me not. My name shall live in the memory of man when the titles of the Northumberlands and the Percys are extinct and forgotten."

How truly his indignant forecast was prophetic is now a matter of history. Few men know much about the once proud families of Northumberland or Percy, but the name of the youth they scornfully disowned lives in the institution he founded, the greatest instrumentality yet devised for "the increase and diffusion of knowledge among men."

Smithson was born in 1765, and received the degree of Master of Arts from Pembroke College at the age of twenty-one. A year later he was admitted a Fellow of the Royal Society, upon the recommendation of his instructors, as being "a gentleman well versed in the various branches of Natural Philosophy, and particularly in Chemistry and Mineralogy." As a student, he was devoted to the study of the sciences, especially chemistry, and his entire life, in fact, was given to scientific research. Twenty-seven papers from his pen were published in "The Philosophical Transactions of the Royal Society" and in "Thompson's Annals of Philosophy," near the close of the eighteenth and the beginning of the nineteenth century, and "all give evidence that he was an assiduous and faithful experimenter."

In this connection, the statement of Professor Clarke, Chief Chemist of the United States Geographical Survey, is in point:

"The most notable feature of Smithson's writings from the standpoint of the analytical chemist, is the success obtained with the most primitive and unsatisfactory appliances. In Smithson's day, chemical apparatus was undeveloped, and instruments were improvised from such materials as lay readiest to hand. With such instruments, and with crude reagents, Smithson obtained analytical results of the most creditable character, and enlarged our knowledge of many mineral species. In his time, the native carbonate and the silicate of zinc were confounded as one species under the name calamine; but his researches distinguished between the two minerals, which are now known as Smithsonite and Calamine, respectively.

"To theory Smithson contributed little, if anything; but from a theoretical point of view, the tone of his writings is singularly modern. His work was mostly done before Dalton had announced the atomic theory; and yet Smithson saw clearly that a law of definite proportions must exist, although he did not attempt to account for it. His ability as a reasoner is best shown in his paper on the Kirkdale Bone Cave, which Penn had sought to interpret by reference to the Noachian Deluge. A clearer and more complete demolition of Penn's views could hardly be written to-day. Smithson was gentle with his adversary, but none the less thorough, for all his moderation. He is not to be classed among the leaders of scientific thought; but his ability and the usefulness of his contributions to knowledge, cannot be doubted."

The life of Smithson was uncheered by domestic affection; he was of singularly retiring disposition, had no intimacies, spent the closing years of his life in Paris, and was long the uncomplaining victim of a painful malady. Professor Langley said of him:

"One gathers from his letters, from the uniform consideration with which he speaks of others, from kind traits which he showed, and from the general tenor of what is not here particularly cited, the remembrance of an innately gentle nature, but also of a man who is gradually renouncing not without bitterness the youthful hope of fame, and as health and hope diminished together, is finally living for the day, rather than for any future."

He died in Genoa, Italy, June 27, 1829, and was buried in the little English cemetery on the heights of San Benigno. The Institution he founded has placed a tablet over his tomb and surrounded it with evidences of continued and thoughtful care.

His will—possibly of deeper concern to mankind than any yet written — bears date October 23, 1826. In its opening clause he designates himself: "Son of Hugh, First Duke of Northumberland, and Elizabeth, heiress of the Hungerfords of Studley, and niece to Charles the proud Duke of Somerset." Herein clearly appears his undying resentment toward those who had denied him the position in life to which he considered himself justly entitled.

The only persons designated in his will as legatees are a faithful servant, for whom abundant provision was made, and Henry James Hungerford, nephew of the testator. To the latter was devised the entire estate except the legacy to the servant mentioned. The clause of the will which has given the name of Smithson to the ages seems to have been almost casually inserted; it appears between the provision for his servant and the one for an investment of the funds.

The clause in his will which was to cause his name "to live in the memory of man when the titles of the Northumberlands and the Percys are extinct and forgotten," was,—

"In the case of the death of my said nephew without leaving a child or children, or the death of the child or children he may have had under the age of twenty-one years, or intestate, I then bequeath the whole of my property subject to the annuity of one hundred pounds to John Fitall (for the security and payment of which I have made provision) to the United States of America, to found at Washington, under the name of the Smithsonian Institution, an establishment for the increase and diffusion of knowledge among men."

Why he selected the United States as his residuary legatee has long been, and will continue to be, the subject of curious inquiry. He had never been in America, had no correspondent here, and nowhere in his writings has there been found an allusion to our country. So far as we know, he could have had no possible prejudice in favor of our system of representative government.

It is a singular fact, however, in this connection, that the pivotal clause in his will bears striking resemblance to the admonition, "Promote as an object of primary importance institutions for the general diffusion of knowledge," contained in the farewell address of President Washington.

The contingency provided for happened; the death of the nephew Hungerford unmarried and without heirs occurred six years after that of the testator. The first announcement to the people of the United States of the facts stated was contained in a special message from President Jackson to Congress, December 17, 1835. Accompanying the message was a letter with a detailed statement, and copy of the will, from our Legation in London. In closing his brief message of transmission, President Jackson says: "The Executive having no authority to take any steps for accepting the trust and obtaining the funds, the papers are communicated with a view to such measures as Congress may deem necessary."

On the first day of July, 1836, a bill authorizing the President to assert and prosecute the claim of the United States to the Smithson legacy became a law. This, however, was after much opposition in Congress; a member of the House indignantly declaring that our Government should receive nothing by way of gift from England, and proposing that the bequest should be denied. The prophetic words of the venerable John Quincy Adams—then a member of the House after his retirement from the Presidency—in advocating the passage of the bill are worthy of remembrance:

"Of all the foundations of establishments for pious or charitable uses which ever signalized the spirit of the age, or the comprehensive beneficence of the founders, none can be named more deserving the approbation of mankind than this. Should it be faithfully carried into effect with an earnestness and sagacity of application and a steady perseverance of purpose proportioned to the means furnished by the will of the founder, and to the greatness and simplicity of his design as by himself declared,— 'the increase and diffusion of knowledge among men,'—it is no extravagance of anticipation to declare that his name will hereafter be enrolled among the benefactors of mankind."

In the execution of this law, the President immediately upon its enactment appointed Richard Rush, a distinguished lawyer of Philadelphia, to proceed to London, and take the necessary steps to obtain the legacy. To the accomplishment of this purpose a suit was soon thereafter instituted by Mr. Rush. The hopelessness of its early termination in an English Chancery Court of that day will at once occur to the readers of Dickens's famous "Jarndyce against Jarndyce." It was truly said, that a chancery suit was a thing which might begin with a man's life, and its termination be his epitaph.

A wiser selection than Mr. Rush could not have been made. He entered upon the work to which he had been appointed, with great determination. In a letter to our Secretary of State just after he had instituted suit, he says:

"A suit of higher interest and dignity, has rarely perhaps been before the tribunals of a nation. If the trust created by the testator's will be successfully carried into effect by the enlightened legislation of Congress, benefits may flow to the United States, and to the human family, not easy to be estimated, because operating silently and gradually throughout time, yet not operating the less effectually. Not to speak of the inappreciable value of letters to individual and social man, the monuments which they raise to a nation's glory often last when others perish, and seem especially appropriate to the glory of a Republic whose foundations are laid in the assumed intelligence of its citizens, and can only be strengthened and perpetuated as that improve."

The successful termination of the suit came, however, sooner than could have been expected; and in May, 1838, the amount of the legacy, exceeding the substantial sum of five hundred thousand dollars, was received and invested as required by law.

The facts stated were communicated by special message from President Van Buren to Congress, in December, 1838. Attention was then called to the fact that he had applied to persons versed in science, for their views as to the mode of disposing of the fund which would be calculated best to meet the intent of the testator, and prove most beneficial to mankind.

During the eight years intervening between this message and the passage of the bill for the incorporation of the Smithsonian Institution, much discussion was had in and out of Congress, as to the best method of making effective the intention of the testator.

In the light of events, some of the many plans suggested are even now of curious interest. The establishment of a magnificent national library at the Capital; the founding of a great university; of a normal school; a post graduate school; and astronomical observatory "equal to any in the world," are a few of the plans from time to time proposed and earnestly advocated.

The act of incorporation in 1846, the appointment of a Board of Regents, and the selection of a Secretary, mark the beginning of the Smithsonian Institution. In the selection of a Secretary, the chief officer of the institution, the regents builded better than they knew. The choice fell upon Professor Joseph Henry of Princeton, then peerless among men of science in America. The appointment was accepted, and the essential features of the plan of organization he proposed were adopted in December, 1847. This plan recognized as

"Fundamental that the terms 'increase' and 'diffusion' should receive literal interpretation in accordance with the evident intention of the testator; that such terms being logically distinct, the two purposes mentioned in the bequest were to be kept in view in the organization of the institution; that the increase of knowledge should be effected by the encouragement of original researches of the highest character; and its diffusion by the publication of the results of original research, by means of the publication of a series of volumes of original memoirs; that the object of the institution should not be restricted in favor of any particular kind of knowledge; if to any, only to the higher and more abstract, to the discovery of new principles rather than that of isolated facts; that the institution should in no sense be national; that the bequest was intended for the benefit of mankind in general, and not for any single nation.

"The accumulation and care of collections of objects of nature and art, the development of a library, the providing of courses of lectures, and the organization of a system of meteorological observation, were to be only incidental to the fundamental design of increasing and diffusing knowledge among men."

In its inception, and in its widening influence during the passing years, those entrusted with the actual management of this institution have conscientiously kept in view the clearly expressed intention of its founder. Following the distinctive but parallel paths, "increase" and "diffusion," the Smithsonian Institution, yet in its infancy, has added largely to the sum of useful knowledge. Its accredited representatives are out upon every pathway of intelligent research and discovery. Under the wise operation of this marvellous instrumentality, long-concealed secrets of nature have been discovered, and it can hardly be doubted that all that is given to man to know will yet be revealed, and it will be permitted him

"To read what is still unread,
In the manuscripts of God."

By indefatigable investigation, and by world-wide publication of the results, mankind has indeed become, as was intended, the beneficiary of the princely bequest.

More fitting words could not be selected with which to close this sketch than those of the gifted and lamented Langley, whose best years were given to scientific research, and whose name is inseparably associated with the Smithsonian Institution:

"What has been done in these two paths the reader may partly gather from this volume—in the former from the various articles by contemporary men of science, describing its activities in research and original contributions to the increase of human knowledge; in the latter, in numerous way—among others from the description of the work of one of its bureaux, that of the International Exchanges, where it may be more immediately seen how universal is the scope of the action of the Institution, which, in accordance with its motto 'PER ORBEM,' is not limited to the country of its adoption, but belongs to the world, there being outside of the United States more than twelve thousand correspondents scattered through every portion of the globe; indeed there is hardly a language, or a people, where the results of Smithson's benefaction are not known, and associated with his name.

"If we were permitted to think of him as conscious of what has been, is being, and is still to be done, in pursuance of his wish, we might believe that he would feel that his hope at a time when life must have seemed so hopeless, was finding full fruition; for events are justifying what may have seemed, at the time, but a rhetorical expression, in the language of a former President of the United States, who has said: 'Renowned as is the name of Percy in the historical annals of England, let the trust of James Smithson to the United States of America be faithfully executed, let the result accomplish his object, the increase and diffusion of knowledge among men, and a wreath more unfading shall entwine itself in the lapse of future ages around the name of Smithson than the united hands of history and poetry have braided around the name of Percy through the long ages past.'"

XII THE OLD RANGER

JOHN REYNOLDS, GOVERNOR OF ILLINOIS, A BORN POLITICIAN—HIS KNOWLEDGE OF THE PEOPLE—HIS AFFECTATION OF HUMILITY—ADMITTED TO THE BAR — HE CONDEMNS A MURDERER TO DEATH—HIS CURIOUS ADDRESS TO ANOTHER MURDERER—BECOMES A MEMBER OF THE LEGISLATURE—ELECTED GOVERNOR —HIS GENEROSITY TO HIS POLITICAL ENEMIES— BECOMES A MEMBER OF CONGRESS—HIS ADMIRATION FOR HIS ASSOCIATES—ELECTED A MEMBER OF THE GENERAL ASSEMBLY OF THE STATE—RETIRES TO PRIVATE LIFE.

This world of ours will be much older before the like of John Reynolds, the fourth Governor of Illinois, again appears upon its stage. The title which he generously gave himself in early manhood, upon his return after a brief experience as a trooper in pursuit of a marauding band of Winnebagoes, stood him well in hand in all his future contests for office. "The Old Ranger" was a *sobriquet* to conjure with, and turned the scales in his favor in many a doubtful contest.

The subject of this sketch was a born politician if ever one trod this green earth. He was a perennial candidate for office, and it was said he never took a drink of water without serious meditation as to how it might possibly affect his political prospects. The late Uriah Heep might easily have gotten a few points in "'umbleness," if he had accompanied the Old Ranger in one or two of his political campaigns.

While Illinois was yet a Territory, his father had emigrated from the mountains of Tennessee and located near the historic village of Kaskaskia. This was at the time the capital of the Territory. The village mentioned was then the most, and in fact, the only, important place in the vast area constituting the present State of Illinois. There were less than five thousand persons of all nationalities and conditions in the Territory, and they mainly in and about Kaskaskia, and southward to the Ohio. Beck's Gazetteer published in 1823—five years after the admission of the State into the Union—contains the following: "Chicago, a village of Pike County, situated on Lake Michigan at the mouth of the Chicago Creek. It contains twelve or fifteen houses, and about sixty or seventy inhabitants."

The acquaintance of John Reynolds with what was then known as "the Illinois Country" began in 1800, and his thorough knowledge of the people and their ways gave him rare opportunities for acquiring great personal popularity. Fairly well educated for the times, gifted with an abundance of shrewdness, and withal an excellent judge of human nature, he soon became a man of mark in the new country. He was at all times and under all circumstances the self-constituted "friend of the people." He affected to be one of the humblest of the sons of men; and his dress, language, and deportment were always in strict keeping with that assumption. For the pride of ancestry he had a supreme contempt. In his "My Own Times," published a few years before his death, he said: "I regard the whole subject of ancestry and descent as utterly frivolous and unworthy of a moment's serious attention."

This recalls what Judge Baldwin said of Cave Burton:

"He was not clearly satisfied that Esau made as foolish a bargain with his brother Jacob as some think. If the birth-right was *a mere matter of family pride*, and the pottage of agreeable taste, Cave was not quite sure that Esau had not gotten the advantage in his famed bargain with the Father of Israel."

Humility was Reynolds's highest card, and when out among the people he was always figuratively clothed in sackcloth and ashes. A few extracts from his book may be of interest:

"I was a singular spectacle when in 1809 I started to Tennessee to college. I looked like a trapper going to the Rocky Mountains. I wore a cream-colored hat made of the fur of the prairie wolf, which gave me a grotesque appearance. I was well acquainted with the mysteries of horse and foot races, shooting matches, and other wild sports of the backwoods, but had not studied the polish of the ball-room and was sorely beset with diffidence, awkwardness, and poverty."

Later, and when out in pursuit of the Indians, he said: "But diffidence never permitted me to approach an officer's tent, or solicit any one for office."

None the less, the office of Orderly Sergeant being thrust upon him, he managed in his humble way to get through with it passably well.

When the State Government was organized in 1818, while shrinking from even the gaze of men, and spurning from the depths of his soul the arts of politicians, he managed in some way to be designated one of the judges of the Supreme Court of the new State. His admiration for the dispensing hand appears as follows: "Wisdom and integrity, with other noble qualities, gave Governor Bond a high standing with his contemporaries. Wisdom and integrity shed a beacon light around his path through life, showing him to be one of the noblest works of God."

Four years prior to this appointment, he had been admitted to the bar, after "undergoing with much diffidence" his examination. This accomplished, he adds: "In the Winter of 1814, I established a very humble and obscure law-office in the French village of Cahokia, the county seat of St. Clair County." The bearing of the one whose meat was locusts and wild honey, and whose loins were girt about with a leathern girdle, was arrogance itself, when compared with the deportment of the later John in the wilderness at the period whereof we write.

That he was orthodox upon what pertained to medical practice will now appear: "It was the universal practice to give the patient of the bilious disease, first, tartar emetic; next day, calomel and jalap; and the third day, Peruvian bark. This was generally sufficient." The latter statement will hardly be questioned.

How his first visitation of the tender passion was mingled with a relish of philosophy is recorded for the benefit of posterity:

"During all my previous life until within a short time before I married, I had not the least intention of that state of existence, and I expressed myself often to my friends to the same effect; but on the subject of matrimony, a passion influences the parties which generally succeeds. Judgment and prudence should be mixed in equal parts with love and affection in the transaction, to secure a lasting and happy union."

With all his diffidence, however, the Old Ranger happened to turn up at the seat of Government in time "to be persuaded by my friends to be a candidate for a Judgeship. It broke in on me like a clap of thunder." The mite of philosophy with which he excused himself for giving way to the urgent demand of his friends is as follows: "Human nature is easier to persuade to mount upwards than to remain on the common level."

His mind, as will appear, was essentially of the strictly practical cast. He no doubt believed with Macaulay that "one acre in Middlesex is worth a principality in Utopia."

That the Republican simplicity of the new Judge followed him from his "very humble and obscure law-office" to the Bench, will now appear:

"The very first court I held was in Washington County, and it was to me a strange and novel business. I was amongst old comrades with whom I had been raised, ranged in the war with them, and lived with them in great intimacy and equality, so that it was difficult to assume a different relationship than I had previously occupied with them. Moreover I detested a mock dignity. Both the sheriff and clerk were rangers in the same company with myself, and it seemed we were still ranging on equal terms in pursuit of the Indians. The sheriff was of the same opinion and very familiar. He opened court sitting astride on a bench in the Court-house, and without rising, proclaimed: 'The court is now open, and our John is on the bench.'"

It may here be mentioned that the first case of importance that came before Judge Reynolds, was the trial of one William Bennett for murder. He had killed his antagonist in a duel in St. Clair County, for which he suffered the death penalty. This is the only duel ever fought in Illinois. No doubt the prompt execution of Bennett did much to discourage duelling in the State.

In reply to the charge that he had acted with unbecoming levity upon the trial of Bennett, the Judge said, "No human being of my humble capacity could have acted with more painful feelings and sympathy than did I on this occasion." Having thus vindicated himself from the serious charge mentioned, he adds:

"I am opposed to capital punishment in any case where the convict can be kept in solitary confinement without pardoning his life; it was extremely painful and awful to me to be the instrument in the hands of the law to pronounce sentence of death upon my fellow-man, extinguishing him forever from the face of the earth, and depriving him of life, which I think belongs to God and not to man."

He consoles himself, however, as he closes his narrative of this sad affair, that "it never did assume the character of a regular and honorable duel." It is very satisfactory also, even at this distant date, to be assured by the Judge that "the prisoner embraced religion, was baptized, and died happy, before spectators to the number of two thousand or more."

Governor Ford, in his history of Illinois, relates the following incident as characteristic of Judge Reynolds. The latter was holding court in Washington County when one Green was found guilty upon an indictment for murder. The court was near the hour of adjournment for the term, when the prosecuting attorney suggested to the court that the prisoner Green be brought in in order that sentence be passed upon him. "Certainly, certainly," said the Judge, and the prisoner was at once brought in from the jail near by.

"Mr. Green," said the Judge in a familiar tone, "the jury in your case have found you guilty. I want you to understand, Mr. Green, and all your friends down on Indian Creek to know, that it is not I who condemns you, but the jury and the law. The law allows you time for preparation, Mr. Green; and so the court wants to know what time it would suit you to be hung?" The prisoner replying that he was ready to suffer at whatever time the court might appoint, the Judge said;

"Mr. Green, you must know that it is a very serious matter to be hung. It can't happen to a man more than once in his life, and you had better take all the time you can get; the court will give you till this day four weeks. Mr. Clerk, look at the almanac and see if this day four weeks comes on Sunday." The Clerk after examination reported that that day four weeks came on Friday. The Judge then said: "Mr. Green, the court gives you till this day four weeks, and then you are to be hanged."

Whereupon the prosecuting officer, the Hon. James Turney, an able and dignified lawyer, said:

"May it please the court, on solemn occasion like the present, when the life of a human being is to be sentenced away for crime by an earthly tribunal, it is usual and proper for courts to pronounce a formal sentence, in which the leading features of the crime shall be brought to the recollection of the prisoner, a sense of his guilt impressed upon his conscience, and in which the prisoner should be duly exhorted to repentance and warned against the judgment in a world to come."

To which the Judge replied: "Oh, Mr. Turney, Mr. Green understands the whole matter as well as if I had preached to him a month. He knows he has got to be hung this day four weeks. You understand it that way, Mr. Green, don't you?"

"Yes," said the prisoner, upon which the Judge again expressing the hope that he and all his friends down on Indian Creek would understand that it was the act of the jury and of the law, *and not of the Judge,* ordered the prisoner to be remanded to jail, and the court adjourned for the term.

For some reason, by no means satisfactorily explained, Judge Reynolds retired from the bench at the end of his four years' term. In "Breese," the first volume of Illinois reports, is an opinion by Judge Reynolds which has been the subject of amusing comment by three generations of lawyers. After giving sundry reasons why there was error in the judgment below, the learned Judge concludes: "Therefore, the judgment *ought to be* reversed; but inasmuch as the court is equally divided in opinion, it is therefore *affirmed.*"

He then resumed the practice of the law, and as he says, "was familiar with the people, got acquainted with everybody, and became somewhat popular. I had no settled object in view other than to make a living, and to continue on my humble, peaceable, and agreeable manner." In view of the aversion already shown to office-holding, the following disclaimer upon the part of the Judge seems wholly superfluous: "I had no political ambition or aspirations for office whatever."

It is gratifying to know that at this time his domestic affairs were in a satisfactory condition: "Plain and unpretending; never kept any liquor in the house—treated my friends to every civility except liquor; used an economy bordering on parsimony."

Under the favorable conditions mentioned, the Judge was enabled to overcome his aversion to holding office, and became a humble member of the State Legislature immediately upon his retirement from the bench. That his "modest aspirations" were on a higher plane than that of ordinary legislators will clearly appear from the following: "I entered this Legislature without any ulterior views, and with an eye single to advance the best interests of the State, and particularly the welfare of old St. Clair County. My only ambition was to acquit myself properly, and to advance the best interests of the country."

Two years later, the aversion of the Old Ranger for office was again overcome, as will appear from the following: "I entered this Legislature, as I had the last, without any pledge or restraints whatever; I then was, and am yet, only an humble member of the Democratic party."

His friends were again on the war-path and the shadow of the chief executive office of the State was now beginning to fall across his pathway. He says:

"It would require volumes to record the transactions of these Legislatures, and of my humble labors in them; but it was my course of conduct in these two sessions of the General Assembly that induced my friends, *without any solicitation on my part*, to offer me as a candidate for Governor. I was urged not by politicians, but by reasonable and reflecting men, more to advance the interest of the State than my own."

If we did not, from his own lips, know how the Judge loathed "the arts of politicians," we might almost be tempted to conclude from the following that he was one of them:

"I traversed every section of the State, and knew well the people. My friends had the utmost confidence in my knowledge of the people, and when I suggested any policy to be observed, this suggestion was consequently carried out as I requested—thus placing all under one leader."

This, it will be remembered, was in 1830, and neither Reynolds nor Kinney, his competitor, had received a party nomination. Both were of the same party, Kinney being a strong Jackson man of the ultra type, and the Judge only a "plain, humble, reflecting Jackson man."

At one time during the campaign it seemed as if there were real danger of this candidate of the "reflecting men of the State" actually falling into the ways and wiles of politicians. "I often addressed the people in churches, in courthouses, and in the open air, myself occupying literally the stump of a large tree; *at times also in a grocery."*

The fiery and abusive hand-bills against his competitor he did not attempt to restrain his friends from circulating, "as they had a right to exercise their own judgment"; but he declares he did not circulate one himself. He moreover felicitates himself upon the fact that his conciliatory course gained him votes.

This noted contest lasted eighteen months, as Reynolds says, and, the State being sparsely populated, he enjoyed the personal acquaintance of almost every voter. The fact, as he further states, that his opponent was a clergyman, was a great drawback to him, and almost all the Christian sects, except his own—the anti-missionary Baptists— opposed him. With a candor that does him credit, the Judge admits "the support of the religious people was not so much *for me*, but *against him."*

No national issues were discussed, but one point urged by Kinney against the proposed Michigan canal was, "that it would flood the country with Yankees." It would be a great mistake to suppose that Reynolds himself wholly escaped vituperation. On the contrary, he claims the credit of being "the best abused man in the State." He relates that one of the stories told on him was, "that I saw a scarecrow, the effigy of a man in a corn-field, just at dusk, and that I said, 'How are you, my friend? Won't you take some of my hand bills to distribute?'"

Some light is shed on the politics of the good old days of our fathers by the following: "The party rancor in the campaign raged so high that neighborhoods fell out with one another, and the angry and bitter feelings entered into the common transactions of life."

If the contest had lasted a year or two longer it is not improbably that our candidate would have fallen from his high "reflecting" state to the low level of artful politician. "It was the universal custom of the times to treat with liquor. We both did it; but he was condemned for it more than myself by the religious community, *he being a preacher of the Gospel."*

Some atonement, however, is made for the bad whiskey our model candidate dispensed by the noble sentiment with which he closes this chapter of his contest: "I was, and am yet, one of the people, and every pulsation of our hearts beats in unison."

Having been elected by a considerable majority as he modestly remarks, our Governor-elect falls into something of a philosophical train of thought, and horror of politicians and their wiles and ways again possessed him. He says:

"It may be considered vanity and frailty in me, but when I was elected Governor of the State on fair, honorable principles by the masses, without intrigue or management of party or corrupt politicians, I deemed it the decided approbation of my countrymen, and consequently a great honor."

The admonition of this sage statesman to the rising generation upon the subject of office-seeking, is worthy of profound consideration:

"But were I to live over again another life, I think I would have the moral courage to refrain from aspiring for any office within the gift of the people. By no means do I believe a person should be sordid and selfish in all his actions, yet cannot a person be more useful to the public if he possesses talents in other situations than in office?"

Some memory of the well-known ingratitude of republics evidently entered like iron into his very soul when his memoirs were written:

"Moreover, a public officer may toil and labor all his best days with the utmost fidelity and patriotism, and the masses who reap the reward of his labors frequently permit him, without any particular fault upon his part, to live and die in his old age with disrespect. Witness the punishment inflicted on Socrates, on our Saviour, and many others for no crime whatever. But this contumely and disrespect ought not to deter *a good and qualified man* from entering the public service, if he is satisfied that the good of the country requires it."

At this point in the career of this eminent public servant, deep sympathy is aroused on account of the conflict between his humility and a not very clearly-defined belief that something was due to the great office to which he had been elevated. As preliminary, however, to accomplishing what was for the best interests of the people it must not be forgotten that "my first object was to soften down the public mind to its sober senses." That no living man was better qualified for the accomplishment of so praiseworthy a purpose will now appear: "It has been my opinion of my humble self, that whatever small forte I might possess was to conciliate and soften down a turbulent and furious people."

This being all satisfactorily accomplished and the abundant reward of the peacemaker in sure keeping for this humble instrument, his efforts were now directed toward the discharge of the duties of the office to which he had so unexpectedly been called.

That this hitherto unquestioned "friend of the people" was now manifesting a slight tendency toward the frailties and vanities of the common run of men, will appear from the following:

"It was my nature not to feel or appear elevated, but I discovered that my appearance and deportment, at times, might look like affected humility or mock modesty, which I sincerely despised, and then *I would straighten up a little.*"

It may be truly said of Reynolds, as Macaulay said of Horace Walpole: "The conformation of his mind was such that whatever was little seemed to him great; and whatever was great, seemed to him little."

Having in his inaugural given expression to the noble sentiment that "proscription for opinion's sake is the worst enemy to the Republic," he at once generously dispelled whatever apprehensions his late opponents might feel as to what was to befall them, by the assurance: "Therefore, all those who honestly and honorably supported my respectable opponent in the last election for Governor shall experience from me no inconvenience on that account." Unfortunately no light is shed upon the interesting inquiry as to what "inconvenience" was experienced by those who had otherwise than "honestly and honorably" supported his respectable opponent in the late contest.

The Black Hawk War was the principal event of the administration of Governor Reynolds. A treaty of peace being concluded, the Indians were removed beyond the Mississippi River. In all this the Governor acquitted himself with credit.

That his aversion to office-holding was in some measure lessening, will appear from the following:

"Being in the office of Governor for some years, I was prevented from the practice of the law, and in the meantime had been engaged in public life until it commenced *to be a kind of second nature to me.* Moreover, I was then young, ardent, and ambitious, so that I really thought it was right for me to offer for Congress; and I did so, in the Spring of 1834."

An "artful politician" would probably have waited until the expiration of his term as Governor. Not so with this "friend of the people." He was not only elected to the next Congress, but the death of the sitting member for the District creating a vacancy, Reynolds was of course elected to that also, and was thus at one time Governor of the State and member elect both to the next and to the present Congress.

His triumph over his "able and worthy competitor" is accounted for in this wise: "I was myself tolerably well informed in the science of electioneering with the masses of the people. I was raised with the people, and was literally one of them. We always acted together, and our common instincts, feelings and interests were the same." He here modestly ventured the opinion that his "efforts on the stump, while *making no pretension to classic eloquence,* yet flowing naturally from the heart, supplied in them many defects."

A mite of self-approval, tinged with a philosophy which appears to have been always kept on tap, closes this chapter of his remarkable career. He says:

"I sincerely state that I never regarded as important the salary of the office, but I entered public office with a sincere desire to advance the best interest of the country, which was my main reward. If a person would subdue his ambition for office and remain a private citizen, he would be a more happy man."

That he must have been the most miserable of men, during the greater part of his long life, clearly appears from the following: "There is no person happy who is in public office, or a candidate for office."

A more extensive field of usefulness now opened up to the Old Ranger as he took his seat in Congress. He had many projects in mind for the benefit of the people—one, the reduction of the price of the public lands to actual settlers; another, the improvement of our Western rivers. But like many other members both before and since his day, he found that "these things were easier to talk about on the stump than to do." He candidly admits: "This body was much greater than I had supposed, and I could effect much less than I had contemplated."

He informs us that he felt like a country boy just from home the first time, as he entered the hall of the law-makers of the great Republic. The city of Washington, grand and imposing, impressed him deeply, but was as the dust in the balance to "the assemblage of great men at the seat of Government of the United States, and at the opening of Congress, when a grand and really imposing spectacle was presented."

His profound admiration for some of his associates upon the broader theatre of the public service found vent in the following eloquent words:

"When the Roman Empire reached the highest pinnacle of literary fame and political power in the reign of Augustus Caesar, the period was called the Augustan age. There was a period that existed eminently in the Jackson administration and a few years after that might be called the Augustan age of Congress. So extraordinary a constellation of great and distinguished individuals may never again appear in office at the seat of government."

If apology were needed for the new members' exalted opinion of his associates, it can readily be found in the fact that among them in the House were John Quincy Adams, John Bell, Thomas F. Marshall, Ben Hardin, James K. Polk, Millard Fillmore, and Franklin Pierce. The first named had been President of the United States, and the last three were yet to hold that great office. At the same time "the constellation of great stars" that almost appalled the Illinois member upon his introduction included, in the Senate, Crittenden, Wright, Cass, Woodbury, Preston, Buchanan, Grundy, Benton, Clay, Calhoun, and Webster.

On finally taking leave of Congress, our member congratulates himself that during seven years of service he was absent from his seat but a single day. That all his humble endeavors were in the interest of the people, of course, goes without saying. He deprecates in strong terms the extravagance of some members of Congress in allowing their expenses to exceed their salaries, and then leaving the capital in debt. That he did nothing of the kind, but practised economy in all his expenses, it is hardly necessary to state. He is not, however, entitled to a patent for the discovery that "the expenses for living at the seat of Government of the United States are heavy."

Being a widower, conditions were now favorable for a little romance to be mingled with the dull cares of state. Near the close of his last term, he says: "I became acquainted with a lady in the District of Columbia, and we, in consideration of mutual love and affection, married. The same tie binds us in matrimonial happiness to the present time." He here admits a fact that might at this later day subject him to Executive displeasure: "Posterity will have an unsettled account against us for having *added nothing to the great reservoir of the human family.*"

It may be of interest to know that while in Congress our member humbly accepted the appointment tendered him by Governor Carlin as Commissioner to negotiate the Illinois and Michigan Canal bonds. His earnest desire to have some one else appointed availed nothing, and in the interest of the great enterprise, upon the success of which the future of the State seemed to hang, he spent the summer of 1839 in Europe. While his mission abroad was fruitless as to its immediate object, it is gratifying to know that our commissioner returned duly impressed with "the immense superiority in every possible manner of our own country, and all its glorious institutions, over those of the monarchies of the old world."

It would be idle to suppose that the retirement of the Old Ranger from Congress was to terminate his career of usefulness to the people. On the contrary, he says: "In 1846, I was elected a member from St. Clair County to the General Assembly of the State. The main object of myself and friends was to obtain a charter for a macadamized road from Belleville to the Mississippi River, opposite St. Louis."

This all satisfactorily accomplished, and the Legislature adjourned, "I turned my time and attention to the calm and quiet of life. With my choice library of one thousand volumes I indulged in the study of science and literature. I soon discovered that the bustle and turmoil of political life did not produce happiness."

Sad to relate, this faithful public servant, worn with the cares of state, was not even yet permitted to lay aside his armor. The happiness of private life, for which his soul yearned as the hart panteth for the water brooks, was again postponed for the hated bustle and turmoil of politics. In 1852, against his remonstrances, he was again elected to the Legislature, and upon the organization of the House unanimously chosen Speaker.

Reluctantly indeed, we now take leave of John Reynolds—the quaintest of all the odd characters this country of ours has known. In doing so, it is indeed a comfort to know that, true as the needle to the pole, his great heart continued to beat in unison with that of the people. Ascending the Speaker's stand, and lifting the gavel, with deep emotion he said—and these are to us his last words: "I have nothing to labor for but the public good. My life has been devoted to promote the public interest of Illinois, and in my latter days it will afford me profound pleasure to advance now, as I have always done in the past, *the best interests of the people.*"

XIII THE MORMON EXODUS FROM ILLINOIS

DELEGATE CANNON AND SENATOR CANNON,
MORMONS—SKETCH OF MORMONISM BY GOVERNOR
FORD—JOSEPH SMITH'S OWN ACCOUNT OF THE ORIGIN
OF HIS CHURCH—HOW "THE BOOK OF MORMON" WAS
MADE—NAUVOO, "THE HOLY CITY"—EFFORTS OF WHIGS
AND DEMOCRATS TO WIN THE VOTES OF THE
MORMONS—VICTORY OF THE DEMOCRATS, AND
CONSEQUENT ANTI-MORMONISM OF THE WHIGS—
JOSEPH SMITH'S PRETENSIONS TO ROYALTY—THE
ORIGIN OF POLYGAMY IN THE MORMON CHURCH—
CONFLICT WITH THE STATE AUTHORITIES —
SURRENDER OF THE LEADERS—ASSASSINATION OF
SMITH—BRIGHAM YOUNG CHOSEN AS HIS SUCCESSOR—
THE EXODUS BEGINS.

Just across the aisle from my seat in the House of Representatives during the forty-sixth Congress sat George Q. Cannon, the delegate from the Territory of Utah. He held this position for many years, and possessed in the highest degree the confidence of the Mormon people. Fifteen years later, when presiding over the Senate, I administered the oath of office to his son, the Hon. Frank J. Cannon, the first chosen to represent the State of Utah in the Upper Chamber of the National Congress. Senator Cannon was then in high favor with "the powers that be" in Salt Lake City, but for some cause not well understood by the Gentile world, is now *persona non grata* with the head of the Mormon Church. The younger Cannon was not a polygamist, and no objection was urged to his being seated upon the presentation of his credentials as a Senator. His father, the delegate, was in theory a polygamist, and had "the courage of his convictions" to the extent of being the husband of five wives, and the head of as many separate households. This, before the days of "unfriendly legislation," was, in Mormon parlance, called "living your religion."

The delegate and the Senator were both men of ability, and possessed in large degree the respect of their associates. The former was in early youth a resident of Illinois, and was of the advance guard of the Mormon exodus to the valley of the Great Salt Lake soon after the assassination of the "prophet." When I first visited Salt Lake City, in 1879, George Q. Cannon, in addition to being the delegate in Congress, was one of the "Quorum of the Twelve," and was in the line of succession to the presidency of the Church. From him I learned much that was of interest concerning the history and tenets of the Mormon people. The venerable John Taylor was then the president of the Church, the immediate successor of Brigham Young. He was in early life a resident with his people in Nauvoo, Illinois, and was a prisoner in the Carthage jail with the "Prophet Joseph" at the time of his assassination, in 1844. President Taylor gave me a graphic description of that now historic tragedy, and of his own narrow escape from the fate of his idolized leader.

A brief notice of this singular people, and of what they did and suffered in Illinois, may not be wholly without interest. Mormonism was the apple of discord in the State during almost the entire official term of the late Governor Ford. More than one little army was, during that period, sent into Hancock County—"the Mormon country"—to suppress disturbances and maintain public order.

Governor Ford says:

"The Church of Jesus Christ of Latter-Day Saints, as this organization is denominated by its adherents, is to be viewed from the antagonistic Gentile and Mormon standpoints.

"Joseph Smith, the founder of the Mormon Church and its prophet, was born in Vermont, in 1805, of obscure parentage. His early education was extremely limited. When he first began to act the prophet, he was ignorant of almost everything which pertained to science; but he made up in natural cunning for many deficiencies of education. At the age of ten, he was taken by his father to Wayne County, New York, where his youth was spent in an idle, vagabond life, roaming the woods, dreaming of buried treasures, and exerting himself to find them by the twisting of a forked stick in his hands, or by looking through enchanted stones. He and his father were 'water witchers,' always ready to point out the exact points where wells could be successfully dug. While leading an idle, profligate life, Joseph Smith became acquainted with Sidney Rigdon, a man of talents and great plausibility. Rigdon was the possessor of a religious romance written some years before by a Presbyterian clergyman. The perusal of this book suggested to Smith and Rigdon the idea of starting a new religion. By them a story was accordingly devised to the effect that golden plates had been found buried near Palmyra, New York, containing a record inscribed on them in unknown characters, which, when deciphered by the power of inspiration, gave the history of the ten lost tribes of Israel in their wanderings through Asia into America, where they had settled and flourished, and where, in due time, Christ came and preached the Gospel to them, appointed his twelve Apostles, and was crucified here, nearly in the same manner he had been in Jerusalem. The record then pretended to give the history of the American Christians for a few hundred years until the wickedness of the people called down the judgment of God upon them, which resulted in their extermination. Several nations from the Isthmus of Darien to the northern extremity of the continent were engaged in continual warfare. The culmination of all this was the battle of Cumorah, fought many centuries ago near the present site of Palmyra, between the Lamanites and the Nephites—the former being the heathen and the latter the Christians of this continent. In this battle, in which hundreds of thousands were slain, the Nephites perished from the earth, except a remnant, who escaped to the southern country. Among this number was Mormon, a righteous man who was divinely directed to make a record of these important events on plates of gold, and who buried them in the earth, to be discovered in future times. 'The Book of Mormon'—none other than the religious romance above mentioned—is the pretended translation of the hieroglyphics said to have been inscribed on the golden plates.

"The account given of himself by the 'prophet' is of far different tenor from the one just given. While yet a youth he became greatly concerned in regard to his soul's salvation; and being deeply agonized in spirit, he sought divine guidance. While fervently engaged in supplication, his mind was taken away from the surrounding objects and enwrapped in a heavenly vision, and he saw two glorious personages similar in form and features and surrounded with a brilliant light, outshining the sun at noonday. He was then informed by these glorious personages that all religious denominations were in error, and were not acknowledged of God as His church and kingdom, and that he, Joseph, was expressly commanded not to go after them. At the same time, he received a promise that the fulness of the Gospel should at some future time be known to him."

Subsequently, on the evening of September 23, 1823, at the hour of six, while he was engaged in prayer, suddenly a light like that of day, only far more pure and glorious, burst into the room, as though the house were filled with fire, and a personage stood before him surrounded with a glory far greater than he had yet seen. This messenger proclaimed himself to be an angel of God, sent with the joyful tidings that the covenant which God had made with ancient Israel was about to be fulfilled; that the preparatory work for the second coming of Messiah was speedily to commence; that the time was at hand for the Gospel to be proclaimed in all its fulness and power to all nations, to the end that a peculiar people might be prepared for the millennial reign. He was further informed that he, Joseph, was to be the instrument in God's hand to bring about this glorious dispensation. The angel also informed him in regard to the American Indians, who they were, and whence they came, with a sketch of their origin, progress, civilization, righteousness, and iniquity, and why the blessing of God had been withdrawn from them as a people. He was also told where certain plates were deposited, whereon were engraved the records of the ancient prophets, who once existed on this continent. And then, to wit, on the last day mentioned, the angel of the Lord delivered into his hands the records mentioned, which were engraved on plates which had the appearance of gold. They were filled with engravings in Egyptian characters and bound together in a volume as the leaves of a book; with the records was found a curious instrument which the ancients called "Urim and Thummim," which consisted of two transparent stones set in the rim of a bow fastened to a breastplate. By the instrumentality of the Urim and Thummim, Joseph was enabled to translate the hieroglyphics aforementioned.

Thus translated, the records mentioned became "The Book of Mormon." The last of the ancient prophets had inscribed these records upon the golden plates by the command of God, and deposited them in the earth, where, fifteen centuries later, they were divinely revealed to Joseph Smith.

It is not pretended that the golden plates are still in existence, but that after being translated by Joseph Smith, by the aid of the wonderful instrument mentioned, they were re-delivered to the angel. The non-production of the plates thus satisfactorily explained, and secondary evidence being admissible, eleven witnesses appeared and testified to having actually seen the plates; three of the number further declaring that they were present when Joseph received the plates at the hands of the angel.

Upon my giving expression, to a high Mormon official, of some lingering doubts as to the absolute authenticity of the above narrative, I was significantly reminded of the words of the immortal bard:

"Disparage not the faith thou dost not know,
Lest, to thy peril, thou aby it dear."

At all events, upon the pretended revelations mentioned, Joseph Smith as "prophet" founded the Church of the Latter-Day Saints, near Palmyra, New York, in 1830. Nor did he lack for followers. The eleven witnesses mentioned, and others, were commissioned and sent forth to proclaim the new gospel, and disciples in large numbers soon flocked to the standard of the "prophet."

The history of delusions from the days of Mahomet to the present time illustrates the eagerness with which men are ever ready to seek out new inventions and to discard the old beliefs for the new. There is no tenet so monstrous but in some breast it will find lodgment.

"In religion
What damned error, but some sober brow
Will bless it and approve it with a text."

In 1833, Mormon colonies were established at Kirtland, Ohio, and in Jackson County, Missouri, but, owing to Gentile persecution, the "saints" at length shook the dust of those unhallowed localities from their feet, and settled in large numbers in Hancock County, Illinois. Here they built Nauvoo, the "Holy City," "the beautiful habitation for man." The Mormon historian says: "The surrounding lands were purchased by the saints, and a town laid out, which was named 'Nauvoo' from the Hebrew, which signifies fair, very beautiful, and it actually fills the definition of the words, for nature has not formed a parallel anywhere on the banks of the Mississippi."

The sacred city, as it was called, soon contained a population of fifteen thousand souls, gathered from all quarters of the globe. Here were built the home of the prophet, the hall of the seventies, a concert hall, and other public institutions. Chief among these buildings was the Temple, described by the same historian as "glistening in white limestone upon the hilltops, a shrine in the wilderness whereat all the nations of the earth may worship, whereat all the people may inquire of God and receive His holy oracles."

This temple, erected at a cost of nearly a million dollars, was at a later day visited by Governor Reynolds, and is thus described by him:

"I was in the Mormon temple at Nauvoo. It was a large and splendid edifice, built in the Egyptian style of architecture; and its grandeur and magnificence truly astonished me. It was erected on the top of the Mississippi bluff, which has a prospect which reached as far as the eye could extend over the country and up and down the river. The most singular appendage of this splendid edifice was the font in which the immersion of the saints was practised. It was composed of marble."

At the time of the Mormon emigration to Illinois, in 1839, the Whig and Democratic parties in the State were in a heated struggle for supremacy. The respective party leaders at once realized that the new importation of voters might be the controlling political factor in the State. To conciliate the Mormons and gain their support soon became the aim of the politicians. This fact is the keynote to the statement of Governor Ford:

"A city charter drawn up to suit the Mormons was presented to the Legislature. No one opposed it, but both parties were active in getting it through. This charter, and others passed in the same manner, incorporated Nauvoo, provided for the election of a mayor, four aldermen, and nine councillors, and gave them power to pass all ordinances necessary for the benefit of the city which were not repugnant to the Constitution. This seemed to give them power to pass ordinances in violation of the laws of the State, and to erect a system of government for themselves. This charter also incorporated the Nauvoo Legion,—entirely independent of the military organization of the State, and not subject to the commands of its officers.

Provision was also made for a court-martial for the Legion, to be composed of its own officers; and in the exercise of their duties they were not bound to regard the laws of the State. Thus it was proposed to establish for the Mormons a Government within a Government, a Legislature with power to pass ordinances at war with the laws of the State. These charters were unheard of, anti-republican and capable of infinite abuse. The great law of the separation of the powers of government was wholly disregarded. The mayor was at once the executive power, the judiciary, and part of the Legislature. One would have thought that these charters stood a poor chance of passing the Legislature of a republican people, jealous of their liberties, nevertheless they did pass both Houses unanimously. Each party was afraid to object to them, for fear of losing the Mormon vote."

Some indications of the hopes and fears of party leaders may be gleaned from the statement of the politic John Reynolds, then a representative in Congress. He thus speaks of the visit of Joseph Smith to the national capital:

"I had recently received letters that Smith was a very important character in Illinois, and to give him the civilities that were due him. He stood at the time fair and honorable, except his fanaticism on religion. The sympathies of the people were in his favor. It fell to my lot to introduce him to the President, and one morning the Prophet Smith and I called at the White House to see the chief magistrate. When we were about to enter the apartments of President Van Buren, the prophet asked me to introduce him as a Latter-day Saint. It was so unexpected and so strange to me that I could scarcely believe he would urge such nonsense on this occasion to the President. But he repeated the request, and I introduced him as a Latter-day Saint, which made the President smile. The Prophet remained in Washington a greater part of the winter, and preached often. I became well acquainted with him. He was a person rather larger than ordinary stature, well proportioned, and would weigh about one hundred and eighty pounds. He was rather fleshy, but was in his appearance, amiable and benevolent. He did not appear to possess barbarity in his nature, nor to possess that great talent and boundless mind that would enable him to accomplish the wonders he performed."

Referring again to the narrative of Ford:

"Joseph Smith was duly installed Mayor of Nauvoo—this *Imperium in Imperio*—he was *ex-officio* Judge of the Mayor's court, and Chief Justice of the Municipal court; and in this capacity he was to interpret the laws he had assisted to make. The Nauvoo Legion was organized with a multitude of high officers. It was divided into divisions, brigades, cohorts, battalions, and companies; and Joseph Smith as Lieutenant-General was the Commander-in-Chief. The common council of Nauvoo passed many ordinances for the punishment of crime. The punishment was generally different from, and much more severe than, that provided by the laws of the State."

That any Legislature would ever, under any stress of circumstances, have conferred—or have attempted to confer—such powers upon a municipality is beyond comprehension. The statement, if unsustained by the official State records, would now challenge belief.

Under the favorable conditions mentioned, the Mormons were now upon the high wave of prosperity in Illinois. Their number had increased to more than twenty thousand in Hancock and the counties adjoining. The owners of large tracts of valuable land, protected by legislation that finds no parallel in any State, courted by the leaders of both parties, and actually holding for a time the balance of political power in the State—they seemed indeed to be "the chosen people," as claimed by their prophet.

It needed no prophet, however, to foretell that this could not long continue. The Mormon leaders failed to realize that to champion the cause of either party would of necessity arouse the fierce hostility of the other, as in very truth it did. Politics, the prime cause of fortune's favors to them in the beginning, proved their undoing in the end.

Joseph Smith had, soon after his removal from Missouri, been arrested upon a requisition from the Governor of that State. From this arrest he was discharged when brought upon a writ of *habeas corpus* before Judge Pope, a Whig. The ground of the decision was, that as Smith was not in Missouri at the time of the attempt upon the life of Governor Boggs, and that whatever he did—if he did anything —to aid or encourage the attempt, was done in Illinois, and not within the jurisdiction of Missouri laws, he was not a fugitive from justice within the provision of the Constitution of the United States. The decision excited much comment at the time, but, as stated by Judge Blodgett, it "has borne the test of criticism, and is now the accepted rule of law in interstate extradition cases."

This for a time inclined the Mormons to the support of the Whig party. Again arrested, the prophet, under similar proceedings, was discharged by a Democratic Judge. This, as Governor Ford says,

"Induced Smith to issue a proclamation to his followers declaring Judge Douglas to be a master spirit, and exhorting them to vote for the Democratic ticket for Governor. Smith was too ignorant to know whether he owed his discharge to the law or to party favor. Such was the ignorance of the Mormons generally, that they thought anything to be law which they thought expedient. All action of the Government unfavorable to them they looked upon as wantonly oppressive, and when the law was administered in their favor they attributed it to partiality and kindness."

The last hope of the Whigs for Mormon support was abandoned in 1843. In the district of which Hancock County was a part, the opposing candidates for Congress were Joseph P. Hoge, Democrat, and Cyrus Walker, Whig, both lawyers of distinction. The latter had been counsel for Smith in the Habeas Corpus proceedings last mentioned. Grateful for the services then rendered, Smith openly espoused the candidacy of Walker in the pending contest. That there were tricks in politics even more than sixty years ago, will now appear. One Backinstos, a politician of Hancock County, declared upon his return from the State capital that he had assurances from the Governor that the Mormons would be amply protected as long as they voted the Democratic ticket. It is hardly necessary to say that the Governor denied having given any such assurance. However, the campaign lie of Backinstos, like many of its kind before and since, proved a "good enough Morgan till after the election." This, it will be remembered, was before the days of railroads and telegraphs, and the Mormon settlement was far remote from the seat of government. A partisan jumble, in which the "saints" were the participants, and the low arts of the demagogues and pretended revelations from God the chief ingredients, is thus described by the historian just quoted:

"The mission of Backinstos produced an entire change in the minds of the Mormon leaders. They now resolved to drop their friend Walker and take up Hoge, the Democratic candidate. A great meeting of several thousand Mormons was held the Saturday before the election. Hiram Smith, patriarch and brother of the prophet, appeared in this assembly and there solemnly announced to the people, that God had revealed to him that the Mormons must support Mr. Hoge. William Law, another leader, next appeared and denied that the Lord had made any such revelation. He stated that to his certain knowledge the prophet Joseph was in favor of Mr. Walker, and that the prophet was more likely to know the mind of the Lord than the patriarch. Hiram again repeated his revelation, with a greater tone of authority, but the people remained in doubt until the next day, Sunday, when the prophet Joseph himself appeared before the assemblage. He there stated that he himself was in favor of Mr. Walker and intended to vote for him; that he would not, if he could, influence any man in giving his vote; that he considered it a mean business for any man to dictate to the people whom they should vote for; that he had heard his brother Hiram had received a revelation from the Lord on the subject; but for his own part, he did not much believe in revelations on the subject of election. Brother Hiram was, however, a man of truth; he had known him intimately ever since he was a boy, and he had never known him to tell a lie. If brother

Hiram said he had received a revelation he had no doubt he had. When the Lord speaks let all the earth be silent."

That the prophet Joseph well understood how to

"By indirections find directions out,"

clearly appears from his cunning expression of faith in the pretended revelation of the patriarch Hiram. The effect of this speech was far-reaching. It turned the entire Mormon vote to Hoge, thereby securing his election to Congress, and at once placed the Whigs in the ranks of the implacable anti-Mormon party then in process of rapid formation. The crusade that now began for the expulsion of the Mormons from the State, was greatly augmented by acts of unparalleled folly upon their own part. In order to protect their leaders from arrest, it was decreed by the City Council of Nauvoo that no writ unless issued and approved by its Mayor should be executed within the sacred city, and that any officer attempting to execute a writ otherwise issued, within the city, should be subject to imprisonment for life, and that the pardoning power of the Governor of the State was in such case suspended. This ordinance when published created great astonishment and indignation. The belief became general that the Mormons were about to set up for themselves a separate Government wholly independent of that of the State. This belief was strengthened by the presentation of a petition to Congress praying for the establishment of a Territorial Government for Nauvoo and vicinity.

Apparently oblivious of the gathering storm, Joseph Smith early in 1844 committed his crowning act of folly by announcing himself a candidate for the high office of President of the United States. Not only this, but as stated by Governor Ford,

"Smith now conceived the idea of making himself a temporal Prince as well as the spiritual leader of his people. He instituted a new and select order of the priesthood, the members of which were to be priests and kings, temporal and spiritual. These were to be the nobility, the upholders of his throne. He caused himself to be crowned and anointed king and priest far above all others. To uphold his pretensions to royalty, he deduced his descent by an unbroken chain from Joseph, the son of Jacob, and that of his wife from some other renowned personage of Old Testament history. The Mormons openly denounced the Government of the United States, as being utterly corrupt, and about to pass away and be replaced by the government of God, to be administered by his servant Joseph. It is at this day certain, also, that about this time, the prophet instituted an order in the Church called the Danite Band. This was to be a body-guard about the person of their sovereign, sworn to obey his commands as those of God himself."

During late years a war of words has been waged within the Mormon church over the question of the responsibility of the prophet Joseph for the introduction of polygamy as a cardinal tenet of its creed. The son of the prophet, it will be remembered, led a revolt against Brigham Young, soon after the succession of the latter to the presidency of the Church, and is now at the head of the Mormon establishment at Plano, Illinois. This branch of the Church rejects the dogma of polygamy, declaring it to be utterly repugnant to the divine revelation to Joseph, and to early Mormon belief and practice.

Upon the contrary, the main body in Utah—of which Joseph F. Smith the nephew of the prophet and son of Hiram the patriarch is now the president—found their belief in the divine character of their peculiar institution upon alleged revelations direct from God to the founder of the Church. The statement of Governor Ford, written nearly sixty years ago, sheds some light upon this controversy:

"A doctrine was now revealed that no woman could get to heaven except as the wife of a Mormon elder. The elders were allowed to have as many of these wives as they could maintain; and it was a doctrine of the Church that any female could be 'sealed up to eternal life' by uniting herself as wife to the elder of her choice. This doctrine was maintained by appeal to the Old Testament scriptures and by the example of Abraham and Jacob and Daniel and Solomon, the favorites of God in a former age of the world."

As the necessary result of the causes mentioned, the followers of the prophet soon found themselves bitterly antagonized by almost the whole anti-Mormon population of the "Military Tract." Charges and counter-charges were made, the arrest of the leaders of the opposing parties followed in rapid succession, and outrages and riots were of daily occurrence. Public meetings were held; all the crimes known to the calendar were charged against the Mormons, and resolutions passed demanding their immediate expulsion from the State. What is known in Illinois history as the "Mormon war" followed closely in the wake of the events just mentioned. Innocent persons were, in many instances, the victims of the folly and of the crimes of unprincipled and brutal leaders.

The events of this period constitute a dark chapter in the history of the State—one that can be recalled only with feelings of horror. The great body of citizens, it is needless to say, favored the rigid maintenance of order and the protection of life and property; but it was the very heyday for the lawless and vicious element of all parties.

That this condition of affairs could not long continue was manifest. The bloody termination, however, came in a manner unexpected to all. Two of the Mormon leaders, William and Wilson Law, were, at the time mentioned, in open revolt against the newly-assumed powers and the alleged practices of the prophet. To strengthen their opposition they procured a printing-press and equipment, and issued from their office in Nauvoo one number of a small weekly, "The Expositor." By order of the Mayor, Smith, and decree of the Council, the press was seized and destroyed, and the Law brothers and their few adherents compelled to flee the Holy City. Immediately upon their arrival at Carthage, they caused warrants to be issued for the arrest of Joseph and Hiram Smith, John Taylor, and others, for the destruction of the printing-press. The almost sovereign powers previously conferred upon the city of Nauvoo now play an important part in this drama. The persons arrested, as above mentioned, were at once brought by writs of *habeas corpus*, issued by the Mayor of Nauvoo, before the Municipal Court and there promptly discharged. Governor Ford, whose righteous soul had been vexed to the limit of endurance by unmerited abuse from Mormon and Gentile alike from the beginning of this controversy, here indulges in a few expressions of justifiable irony. Of these proceedings he says:

"It clearly appeared both from the complaints of the citizens and the admissions of the Mormons, that the whole proceedings of the Mayor, Council, and Municipal Court were illegal and not to be endured in a free country; but some apology might be made for the court, as it had been repeatedly assured by some of the ablest lawyers in the State of both political parties, when candidates before that people, that it had full and complete power to issue writs of *habeas corpus* in all cases whatever."

> "In law, what plea so tainted and corrupt,
> But, being seasoned with a gracious voice,
> Obscures the show of evil."

The incidents mentioned added quickly fuel to the flame. A new warrant was issued by a magistrate in Carthage for the arrest of the Mormon leaders and placed in the hands of an officer of the State for execution. The latter at once summoned the citizens of the county, as a *posse comitatus*, to aid in the arrests. At this critical moment Governor Ford, in the interest of peace, reached Carthage, the county seat. Upon his arrival he found the situation truly alarming. Several hundred armed men from the country around had hastily assembled and were encamped upon the public square. By order of the Governor, this force was organized into companies and placed under the immediate command of officers of his appointment. At the conclusion of a speech by the Governor, the officers and men pledged themselves to aid him in upholding the laws, and in protecting the Mormon prisoners when brought to Carthage for trial.

Meanwhile, Smith as lieutenant-general had called out the Nauvoo Legion and proclaimed martial law in that city. The Mormons from the country promptly obeyed the call of their leader and marched to his assistance, and Nauvoo became at once a vast military camp. Governor Ford now demanded of the Mormon leaders the return of the State arms furnished at the time of the organization of the Legion, this demand, if not promptly complied with, to be enforced by an immediate attack upon Nauvoo by the assembled forces encamped at Carthage.

Appreciating now for the first time the hopelessness of a conflict with State authorities, a number of the weapons were surrendered and the Smiths, accompanied by Taylor and Richards, two other Mormon leaders, went to Carthage and surrendered themselves to the officer holding the warrant for their arrest. Upon giving bond for their appearance, they were at once released on charge of riot. A new complaint, charging them with treason— in levying war against the State, declaring martial law in Nauvoo, and ordering out the Legion to resist the execution of lawful process—was immediately lodged against them, a warrant duly issued, the prisoners rearrested and committed to the common jail of the county. On the evening following this arrest, the guards stationed at the jail for the protection of the prisoners were attacked and overpowered by a mob of several hundred persons. Governor Ford states:

"An attempt was now made to break open the door; but Joseph Smith, being armed with a six-barrel pistol furnished by his friends, fired several times as the door was burst open and wounded three of the assailants. At the same time, several shots were fired into the room, wounding John Taylor and killing Hiram Smith. Joseph Smith now attempted to escape by jumping out of the second-story window; but the fall so stunned him that he was unable to rise, and being placed by the conspirators in a sitting posture, they despatched him by four balls shot through his body."

Thus perished, at the age of thirty-nine, the founder and prophet of the Mormon Church. Contradictory statements as to his real character have come down to the present generation. The estimate of Governor Ford, who knew him well, is as follows:

"He was the most successful impostor in modern times; a man who, though ignorant and coarse, had some great natural parts which fitted him for temporary success, but which were so obscured and counteracted by the inherent corruptness of his nature that he never could succeed in establishing a system of policy which looked to permanent success in the future. It must not be supposed that the pretended prophet practised the tricks of a common impostor; that he was a dark and gloomy person with a long beard, a grave and severe aspect, and a reserved and saintly carriage of his person. On the contrary, he was full of levity, even to boyish romping; dressed like a dandy, and at times drank like a sailor and swore like a pirate. He could, as occasion required, be exceedingly meek in his deportment, and then, again, be as rough and boisterous as a highway robber; being always able to prove to his followers the propriety of his conduct. He always quailed before power, and was arrogant to weakness. At times he could put on an air of a penitent, as if feeling the deepest humility for his sins, and suffering unutterable anguish, and indulging in the most gloomy foreboding of eternal woe. At such times he would call for the prayers of the brethren in his behalf with a wild and fearful anxiety and earnestness. He was six feet high, strongly built, and uncommonly full muscled. No doubt he was as much indebted for his influence over an ignorant people to the superiority of his physical vigor as to his great cunning and intellect."

Of a wholly different tenor is the tribute of Parley P. Pratt, the poet and historian of the Mormon Church:

"President Smith was in person tall and well built, strong and active; of a light complexion, light hair, blue eyes, and of an expression peculiar to himself, on which the eye naturally rested with interest and was never weary of beholding. His countenance was very mild, affable, and beaming with intelligence and benevolence mingled with a look of interest and an unconscious smile of cheerfulness, and entirely free from all restraint or affectation of gravity; and there was something connected with the serene and steady penetrating glance of his eye, as if he would penetrate the deepest abyss of the human heart, gaze into eternity, penetrate the heavens, and comprehend all worlds. He possessed a noble boldness and independence of character; his manner was easy and familiar, his rebuke terrible as the lion, his benevolence unbounded as the ocean, his intelligence universal, and his language abounding in original eloquence peculiar to himself."

For a brief period following the assassination of the Smiths, comparative quiet prevailed in the Mormon country. The selection of a successor to their murdered prophet, was now the absorbing question among the Mormon people. Revelations were published that the prophet, in imitation of the Saviour, was to rise from the dead, and some even reported that they had seen him attended by a celestial army coursing the air on a great white horse.

Sydney Rigdon now aspired to be the head of the Church as the successor to the martyred prophet. His claims were verified by a pretended revelation direct from heaven. He was, however, at once antagonized by the "quorum of the Twelve," and after a bitter struggle, Apostle Brigham Young was chosen, and Rigdon expelled from the Church and "given over to the buffetings of Satan."

The quiet immediately succeeding the tragedy was of short duration. It was only the calm which precedes the storm. While his followers were invoking the vengeance of the law upon the murderers of the prophet, the anti-Mormons were quietly organizing a crusade for the expulsion of the entire Mormon population from the State. The trial of the assassins of the Smiths resulted in their acquittal, as was to have been expected when the intense anti-Mormon feeling existing throughout the immediate country is taken into account. The result is even less surprising when it is remembered that the principal witness for the prosecution supplemented his testimony of having seen the crime committed, by the remarkable declaration that immediately upon the death of Joseph, "a bright and shining light descended upon his head, that several of the conspirators were stricken with total blindness, and that he heard supernatural voices in the air confirming the divine mission of the murdered prophet."

In the narration of these exciting events, the names of men who at a later day achieved national distinction frequently occur. The Hon. O. H. Browning, since Senator and member of the Cabinet, was chief counsel for the alleged murderers of the Smiths. He was at the time a distinguished Whig leader, and one of the most eloquent men in the State. The disorder and outrages that followed the acquittal just mentioned called Governor Ford again to the seat of war. He says:

"When informed of these proceedings, I hastened to Jacksonville, where in a conference with General Hardin, Judge Douglas, and Mr. McDougal the Attorney-General of the State, it was agreed that these gentlemen should proceed to Hancock County in all haste with whatever force had been raised, and put an end to these disorders. It was also agreed that they should unite their influence with mine to induce the Mormons to leave the State. The twelve apostles had now become satisfied that the Mormons could not remain, or, if they did, that the leaders would be compelled to abandon the sway they exercised over them. Through the intervention of General Hardin, acting on instructions from me, an agreement was made between the hostile parties for the voluntary removal of the greater part of the Mormons across the Mississippi in the spring of 1846."

Of the advisors of the Governor in the adjustment mentioned, Douglas and McDougall were at a later day distinguished Senators, respectively from Illinois and California, and Hardin was killed while gallantly leading his regiment at the battle of Buena Vista.

To the peaceable accomplishment of the purposes mentioned, a small force under a competent officer was stationed for a time in Hancock County.

The Governor justly felicitates himself that thereby "the greater part of the Military Tract was saved from the horrors of civil war in the winter time, when much misery would have followed by the dispersion of families and the destruction of property."

The Mormon exodus from Illinois, once the "land of promise," now began in terrible earnest. Many farms and homes and large quantities of personal effects were hastily disposed of at a great sacrifice. The speeding was far different from the welcome but a few years before so heartily extended to the incoming "saints." The "Holy City" and sacred temple soon to be destroyed were abandoned for perilous journeyings in the wilderness. The chapter that immediately follows in the history of this people is indeed pathetic. The terrible sufferings of the aged and infirm, of helpless women and children, as the shadows of the long night of winter gathered about them on their journey, can never be adequately told. But, inspired with the thought that they were the Israel of God, that Brigham Young was their divinely appointed leader, that the pillar of cloud by day and of fire by night ever went before them on their journeyings, they patiently endured all dangers and hardships.

High upon the western slope of the Wasatch hard by the old wagon trail which led down into the valley stands a huge rock around whose base the Mormon leader assembled his followers just as the last rays of a summer sun were falling upon the mountains. In stirring words he recalled their persecutions and trials, told them that their long pilgrimage, the weary march by day and lonely vigil by night, were now ended, and their Canaan the great valley which stretched out before them.

Upon a visit to Salt Lake City nearly a third of a century ago, I attended service in the great Tabernacle when it was filled to overflowing, and yet so excellent were its acoustic arrangements that every word of the speaker and every note of the organ could be heard distinctly. The surroundings were indeed imposing. Upon the great platform sat the President and his Council, the twelve apostles, the seventy elders, with an innumerable army of bishops, teachers, deacons, and other functionaries constituting the lower order of the Mormon hierarchy. The sermon was delivered by the famous Orson Pratt, the Saint Paul of the Mormon Church, a venerable patriarch of four score years, and yet, withal, a man of wonderful power.

As our little party passed in front of the speaker's platform to reach the door, he halted in his discourse, and stated to the audience that the strangers within their gates were leaving because of the near departure of their train and not because of any disrespect to the service. Then, bowing his aged head, he invoked the blessing of the God of Abraham, of Isaac, and of Jacob, upon the Gentile strangers, and prayed "that their long journey might be ended in safety, and that in the fulness of time, having witnessed the manifestations of Almighty Power, they might return again, not as sojourners, but as fellow-citizens with the saints, to dwell in the Holy City."

XIV A KENTUCKY COLONEL

COL. WINTERSMITH'S GREAT POPULARITY—HIS ADMIRATION FOR MR. CLAY —HIS MARVELLOUS MEMORY—HIS WIT AND HUMOR.

Few men were better known in Washington, a quarter of a century and more ago, than Colonel Dick Wintersmith of Kentucky. He had creditably filled important positions of public trust in his native State. His integrity was beyond question, and his popularity knew no bounds. Without the formality of party nomination, and with hardly the shadow of opposition at the polls, he had held the office of State Treasurer for nearly a score of years. An ardent Whig in early life, he was a devout worshipper at the shrine of Henry Clay. In the later years of his life, he would often with the deepest emotion refer to himself as "the last of the old guard." He never tired of relating interesting incidents of Mr. Clay. It was his glory that he had accompanied "the great pacificator" to Washington, when, with the fond hope of being able by his historic "compromise" to pour oil on the troubled waters, he returned to the Senate for the last time.

Wintersmith was the close friend of Theodore O'Hara, and stood beside him when at the unveiling of the monument to the Kentuckians who had fallen at Buena Vista he pronounced his now historic lines beginning—

"On fame's eternal camping-ground
Their silent tents are spread."

Colonel Wintersmith knew, as he knew his children, two generations of the public men of Kentucky. His memory was a marvel to all who knew him. He could repeat till the dawn, extracts from famous speeches he had heard from the lips of Clay, Grundy, Marshall, and Menifee. More than once, I have heard him declaim the wonderful speech of Sargent S. Prentiss delivered almost a half-century before, in the old Harrodsburg Court-house, in defence of Wilkinson for killing three men at the Galt House.

It is hardly necessary to say that the Colonel was the soul of generosity. It was a part of his living faith that—

"Kind hearts are more than coronets."

That he was possessed in no stinted measure of wit and its kindred quality, humor, will appear from an incident or two to be related.

The Hon. Ignatius Donnelly, member of Congress from Minnesota, had written a book to prove that Lord Bacon was the veritable author of the plays usually accredited to Shakespeare. Soon after the appearance of Donnelly's book, he met Colonel Wintersmith on Pennsylvania Avenue.

After a cordial greeting, the Colonel remarked, "I have been reading your book, Donnelly, and I don't believe a word of it."

"What?" inquired Donnelly, with great surprise.

"Oh, that book of yours," said the Colonel, "in which you tried to prove that Shakespeare never wrote 'Hamlet' and 'Macbeth' and 'Lear' and all those other plays."

"My dear sir," replied Donnelly with great earnestness, "I can prove beyond all peradventure that Shakespeare never wrote those plays."

"He did," replied Wintersmith, "he did write them, Donnelly, *I saw him write three or four of them, myself.*"

"Impossible!" replied Donnelly, who was as guiltless of anything that savored of humor as the monument recently erected to the memory of Hon. John Sherman, "impossible, Colonel, that you could have seen Shakespeare write those plays; they were written three hundred years ago."

"Three hundred years, three hundred years," slowly murmured the Colonel in pathetic tone, "is it possible that is has been so long? *Lord, how time does fly!*"

The Colonel often told the following with a gravity that gave it at least the semblance of truth. Many years ago, his State was represented in part in the Upper House by a statesman who rarely, when in good form, spoke less than an entire day. His speeches, in large measure, usually consisted of dull financial details, statistics, etc. He became in time the terror of his associates, and the nightmare of visitors in the galleries. His "Mr. President," was usually the signal for a general clearing out of both Senate Chamber and galleries.

"Upon one occasion," said Colonel Dick, "I was seated in the last tier in the public gallery, when my Senator with books and documents piled high about him solemnly addressed the Chair. As was the wont, the visitors in the gallery as one man arose to make their exit. With a revolver in each hand, I promptly planted myself in front of the door, and in no uncertain tone ordered the crowd to resume their seats, and remain quietly until the Senator from Kentucky had concluded his remarks. They did so and no word of complaint reached my ears. Hour after hour during the long summer day the speech drew itself along. At length as the shadows were lengthening and the crickets began to chirp, the speech ended and the Senator took his seat. I promptly replaced my pistols and motioned the visitors to move out. They did so on excellent time. As the last man was passing out, he quietly remarked to me, 'Mister, that was all right, no fault to find, but *if it was to do over again, you might shoot.*'"

XV FORGOTTEN EVENTS OF THE LONG AGO

THE WRITER MEETS MISS GRAHAM, SISTER-IN-LAW OF MR. GILES, A REPRESENTATIVE IN THE DAYS OF WASHINGTON—HIS MEETING WITH THE DAUGHTER OF THOMAS W. GILMER, SECRETARY OF THE NAVY UNDER PRESIDENT TYLER—THE SECRETARY KILLED, AND THE PRESIDENT ENDANGERED BY AN EXPLOSION— SPECULATION AS TO POSSIBLE POLITICAL CHANGES HAD THE PRESIDENT BEEN KILLED.

During my sojourn in Washington I visited the "Louise Home," one of the splendid charities of the late W. W. Corcoran. Two of the ladies I there met were Miss Graham and Miss Gilmer. The turn of Fortune's wheel had brought each of them from once elegant Virginia homes to spend the evening of life in the Home which Mr. Corcoran had so kindly and thoughtfully provided. It was in very truth the welcome retreat to representatives of old Southern families who had known better days. Here in quiet and something of elegant leisure, the years sped by, the chief pastime recalling events and telling over again and again the social triumphs of the long ago. Thus lingering in the shadows of the past, sadly reflecting, it may be, in the silent watches, that—

"The tender grace of a day that is dead
Will never come back to me,"

these venerable ladies were in sad reality "only waiting till the shadows had a little longer grown."

There was something pathetically remindful of the good old Virginia days in the manner in which Miss Graham handed me her card and invited me to be seated. Looking me earnestly in the face, she said, "Mr. Vice-President, you must have known my brother-in-law, Governor Giles."

"Do you mean Senator William B. Giles of Virginia?" I inquired.

"Yes, yes," she said, "did you know him?"

"No, madam," I replied, "I did not; he was a member of Congress when Washington was President; that was a little before my day. But is it possible that you are a sister-in-law of Governor Giles?"

"Yes, sir," she answered, "he married my eldest sister and I was in hope that you knew him."

I assured her that I had never known him personally, but that I knew something of his history: that he was a soldier of the Revolution; that he began his public career with the passing of the old Confederation and the establishment of the National Union; that as Representative or Senator he was in Congress almost continuously from the administration of Washington to that of Jackson. I then repeated to her the words Mr. Benton, his long-time associate in the Senate, had spoken of her brother-in-law: "Macon was wise, Randolph brilliant, Gallatin and Madison able in argument, but Giles was the ready champion, always ripe for the combat." And I told her that John Randolph, for many years his colleague, had said: "Giles was to our House of Representatives what Charles James Fox was to the British House of Commons—the most accomplished debater our country has known."

I might have said to Miss Graham, but did not, that her brother-in-law, then a member of the House, had voted against the farewell address of that body to President Washington upon his retirement from the great office. Strange indeed to our ears sound the words that even mildly reflect upon the Father of his Country. Of this, however, we may be assured, that the Golden Age of our history is but a dream; "the era of absolute good feeling,"—the era that has not been.

"Past and to come seem best;
Things present, worst."

Before condemning Mr. Giles too severely the words of Edmund Burke may well be recalled: "Party divisions, whether upon the whole operating for the best, are things inseparable from free Government." Party divisions came in with our Constitution; partisan feeling almost with our first garments.

In this connection it will be remembered that this country has known no period of more intense and bitter party feeling than during the administration of the immediate successor of Washington, the period which witnessed the downfall of the Federal party, and the rise of the party of Jefferson. It was after the election but before the inauguration of John Adams, that the following words were spoken of President Washington by the brother-in-law of the little old lady to whom I have referred:

"I must object to those parts of the address which speak of the wisdom and firmness of the President. I may be singular in my ideas, but I believe his administration has neither been firm nor wise. I must acknowledge that I am one of those who do not think so much of the President as some others do. I wish that this was the moment of his retirement. I think that the Government of the United States can go on without him. What calamities would attend the United States, and how short the duration of its independence, if but one man could be found fitted to conduct its administration! Much had been said and by many people about the President's intended retirement. For my own part, I feel no uncomfortable sensations about it."

As I thus recalled the man whose public life began with that of Washington, his kinswoman at my side seemed indeed the one living bond of connection between the present and the long past, that past which had witnessed the Declaration of Independence, the War of the Revolution, and the establishment of the Federal Government.

The younger, by many years, of the two ladies, was the daughter of the Hon. Thomas W. Gilmer, a distinguished member of Congress during the third decade of the century, later the Governor of Virginia, and at the time of his death the Secretary of the Navy. The mention of his name recalls a tragic event that cast a pall over the nation and shrouded more than one hearthstone in deepest gloom. During later years, the horrors of an internecine struggle that knows no parallel, the assassination of three Presidents of the United States, and the thousand casualties that have crowded in rapid succession, have almost wiped from memory the incident now to be mentioned.

The pride of the American Navy, the man-of-war *Princeton,* Commodore Stockton in command, was lying in the Potomac just below Washington, on the morning of February 28, 1843. The day was beautiful, and the distinguished commander, who had known much of gallant service, had invited more than one hundred guests to accompany him on a sail to a point a few miles below Mount Vernon. Among the guests were President Tyler and two members of his Cabinet; Mr. Upshur, Secretary of State, and Mr. Gilmer, Secretary of the Navy; the widow of Ex-President Madison; Mr. Gardner, a prominent citizen of New York, and his accomplished daughter; Commodore Kennan; and a number of Senators and Representatives. Commodore Stockton was anxious to have his guests witness the working of the machinery of his vessel and to observe the fire of his great gun, his especial pride. Mr. Gardner and his daughter were guests at the Executive Mansion; and to the latter, the President—then for many years a widower —was especially attentive. Officers and guests were all in the best of sprits, and nothing seemed wanting to make the occasion one of unalloyed pleasure. Upon the return, and when almost directly opposite Mount Vernon, the company were summoned by the Commodore from the dinner table to witness the testing of the gun. Preceded by an officer, the guests were soon assembled in proximity to the gun. A place at the front was reserved for the President, but just as he was advancing, his attention was directed by his fair guest to some object on the shore. This for a moment arrested his progress, and prevented his instant death, for at this critical moment the gun exploded, causing the immediate death of more than twenty persons, and serious injuries to many others. Among the injured were Senator Benton and Commodore Stockton. The list of the dead included Secretary of State Upshur, Secretary of the Navy Gilmer, Commodore Kennan—one of the heroes of the second war with Great Britain,—and Mr. Gardner, the father of the lady whose timely interposition had caused the moment's delay which had saved the President from the terrible fate of his associates. Upon the return of the *Princeton* to Washington the dead were removed to the Executive Mansion, and the day, so auspicious in the beginning, ended in gloom.

Something in the way of romance is the sequel to that sad event. A few months later Miss Gardner, the fair guest of the President upon the ill-fated *Princeton,* became his bride, and during the remainder of his term of office did the honors of the Executive Mansion.

The thousands of visitors who have, during the past sixty years, passed through the spacious rooms of that Mansion, have paused before a full-length portrait of one of the most beautiful of women. Possibly the interest of no one who gazed upon her lovely features was lessened when told that the portrait was that of the wife of President Tyler, the once charming and accomplished Miss Gardner, whose name is so closely associated with the long-ago chapter of sorrow and of romance.

A thought pertaining to the domain of the real rather than of the romantic is suggested by the sad accident upon the *Princeton.* But for the trifling incident which detained President Tyler from the side of his Cabinet officers at the awful moment, the administration of the Government would have passed to other hands. As the law then stood, the Speaker of the House of Representatives would have succeeded to the Presidency; and how this might have changed the current of our political history is a matter of at least curious speculation.

Remembering that—

"Two stars keep not
Their motion in one sphere,"

might not the removal of one have healed the widening breach in the Whig party? What might have been its effect upon the grand Internal Improvement Scheme—the darling project of Henry Clay? what upon the determination of the Oregon Boundary Question—whether by diplomacy or war? and how might the destiny of the "Lone Star," the Republic of Texas, have been changed? What might have been the effect upon the political fortunes of Tyler's great antagonist, around whom the aggressive forces of the party he had founded were even then gathering for a life-and-death struggle against a comparatively obscure rival in the Presidential campaign of 1844?

Trifles light as air are sometimes the pivots upon which hinge momentous events. The ill-timed publication of a personal letter defeated Cass in 1848; and within our day the utterance of a single word, unheard by the candidate to whom it was addressed, lost the Presidency to Blaine.

The antagonism of Tyler and his adherents eliminated, it is within the bounds of probability that Henry Clay would have triumphed in his last struggle for the Presidency. If so, what change might not have been wrought in the trend of history? Under the splendid leadership of the "great pacificator," what might have been the termination of vital questions even then casting their dark shadows upon our national pathway?

With Clay at the helm, himself the incarnation of the spirit of compromise, possibly—who can tell?—the evil days so soon to follow might have been postponed for many generations.

XVI ROBERT G. INGERSOLL

MR. INGERSOLL'S ELOQUENCE WHILE A YOUNG MAN— HIS CANDIDACY FOR CONGRESS—HIS AGNOSTICISM A HINDRANCE TO HIS POLITICAL ADVANCEMENT —HIS ORATION AT THE FUNERAL OF HIS BROTHER.

It was in April, 1859, that for the first time I met Robert G. Ingersoll. He came over from his home in Peoria to attend the Woodford Circuit Court. He was then under thirty years of age, of splendid physique, magnetic in the fullest significance of the word, and one of the most attractive and agreeable of men. He was almost boyish in appearance, and hardly known beyond the limits of the county in which he lived. He had but recently moved to Peoria from the southern part of the State.

To those who remember him it is hardly necessary to say that even at that early day he gave unmistakable evidence of his marvellous gifts. His power over a jury was wonderful indeed; and woe betide the counsel of but mediocre talents who had Ingersoll for an antagonist in a closely contested case.

The old Court-house at Metamora is yet standing, a monument of the past; the county seat removed, it has long since fallen from its high estate. In my boyhood, I have more than once heard Mr. Lincoln at its bar, and later was a practitioner there myself—and State's Attorney for the Circuit,—when Mr. Ingersoll was attendant upon its courts. Rarely at any time or place have words been spoken more eloquent than fell from the lips of Lincoln and Ingersoll in that now deserted Court-house, in the years long gone by.

The first appearance of Mr. Ingersoll in the political arena was in the Presidential struggle of 1860. In his later years he was a Republican, but in the contest just mentioned he was the earnest advocate of the election of Mr. Douglas to the Presidency and was himself the Democratic candidate for Congress in the Peoria District. His competitor was Judge Kellogg, a gentleman of well-known ability and many years' experience in Congress. Immediately upon his nomination, Ingersoll challenged Kellogg to a series of joint debates. The challenge was accepted, and the debates which followed were a rare treat to the throngs who heard them. The discussion turned upon the vital issues yet pending at the outbreak of the Civil War, issues which were to find their final determination on the field of battle. Possibly, with the exception of the historic debates two years earlier, between Lincoln and Douglas, the country has known no abler discussion of great questions. It was then for the first time that Ingersoll displayed the marvellous forensic powers that at a later day—and upon a different arena—gave him world-wide renown.

It was at a period subsequent to that just mentioned that he became an agnostic. I recall no expression of his during the early years of our acquaintance that indicated a departure from the faith in which he had been reared. That his extreme views upon religious subjects, and his manner, exceedingly offensive at times, of expressing them, formed an insuperable barrier to his political advancement, cannot be doubted. But for his unbelief, what political honors might have awaited him cannot certainly be known. But recalling the questions then under discussion, the intensity of party feeling, and the enthusiasm that his marvellous eloquence never failed to arouse in the thousands who hung upon his words, it is probable that the most exalted station might have been attained. To those familiar with the political events of that day, it is known that the antagonism aroused by his assaults upon the citadel of the faith sacred to the many, compassed his defeat in his candidature in 1868 for the Governorship of Illinois. His explanation was, that his defeat was caused by a slight difference of opinion between himself and some of the brethren upon the highly exciting question of total depravity.

Some years later, the nominee of his party for the Presidency was exceedingly obnoxious to him. Meeting the Colonel the morning after the adjournment of the convention I inquired, "Are you happy?" To this he replied, that he was somewhat in the condition of a very profane youth who had just got religion at a backwoods camp-meeting. Soon after his conversion, the preacher, taking him affectionately by the hand, inquired: "My young friend, are you very happy?" "Well, parson," replied the only half-converted youth, "I am not damn happy, just *happy*, that's all."

His only brother was for many years a Representative in Congress from Illinois. Clark Ingersoll was himself able and eloquent, but overshadowed by the superior gifts of his younger brother, the subject of this sketch. The death of the former was to Colonel Ingersoll a sorrow which remained with him to the last. The funeral occurred in Washington in the summer of 1879, and of the pall-bearers selected by Colonel Ingersoll for the last sad service to his brother, were men well known in public life, one of whom but two years later, while President of the United States, fell by the hand of an assassin.

From a Washington paper of the day succeeding the funeral of Clark Ingersoll, the following is taken: "When Colonel Ingersoll ceased speaking the pall-bearers, Senator Allison, Senator David Davis, Senator Blaine, Senator Voorhees, Representatives Garfield of Ohio, Morrison, Boyd, and

Stevenson of Illinois, bore the casket to the hearse and the lengthy *cortege* proceeded to the Oak Hill Cemetery where the remains were interred."

The occasion was one that will not easily pass from my memory. There was no service whatever save the funeral oration which has found its way into all languages. I stood by the side of Colonel Ingersoll near the casket during its delivery, and vividly recall his deep emotion, and the faltering tones in which the wondrous sentences were uttered. It is probable that this oration has no counterpart in literature. It seemed in very truth the knell of hope, the expression of a grief that could know no surcease, the agony of a parting that could know no morrow.

In such an hour how cheerless and comfortless these words:

"Life is a narrow vale between the cold and barren peaks of two eternities. We strive in vain to look beyond the heights. We cry aloud, and the only answer is the echo of our wailing cry.

"Every life, no matter if its every hour is rich with love, and every moment jewelled with a joy, will at its close become a tragedy as sad and deep and dark as can be woven of the warp and woof of mystery and death."

And yet in those other words, "But in the night of death, hope sees a star, and listening love can hear the rustle of a wing," and, "while on his forehead fell the golden dawning of a grander day," there is a yearning for "the touch of a vanished hand," and a hope that no philosophy could dispel of a reunion sometime and somewhere with the loved and lost.

Two decades later, again "the veiled shadow stole upon the scene," and the sublime mystery of life and death was revealed. The awful question, "If a man die shall he live again?" was answered, and to the great agnostic *all was known*.

XVII A CAMP-MEETING ORATOR

**PETER CARTWRIGHT, METHODIST PREACHER—HIS
FEARLESSNESS AND ENERGY— HIS OLD-FASHIONED
ORTHODOXY—HOW HE CONVERTED A PROFANE
SWEARER —HIS ATTENDANCE AT A BALL—OLD-TIME
CAMP-MEETINGS—CARTWRIGHT'S AVERSION TO OTHER
SECTS—CONVERSION OF A DESPERADO INTO A
PENITENT —CARTWRIGHT MR. LINCOLN'S COMPETITOR
FOR REPRESENTATIVE—HIS SPEECH AT A DEMOCRATIC
STATE CONVENTION.**

The Rev. Peter Cartwright was a noted Methodist preacher of pioneer days in Central Illinois. Once seen, he was a man never to be forgotten. He was, in the most expressive sense of the words, *sui generis;* a veritable product of the times in which he lived, and the conditions under which he moved and had his being. All in all, his like will not appear again. He was converted when a mere youth at a camp-meeting in southern Kentucky; soon after, he was licensed to preach, and became a circuit rider in that State, and later was of the Methodist vanguard to Illinois. It was said of him that he was of the church *military* as well as "the church militant." He was of massive build, an utter stranger to fear, and of unquestioned honesty and sincerity. He was gifted with an eloquence adapted to the times in which he lived, and the congregations to which he preached. There would be no place for him now, for the untutored assemblages who listened with bated breath to his fiery appeals are of the past.

"For, welladay! Their day is fled,
Old times are changed, old manners gone."

The narrative of his tough conflicts with the emissaries of Satan is even now of the rarest reading for a summer's day or a winter's night. How he fought the Indians, fought the robbers, swam rivers, and threaded the prairies, in order that he might carry the Gospel to the remotest frontiersmen, was of thrilling interest to many of the new generation as his own sands were running low. He literally took no thought of the morrow, but without staff and little even in the way of scrip unselfishly gave the best years of a life extending two decades beyond the time allotted, to the service of his Master.

Until the Judgment leaves are unfolded the good which this man and many of his co-laborers did in the new country will never be known. A journey of days on horseback to fill an appointment, to perform a marriage ceremony, preach a funeral sermon, or speak words of hope and comfort to the sick or the bereaved, was part of the sum of a life of service that knew little of rest.

There would probably be few pulpits open to Peter Cartwright in these more cultivated times. Old things have passed away; the pioneer in his rough garb, with axe upon his shoulder, and rifle in hand, is now but a tradition, while the border line of civilization has receded westward to the ocean.

None the less, the typical minister of to-day would have had very scant welcome in the rude pulpits of the days of which we write. His elegant attire, conventional manners, written sermons, and new theology, would have been sadly out of place in the camp-meeting times, for be it remembered that Cartwright called things by their right names. He gave forth no uncertain sound. His theology was that of the Fathers. We hear little in these modern days of "The fire that quencheth not" and of "total depravity" and of "the bottomless pit." Such expressions are unfitted for ears polite. Higher criticism, new thought, and all kindred ideas and suggestions,

"Sapping a solemn creed with solemn sneer,"

were believed by Cartwright and his contemporaries to be mere contrivances of Satan for the ensnaring of immortal souls. His abhorrence of all these "wiles of the devil," and his scorn for their advocates, knew no bounds.

His preaching was of the John Wesley, George Whitefield, and Jonathan Edwards type. Mingled with his denunciations of sin, his earnest exhortations to repentance, his graphic description of the New Jerusalem, with its "streets of gold, walls of jasper, and gates of pearl," and of the unending bliss of the redeemed, were expressions now relegated to the limbo of the past. Little time, however, was wasted by the Rev. Peter in picking out soft words for fear of giving offence. To his impassioned soul "the final doom of the impenitent," the "torment of the damned," and "hell fire" itself, were veritable realities. And so indeed, when rolling from his tongue, did they appear, not alone to the rapt believer, but oftentimes to the ungodly and the sinner as well.

More than one marvellous conversion under his ministration is recorded by Brother Cartwright in the autobiography written in the closing years of his life. At one time in crossing a stream, he was deeply offended by the profanity of the boatman. The kindly admonition and the gentle rebuke of the minister apparently added zest and volume to the oaths of the boatman. Suddenly seizing the offender, the irate preacher ducked him into the river, and turned a deaf ear to his piteous appeals for succor until the half-drowned wretch had offered a prayer for mercy and made profuse promises of repentance. Hopeful conversion, and an ever-after life of Christian humility, were the gratifying sequels to the baptism so unexpectedly administered.

Another experience no less remarkable occurred when, during the early years of his ministry, he was crossing the mountains on his way to the General Conference. At a tavern by the wayside, where he had obtained lodging for the night, he found preparations in progress for a ball to come off that very evening. The protestation of the minister against such wickedness only aroused the ire of the landlord and his family. The dance promptly began at the appointed time.

"Soft eyes looked love to eyes which spake again,
And all went merry as a marriage-bell."

There being but a single room to the house, and a storm raging without, the outraged and indignant minister was the unwilling witness to the ebb and flow of this tide of ungodliness. At length, as partners were being chosen for the Virginia Reel, a beautiful girl approached the solitary guest and requested his hand for the set just forming. The minister arose and intimated a ready compliance with her request, at the same time assuring her that he never entered upon any important undertaking without first invoking God's blessing upon it; and seizing her by the hand he fell upon his knees and with the voice of one born to be obeyed commanded silence and began his prayer. The dance was immediately suspended, and a solemnity and horror, as if the presage of approaching doom, fell upon the startled assemblage. Above the agonizing sobs of the lately impenitent revellers was heard, as was that of the ancient prophet above the din of the worshippers of Baal, the voice of the man of God in earnest appeals to the throne of grace for mercy to these "hell-deserving sinners."

An hour passed; lamentation and groans of sin-sick soul mingled meanwhile with the fervent exhortations and appeals of the man of prayer. Suddenly and in rapid succession shout after shout of victory from redeemed souls ascended, and as if by magic the late abode of scoffers became indeed a very Bethel. The incidents mentioned, and others scarcely less remarkable, will be found in Mr. Cartwright's autobiography. The present generation knows but little of the old-time camp-meeting; as it existed in the days and under the administration of Peter Cartwright and his co-laborers, it is verily a thing of the past.

"New occasions teach new duties;
Time makes ancient good uncouth."

Seventy years and more ago, the country new, the population sparse, the settlements few and far between, the camp-meeting was of yearly and, as it was believed, of necessary occurrence. It was, especially with the early Methodists, a recognized instrumentality for preaching the Gospel for the conversion of souls.

A convenient spot—usually near a spring or brook—being selected, a rude pulpit was erected, rough seats provided, a log cabin or two for the aged and infirm hastily constructed, and there in the early autumn large congregations assembled for worship. For many miles around, and often from neighboring counties, the people came, on horseback, in wagons, and on foot. Each family furnished its own tent, the needed bed-clothing, cooking utensils, and abundant provisions for their temporary sojourn in the wilderness. It was no holiday occasion, no time for merry making. It was often at much sacrifice and discomfort that such meetings were held, and preachers and people alike were in terrible earnest. Rigid rules for their government were formulated and enforced, and a proper decorum required and observed. Woe betide the wretch who attempted to create disturbance, or depart from the strictest propriety of deportment. Not infrequently in the early camp-meetings of Kentucky and Tennessee there were stalwart men keeping guard over these religious gatherings, who had in their younger days hunted the savage foe from his fastness, faced Tecumseh at Tippecanoe and the Thames, possibly been comrades of "Old Hickory" through the Everglades and at New Orleans.

A sufficient time being set apart for meals and the needed hours of rest, the residue was in the main devoted to public or private worship. Family prayer-meetings were held in each tent at the early dawn; public preaching by the most gifted speakers during two hours or more of the forenoon. After a hasty midday meal the public services were resumed, to be followed at the appointed time by meetings for special prayer, class meetings, and love feasts, all conducted with the greatest possible solemnity; and the exercises, after supper had been served and the candles lighted, concluded for the day with an impassioned sermon from the main stand. During the last-mentioned service especially, the scene presented was truly of a weird and picturesque character. The flickering lights of the camp, the dark forest around, the melodious concert of a thousand voices mingling in sacred song, the awe-inspiring, never-to-be-forgotten hymn,

"Come, humble sinner, in whose breast
A thousand thoughts revolve,"

the fervid exclamations as convicted sinners gathered around the mourners' bench and the shouts of joy heard far beyond the limits of the camp as peace found lodging in sin-distracted souls, all impressed the memory and heart too deeply for even the flight of years wholly to dispel.

It need hardly be added that these scenes, of which but feeble description has been given, marked the hour of triumph of the truly gifted of the revival preachers of camp-meeting times. The echoes will never awake to the sound of such eloquence again. The orator and the occasion here met and embraced. In very truth, the joys of the redeemed, and the horrors of lost souls, were depicted in colors that only lips "touched with a live coal from the altar" could adequately describe. In the presence of such lurid imagery, even the inspired revelation of the apocalyptic vision seems but sober narrative of commonplace events.

With camp-meetings and their thrilling incidents of two generations ago in our Western country, the name of Peter Cartwright is inseparably associated. He was the born leader; *par excellence,* the unrivalled orator. Since the passing of Whitefield and Asbury a greater than he had not appeared. To those who have never attended an old-time camp-meeting the following quotation from Mr. Cartwright's autobiography may be of interest:

"The meeting was protracted for weeks and was kept up day and night. Thousands heard of the mighty work, and came on foot, on horseback, and in wagons. It was supposed that there were in attendance at different times from twelve to twenty-five thousand. Hundreds fell prostrate under the mighty power of God, as men slain in battle; and it was supposed that between one and two thousand souls were happily and powerfully converted to God during the meetings. It was not unusual for as many as seven preachers to be addressing the listening thousands at a time, from different stands. At times, more than a thousand persons broke out into loud shouting, all at once, and the shouts could be heard for miles around."

Strange as the following may sound to the present generation, it is one of the many experiences recorded by Cartwright:

"The camp-meeting was lighted up, the trumpet blown, I rose in the stand and required every soul to leave the tents and come into the congregation. There was a general rush to the stand. I requested the brethren, if ever they prayed in their lives, to pray now. My voice was strong and clear, and my preaching was more of an exhortation than anything else. My text was: 'The gates of hell shall not prevail.' In about thirty minutes the power of God fell upon the congregation in such a manner as is seldom seen; the people fell in every direction, right and left, front and rear. It was supposed that not less than three hundred fell like dead men in mighty battle; and there was no need of calling mourners, for they were strewed all over the camp ground. Loud wailings went up to Heaven from sinners for mercy, and a general shout from Christians so that the noise was hear afar off."

That it was by no means an unusual occurrence for those who came to scoff to remain to pray will appear from the same book:

"Just as I was closing up my sermon and pressing it with all the force I could command, the power of God suddenly was displayed, and sinners fell by scores all through the assembly. It was supposed that several hundred fell in five minutes; sinners turned pale; some ran into the woods; some tried to get away, and fell in the attempt; some shouted aloud for joy."

The horror of Brother Cartwrights for "immersionists" and Calvinists of every degree, appears throughout his entire book. That his righteous soul was often sorely vexed because of them is beyond question. That his cup had not been drained to the dregs will appear from a new element he encountered when sent across the Ohio to the Scioto conference.

"It was a poor and hard circuit at that time, and the country round was settled in an early day by a colony of Yankees. At the time of my appointment I had never seen a Yankee, and I had heard dismal stories about them. It was said they lived almost entirely on pumpkins, molasses, fat meat, and Bohea tea; moreover that they could not bear loud and zealous sermons, and that they had brought on their learned preachers with them, and were always criticising us poor backwoods preachers."

The "isms" our circuit-rider now encountered would have appalled a less resolute man. He seems, however, to have gotten along fairly well except with one "female," who, from all accounts, was given over in about equal parts to "universalism" and "predestinarianism." This troublesome female, that he candidly admitted he had *a hard race to keep up with*, he has left impaled for all time as a "thin-faced, Roman-nosed, loquacious, glib-tongued Yankee."

Something of the antagonism of the different persuasions in the good old pioneer days, may be gathered from the tender farewell taken by Brother Cartwright of a former associate, one Brother D., "who left the Methodists, joined the Free-will Baptists, left them and joined the New Lights, and then moved to Texas, where I expect the devil has him in safe keeping long before this time!"

It would be idle to suppose that Peter Cartwright was a mere visionary or dreamer. Nothing could be farther from the truth. He was abundantly possessed with what, in Western parlance, is known as "horse sense." He was a student of men, and kept in close touch with the affairs of this world. His shrewdness, no less than his courage, was a proverb in his day. Upon one occasion, at the beginning of his sermon before a large audience, he was more than once interrupted by the persistent but ineffectual attempt of a saintly old sister to shout. Annoyed at length, turning to her he said:

"Dear sister, never shout as a matter of duty; when you can't help it, then shout; *but never shout as a mere matter of duty!"*

At a camp-meeting on the banks of the Cumberland in the early years of the last century, an attempt was made by a band of desperadoes to create a disturbance. To this end their leader, a burly ruffian, stalked to the front of the pulpit, and with an oath commanded Cartwright to "dry up." Suspending divine service for a few minutes, and laying aside his coat, the preacher descended from the pulpit and springing upon the intruder, felled him to the earth and belabored him until the wretch begged for mercy. The precious boon was withheld until the now penitent disturber, after promising to repent, had been given the humblest seat in the "amen corner." This all satisfactorily completed, and his garment replaced, the minister, scarcely ruffled by the trifling incident, re-entered the pulpit, and with the words, "As I was saying, brethren, when interrupted," continued his discourse.

This little sketch would be unpardonably incomplete if the important fact were withheld that Peter Cartwright had a relish for politics, as well as for salvation. He was more than once a member of the General Assembly of Illinois, and be it said to his eternal honor his speech and vote were ever on the side of whatever conduced to the best interests of the State. In him the cause of education, and the asylums for the unfortunate, had ever an earnest advocate.

Though many years his senior, he was the contemporary of Abraham Lincoln, and a resident of the same county. Mr. Lincoln was, in 1846, the Whig candidate for Representative in Congress. The district was of immense area, embracing many counties of Central Illinois. Newspapers were scarce, and the old-time custom of joint discussions between opposing candidates for high office were still in vogue. Mr. Lincoln's unsuccessful competitor was none other than the subject of this article. The great Whig leader and his Democratic antagonist—"My friend the Parson," as Mr. Lincoln familiarly called him—were soon engaged in joint debate. It is to be regretted that there is no record of these debates. There is probably no man now living who heard them. But what rare reading they would be at this day, if happily they had been preserved. The earnest, inflexible parson,— even then "standing upon the Western slope,"—backed by his party, then dominant in the national government, upon the one side; the comparatively youthful lawyer, whose fame was yet to fill the world, upon the other. No doubt, daily upon "the stump" and at night at the village taverns, the changes were rung upon the then all-absorbing subjects, the Walker Tariff, the War with Mexico, and the Wilmot Proviso. These questions belong now to the domain of history; as do indeed issues of far greater consequence, upon which Lincoln and an antagonist more formidable than Cartwright crossed swords a dozen years later.

At the Democratic State Convention, which assembled in Springfield in the early spring of 1860, a resolution instructing the Illinois delegates to support Stephen A. Douglas for nomination to the Presidency at the approaching National Convention was adopted amidst great enthusiasm. Immediately upon its adoption, a delegate called attention to the fact that the venerable Peter Cartwright was present, and said he knew the Convention would be glad to hear a word from him. Immediately "Cartwright," "Cartwright," "Cartwright," was heard from all parts of the chamber. From his seat, surrounded by the Sangamon County delegates, near the central part of the hall, Mr. Cartwright arose, and with deep emotion, and scarcely audible voice, began:

"My friends and fellow-citizens, I am happy to be with you on the present occasion. My sun is low down upon the horizon, and the days of my pilgrimage are almost numbered. I have lived in Illinois during the entire period of its history as a State. I have watched with tender interest its marvellous growth from its feeble condition as a Territory, until it has reached its present splendor as a State. I have travelled over its prairies, slept with only the canopy of heaven for a covering; I have followed the trail of the Indians, fought the desperadoes, swam the rivers, threaded the almost pathless forests, in order that I might carry the tidings of the blessed Gospel to the loneliest cabin upon the border. Yes, my friends, for seventy long years, amid appalling difficulties and dangers, I have waged an incessant warfare against the world, the flesh, the devil, *and all the other enemies of the Democratic party!"*

XVIII CLEVELAND AS I KNEW HIM

CLEVELAND'S SPEECH ACCEPTING HIS NOMINATION—
MR. BLAINE'S FRUITLESS TOUR AS A CANDIDATE—
CLEVELAND'S INSIGHT INTO HUMAN CHARACTER—HIS
TARIFF-REDUCTION MESSAGE—WITHDRAWAL OF THE
HAWAIIAN ANNEXATION TREATY—HIS VENEZUELAN
MISSION—HIS ACQUAINTANCE WITH THE SCIENCE OF
GOVERNMENT—HIS QUALIFICATIONS FOR SOCIAL LIFE
AND FOR SERVING THE COUNTRY.

Upon the adjournment of the Democratic National Convention of 1884, which had nominated Mr. Cleveland for the Presidency, in company with other delegates I visited him at the Executive Mansion at Albany, New York. The Hon. William F. Vilas was the chairman of our committee, and the purpose of the visit to notify Mr. Cleveland, officially, of his nomination to the great office. I saw him then for the first time.

He was then Governor of New York, having been but recently elected by an unprecedented majority. I recall him distinctly on this occasion as he responded to the eloquent speech of Colonel Vilas. Standing near him at the time were three men well known at a later date as members of his cabinet and his closest friends, Daniel Manning, William C. Whitney, and Daniel S. Lamont.

Cleveland's response to the speech of notification was in dignified, forceful phrase, and at once challenged public attention and gave the keynote to the memorable contest which immediately followed. In some of its aspects it was a Presidential struggle the like of which we may not again witness. As the day of election drew near, the excitement increased in intensity, and no efforts that gave hopes of success were spared by the opposing party managers.

The defection from his ranks by what in campaign publications of the day was known as the "mugwump" element, caused Mr. Blaine to venture upon a hazardous tour of speech-making. Enthusiastic audiences gathered around the brilliant Republican candidate during his Western tour. This, however, as the sequel showed, was time and energy wasted; Illinois and Ohio were safely in the Republican column, and the real battle-ground was New York state. Homeward bound at length from this strenuous pilgrimage demanded by no party necessity, Mr. Blaine was fated during his brief sojourn in New York to listen to the now historical words of Burchard, words which in all human probability proved the political undoing of the candidate to whom, with the best intentions, they were earnestly addressed.

New York, as has been its wont before and since, proved the pivotal State. For many days after the election the result was still in doubt. Party feeling was intense, and the result hinged upon the narrow margin in the vote of Blaine and Cleveland in one State.

During the strenuous days that passed from the election until the authoritative announcement of the result, one man alone, amid the high tide of party passion, remained calm. To all appearances unmoved, Grover Cleveland sat in his office day after day, no detail of official duty failing to receive his careful attention. The fact just stated is explanatory of much in his subsequent career.

When first nominated for the Presidency, Mr. Cleveland had little personal knowledge of public men outside of his own State. How rapidly he acquired the information necessary to a successful administration of the government was indeed a marvel. It was no "Cleveland luck" or haphazard chance that called into his first Cabinet such men as Bayard, Manning, Garland, Vilas, and Whitney. It can safely be asserted that Mr. Cleveland was an excellent judge of men and of their capacity for the particular work assigned them. As if by intuition, he thoroughly understood after a single interview the men with whom he was brought in contact. As an object lesson a better appointment to high office has rarely been made than that of Fuller to the chief justiceship of the great court. No less fortunate was his selection of Vilas to the responsible position of Postmaster-General. And yet both of these gentlemen were personally strangers to Mr. Cleveland when he was first named for the Presidency. His appointments to important diplomatic positions likewise strikingly illustrated his aptness in forming a correct estimate of men from whom his appointees were to be chosen.

No incumbent of the Presidency was ever less of a time-server than Cleveland. "Expediency" was a word scarcely known to his vocabulary. Recognizing alike the dignity and responsibility of the great office, he was in the highest degree self-reliant. None the less he at all times availed himself of the wise counsel of his official advisers. In matters falling within their especial province their determination was, except in rare instances, conclusive. In no sense was his mind closed against the timely counsel of his friends. Far from being opinionated, in the offensive sense of the word, the ultimate determination, however, was after "having taken counsel from himself."

The incident contributing perhaps more than any other to his defeat in 1888 was his tariff-reduction message to Congress one year prior to that election. An abler state paper has rarely been put forth. It was a clear, succinct presentation of existing economic conditions; in very truth an unanswerable argument for tariff reduction. It is not yet forgotten how promptly this message was denounced by the entire opposition press as a "free-trade manifesto," and how this cry increased in voice and volume until the close of the Presidential contest. And yet, in sending this message to Congress, Mr. Cleveland was entirely consistent with himself. Its utterances were in clear accord with the platform upon which he had been nominated and with his letter of acceptance. It is one of the anomalies of politics that the clear-cut sentences measurably instrumental in compassing his defeat in 1888, were upon the banners of his triumphant partisans in the campaign of 1892.

In the year last named, Mr. Cleveland was for the third time the candidate of his party for the Presidency. His nomination, by a two-thirds vote, was upon the first ballot, and marked an era in the history of national conventions. His candidacy was bitterly antagonized by the delegation from his own State, his name being presented by Governor Abbott of New Jersey. It is a fact of much significance that neither in the platform upon which he was nominated, nor in the letter of acceptance, was there the slightest departure from his emphatic utterances upon the tariff in the memorable message of 1887. The salient issues of the campaign were "tariff reform" and hostility to the then pending "Force bill." From first to last Mr. Cleveland was in close consultation with the leaders of his party and advised as to every detail of the contest. The result was a vindication of his former administration and an unmistakable endorsement of the tenets of the Democratic faith.

In this brief sketch, there can be but slight reference to the important questions which now for four years engaged his attention. Almost his first official act after his second inauguration was the withdrawal from the Senate of the Hawaiian Annexation Treaty recently submitted by President Harrison for ratification. Firmly believing that the late United States Minister to the unfortunate island had at least acquiesced in the overthrow of the Hawaiian Government, President Cleveland, with the hope that he might measurably repair the wrong, recalled the Annexation Treaty, as stated. In his message of withdrawal were the words: "A great wrong has been done to a feeble and independent State." This almost forgotten incident is now recalled only to emphasize the spirit of justice that characterized his dealings with foreign Governments.

And yet history will truly say of him that, while just to other Governments, no President has more firmly maintained the rights of his own. This assertion finds verification in the Venezuelan message, which, for the moment, almost startled the country. By many it was for the time believed to be the prelude to war. In very truth, as the sequel proved, it was a message of peace. It was a critical moment, and the necessity imperative for prompt, decisive action. If the Monroe Doctrine was to be maintained, Great Britain could not be permitted arbitrarily to divest Venezuela of any portion of her territory. The arbitration proposed by President Cleveland, resulting in peaceable adjustment, established what we may well believe will prove an enduring precedent. One sentence of the memorable message is worthy of remembrance by the oncoming generations: "The Monroe Doctrine was intended to apply to every stage of our national life, and cannot become obsolete while our Republic endures."

I had excellent opportunities to know Mr. Cleveland. I was a member of the first and third conventions which named him for the Presidency, and actively engaged in both the contests that resulted in his election. As assistant Postmaster-General during his first term, and Vice-President during the second, I was often "the neighbor to his counsels." I am confident that a more conscientious, painstaking official never filled public station. In his appointments to office his chief aim was to subserve the public interests by judicious selections. The question of rewarding party service, while by no means ignored, was immeasurably subordinate to that of the integrity and efficiency of the applicant. He was patriotic to the core, and it was his earnest desire that the last vestige of legislation inimical to the Southern States should pass from the statute books. He did much toward the restoration of complete concord between all sections of the country.

Mr. Cleveland possessed a kind heart, and was ever just and generous in his dealings. Wholly unostentatious himself, the humblest felt at ease in his presence. Possibly no incumbent of the great office was more easily accessible to all classes and conditions. Courteous at all times, no guards were necessary to the preservation of his dignity. No one would have thought of an undue familiarity.

He was a profound student of all that pertained to human affairs. He had given deep thought to the science of government, and was familiar with the best that had been written on the subject. Caring little for the light literature of the day, his concern was with the practical knowledge bearing upon existing conditions and that might aid in the solution of the ever-recurring problems confronting men in responsible positions. He loved to talk of the founders of the Government, and of the matchless instrument, the result of their wise deliberations, declared by Gladstone, "the most wonderful work ever struck off at a given time from the brain and purpose of man." The Constitution was in very truth "the man of his counsel," and, in my opinion, no statesman in ancient or modern times so challenged his profound admiration as did James Madison.

Mr. Cleveland was sociable in the best sense of that word, and the cares of state laid aside, in the company of friends he was an exceedingly agreeable companion. While by no means the best of story-tellers himself, he had a keen appreciation of the humorous and ludicrous phases and incidents of life. I shall not soon forget an evening I spent with him in company with Governor Proctor Knott of Kentucky. The greatest story-teller of the age was at his best, and the delight of the occasion was, as Cleveland declared, "beyond expression."

More than once I have been a guest in his home. During the campaign of 1892, when his associate on the national ticket, I spent some days in conference with him at Gray Gables. The memory of that long-ago visit lingers yet. He was the agreeable host, the gentleman; more than that, the tender, considerate husband, the kind, affectionate father. It has never been my good fortune to cross the threshold of a more delightful home.

I saw Mr. Cleveland last upon the occasion of his visit to Arbor Lodge, Nebraska, to deliver an address at the unveiling of a statue of the late Sterling Morton, former Secretary of Agriculture. The address was worthy of the occasion, and indeed a just and touching tribute to the memory of an excellent man, an able and efficient Cabinet Minister. In my last conversation with Mr. Cleveland upon the occasion mentioned, he spoke feelingly of our old associates, many of whom had passed away. I remember that the tears came to his eyes when the name of Colonel Lamont happened to be mentioned.

During our stay at Arbor Lodge, the beautiful Morton home, by invitation of the superintendent, Mr. Cleveland visited the State Asylum for the Blind at Nebraska City. In his brief address to the unfortunate inmates of the institution, Mr. Cleveland mentioned the fact that in his early life he had been for some time a teacher in an asylum for the blind, and spoke of his profound interest in whatever concerned their welfare. I have heard him many times, but never when he appeared to better advantage, or evinced such depth of feeling as upon this occasion.

The passing of Cleveland marks an epoch. He was indeed a striking figure in American history. Take him all in all, we may not look upon his like again. The "good citizenship," an expression frequently on his lips, to which he would have his countrymen aspire, was of the noblest, and no man had a clearer or loftier conception of the responsible and sacred character of public station. With him the oft-quoted words, "A public office is a public trust," was no mere lip-service. His will be a large place in history. His administration of the government will safely endure the test of time.

"Whatever record leaps to light,
He never can be shamed."

In victory or defeat, in office or out, he was true to his own self and to his ideals. His early struggles, his firmness of purpose, his determination that knew no shadow of wavering, his exalted aims, and the success that ultimately crowned his efforts have given him high place among statesmen, and will be a continuing inspiration to the oncoming generations of his countrymen.

XIX A UNANIMOUS CHOICE FOR SPEAKER

A MEETING OF PROSPECTIVE SPEAKERS—DR. ROGERS WITHIN SIGHT OF THE GOAL OF HIS AMBITION—HE STATES THE GROUND OF HIS HOPE—THE FOUNDATION PROVES TO BE ONLY SAND—A TEMPEST CALMED BY THE DOCTOR.

At a banquet in Washington in the winter of 1880-81, a large number of Representatives were present. Among the number were Reed, McKinley, Cannon, and Keifer. These gentlemen were all prospective candidates for the Speakership of the then recently elected House of Representatives. The best of feeling prevailed, and the occasion was one of rare enjoyment and mirth. Each candidate in turn was introduced by the toast-master as "the Speaker of the next House," and in his speech each claimed all the others as his enthusiastic and reliable supporters. The apparent confidence of each candidate in the support of his rivals reminded Mr. Cannon of the experience of an Illinois legislator, which he requested his colleague from the Bloomington district to relate.

That the reader may appreciate the incident then related, some mention must be made of Dr. Thomas P. Rogers of Bloomington. He was a gentleman of the old school, a politician from the beginning, of inflexible integrity and an earnestness of purpose that knew no shadow of turning. He was as devoid of any possible touch of humor as was his own marble bust of Thomas Jefferson. He was the personal friend of Lincoln and of Douglas, and the political follower of the latter. The fondness of a mother for her first-born hardly exceeded that of Dr. Rogers for the party of his choice. Any uncomplimentary allusion to his "principles" was considered a personal injury, and his devotion to party leaders, from Jackson to Douglas, savored of idolatry. Some camp-meeting experiences in early life had given zest and tone to his style of oratory, which stood him well in hand in his many political encounters of a later day.

For three consecutive terms the Doctor had been a member of the Legislature, and his record from every point of view was without a blemish. At his fourth election, it was found that for the first time in a decade or more his party had secured a majority in the House, to which the Doctor had just been elected. The goal of his ambition was the Speakership, and it truly seemed that his hour had now come.

Soon after these facts were known beyond peradventure, the Doctor came one day into my office. After election matters had been talked over at length and with much satisfaction, the Doctor modestly intimated a desire to be a candidate for the Speakership. I at once gave him the promise of my earnest support and inquired whether he had any friends upon whom he could rely in the approaching caucus. He assured me that there were four members of the last House re-elected to this, upon whom he knew he could absolutely depend under all circumstances. Upon my inquiry as to their names, he said:

"Hadlai,"—the Doctor, it may be here mentioned, had from my boyhood kindly given me the benefit of an "H" to which I laid no claim and was in no way entitled—"Hadlai, you take your pencil and take down their names as I give them to you."

I at once took my seat, and pencil in hand, looked inquiringly toward the Doctor.

"Hadlai," he continued, "put down Heise of Cook. John and I have been friends for more than thirty years; I worked for him for a delegate-at-large to the last National Convention, and he told me then, 'Doctor, if there is anything I can do for you, just let me know.'"

To which I replied, "Heise of Cook, dead sure," and his name was at once placed in the Rogers column.

"Now, Hadlai," continued the Doctor, "there is Armstrong of La Salle; Wash and I were boys together in Ohio, and sat side by side in the Charleston Convention when we were trying to nominate Douglas. He has told me more than once that if ever we carried the House, he was for me for Speaker above any man on earth." At which I unhesitatingly placed Armstrong of La Salle in the same column with Heise of Cook.

"Now, Hadlai," continued the Doctor, after a moment's pause, "there is Cummins of Fulton; I helped elect Jim Chairman of the last State Convention, and he has told me again and again that he hoped he would live to see me Speaker, so I can count on Jim without doubt."

I at once placed Cummins in the column of honor with Heise and Armstrong, and calmly awaited further instructions.

"Now, Hadlai, there is Moore of Adams; Alf got into trouble over a bill he had in the last Legislature; he could neither get it out of the committee, nor the committee to take any action, so he came over to my seat terribly worried, and says he, 'Doctor, for God's sake, get me out of this!' I did, Hadlai, and Alf was the most grateful man you ever saw on earth, and told me then, 'Doctor, I would get up at two o'clock at night to do you a favor.' I can safely count on him."

It is needless to say that Moore of Adams rounded out the quartette of faithful supporters.

"Now, Hadlai," remarked the Doctor, after contemplating with apparent satisfaction the list I had handed him, "if you will give me some paper and envelopes and a pen and some stamps, if you have them handy, I will write to all of them now." The articles mentioned were produced, the letters written, stamped, and duly mailed, and the good Doctor departed in an exceedingly comfortable frame of mind.

Time passes, as is its wont; but for some weeks I neither saw nor heard from the Doctor. Meeting him on the street at length, I at once inquired whether he had received replies to his letters.

"Come into the office, Hadlai, and I will explain." Pained to observe that the tone and air of confidence so perceptible in our last interview was lacking, I followed with some misgiving into his office.

"Yes, Hadlai," he slowly began, "I have heard from all of them. Heise of Cook [the familiar appellations of the former interview were wanting] writes assuring me that there is no man living for whom he entertains a more profound respect then for myself, Hadlai; but that owing to unforseen complications arising in his county, he has reluctantly consented *to allow his own name* to be presented to the caucus."

The name of Heise of Cook was immediately stricken from the head of the list. Then a reverie into which the Doctor had fallen was at length disturbed by my inquiry, "What about Armstrong?"

"Yes, Hadlai, Armstrong of La Salle writes me that in his judgment there is no man living so deserving of the gratitude of the party, or so well qualified for the office of Speaker as myself, but that the pressure from his constituents has been so great that he has *finally consented to allow his own name* to be presented to the caucus."

"Fare-you-well, Mr. Armstrong," was my hurried observation, as the name of that gentleman disappeared from my list.

Arousing the Doctor at length from the reverie into which he had again fallen, I ventured to inquire as to the state of mind of Mr. Cummins.

"Yes, Hadlai, Cummins of Fulton says that in a certain contingency *he will himself be a candidate,* and Moore of Adams writes me that *he is a candidate!*"

It may not be out of place to supplement this little narrative by relating an incident that illustrates the fact that a man wholly devoid of any sense of humor himself may at times be the unconscious cause of amusement in others.

Imprimis: The Doctor, while a member of the General Assembly, voted for a measure known in local parlance as "the Lake Front Bill." The criticisms which followed vexed his righteous soul, and he patiently awaited the opportunity for public explanation and personal vindication.

Now it so fell out that at the time whereof we write there was much excitement—a tempest in a tea-pot—in the little city of Bloomington, over a change in "readers" recently ordered in the schools by the Board of Education. After much discussion on the streets and at the corners, a public indignation meeting was called for Saturday evening at the east door of the Court-house. Meanwhile the indignation against the offending Board intensified, and there was some apprehension even of serious trouble. At the appointed time and place, the meeting assembled and was duly organized by the selection of a Chairman. Calls at once began for well-known orators at the bar and upon the hustings. "Ewing," "Fifer," "Rowell," "Prince," "Lillard," "Phillips," "Kerrick," "Weldon," were heard from the crowd in rapid succession. It was like "calling spirits from the vasty deep." No response was given, no orator appeared; and, as is well known, an indignation meeting without an orator is as impossible as "Hamlet" with the Prince of Denmark omitted.

But sure enough—

"Fortune sometimes brings in boats that are not steered."

At the auspicious moment, from the rear of the crowd Tom Hullinger called out, "Doctor Rogers, Doctor Rogers!" The hour had struck. Without waiting further call, the Doctor promptly took the stand and waiving the formality of an introduction, began:

"I am deeply gratified to have this opportunity to explain to my fellow-citizens who have known me from my early manhood my vote upon the Lake Front Bill," *and a two-hour vindication immediately followed.* No allusion being made to the object of the meeting, or the change of school-books, of which the Doctor knew as little and cared as little as he did of the thirteenth century controversy between the Guelphs and the Ghibellines, with the waning hours the excitement subsided. The change of readers became a dead issue; the era of good feeling was restored; and to this blessed hour, except in a spirit of mirth, *the school-book question has never been mentioned.*

XX A LAWYER OF THE OLD SCHOOL

JUDGE ARRINGTON, THE IDEAL LAWYER—EULOGIZED BY
OTHER JUDGES—BOOKS HIS EARLY COMPANIONS—
BECOMES SUCCESSIVELY A METHODIST PREACHER, A
LAWYER, AND A JUDGE—WRITES SOME SKETCHES OF
LIFE IN THE SOUTHWEST —HIS APOSTROPHE TO WATER
RECITED BY GOUGH.

In the old Supreme Court-room at Ottawa, almost a half-century ago, I saw and heard Judge Alfred A. Arrington for the first time. For two hours I listened with the deepest attention to his masterly argument in a cause then exciting much interest because of the large amount involved. The dry question of law under discussion, "as if touched by the enchanter's wand," was at once invested with an interest far beyond its wont. As I listened to the argument of Judge Arrington, and witnessed the manner of its delivery, he appeared in the most comprehensive sense the ideal lawyer. He seemed, indeed, as he probably was, the sole survivor of the school of which Wirt and Pinckney were three generations ago the typical representatives. His dignified bearing, old-time apparel, and lofty courtesy toward the Court and opposing counsel, all strengthened this impression. He had a highly attractive appearance, and as was said by a contemporary, "to crown all, a massive Websterian forehead, needing no seal to give the world assurance of a man."

"Sage·he stood,
With Atlantean shoulders, fit to bear
The weight of mightiest monarchies; his look
Drew audience and attention still as night
Or summer's noontide air."

Since then I have listened to advocates of national renown in our great court and in the Senate sitting as a High Court of Impeachment, but at no time or place have I heard an abler, more scholarly, or more eloquent argument than that of Judge Arrington in the old court-room at Ottawa, Illinois, on that day long gone by.

The most eminent members of the Chicago bar were the eulogists of Judge Arrington when he passed to his grave, near the close of the great Civil War. Judge Wilson, in presenting resolutions in honor of the deceased, voiced the sentiments of his associates when he said:

"For more than thirty years at the bar and upon the bench, I have been associated with the legal profession; and I may say without offence that of the many able men I have known I regard Judge Arrington, take him all in all, as the ablest."

The venerable Judge Drummond said:

"I have rarely heard a man whose efforts so constantly riveted the attention from the beginning to the close of his discourse. For while he trod with firm and steady steps the path of logic, his vivid imagination was constantly scattering on each side flowers of fragrant beauty, to the wonder and delight of all who heard him. He was a great lawyer in the highest and largest sense of the term —great in the extent and thoroughness of his legal learning, in the vigor and acuteness of his reasoning, and in the power of his eloquence."

The Hon. Melville W. Fuller, the present Chief Justice of the United States, said:

"When he arose to discuss a question, he exhibited a perfect knowledge of every phase in which it could be presented; and men never grew weary (especially if the argument involved Constitutional construction, in which department he stood *primus inter illustres*) of admiring the amplitude of his legal attainments, the accuracy of his learning, the compactness of his logic, and the majestic flow of his eloquence, and more than all, that firmness and breadth of mind which lifted him above the ordinary contest of the forum.

"It is a source of the deepest consolation that he found peace at the last; that the grand spirit, before it took its everlasting flight, reposed in confidence on the Book of Books; that its departure was illumined by that precious light which ever renders radiant the brief darkness 'twixt mortal twilight and immortal dawn."

And yet, alas, his name has now almost passed from the memories of men; the veil of time has settled over him; no distinct image is recalled by the mention of his name. How suggestive this, of the ephemeral fame of even a great lawyer:

  "Swift as shadow, short as any dream
  Brief as the lightning in the collied night."

Words long since uttered by an eminent jurist have not lost their significance:

"There is, perhaps, no reputation that can be achieved amongst men that is so transitory, so evanescent, as that of a great advocate. The very wand that enchants us is magical. Its effects can be felt; it influences our actions; it controls and possesses us; but to define it, or tell what it is, or how it produces these effects, is as far beyond our power as to imprison the sunbeam. In the presence of such majestic power we can only stand awed and silent."

There was much of romance, and somewhat of mystery, that gathered about the life of Judge Arrington. Born of humble parentage in the pine forests of North Carolina, with no advantages other than those common in the remoter parts of our country a century ago, from the beginning he apparently dwelt apart from the conditions surrounding him. At an early age he removed with his father's family to the then wilds of the Southwest.

There, upon the very border line of civilization, his associates for a time were the advance guard, the adventurers and soldiers of fortune that in a large measure constituted the civilization of the southwestern frontier during the early years of the last century. With his early environment, his subsequent career seems a marvel. It can only be explained upon the supposition that through with them, he was not of them.

"His soul was like a star, and dwelt apart."

His companions were his books. Denied the advantages of early scholastic training, he was, from the beginning, an omnivorous reader. He cared little for the allurements and excitement of society. At the age of seventeen, he joined the Methodist Episcopal Church, and was soon after licensed to preach. For four years he rode the circuit, enduring all the discomforts and dangers then and there incident to his calling. His field may be called the *Ultima Thule,* bordering upon the Rio Grande and inhabited by Indians. Untutored audiences were stirred to the depths by his fervid appeals. Church buildings were yet in the future; the congregations assembled in God's first temples, and listened with rapt attention to the fiery eloquence of the delicate, youthful messenger, whose soul seemed on fire.

A gentleman who had heard Arrington writes:

"He was then young, delicate, as brilliant as a comet, and almost as erratic. Without research or mental discipline, he could electrify an audience beyond all living men, and arouse in the minds of those who heard him the wildest enthusiasm."

For some cause, possibly never to be explained, he suddenly abandoned the ministry, began the study of the law, and when a little past the age of twenty-one, was admitted to the bar. After some years of successful practice in the rude frontier courts of Arkansas, he removed to Texas, where he was soon appointed a judge, and assigned to the Rio Grande circuit. In addition to his judicial labors, he now wrote and published some graphic and interesting sketches of border life, vivid pictures of conditions then existing in the Southwest among a people the like of which we shall not see agin, a people upon whom the restraints and amenities of civilized life sat but lightly, who were in large degree a law unto themselves, and with whom revenge was virtue.

One of his publications, "Paul Denton," still has a place in many of our libraries. It is, in part, a narrative of the thrilling experiences of an early Methodist circuit-rider—presumably himself —upon the southwest border. In this will be found his marvellous apostrophe to water, which, as was said by Judge Dent, "was so familiar to the lecture-going public of the last generation owing to its frequent declamation from the rostrum by the temperance lecturer, Gough."

The hero of the book, Paul Denton, had been announced to preach at a famous Spring, where "plenty of good liquor" was promised to all who would attend. During the sermon, a desperado demanded: "Mr. Denton, where is the liquor you promised?"

"There!" answered the preacher in tones of thunder, and pointing his motionless finger at a spring gushing up in two strong columns from the bosom of the earth with a sound like a shout of joy. "There," he repeated, "there is the liquor which God the Eternal brews for all his children. Not in the simmering still over the smoky fires choked with poisonous gases, surrounded with stench of sickening odors and corruptions, doth your Father in heaven prepare the precious essence of life—pure cold water; but in the green glade and grassy dell, where the red-deer wanders and the child loves to play, there God brews it; and down, low down, in the deepest valleys, where the fountains murmur, and the rills sigh, and high upon the mountain-tops where the naked granite glitters like gold in the sun, where the storm-cloud broods and the thunder-storms crash; and far out on the wide, wild sea, where the hurricane howls music and the big waves roll the chorus, sweeping the march of God—there he brews it, the beverage of life, health-giving water.

"And everywhere it is a thing of life and beauty—gleaming in the dew-drop; singing in the summer rain; shining in the ice gem till the trees all seem turned to living jewels; spreading a golden veil over the sun or a white gauze around the midnight moon; sporting in the glacier; folding its bright snow-curtain softly about the wintry world; and weaving the many-colored bow whose warp is the rain-drops of earth, whose woof is the sunbeam of heaven, all checkered over with the mystic hand of refraction.

"Still it is beautiful, that blessed life-water! No poisonous bubbles are on its brink; its foam brings not murder and madness; no blood stains its liquid glass; pale widows and starving orphans weep not burning tears into its depths; no drunkard's shrieking ghost from the grave curses it in the world of eternal despair. Beautiful, pure, blessed, and glorious. Speak out, my friends, would you exchange it for the demon's drink, alcohol?"

In Calvary Cemetery, Chicago, rests all that is mortal of Judge Arrington.

"Tread lightly on his ashes, ye men of genius, for
he was your kinsman!
Weed clean his grave, ye men of goodness, for
he was your brother!"

XXI HIGH DEBATE IN THE MOUNTAINS

COLONEL WOOLFORD, A HERO UNDER GENERAL ZACHARY TAYLOR—HIS MANNER OF FIGHTING—HIS DEFENCE OF A YOUTH CHARGED WITH MURDER—HE MAKES A SPEECH THAT INFURIATES GENERAL FRY.

One of the men not easily forgotten was the Hon. Frank Woolford, a member of Congress from the mountains of Kentucky nearly a quarter of a century ago. He was without reservation a typical mountaineer. He practised law in the local courts, and was prominent in the politics of his State. His style of oratory bore little resemblance to that of the British House of Lords. He had been a soldier in two wars, and his dauntless courage and inexhaustible good humor made him the idol of his comrades. He had been of the heroic band of "Old Rough and Ready" that repelled the charge of twenty thousand lancers under Santa Ana at Buena Vista. He was as brave as Marshal Ney, and it was said of him that the battle-field was his home as the upper air was that of the eagle.

He promptly espoused the cause of the Union at the outbreak of the Civil War and was chosen Colonel of a mounted regiment gathered from his own and adjacent counties. He knew how to fight, but of the science of war as taught in the schools he was as ignorant as the grave. It was said that his entire tactics were embraced in two commands: "Huddle and fight," and "Scatter." When the first was heard his men "huddled and fit"; and when retreat was the only possible salvation, the command to "scatter" was obeyed with equal alacrity. Each man was now for himself, and "devil take the hindmost" for a time, but the sound of Woolford's bugle never failed to secure prompt falling into line at the auspicious moment. "Woolford's cavalry" was the synonym for daring, even at the time when the recital of the deeds of brave men filled the world's great ear.

Woolford and his troopers were in the thickest of the fight at Mill Spring, where Zollicoffer fell; later, they hung upon the flanks of Bragg on his retreat southward from the bloody field of Perryville. More than once during those troublous times our hero was a "foeman worthy the steel" of John Morgan, Forrest, and the gallant Joe Wheeler of world renown.

At the close of the war, Colonel Woolford returned to his mountain home and was in due time elected a Representative in Congress. Years later, with life well rounded out, he met the only foe to whom he ever surrendered, and lamented by all, passed to the beyond.

Some faint idea of Colonel Woolford's style of eloquence at the bar may possibly be gathered from the following. He was retained to defend a half-grown, illiterate youth under indictment for murder. The crime was committed near "Jimtown," but by a change of venue the trial took place at Danville, in the neighboring county of Boyle. Danville, it must be remembered, was the Athens of Kentucky. It was the seat of Centre College, of a Presbyterian theological Seminary, and of more than one of the public institutions of the State. It was the home of men of prominence and wealth, and for three generations had been renowned for the high character, attainments, and culture of its people.

In his speech to the jury in behalf of his unfortunate client, the Colonel insisted that the poor boy at the bar of justice, born and reared in the mountains, without any of the advantages of churches and schools, was not to be held in the same degree responsible as if his lot had been cast in Danville. In his argument he said:

"Here you have your schools, your Centre College, your Theological Seminary, your churches. Every third man you meet on the streets is a minister of the Gospel, and the others are all teachers in the Sunday school. Here you have your great preachers, Young, Green, Humphreys, Yerkes, Robertson, Breckenridge—in fact, Presbyterianism to your hearts' content in the very air. But this poor boy has known nothing of these things. O gentlemen, what might not this poor boy have been, and what might not poor Jimtown have been, with all these advantages?"

Throwing up his arms, in tragic tones he exclaimed:

"Oh, Jimtown! Jimtown! Had the mighty things that have been done in Danville been done in thee, thou wouldst long since have repented in sackcloth and ashes!"

The incident which I shall now relate was told me by my kinsman, General S. S. Fry of Danville. He and Colonel Woolford were friends from boyhood, and comrades in the Mexican and Civil wars. Their party affiliations, however, were different, General Fry being a Republican, and Colonel Woolford a Democrat.

During the reconstruction period, soon after the close of the Civil war, a barbecue was given to the Colonel, then a candidate for Congress, in one of the mountain counties of his district. As a matter of course, the Colonel was to be the orator of the occasion.

In order, if possible, to counteract the evil effect of his speech, the Republican State Committee requested General Fry to attend the barbecue, and engage Colonel Woolford in public debate. In compliance with this request, General Fry, after a horseback ride of many hours, put in an appearance at the appointed time and place. The attendance was general; the people of the entire county, of both sexes and of all ages and conditions, were there. The barbecue was well under way when General Fry arrived. A table of rough boards and of sufficient length had been constructed, and was literally covered with savory shote and mutton just from the pit where barbecued. These viands were abundantly supplemented with fried chicken, salt-rising bread, beaten biscuit, "corn dodgers," and cucumber pickles. To this add several representatives of the highly respectable pie family, and possibly an occasional pound cake, and the typical barbecue is before you.

General Fry, upon his arrival, was warmly greeted by Colonel Woolford, whose hearty invitation *to partake* was not limited to the viands mentioned. The feast being at length happily concluded, and the crowd assembled around the speaker's stand, Colonel Woolford said to his old-time comrade; "Now, General Fry, you just go ahead and speak just as long as you want to. The boys have all heard me time and again, and I have nothing new to tell them, but they will be glad to hear you. When you get through, of course, if there is a little time left, I may say 'howdy' to the boys, and talk a little while, but you just go ahead."

After formal introduction by the Colonel, General Fry did "go ahead," and discuss the financial question, the tariff, reconstruction, and dwelt earnestly and at length upon the magnanimity of the Republican party toward the men lately in rebellion against the Government. Since the surrender at Appomattox, no life had been taken, no one punished, no man ever put on his trial. It was without a parallel in history, and as a matter of simple gratitude, the Republican party was entitled to the support of the entire Southern people for such magnanimity.

The speech at length concluded, Colonel Woolford arose and without even the formality of saying "howdy," or honoring finance or tariff with the briefest mention, proceeded:

"General Fry has dwelt long and loud upon the magnanimity of the Republican party. He has told you that when the war was over and the last rebel had laid down his arms, a hand-shaking took place all around, everybody was forgiven, and the peace of heaven came down like a dove upon the whole Southern people. Yes—a hell of a magnanimity it was! How did they show the magnanimity that General Fry talks so much about? You all remember Stonewall Jackson, one of the grandest men God ever made. This same magnanimous Republican party took him prisoner, tried him by a drumhead court-martial, and shot him down like a mad dog after he had surrendered up his sword."

At which Colonel Fry interposed:

"Why, Colonel Woolford, you ought not to make such a statement as that. Stonewall Jackson was accidentally shot by one of his own men in battle, and his memory is honored by all the people North and South."

To this the Colonel replied:

"Don't try to deceive these people. We don't put on style and wear store clothes like you big folks down about Danville, but we live in our plain way, wear our home-spun and eat our hog and hominy; but if there is anything on earth that these people do love, it is the *truth*. What did this same magnanimous Republican party that General Fry had told you so much about do with General Robert E. Lee? I knew General Lee, I served with him in Mexico, and although we fought on different sides in the last war, I always respected him as a brave soldier. Well, after he had surrendered at Appomattox, and his men had all laid down their arms, what did this same magnanimous party that General Fry talked so much about do with General Lee? Why, they tried him by a drumhead court-martial *and shot and quartered him right on the spot!*"

Again interrupting, General Fry indignantly exclaimed:

"It is an outrage, Colonel Woolford, to attempt to deceive these people by such statements. General Lee was never even imprisoned, and is still alive, the president of a college in Virginia, and highly esteemed by everybody."

The Colonel answered:

"Now, General Fry, you have been treated like a gentleman ever since you came to these mountains; we gave you the best we had to eat, gave you the last drop out of the bottle, and listened quietly to you just as long as you wanted to speak. We don't wear Sunday clothes, General Fry, like you do down in Danville, but just live in our plain way in our log cabins, and eat our hoe-cake, and say our prayers, but if there is anything on God's earth that we do love, it is the *truth*. It is wrong for you, General Fry, to try and fool these people. Yes, this same magnanimous party that General Fry has been telling you about, what did they do with poor old Jeff Davis after he was captured? Now, I never was fond of old Jeff myself, and I fought four years against him in the last war. But I was on the same side with him in Mexico, I saw him head the charge of the Mississippi rifles, and drive back the Mexican lancers after McKee and Clay and Hardin had been killed at Buena Vista, and I know he was no coward. Well, after he was in prison and as helpless as a child, what did they do with him? Why, they just took him out, and without even giving him a drumhead trial, tied him up and *burned him to ashes at a stake!*"

Fry sprang to his feet, exclaiming:

"Great God! Jeff Davis is still alive, at his home in Mississippi, and has never even been tried; it is damnable to make such statements to these people, Colonel Woolford!"

The Colonel thereupon, with a deeply injured air, said:

"General Fry, you and I have been friends a life-time. We hooked watermelons, hunted coons, and attended all the frolics together when we were boys. We slept under the same blanket, belonged to the same mess, and fought side by side at Palo Alto and Cerro Gordo; we shed our blood on the same battlefields when fighting to save this glorious Union. I have loved you, General Fry, like a brother, but this is too much, it is putting friendship to a turrible test; it is a little more than flesh and blood can stand."

Pausing for a moment, he apparently recovered himself from the deep emotion he had just shown, then quietly resuming, he said, "What I have said about the way they treated old Jeff is true, and here is my witness." He called out, "Bill, tell the General what you saw them do with old Jeff."

Bill, a tall, lank, one-gallowsed mountaineer, leaning against a sapling near by, promptly deposed that he was present at the time, saw old Jeff led out, tied to a stake and finally disappear in a puff of smoke. At this, General Fry, without the formality of a farewell, immediately shook the mountain dust from his feet, mounted his horse, and, looking neither to the right nor to the left, retraced his steps to Danville, and without delay informed the State Committee that if they wanted *any further joint debates with old Frank Woolford*, they would have to send some one else.

Years after, seated at my desk in the Postoffice Department in Washington, after I had appointed a few cross-road postmasters for Congressman Woolford, I ventured to inquire of him whether he had ever had a joint debate with General Fry. With a suppressed chuckle, and a quaint gleam of his remaining eye, he significantly replied, *"It won't do, Colonel, to believe everything you hear!"*

XXII THE SAGE OF THE BAR

WITTY SAYINGS OF MR. EVARTS—HE DEFENDS
PRESIDENT JOHNSON BEFORE THE COURT OF
IMPEACHMENT—DIFFERENT OPINIONS AS TO THE REAL
CHARACTER OF THAT TRIBUNAL—MR. BOUTWELL'S
ATTEMPT TO INDICATE THE PUNISHMENT MERITED BY
THE PRESIDENT—MR. EVARTS'S REPLY—EXCHANGE OF
COURTESIES BY MEMBERS OF THE HOUSE.

The late William M. Evarts, at one time the head of the American bar, said many things in his lighter moments worthy of remembrance.

Upon his retirement from the bar to accept the position of Secretary of State, a farewell dinner was given him by prominent lawyers of New York. The appointments, viands, etc., it is needless to observe were all after the most approved style. Somewhat out of wont, however, a magnificent goose with all its appurtenances and suitably dished was placed immediately in front of the guest of honor.

The grosser part of the feast concluded, the toast was proposed: "The Sage of the Bar." Slowly arising, Mr. Evarts surveyed for a moment the dish before him, and began: "What a wonderful transition! An hour ago you beheld a goose stuffed with sage; *you now behold a sage stuffed with goose!*"

It is not entirely forgotten that during the administration of which Mr. Evarts was a part, total abstinence was faithfully enforced in the great dining-room of the Executive Mansion upon all occasions. To those who knew the Secretary of State, it is hardly necessary to say that he had little sympathy with this arrangement, that to him it was a custom "more honored in the breach than the observance."

Now it so happened that at a state dinner, upon a time, a mild punch in thimbleful instalments was served to the guests in lieu of more generous beverages. Raising the tiny vessel and bowing to the Austrian Ambassador at his side, Mr. Evarts in undertone significantly observed, "Life-saving station!"

To a "candid friend"—from whom God preserve us—who once took him to task for his lengthy and somewhat involved sentences, Evarts replied, "Oh, you are not the first man I ever encountered *who objected to a long sentence.*"

During his official term above mentioned, Mr. Evarts accompanied a prominent member of the British Parliament to Mount Vernon. Standing in front of the old mansion, so dear to all American hearts, the distinguished visitor, looking across to the opposite shore, remarked: "I read in a history that when Washington was a boy he threw a dollar across the Potomac; remarkable indeed that he could have thrown a dollar so far, a mile away across the Potomac; very remarkable indeed, I declare." "Yes," replied Evarts, "but you must remember that *a dollar would go a great deal farther then than it does now.*"

This incident being told to a member of Congress of Hibernian antecedents, he immediately replied: "Yes, he might have told the Britisher that when Washington was a boy he sure enough threw a dollar across the Potomac, and when he got to be a grown-up man, *he threw a sovereign across the Atlantic.*"

Mr. Evarts was counsel for President Johnson in his famous arraignment before the Senate, sitting as a High Court of Impeachment. His speech, lasting many hours, was an able and exhaustive discussion of the salient questions involved in the trial. The leading managers upon the part of the House of Representatives were Benjamin F. Butler, George S. Boutwell, and John A. Bingham. The retort courteous was freely indulged in many times by the managers and counsel from the beginning to the close of the long-drawn-out prosecution.

It is a singular fact, and to this generation renders the entire proceeding measurably farcical, that the managers upon the part of the House, and the counsel for the impeached President, were at cross-purposes from the beginning as to the real character of the tribunal before which they were appearing. The latter regarded it as a court, and constantly addressed its presiding officer, the Chief Justice of the United States, as "Your Honor"; while the former insisted that it was only the Senate, and continually addressed the Chief Justice as "Mr. President."

The issues involved were likewise argued by the opposing counsel from wholly different standpoints. The contention of the defence as stated by counsel was:

"We are then in a court. What are you to try? You are to try the charges contained in these articles of impeachment, and nothing else. Upon what are you to try them? Not upon common fame; not upon the price of gold in New York, or upon any question of finance; not upon newspaper rumor; not upon any views of party policy; you are to try them upon the evidence offered here and nothing else, by the obligation of your oaths."

The contrary contention as stated by one of the managers was as follows:

"We define, therefore, an impeachable high crime or misdemeanor, to be one in its nature or consequences subversive of some fundamental or essential principle of government, or highly prejudicial to the public interest; and this may consist of a violation of the Constitution, of law, or of duty by an act committed or omitted, or without violating positive law, by the abuse of discretionary powers from improper motives, or for any improper purpose."

With gulf as broad between managers and counsel as that separating Dives and Lazarus, not only as to the issues to be tried, but as to the nature of the functions and designation of the tribunal before which they were appearing, and with the decision of the Chief Justice upon questions of law arising continually over-ruled by the majority of the Senators, it may reasonably be supposed that there was much in the way of "travelling out of the record" in the heated discussion which followed.

The associates of Mr. Evarts—Stanberry, Curtis, Groesbeck, and Nelson— were the most solemn of men, and whatever there was "bright with the radiance of utterance" to lessen the tension of the protracted struggle, came from his own lips.

Near the close of his speech, Manager Boutwell, in attempting to indicate the punishment merited by the accused, said:

"Travellers and astronomers inform us that in the southern heavens near the Southern Cross there is a vast space which the uneducated call a hole in the sky, where the eye of man, with the aid of the telescope, has been unable to discover nebula, or asteroid, planet, comet, star or sun. In that dreary, cold, dark region of space, which is only known to be less than infinite by the evidences of creations elsewhere, the Great Author of celestial mechanism has left the chaos which was in the beginning. If this earth were capable of the sentiments and emotions of justice and virtue which in human mortal beings are the evidences and the pledge of our divine origin and immortal destiny, it would heave and throw with the energy of the elemental forces of nature, and project this enemy of two races of men into that vast region, there forever to exist in a solitude eternal as life, or as the absence of life, emblematical of, it not really, that outer darkness of which the Saviour of Man spoke in warning to those who are the enemies of themselves, of their race, and of their God."

To the above Mr. Evarts replied:

"I may as conveniently at this point of the argument as at any other pay some attention to the astronomical punishment which the learned and honorable manager, Mr. Boutwell, thinks would be applied to this novel case of impeachment of the President. Cicero, I think it is, who says that a lawyer should know everything, for sooner or later there is no fact in history, in science, or of human knowledge, that will not come into play in his argument. Painfully sensible of my ignorance, being devoted to a profession which sharpens and does not enlarge the mind, I yet can admit without envy the superior knowledge evinced by the honorable manager. Indeed, upon my soul, I believe he is aware of an astronomical fact of which many professors of that science are wholly ignorant. Nevertheless, while some of his honorable colleagues were paying attention to an unoccupied and unappropriated island on the surface of the seas, Mr. Manager Boutwell, more ambitious, had discovered an untenanted and unappropriated region in the skies reserved, he would have us think, in the final counsels of the Almighty as the place of punishment for convicted and deposed American Presidents. At first I thought that his mind had become so enlarged that it was not sharp enough to discover that the Constitution had limited the punishment, but on reflection I saw that he was as legal and logical as he was ambitious and astronomical, for the Constitution has said 'removal from office,' and has put no distance to the limit of removal, so that it may be, without shedding a drop of his blood, or taking a penny of his property, or confining his limbs, instant removal from office, and transportation to the skies. Truly this is a great undertaking and if the learned manager can only get over the obstacles of the laws of nature, the Constitution will not stand in his way. He can contrive no method but that of a convulsion of the earth, that shall project the deposed President to this infinitely distant space; but a shock of nature of so vast energy and for so great a result on him, might unsettle even the footing of the firm members of Congress. We certainly need not resort to so perilous a method as that. How shall we accomplish it? Why, in the first place, nobody knows where that space is but the learned manager himself, and *he is the necessary deputy to execute the judgment of the court.*"

Two of the managers, Butler and Bingham, were at sword's points, and had but recently assailed each other with great bitterness in the House. How all this was turned to account by the counsel will now appear. In vindicating the President against the charge of undignified utterances and impropriety of speech in recent public addresses, Mr. Evarts candidly admits that the Executive, whose early educational advantages had been meagre indeed, and who was confessedly untaught of the schools, "had gotten into trouble by undertaking to be logical with a metaphor."

He insisted, however, that the President should be bound by no higher standard of propriety of speech than that set by the House of which the Honorable Managers were members. The rule governing the House in such matters will readily appear from a recent exchange of courtesies between the two distinguished members referred to above, Mr. Bingham and Mr. Butler. The former said:

"I desire to say, Mr. Speaker, that it does not become a gentleman who recorded his vote fifty times for Jefferson Davis as his candidate for President of the United States, to undertake to damage this cause by attempting to cast an imputation either upon my integrity or my honor. I repel with scorn and contempt any utterance of that sort from any man, *whether he be the hero of Fort Fisher, not taken, or of Fort Fisher, taken!*"

To which Mr. Butler replied:

"But if during the war, the gentleman from Ohio did as much as I did in that direction, I shall be glad to recognize that much done. But the only victim of the gentleman's prowess that I know of was an innocent woman on the scaffold, one Mrs. Surratt. I can sustain the memory of Fort Fisher if he and his present associates can sustain him in shedding the blood of a woman tried by a military commission *and convicted, in my judgment, without sufficient evidence!*"

To which Mr. Bingham replied: "I challenge the gentleman, I dare him anywhere, in this tribunal or any tribunal, to assert that I spoliated or mutilated any book. Why, sir, such a charge without one tittle of evidence is only fit to come from a man *who lives in a bottle, and is fed with a spoon!*"

"Now, what under heavens that means," protested Evarts, "I do not know, but it is within the common law of courtesy in the judgment of the House of Representatives."

XXIII "THE GENTLEMAN FROM MISSISSIPPI"

JOHN ALLEN, MEMBER OF CONGRESS—HE PAYS A COMPLIMENT TO GENERAL WHEELER—HIS MODEST LUNCH—A SOUTHERNER'S VIEW OF PREDESTINATION — A SKULKER'S OBJECTION TO BE SHOT BY A "LOW-DOWN YANKEE"—JOHN ALLEN'S TILT WITH COLONEL FELLOWS.

The subject of this brief sketch is still in life, very much so; and that he

"Shall live the lease of nature, pay his breath
To time and mortal custom"

is the prayer of friends and political foes alike. Who does not know or has not heard of "Private John Allen," the sometime member of Congress from Mississippi? A more charming gentleman or delightful companion for the hours of recreation and gladness has rarely appeared in this old world. He was, while in his teens, a private soldier in the Confederate army, later was a practising lawyer, and in time "reluctantly yielding to the earnest solicitations of his friends," generously consented to serve a few terms in Congress. From his first entrance into the House, he was well known to all its members. No one needed an introduction—they all knew John Allen.

Upon the conclusion of his first speech, which possibly referred to the improvement of the Tombigbee River, he modestly remarked: "Now I am through my speech for this time, Mr. Speaker, *and will immediately retire to the cloak-room to receive the congratulations of my friends."*

Speaker Reed, with whom he was a great favorite, never failed to "recognize" John, and in fact by common consent he was always entitled to the floor. This fact will shed some light upon the following incident. During the roll-call of the House upon a motion to adjourn at a late hour of a night session, Mr. Allen passed down the aisle, with hat and overcoat upon his arm, and, stopping immediately in front of the Clerk's desk, said "Mr. Speaker, —— "

"For what purpose," said Reed, "does the gentleman from Mississippi interrupt the roll-call?"

"Mr. Speaker," continued Allen, "I rise to a parliamentary inquiry. I want to know how General Wheeler voted on this motion." To this "parliamentary inquiry" the Speaker after ascertaining the fact replied that the gentleman from Alabama had voted "aye."

"Well, then, Mr. Speaker," said John, "just put me down the same way with General Wheeler; I followed him four years, and *he never led me into danger yet.*"

Seated one day in the Senate restaurant, I observed Mr. Allen standing at the entrance. Upon my invitation, he took a seat at my table. "What will you have, John?" said I. With an abstracted air, and the appearance of being extremely embarrassed by his surroundings, he replied, "It makes mighty little difference about me anyway," and turning to a waiter he slowly drawled out, "Bring me some terrapin and champagne." Then, in an apologetic tone he quietly observed, "I got used to that durin' the Wah."

After a moment's pause, he continued, "By the way, did you ever hear the expression 'before the Wah'?" I intimated that the expression had not wholly escaped me.

"I heard it once under rather peculiar circumstances," said John. "Down in the outskirts of my deestrict, there is an old-time religious sect known as the 'hard-shell' or 'iron-jacket' Baptists; mighty good, honest people, of course, but old-fashioned in their ways and everlastingly opposed to all new-fangled notions, such as having Temperance societies, Missionary societies, and Sunday schools. They would, however, die in their tracks before they would ever let up on the good old church doctrines, especially predestination. Oh, I tell you they were predestinarians from away back. John Calvin with his vapory views upon that question would not have been admitted even on probation. Sometimes the preacher during his sermon, turning to the Amen corner would inquire: 'When were you, my brother, predestinated to eternal salvation, or eternal damnation?'

"Well, the answer that had come down from the ages always was, 'From the foundation of the world.'

"When I was making my first race for Congress, I spoke in that neighborhood one Saturday, and stayed all night with one of the elders, and on Sunday of course I went to church. During the sermon, the preacher while holding forth as usual on his favorite doctrine, suddenly turning to a stranger who had somehow got crowded into the Amen corner, said: 'My brother, when were you predestinated to eternal salvation or eternal damnation?' To which startling inquiry the stranger, terribly embarrassed, hesitatingly answered: 'I don't adzactly remember, Parson, but *I think it was befo' the Wah.*'"

A comrade of John in Company G was a tow-headed, lantern-jawed fellow who never failed somehow to get to the rear and to a place of comparative safety at the first intimation of approaching battle. He was proof alike against the gibes of his comrades and the threats of his officers. Upon one occasion the approach of the enemy was heralded by a few shells bursting suggestively near the spot where Company G was stationed. The tow-headed veteran immediately began preparations to retire. With threatening mien, levelled revolver, and oaths that would have done no discredit to "our army in Flanders," the Captain ordered the skulker back into line, upon pain of instant death. Leaning upon his musket, and with familiar gaze upon his irate superior, the culprit slowly drawled: "I don't mine bein' muddered by a high-tone Southern gentleman like you, Cappen, but dam if I'm gwyen to eternally disgrace my family by lettin' one of them low-down Yankees shoot me!"

Allen was no exception to the rule that men gifted like himself are subject to occasional seasons of gloom, but his greeting usually came as a benediction. At the banquet table, when dull care was laid aside and he was surrounded by genial companions,—"for 'tis meet that noble minds keep ever with their likes"—his star was at its zenith. Then indeed, all rules were suspended; no point of order suggested—"The man and the hour had met." His marvellous narratives of quaint incidents and startling experiences, his brilliant repartee, sallies of wit, banter, and badinage have rarely been heard since the days of the Round Table or the passing of "the Star and Garter."

Once, however, John Allen confessedly met his match in the person of the Hon. John R. Fellows, who had been Colonel of an Arkansas regiment in the Confederate service; later a prominent leader of Tammany Hall, and was at the time mentioned, a Representative in Congress from New York. He was the "Prince Rupert of Debate," and was gifted with eloquence rarely equalled. At a banquet given in his honor upon his retirement from Congress, a hundred or more of his associates were guests, including, of course, the subject of this sketch. Men high in councils of State, leaders of both parties, and of both Houses, had gathered around the board, and good-fellowship and mirth reached the high-water mark. By common consent Fellows and Allen were in undisputed possession of the floor. Such passages-at-arms no pen can describe. Even "John Chamberlain's" in its palmiest days has never known the like.

Near the close Allen said:

"There is one thing I would like to have Colonel Fellows explain. He was captured the first year of the war, and never exchanged, but held as a prisoner by the Federals until the war was over. I was taken prisoner five times, and always promptly exchanged. I would like Colonel Fellows to explain how it was that he was kept in a place of safety, while I was always at the front?"

When the applause which followed had subsided, Colonel Fellows arose and said:

"I am grateful to my friend from Mississippi for giving me an opportunity to explain that part of my military record which I apprehend has never been sufficiently clear. It is true. I was taken prisoner the first year of the war, and the enemy, well knowing the danger of my being at large, persistently refused to release me until peace was restored. Had I been promptly exchanged, *the result of that war might have been different!* But why it was, that my friend from Mississippi was so repeatedly and promptly exchanged is a question that until yesterday I have never been able to understand. It has given me deep concern. I have pondered over it during the silent watches of the night. Yesterday, however, my mind was completely set at rest upon that question by reading the correspondence—to be found in Volume 748, page 421 of the 'Record of the War of the Rebellion'—between President Lincoln and President Davis relating to the exchange of Private John Allen of Company G, Fourteenth Mississippi Volunteers. The correspondence covers many pages of this valuable publication, but I will read only the closing communication."

And while John with a new supply of terrapin before him was listening intently, Fellows carefully adjusting his eye-glasses and taking a letter from his pocket, continued:

"The letter I will read from President Lincoln concluded the correspondence, and is as follows: *'Dear Jeff:* With this I return you Private John Allen of Company G, Fourteenth Mississippi. I require no prisoner in exchange. The Lord's truth is, Jeff, *I had rather fight John than feed him!'*"

XXIV AN OLD-TIME COUNTRY DOCTOR

THE WRITER AT HIS INN, THE TRAVELLER'S HOME— DOCTOR JOHN, ONE OF HIS EARLIEST ACQUAINTANCES—THE DOCTOR'S LIBERALITY IN ADMINISTERING MEDICINE—A DISAPPOINTMENT IN EARLY LIFE—THE DOCTOR'S IGNORANCE OF THE "SOLAR SYSTEM"—A DIFFICULTY WITH THE LANDLADY— A QUESTION OF ORTHOGRAPHY—THE DOCTOR AS A MEMBER OF A TOTAL-ABSTINENCE SOCIETY.

Upon my admission to the bar in 1858, I located at Metamora, a village of five hundred inhabitants, about forty miles northwest of Bloomington. It was beautifully and *quietly* situated, eight miles from the railroad, and was at the time the county-seat of Woodford County, one of the finest agricultural portions of Illinois.

Metamora contained many delightful families, and a cordial welcome was accorded me. The old tavern, "Traveller's Home," was mine inn, and as a hostelry it possessed rare advantages. The one that chiefly recommended it to me was its extremely moderate charges. Two dollars and a half per week for board and lodging, "washing and mending" included, were the inviting terms held out to all comers and goers. There was much, however, in the surroundings, appointments, etc., of this ancient inn, little calculated to reconcile delicately toned mortals to things of sense. It was of this place of entertainment that Colonel Ingersoll spoke when, in his description of the tapestry of Windsor Castle, he said that it reminded him of a Metamora table-cloth *the second week of court.*

The dear old tavern has fallen a victim to the remorseless tooth of time, but, in the palmy days of Metamora, when it was the county-seat, and the Spring and Fall terms of court were as regular in their coming as the seasons themselves, the old tavern was in its glory, and for all "transients" and "regulars" it was the chief objective point. For a decade or more its walls gave shelter to Judge Treat, Judge Davis, Mr. Lincoln, General Gridley, Judge Purple, and more than once to General Shields and Stephen A. Douglas. At a later date it was upon like occasion the stopping place of Colonel Ingersoll, John Burns, Judge Shaw, James S. Ewing, Robert E. Williams, Judge Richmond, and other well-known members of the bar.

One of my earliest acquaintances in Metamora, and one not soon to be forgotten, was Doctor John—familiarly called "Doc," except upon state occasions. As I write, the vision of the Doctor arises before me out of the mists of the shadowy past. His personal appearance was indeed remarkable. Standing six feet six in his number elevens, without an ounce of superfluous flesh, a neck somewhat elongated and set off to great advantage by an immense "Adam's apple," which appeared to be constantly on duty, head large and features a trifle exaggerated, and with iron gray locks hanging gracefully over his slightly stooped shoulders, the Doctor would have given pause to the McGregor, even with foot upon his native heather. He first saw the light of day in the "Panhandle" of the Old Dominion; the part thereof afterwards detached for the formation of the new State. How this all came about was to the Doctor as inexplicable as the riddle of the Sphinx; but he scouted the thought that he had ever ceased to be a son of "the real old Virginny." He claimed to be a descendant of one of "the first families," and there lingered about him in very truth much of the chivalric bearing of the old cavalier stock. No man living could possibly have invited a gentleman "to partake of some spirits" or "to participate in a glass of beer," in a loftier manner than did the Doctor. Not himself a member of the visible church, nor even an occasional attendant upon its service, the heart of the Doctor nevertheless, like that of the renowned Cave Burton, responded feelingly to every earnest supplication "for the preservation of the kindly fruits of the earth to be enjoyed in due season." And with the Doctor, as with Cave, the question of the *quantity* of the kindly fruits thus preserved was of far greater moment than any mere matter of sentiment as to their *quality*.

The intellectual attainments of the Doctor, it must be admitted, were not of the highest order. He was a student of men rather than of books. He had journeyed but little along the flowery paths of literature. He never gave "local habitation or name" to the particular Medical College which had honored him with its degree. He was, as he often asserted, of the "epleptic" school of medicine. In reply to my inquiry as to what that really was, he solemnly asservated that it was the only school which permitted its practitioners to accept all that was good, and reject all that was bad, of all the other schools. In his practice he had a supreme contempt for what he called "written proscriptions," and often boasted that he never allowed one of them to go out of his office. He infinitely preferred to compound his own medicines, which, with the aid of mortar and pestle, he did in unstinted measure in his office. On rainy days and during extremely healthy seasons, his stock was thereby largely augmented. In administering his "doses" his generous spirit manifested itself as clearly as along other lines. No "pent-up Utica" contracted his powers. It has been many times asserted, and with apparent confidence, that no patient of his ever complained of not having received full measure. There were no Oliver Twists among his patients. It was a singular fact in all the professional experience of this eminent practitioner, that his patients, regardless of age or sex, were all afflicted with a like malady. Many a time as he returned from a professional visit, mounted on his old roan, with his bushel measure medicine bag thrown across his saddle, in answer to my casual inquiry as to the ailment of his patient, he gave in oracular tones, the one all-sufficient reply, *"only a slight derangement of the nervous system."*

He never quite forgave Mr. Lincoln the reply he once made to an ill-advised interruption of the Doctor during a political speech. "Well, well, Doctor," replied Mr. Lincoln, good-humoredly, "I will take anything from you *except your medicines."*

The Doctor was a bachelor, and his "May of life" had fallen into the sear and yellow leaf at the time of which we write. He was still, however, as he more than once assured me, an ardent admirer of "the opposing sect."

In one of his most confidential moods, he disclosed to me the startling fact that he had in early life been the victim of a misplaced confidence. In an unguarded moment he entrusted the idol of his heart to the safe keeping of a friend, in the whiteness of whose soul he trusted as in a mother's love, while he, the confiding Doctor, journeyed westward to seek a home.

"He knew not the doctrine of ill-doing,
    Nor dreamed that any did."

Alas for human frailty, "the badge of all our race." Upon his return after an absence of several moons, he found to his unspeakable dismay that that same "friend" had taken to wife the idol whose image had so long found lodgment in the Doctor's own sad heart. Too late he realized, as wiser men have done before and since, that

"Friendship is constant in all other things
    Save in the office and affairs of love."

The Doctor was much given at times to what he denominated "low down talks" such as are wont when kindred souls hold close converse. Seated in my office on one occasion, at the hour when churchyards yawn, and being as he candidly admitted in a somewhat "reminiscent" mood, he unwittingly gave expression to thoughts beyond the reaches of our souls, when I made earnest inquiry, "Doctor, what in your judgment as a medical man is to be the final destination of the human soul?" The solemn hour of midnight, together with the no less solemn inquiry, at once plunged the Doctor into deep thought. First carefully changing his quid from the right to the left jaw, he slowly and as if thoughtfully measuring his words, replied: "Brother Stevenson, *the solar system are one of which I have given very little reflection."*

It is a sad fact that in this world the best of men are not wholly exempt from human frailties. Even in the noble calling of medicine there have been at times slight outcroppings of a spirit of professional jealousy. That the subject of these brief chronicles was no exception to this infirmity will appear from a remark he once made in regard to a professional contemporary whose practice had gradually encroached upon the Doctor's beat. Said he: "They talk a good deal about this Doc Wilson's practice; but I'll 'low that my books will show a greater degree of mortality than what hisn will."

The Doctor was one of the regular boarders at the historic inn already mentioned. By long and faithful service he had won the honored position of chief boarder, and his place by common consent was at the head of the table. No one who ever sat at that delightful board could forget the dignified manner in which the Doctor would take his accustomed seat, and without unnecessary delay proceed to appropriate whatever viands might be within his reach. As a matter of especial grace upon the part of the good landlady, an old-fashioned corn pone and a pitcher of sweet milk appeared occasionally upon the supper table of this most excellent inn. Such visitations were truly regarded, even by the veterans, as very oases in the desert of life. Now, it so happened, that upon a cold December evening, between the first and second tolling of the supper bell, the boarders in anxious expectancy were awaiting the final summons, in a small chamber hard by the dining-room. To this assembly the writer hereof remarked: "It seems to me, gentlemen, that it has been a long time since we have been favored with pone bread and sweet milk. I therefore move that Doctor John be appointed a committee of one to request Mrs. Sparks to have these delicacies for supper to-morrow night."

A hearty second was immediately given by Whig Ewing, Esq., at a later day distinguished both as an orator and a Judge. Without shadow of opposition the resolution was adopted, and upon summons the boarders were almost immediately thereafter in their accustomed places at the table. Turning to the landlady as she slowly approached with a platter of cold biscuits, the Doctor in most conciliatory tones said: "Mrs. Sparks, at a regular meeting of the borders held this evening I was appointed a committee of one to invite you to have corn pone and sweet milk to-morrow evening." A deep frown at once encircled the fair brow of our hostess. Unlike that of the late Mrs. Tam O'Shanter, her wrath needed no nursing to keep it warm. Advancing a step, and with apparent effort suppressing her emotion, she slowly articulated *"What did you say, Doctor?"* Presaging danger in the very air, the Doctor repeated in husky tones, "At a regular meeting of the boarders held this evening, I was appointed a committee of one to invite you to have corn bread for supper to-morrow evening." At the repetition the frown upon the brow of the fair one darkened and deepened. Advancing a step nearer the object of her wrath, she said, "If *you* or any of the *other* boarders are dissatisfied with my house, you can leave, *and leave now!*"

With the thermometer at zero and Peoria seventeen miles away, and the Illinois out of its banks, there was little that was comforting in her words. The stillness of the grave was upon that little assembly. At length, to relieve the strain of the situation, if possible, the writer inquired, "What was your remark, Doctor John?" to which the Doctor, in a tome somewhat hopeful but by no means confident, replied, "I was just remarking to our beloved landlady, brother Stevenson, that at a regular meeting of the boarders held this evening I was appointed a committee to invite her to have corn bread for supper to-morrow night." To which I modestly replied, "Well, if any such meeting as that was ever held, *it is very strange that I heard nothing about it.*" This kindly observation only deepened the gloom, and perceptibly lessened the distance between the irate hostess and the chief boarder. The latter in sheer desperation at length appealed for succor to Ewing, who until this moment, strangely enough, had been an attentive listener. Thus appealed to, the latter, with Prince Albert buttoned to the very top, and with the statesman's true pose, said:

"I beg to assure you, Mrs. Sparks, that I am profoundly ignorant of any such meeting of the boarders as has been indicated. Had I been apprised that such meeting was contemplated I would have attended and used by utmost endeavor to secure the defeat of its ill-timed resolution. Let me say further, madam, that I am not fond of corn bread. The biscuits with which we are nourished from day to day are exactly to my taste, and even if they were a few degrees colder I would cherish them still the more fondly. In the years gone by, madam, I have been a guest at the Astor, the Galt, the St. Charles, and at the best hotels in London and upon the continent of Europe. None of them in my humble judgment are comparable to this. I assure you solemnly, madam, that I have lingered in this village month after month only because of my reluctance to tear myself away from your most excellent hotel."

With finger raised, step advanced, and eye fixed uncharitably upon the offending physician, the gentle hostess in voice little above a whisper, said, *"Doc, I think you made that up out of whole cloth."* The crisis was reached; flesh and blood could endure no more. The Doctor rose, and waiving all formalities and farewells, "stood not upon the order of his going."

For reasons unnecessary to explain, I did not seek the Doctor that evening nor the following day. Morning and noon came and went, but the chief boarder did not appear. The vacant chair was to those who lingered a pathetic reminder of the sad departure. When, upon the following evening, the surviving boarders gathered to their accustomed places, they beheld in wonderment a splendid pone, savory and hot, flanked upon its left by the old yellow pitcher filled to its brim with rich, sweet milk.

A moment later, and all eyes were turned to the open door through which a once familiar figure moved to his seat. Suddenly stretching both arms to the middle of the table, with one hand the good Doctor grasped the pone, and with the other the pitcher, and holding both aloft as he gazed upon each boarder in turn, exclaimed, "I understand the boarders are not fond of corn bread." In the twinkling of an eye, the Doctor, *the pitcher, the pone had all disappeared from the dining-room,* and the latter two were ne'er heard of more. The poetic justice of the situation, however, was so complete, that no word of complaint was ever uttered.

Some weeks after the events last narrated, I heard the sound of many voices accompanied by peals of laughter coming from the office of Doctor John. Stopping at his door, I soon learned that the tumult was occasioned by a discussion as to whether the Doctor could spell "sugar" correctly. The faction adverse to the physician was led by one William Hawkins, a country schoolmaster. The latter and his allies bantered and badgered the old Doctor to their hearts' content. Rendered desperate at length by their merciless gibes, the Doctor, taking from his vest pocket a five-dollar bill— one I had loaned him an hour before with which to pay a couple of weeks' boards—he offered to bet the full amount that he could spell the word correctly. A like amount being at length raised by the adverse faction, the question at once arose as to who should be the arbiter. Observing me for the first time as I stood at the door, the Doctor declared his willingness to accept me as "empire." It may here be remarked that the honorable office to which I was thus nominated is sometimes called "umpire." Webster, Worcester, and possibly other lexicographers give the latter pronunciation the preference. But the Doctor being "an old settler" and much better acquainted in that locality than either of the other authorities, his preference will be recognized, and "empire" it will be to the end of this chapter. At all events my nomination—for the first and only time—was unanimously concurred in. Stepping at once into the office and confronting the leaders of the opposing faction, I stated candidly that while I highly appreciated the distinction tendered, still I was unwilling to accept the responsible position of "empire" save upon the explicit agreement that, *whatever the decision,* there should be no complaint or grumbling upon the part of the disaffected or disgruntled hereafter; that "empires" after all were only men and liable to the mistakes and errors incident to our poor humanity. To the end, therefore, that an "empire" act with proper independence, it was all important that his decision pass unchallenged. These reasonable requirement being readily acquiesced in, the office was accepted and the money hazarded by each faction carefully deposited in the "empire's" vest pocket. The arbiter now solemnly addressing the principal actor said: "Doctor, the word is, 'sugar'; *proceed to spell.*"

The Doctor immediately stood up. The psychological question, if it be such, is here presented whether *standing* is the more eligible position for the severe mental effort indicated above. Waiving all discussion upon this interesting point, the fact is here faithfully chronicled that the Doctor stood up. Looking neither to the right nor to the left, but standing majestically in the middle of the room, and presenting in some of its characteristics the beauty and symmetry of an inverted L, the Doctor began, "S-h-o-o-g ——" whereupon the little schoolmaster burst into loud laughing. Solemnly warning him against the repetition of such conduct, the arbiter reminded him that such manifestations in the very presence of the "empire," were in some countries punished with immediate death, and again significantly warned him against its recurrence. At the same time the Doctor was reminded that he had not yet completed the spelling of the word. The Doctor replied, "If it is all the same to you, Mr. Empire, I believe I will begin all over again." Permission being granted, the spelling was resumed: "S-h-o-o-g-o-r." To this the arbiter responded, "You have spelled the word correctly, Doctor," and *immediately handed him the stakes.*

One of the interesting events occurring during my residence in Metamora, was a noted temperance revival under the auspices of "the Grand Worthy Deputy" of a well-known temperance organization. A lodge was duly organized, and a profound interest aroused in the good work. During the visit of the excellent lady who bore with becoming modesty the somewhat formidable title above given, the interest deepened, meetings were of nightly occurrence, and large numbers were gathered into the fold. For many days ordinary pursuits were suspended, and the grand cause was the only and all-absorbing topic of conversation.

Chief among the initiated was our old friend Doctor John. His conversion created a profound sensation, and it veritably seemed for a time as though a permanent breach had been effected in the ramparts of Satan. It was even boasted that the Presbyterian clergyman, one saloon keeper, and the writer of these truthful annals were, as Judge Tipton would say, "substantially" the only adherents remaining to His Satanic Majesty. The pressure was, however, soon irresistible, and the writer, deserting his sometime associates, at length passed over to the _un_silent majority.

The Doctor was the bearer of my petition, and in due time and as the sequel will show, for only a short time, I was in good and regular standing. As explanatory of the sudden termination of what might under happier auspices have proved an eminently useful career, it may be casually mentioned that upon the writer's first introduction into the lodge, in answer to the official inquiry solemnly propounded, "Why do you seek admission into our honorable order?" he unwittingly replied, *"Because Doctor John joined."*

This was for the moment permitted to pass, and the exercises of the session reached the high-water mark of entertainment. At some time during the evening, by way of "exemplifying the work," Doctor John had for the second time taken the solemn vow henceforth and forever to abstain from the use of all fluids of alcoholic, vinous, or fermented character.

The hour for separation at length drew nigh. Thus far all had gone merry as a marriage bell. All signs betokened fair weather. Barring the temporary commotion occasioned by the uncanonical reply of the writer above given, not a ripple had appeared upon the surface. It was at length announced that this was the last evening that the Grand Worthy Deputy could be with us, as she was to leave for her distant home by the stage coach in the early morning. Splendidly set off in her great robes of office, her farewell words of instruction, encouragement, and admonition, were then most tenderly spoken. Before pronouncing the final farewell—"that word which makes us linger"—she calmly remarked that this would be her last opportunity to expound any constitutional question that might hereafter arise pertaining to the well-being of the order, and that she would gladly answer any inquiry that any brother or sister about the lodge might propose. Her seat was then resumed, and silence for the time reigned supreme. At length, amid stillness that could no longer be endured, she arose and advancing to the front of the platform, repeated, in manner more solemn than before, the invitation above given. Still there was no response. It all seemed formidable and afar off. In the hope that he might in some measure dispel the embarrassment, the unworthy chronicler of these important events, from his humble place in the northwest corner of the lodge, for the first and last time addressed the chair. Permission being graciously given him to proceed, he candidly admitted that he had no constitutional question himself to propound, but that Brother John was in grave doubt touching a question upon which he would be glad to have the opinion of the chair.

"I understand," continued the speaker, "from the nature of the pledge that if any brother, or sister even for that matter, should partake of liquors alcoholic, vinous, or fermented, he or she would be liable to expulsion from the order. Am I correct?"

"That is certainly correct, Brother Stevenson," was the prompt reply in no uncertain tone.

"I so understand it," continued the speaker, "and so does Brother John. What he seeks to know is this: If in an unguarded moment he should hearken to the voice of the tempter, and so far forget his solemn vows as to partake of alcoholic, vinous, or fermented liquors, and be expelled therefor, would he thereby be wholly beyond the pale of the lodge, or would he *by virtue of his second obligation taken this night,* have another chance, and still retain his membership in the order?"

The official answer, in tone no less uncertain than before, was instantly given.

"No, sir, if Brother John *or you either,* should drink one drop of the liquors mentioned and be expelled therefor, you would both be helplessly beyond the pale of the lodge, even though you had *both taken the obligation a thousand times!"*

As the ominous applause which followed died away, Brother John, half arising in his seat, vehemently exclaimed,

"Mrs. Worshipful Master, *I never told him to ask no such damn fool question!"*

XXV A QUESTION OF AVAILABILITY

A POLITICAL BANQUET IN ATLANTA, GA.—GENERAL GORDON PROPOSED "THE DEMOCRACY OF ILLINOIS"— THE WRITER'S RESPONSE—A DESIRE IN ILLINOIS TO NOMINATE THE HON. DAVID DAVIS FOR PRESIDENT.

About the year of grace 1889, a number of distinguished statesmen were invited to attend a political banquet to be given by the local Democratic Association of the splendid city of Atlanta, Georgia. Among the guests were Representative Flower of New York and General Collins of Massachusetts; the chief guest of the occasion was the Hon. David B. Hill, then the Governor of New York. The banquet was under the immediate auspices of the lamented Gordon, and of Grady of glorious memory. The board literally groaned under the rarest viands, and Southern hospitality was at its zenith. It was, all in all, an occasion to live in memory. I was not one of the invited guests of the committee, but being in a neighboring city was invited by Mr. Grady to be present.

At the conclusion of the feast, a toast was proposed to "The Gallant Democracy of New York." Glasses were touched and the enthusiasm was unbounded. The toast was of course responded to by the distinguished Governor of the Empire State. He was at his best. His speech, splendid in thought and diction, was heard with breathless interest.

The keynote was struck, and speech after speech followed in the proper vein. There was no discordant note, the burden of every speech being the gallant Democracy and splendid statesmanship of the great State of New York.

When the distinguished guests had all spoken, the master of ceremonies, General Gordon, proposed a toast to "The Democracy of Illinois," and called upon me to respond. I confessed that I was only an average Democrat from Illinois; that way out there we were content to be of the rank and file, and of course to follow the splendid leadership and the gallant Democracy of which we had heard so much. To vote for a New York candidate had by long usage become a fixed habit with us, in fact, we would hardly know how to go about voting for a candidate from any other State; and I then related an incident on the question of supporting the ticket, which I thought might be to the point.

In 1872, in the portion of Illinois in which I live, there was an earnest desire on the part of conservative Democrats and liberal Republicans, to elect the Hon. David Davis to the Presidency. He had been a Whig in early life, brought up in the school of Webster and Clay, and was later the devoted personal and political friend of Mr. Lincoln. An earnest Union man during the war, he had at its close favored the prompt restoration to the Southern people of all their rights under the Constitution. As a judge of the Supreme Court, he had rendered a decision in which human life was involved, in which he had declared the supremacy of the Federal Constitution *in war as well as in peace.* Believing that he would prove an acceptable candidate, I had gladly joined the movement to secure his nomination at the now historic convention which met at Cincinnati in May, 1872. For many weeks prior to the meeting of that convention, there was little talked of in central Illinois but the nomination of Judge Davis for President. Morning, noon, and night, "Davis, Davis, Davis," was the burden of our song.

He did not, as is well known, receive the nomination, that honor, of course, passing to a distinguished Democratic statesman of New York.

Two or three days before I was to leave my home for the Cincinnati convention, an old Democratic friend from an adjoining county came into my office. He was an old-timer in very truth. He was born in Tennessee, had when a mere boy fought under Jackson at Talladega, Tallapoosa, and New Orleans, had voted for him three times for the Presidency, and expected to join him when he died. He had lived in Illinois since the "big snow," and his party loyalty was a proverb.

As I shook hands with him when he came into my office, he laid aside his saddle-bags, stood his rifle in the corner, took off his blanket overcoat, and seating himself by the fire, inquired how my "folks" all were. The answer being satisfactory, and the fact ascertained by me that his own "folks" were well, he asked.

"Mr. Stevenson, who are you fur fur President?"

Unhesitatingly and earnestly I replied, "Davis."

A shade, as of disappointment, appeared for a moment upon his countenance, but instantly recovering himself, he said, "Well, if they nominate him, we will give him the usual majority in our precinct, but don't you think, Mr. Stevenson, *it is a leetle airly to bring old Jeff out?"*

XXVI A STATESMAN OF A PAST ERA

ZEBULON B. VANCE, THE IDOLIZED GOVERNOR OF NORTH CAROLINA—HIS LEARNING AND HIS HUMOR— HE RECALLS MEN AND MATTERS OF THE OLDEN TIME— HE SUITS HIS CREED TO HIS AUDIENCE—HIS SPEECH IN FAVOR OF HORACE GREELEY.

A name to conjure with in the old North State is Zeb Vance. What Lee was to Virginia, Hendricks to Indiana, Clay to Kentucky, and Lincoln to Illinois, Zebulon B. Vance was for a lifetime to North Carolina. He was seldom spoken of as Governor, or Senator, but alike in piny woods and in the mountains, he was familiarly called "Zeb Vance." He was the idol of all classes and conditions. A decade has gone since he passed to the grave, but his memory is still green. A grateful people have erected a monument to commemorate his public services, while from the French Broad to the Atlantic, alike in humble cabin and stately home, his name is a household word.

"He had kept the whiteness of his soul,
And thus men o'er him wept."

The expression "rare," as given to Ben Jonson, might with equal propriety be applied to Senator Vance. Deeply read in classic lore, a profound lawyer, and an indefatigable student from the beginning in all that pertained to human government, he was the fit associate of the most cultured in the drawing-room or the Senate. None the less, with the homely topics of everyday life for discussion, he was equally at home, and ever a welcome guest at the hearthstone of the humblest dweller in pine forest and mountain glen of his native State.

Of all the men I have ever known, Vance was *par excellence* the possessor of the wondrous gift of humor. It was ingrained; literally a part of his very being. He once told me that he thought his fame for one generation, at least, was secure, inasmuch as one-half of the freckled-faced boys and two-thirds of the "yaller" dogs in North Carolina had been named in his honor.

Upon one occasion in the Senate, a bill he had introduced was bitterly antagonized by a member who took occasion in his speech, while questioning the sincerity of Vance, to extol his own honesty of purpose. In replying to the vaunt of superior honesty by his opponent, Vance quoted the old Southland doggerel:

"De darky in de ole camp ground
Dat loudest sing and shout
Am gwine to rob a hen-roost
Befo' de week am out."

The summer home of Senator Vance during the later years of his life was in his native county of Buncombe, about twenty miles from Asheville, where for some days I was his guest, many years ago. Leaving the cars at the nearest station and following the trail for a dozen miles, I found the Senator snugly ensconced in his comfortable home at the top of the mountain. He was alone, his family being "down in the settlements," as he told me. An old negro man *to whom Vance once belonged,* as he assured me, was housekeeper, cook, and butler, besides being the incumbent of various other offices of usefulness and dignity.

The first inquiry from Vance as, drenched with rain, I entered his abode and approached a blazing fire, was, "Are you *dry?"* It would only gratify an idle curiosity to tell how the first moments of this memorable visit passed. Suffice it to say that old-time Southern hospitality was at its best, and so continued till the morning of the fifth day, when I descended in company with my host to the accustomed haunts of busy men.

The days and evenings passed with Vance at the cheerful fireside of his mountain home still live in my memory. He literally "unfolded himself," and it was indeed worth while to listen to his description of the quaint times and customs with which he was familiar in the long ago, to hear of the men he had known and of the stormy events of which he had been a part.

His public life reached back to a time anterior to the war. He was in Congress when its Representatives assembled in the Old Hall, now the "Valhalla" of the nation. Events once of deep significance were recalled from the mists of a long past; men who had strutted their brief hour upon the stage and then gone out with the tide were made to live again. Incidents once fraught with deep consequence but now relegated to the by-paths of history, were again in visible presence, as if touched by the enchanter's wand.

The scenes, of which he was the sad and silent witness, attendant upon the withdrawal of his colleagues and associates from both chambers of the Capitol, and the appeal to the sword—precursors of the chapter of blood yet to be written—were never more graphically depicted by mortal tongue.

I distinctly recall, even at this lapse of time, some of the incidents he related. When first he was a candidate for Congress, far back in the fifties, his district embraced a large portion of the territory of the entire western part of his State. Fully to appreciate what follows, it must be remembered that at that time there was in the backwoods country, and in the out-of-the-way places, far off from the great highways, much of antagonism between the various religious denominations. At times much of the sermons of the rural preachers consisted of denunciations of other churches. By a perusal of the autobiography of the Rev. Peter Cartwright, it will be seen that western North Carolina was only in line with other portions of the great moral vineyard. The doctrines peculiar to the particular denomination were preached generally with great earnestness and power. "Blest be the tie that binds our hearts in Christian love," was too seldom heard in the rural congregations. In too many, indeed, Christian charity, even in a modified form, was an unknown quantity.

Under the conditions mentioned, to say that seekers of public place obeyed the Apostolic injunction to be "all things to all men" is only to say that they were—*candidates.*

It so fell out that our candidate for Congress at the time mentioned was quietly threading his way on horseback to meet his appointment. Far out from the county seat, in a wild and sparsely populated locality, at a sudden turn in the road he found himself in the immediate presence of a worshipping congregation in God's first temple. It was what is known in mountain parlance as a "protracted meeting." The hour was noon, and the little flock had just been called from labor to refreshment. The cloth was spread in the shade of a large tree, and liberally supplied with ham, fried chicken, salt-rising bread, corn dodgers, cucumber pickles, and other wholesome edibles. When Vance appeared upon the scene, the leader of the little flock at once greeted him with cordial invitation to "light and take a bite with us." The candidate accepted the invitation, and fastening his horse to a convenient tree, approached the assembled worshippers, introducing himself as "Zeb Vance, Whig candidate for Congress." The thought uppermost in his soul as he shook hands all around and accepted the proffered hospitality was, "What denomination is this? Methodist? Baptist? *What?*" As soon as this inquiry could be satisfactorily answered, he was, of course, ready to join; his "letter" was ready to be handed in. But as he quickly scanned the faces about him, he could get no gleam of light upon the all-important question. Suddenly his meditations were ended, the abstract giving way to the concrete, by the aforementioned leader abruptly inquiring, "Mr. Vance, what persuasion are you of?"

The hour had struck. The dreaded inquiry must be answered satisfactorily *and at once.* That Vance was equal to the emergency will be seen from the sequel.

Promptly laying down the chicken leg, the chunk of salt-rising bread, and cucumber pickle with which he had been abundantly supplied by one of the dear old sisters, and assuming an appropriate oratorical pose, with his eyes intent upon his interrogator, he began:

"My sainted grandfather was, during the later years of his long and useful life, a ruling elder in the Presbyterian Church." The gathering brow and shaking head of the local shepherd would even to a less observing man than the candidate have been sufficient warning that he was on the wrong trail. "But," continued the speaker, "my father during long years of faithful service in the Master's cause was an equally devout member of the Methodist Episcopalian Church."

The sombre aspect of the shepherd, with the no less significant shake of the head, was unmistakable intimation to our candidate that danger was in the very air. Rallying himself, however, for the last charge, with but one remaining shot in his locker, the orator earnestly resumed: "But, when *I* came to the years of maturity, and was able, after prayer and meditation, to read and understand that blessed book myself, I came to the conclusion *that the old Baptist Church was right.*"

"Bless God!" exclaimed the old preacher, seizing Vance by the hand. "He is all right, brethren! Oh, you'll get all the votes in these parts, Brother Vance!"

Talking along religious lines at the time of the visit mentioned, he illustrated the difference between profession and practice. "Now, there is my brother Bob," referring to General Robert B. Vance; "he is, you know, a Methodist, and believes in falling from grace, *but he never falls,* while I am a Presbyterian, and don't believe in falling from grace, *but I am always falling!*"

The first wife of Senator Vance was a Presbyterian. Some years after her death, he was married to an excellent lady, a devoted member of the Roman Catholic Church. Soon thereafter, he was taken to task by an old Presbyterian neighbor, who expressed great surprise that he should marry a Catholic. "Well," replied the Senator with imperturbably good humor, "the fact is, Uncle John, as I had tried Rum, and tried Rebellion, I just thought I would try Romanism too!"

Many years ago, near the western border of Buncombe County, lived an old negro who had in early life been a member of the family of the father of Senator Vance. In a little cabin at the foot of the mountain, "Uncle Ephraim," as the old negro was familiarly called, was, as he had been for two or three decades, "living on borrowed time." How old he was no man could tell. When in confidential mood, he would sometimes tell of the troubles he and his old master used to have with the Tories during the Revolutionary War.

Mr. Vance, in his first race for Congress, having finished his speech at the cross-roads near by, visited the old man, from whom, of course, he received a warm welcome. In reply to the inquiry of his visitor as to how he was getting along, the old negro slowly replied:

"Mighty po'ly, mighty po'ly, Mause Zeb, mighty po'ly forninst the things of dis world, but it's all right over yander, over yander."

"What church do you belong to, Uncle Ephraim?" said Vance.

"Well, Mause Zeb, I's a Presbyterian."

"Uncle Ephraim," said Vance with great solemnity, "do you believe in the doctrine of *election?*"

After a pause and with equal solemnity, the old man responded: "Mause Zeb, I don't pertend to understand fully the ins and outs of dat doctrine, but 'cordin' to my understandin', it's de doctrine of de Bible, and I bleebes it."

"Uncle Ephraim," said Vance, "do you think I have been *elected?*"

"Mause Zeb," said the old man in pathetic tone, "ef it's jest de same to you, I would a leetle ruther you would wifdraw dat question. I's poorty ole and gittn' a little too near de grabe to tell a lie, but de fac am, I bin livin' round in dese parts nigh onto a hundred years and knowed a heap of de big mens dat's dead and gone, and I neber yet knowed nor hear tell of no man bein' 'lected, *what wan't a candidate.*"

Like many other orators of his party, Senator Vance found the position of champion of the Democratic nominee for President in 1872 one of extreme embarrassment. A story he occasionally told, however, relieved the situation greatly. He said: "My fellow-citizens, I am somewhat in the position of an old-time illiterate backwoods preacher, who was with great difficulty able to read off, after a fashion, one favorite hymn at which his book always opened at the opportune moment. One Sunday morning, just before the beginning of the services, some mischievous boys, not having the fear of the Lord before their eyes, got hold of the book and pasted 'Old Grimes' over the favorite hymn. At the auspicious moment the book opened at the accustomed place, and the old preacher, after properly adjusting his glasses, slowly began: 'Old Grimes is dead, that good old man.' Amazed beyond description, the preacher instantly suspended the reading, carefully wiped off his glasses, looked appealingly to the congregation, and again solemnly and slowly began: 'Old Grimes is dead, that good old man.' The congregation now equally astonished with himself, the aged pastor suspended the reading, carefully removed his glasses, and laying down the book, solemnly observed: 'My beloved friends, I have been a-readin' and asingin' outen this blessed book for nigh onto forty year, and I never seed this hymn in thar before; but it's *in thar,* brethren, and we'll sing it through if it smashes up this meetin'!'

"Now," continued Vance, "my beloved brethren, I have been a-readin' and a-votin' of the Democrat ticket nigh onto forty year, and I never seed the name of old Horace Greeley on a Democrat ticket before; but it's *on thar,* brethren, and we'll vote it through if it kills us—*and it does come devilish near killing the most of us!"*

XXVII NOT GUILTY OF PREACHING THE GOSPEL

THE "DRAKE CONSTITUTION" IN MISSOURI—THE CRIME OF PREACHING THE GOSPEL—A PROVISION OF THIS CONSTITUTION FOUND TO BE A VIOLATION OF THE CONSTITUTION OF THE UNITED STATES—MINISTERS OF VARIOUS SECTS TRIED FOR PREACHING WITHOUT FIRST TAKING AN OATH TO SUPPORT THE "DRAKE CONSTITUTION"—THE JUDGE FINDS THAT NOT ONE OF THEM HAS PREACHED THE GOSPEL.

The "holding" of a *nisi prius* judge upon one of the western circuits of Missouri, near the close of the Civil War, is without a precedent, and it is quite probable that no occasion will ever arise for citing it as an authority. It will remain, however, a case in point of how a "horse-sense" judge can protect the innocent against unusual and unjust prosecution.

What is known in Missouri history as the "Drake Constitution" had then but recently supplanted the organic law under which the State had for a long time had its being. No counterpart of the Constitution mentioned has ever been framed in any of the American States. It could have been only the product of the evil days when "judgment had fled to brutish beasts, and men had lost their reason." Possibly at no time or place in our history has there been more emphatic verification of the axiom, "In the midst of arms, the laws are silent."

The "Drake Constitution" was formulated at a time when fierce passion was at its height, when the sad consequences of civil war were felt at every fireside, when neighbor was arrayed against neighbor, the hand of brother uplifted against brother, and "a man's foes were they of his own household." As is well known, certain provisions of this Constitution were, at a later day—upon a writ of error—set aside by the Supreme Court of the United States as being in violation of the Federal Constitution. One of the thirty distinct affirmations or tests of the Drake Constitution was to the effect that, if any minister or priest should be guilty of the crime of preaching the Gospel, or of solemnizing the rite of marriage, without first having taken an oath to support said Constitution, he should, upon conviction, be subjected to a fine of not less than five hundred dollars, imprisonment for six months in the common jail, or both.

Under the provision indicated, a Catholic priest was convicted in one of the circuit courts of Missouri, and duly sentenced to fine and imprisonment.

Upon his appeal, the Supreme Court of the United States reversed the decision of the lower court, and virtually abrogated the provision of the Constitution under which the accused had been convicted. The great court of last resort decided the test oath, imposed as above mentioned, to be a violation of that provision of the Constitution of the United States which declares, "No State shall pass any bill of attainder, or *ex post facto* law." It held a bill of attainder to be "a legislative act which inflicts punishment without a judicial trial"; and an *ex post facto* law "one which imposes a punishment for an act which was not punishable at the time it was committed; or imposes additional punishment to that then prescribed." The court said: "The oath thus required is, for its severity, without any precedent that we can discover. In the first place, it is retrospective; it embraces all the past from this day; and if taken years hence, it will also cover all the intervening period. . . . It allows no distinction between acts springing from malignant enmity, and acts which may have been prompted by charity, or affection, or relationship. . . . The clauses in question subvert the presumption of innocence, and alter the rules of evidence which heretofore, under the universally recognized principles of the common law, have been supposed to be fundamental and unchangeable. They assume that the parties are guilty; they call upon the parties to establish their innocence; and declare that such innocence can only be shown in one way—by an inquisition in the form of an expurgatory oath into the consciences of the parties." And then, as preliminary to the discharge of the priest from long imprisonment, the court concluded its opinion with a pertinent question from the writings of Alexander Hamilton: "It substitutes for the established and legal mode of investigating crimes and inflicting forfeitures, one that is unknown to the Constitution, and repugnant to the genius of our law."*

[*Footnote: Fourth Wallace Reports.]

During the period extending from the promulgation of the Drake Constitution to the setting aside of some of its obnoxious provisions as heretofore mentioned, an old-time judge still held court on one of the Missouri circuits. He had somehow been overlooked in the political upheaval to which the State had been subjected. He had come down from a former generation, and, unabashed by the clash of arms, still served sturdily on his wonted way. The rife spirit that boded destruction to ancient landmarks had passed him by; Magna Charta and the Bill of Rights were to him abiding verities.

Now it so fell out that during the period mentioned, while presiding in one of the border counties of his circuit, he was greatly astonished, at the opening of his court upon a certain morning, to find half a dozen ministers of the Gospel, all of whom were personally known to him, snugly seated in the prisoners' box.

With characteristic brusqueness, the judge at once demanded of the attorney for the Commonwealth why these men were under arrest. The not unexpected reply was, that they had been indicted for preaching without first taking an oath to support the Constitution of the State of Missouri.

"Ah, Mr. Prosecutor, a very serious offence, a very serious offence indeed. The makers of our fundamental law have wisely provided that no man shall be permitted to preach the Gospel until he has first taken an oath to support the Constitution of the State of Missouri. It is the duty of this court to see to it that this wholesome provision of our Constitution is duly enforced."

Addressing himself now to the prisoner nearest him, His Honor inquired: "Is it possible, sir, that you have been guilty of the crime of preaching the Gospel without having first taken an oath to support the Constitution of the State of Missouri?" The prisoner, a tall, venerable-appearing gentleman, in typical black, quietly replied that he could not conscientiously take the required oath, but had only continued in the pastoral work in which he had been for a lifetime engaged.

"A mere subterfuge, a mere subterfuge, Mr. Prosecutor," observed the judge, as with apparent fierceness his eyes were fixed upon the offender. "This prisoner cannot be permitted, sir, to interpose his conscience as a barrier against the enforcement of this salutary provision of our most excellent Constitution. He must be punished, sir, he must be punished."

After reading aloud the penalty imposed for the commission of the offence mentioned, and with pen in hand as if about to make the appropriate entry upon the docket, His Honor again turned to the prisoner and inquired:

"Of what church are you a minister?" The steady reply, as of one prepared for the worst, was,

"I am a Presbyterian, Your Honor."

"Presbyterian! Presbyterian!" quickly observed the sage interpreter of the law. "Oh, you preach the tenets and doctrines of the Presbyterian Church, do you?" An affirmative reply was modestly given.

"You preach," continued His Honor in apparent amazement, "the doctrine of infant baptism, and of the final perseverance of the saints, do you?" An answer like the last being given, the judge remarked:

"You appear to be a man of intelligence, but don't you know, sir, that *that* isn't the Gospel? He has not been guilty of preaching the Gospel, Mr.

Prosecutor, *and will have to be discharged.* You can go, sir, but if this court ever hears that you have been actually guilty of preaching *the Gospel,* you will be punished to the full extent of the law."

Addressing himself now to the comparatively youthful occupant of the lately vacated seat, His Honor inquired:

"What is *your* church, sir?"

In a manner by no means aggressive, and with tones the counterpart of the humblest that ever came from an Amen corner, the reply was,

"I am a Methodist, may it please the Court."

Eying the prisoner keenly, and with a manner expressive of surprise to which all that had gone before seemed indifference itself, his Honor, with apparent difficulty, at length ejaculated:

"A Methodist, a Methodist, Mr. Prosecutor. Oh, you preach the doctrine of the Methodist Church, do you?—infant baptism, and falling from grace?" To these hurried interrogatories, an affirmative was meekly but distinctly given.

"Well, don't you know that *that* isn't the Gospel? He is not guilty of preaching the Gospel, Mr. Prosecutor, and will have to be discharged. You can go, sir, but if this Court ever learns that you have been really guilty of preaching the Gospel without first taking an oath to support the Constitution of the State of Missouri, you will have to be punished, sir; the Court will see that there is no evasion of this salutary provision of our most excellent Constitution. *Go, sir.*"

A clean-shaven, benevolent-looking gentleman of middle age was next in evidence. He had but recently assumed his present pastorate and was a deeply interested and attentive observer of all that was happening. In reply to the inquiry from the bench, he answered that he was a Universalist.

"A Universalist!" replied the judge, almost astounded beyond the power of expression. Recovering himself, he at length inquired:

"You preach the doctrine of universal salvation, do you?"

A slight bow indicated such to be the fact.

"You preach," continued his Honor, with warmth well suited to the subject-matter, "that there is no hell?"

A bow, much more emphatic, was unmistakable evidence that its author was a man who had the courage of his convictions.

"He doesn't believe that *there is any hell*, Mr. Prosecutor," thundered the judge, "he will have to be discharged; it is no violation of the Constitution of the State of Missouri to preach such infernal nonsense as that."

The official admonition, "Depart, sir," was promptly obeyed, and the apostle of the broad highway followed quickly in the wake of the aforementioned disciples of Calvin and Wesley, in the "narrow path" which led straightway out of the crowded court-room.

In rapid succession the two remaining prisoners on the front bench were questioned, and each in turn found "not guilty" of preaching the Gospel. An avowal of his belief in the tenet of "the Apostolic succession" instantly resulted in the acquittal of the first, while the second was with equal promptness found "not guilty" upon his admission that he preached the doctrine of "regeneration by ——" There was much confusion in the court-room at this moment, and the reporter failed to catch the concluding words of the confession. Finding himself, moreover, getting into *deep water*, he thoughtfully left on record that both the Episcopalian and the Christian pastor left the court-room with the admonition ringing in their ears, that if they were ever actually found guilty *of preaching the Gospel* they should be duly punished.

A lone prisoner remained in the dock. The days of the years of his pilgrimage were not few, and quite probably, except in a figurative sense, not evil. He was of sturdy build, quiet manners, and his countenance was indicative of great sincerity. In a voice extremely deferential he stated that he had once ministered to a dying Confederate, and it was impossible for him to take the required oath that he had never expressed any sympathy for any person who had ever been engaged in the Rebellion.

"Of what church are you a minister?" interrupted the judge.

"The Baptist Church," was the answer.

"The Baptist Church," instantly repeated the judge, and looking very earnestly at the accused, he asked;

"Do you preach the doctrines of the Baptist Church?"

An affirmative answer having been given, His Honor said:

"Upon his own confession he is guilty, Mr. Prosecutor: the Court holds the Baptist *to be the true church,* and this defendant has been guilty of preaching the Gospel without first taking the oath to support the Constitution of the State of Missouri. He will have to be punished."

Addressing the prisoner, he said: "You will have to be punished, sir; this Court can permit no excuse or evasion."

The graveyard stillness that now fell upon the little assemblage was at length broken by His Honor reading aloud the prescribed punishment for preaching the Gospel without first having taken the required oath.

"Yes, a fine of five hundred dollars or six months in the common jail, *or both*. A clear case, Mr. Prosecutor, this prisoner must be made an example of; hand me the docket, Mr. Clerk. Yes, the full penalty."

Then, before making the fatal entry, suddenly turning to the prisoner, he demanded:

"How long have you been preaching the Gospel?"

In hardly audible accents, the answer tremblingly given was,

"I have been trying to preach the Gospel ——"

"Only *trying* to preach the Gospel, only *trying* to preach the Gospel!" exclaimed the judge. "There is no law, Mr. Prosecutor, against merely *trying* to preach the Gospel. You can go, sir; but if this Court ever hears that you have succeeded in actually *preaching* the Gospel, you will be punished, sir!"

XXVIII AMONG THE ACTORS

THE GIVING OF PLEASURE THE ACTOR'S AIM—PRAISE OF
NOTABLE ACTORS
—BARRETT, FORREST, McCULLOUGH, EDWIN BOOTH, WILKES
BOOTH, JEFFERSON,
IRVING—MACBETH'S PRAISE OF SLEEP.

On the evening of October 27, 1908, a meeting was held in the Grand
Opera House, Chicago, Illinois, in the interest of the Democratic
candidates in the campaign then pending. The meeting began a few minutes
after midnight, and the immense audience consisted, in a large measure, of
actors and actresses and their attendants from the various theatres of the
city.

After an eloquent political speech of the Hon. Samuel Alschuler and a
stirring recitation by one of the actors, I was introduced, and spoke as
follows:

"I am grateful for the opportunity under such happy auspices, to bid you
good-morning. I would count myself fortunate, indeed, could I contribute
even the smallest mite to the enjoyment of those who have in such
unstinted measure dispensed pleasure to so many of the human family, to
the representatives of a profession which, struggling up through the
centuries, has at last found honored and abiding place in a broader
civilization, a calling whose sublime mission it is to give surcease to
harassing care, to smooth out the wrinkles from the brow, bring gladness to
the eye, to teach that

'Behind the clouds is the sun still smiling';

in a word, to add to the sum of human happiness.

"It has been my good fortune, in the happy years gone by, to have had the
personal acquaintance of some of the most eminent of your profession.
Under the witchery of this inspiring presence, 'the graves of memory render
up their dead.' Again I hear from the lips of Barrett: 'Take away the sword;
States can be saved without it!' 'How love, like death, levels all ranks, and
lays the shepherd's crook beside the sceptre!'

"Who that ever saw Forrest 'sitting as if in judgment upon kings' could
forget that superb presence? In the silent watches, even yet, steal upon us in
ominous accents the words, 'Put out the light, and then put out the light!'
Complimented upon the manner in which he played Lear, he angrily
exclaimed: 'Played Lear, played Lear? I *play* Hamlet, I *play* Macbeth, I *play*

Othello; but I *am* Lear!' Possibly the art of the tragedian has known no loftier triumph than in Forrest's rendition of Lear's curse upon the unnatural daughter:

'Let it stamp wrinkles in her brow of youth;
With cadent tears fret channels in her cheeks;
Turn all her mother's pains and benefits
To laughter and contempt!'

"A third of a century ago, I made the acquaintance of John McCullough, then at the very zenith of his fame. In even measure as was the elder Booth Richard the Third, Forrest, King Lear, or Edwin Booth, Hamlet, so was McCullough the born Macbeth. When I first saw him emerge with dishevelled hair and bloody hands from the apartment of the murdered king, I was, I confess, in mortal dread of the darkness. I have heard another since of even greater repute in that masterful impersonation, but with me to the last, John McCullough will remain the veritable Macbeth. His are the words that linger:

'I go, and it is done; the bell invites me,
Hear it not, Duncan; for it is the knell
That summons thee to heaven or to hell.'

"Edwin Booth has stepped from the stage of living men, and when in the tide of time will such a Hamlet again appear? To him Nature had been prodigal of her choicest blessings. Every gift the gods could bestow to the full equipment of the interpreter, the actor, the master, was his.

'He was a man, take him for all in all,
We shall not look upon his like again.'

Many moons will wax and wane before from other lips, as from his, will fall:

'Or that the Everlasting had not fixed
His canon 'gainst self-slaughter.'

or, giving expression to thoughts from the very depths, which have in all the ages held back from such dread ending:

'To die, to sleep;
To sleep! perchance to dream; aye, there's the rub;
For in that sleep of death what dreams may come,
When we have shuffled off this mortal coil,
Must give us pause.'

"The ever-abiding memory that his brother was the real actor in a tragic scene that gave pause to the world, burdened the heart and mellowed the tone of Edwin Booth, and no doubt linked him in closer touch with what has, as by the enchanter's wand, been portrayed of the 'melancholy Dane.'

"Two years before the assassination of President Lincoln I heard Wilkes Booth as Romeo at the old McVicker. The passing years have not wholly dimmed his

'Night's candles are burnt out, and jocund day
Stands tiptoe on the misty mountain-tops,'

and then, as if forecasting a scene to strike horror even in 'States unborn and in accents yet unknown,' the exclamation:

'I must be gone and live,
Or stay and die!'

"High on the list of the world's benefactors write the name of Joe Jefferson, as one who loved his fellow-men. Whatever betide, his fame is secure. 'Age cannot wither'; it was in very truth high privilege to have known him; to have met him face to face.

"There come moments to all when we gladly put aside the masterpieces of the great bard, and find solace in simpler lays; such as, it may be, appear of kinship with the happenings of daily life. The mighty thoughts of the former unceasingly suggest life's endless toil and endeavor.

"In words that have touched many hearts our own poet suggests:

'Read from some humbler poet,
Whose songs gushed from his heart;
. . . .
Such songs have power to quiet
The restless pulse of care.'

"And so, there are times when the stately rendition of the masterpieces, even with the greatest tragedians in the role, weary us, and we give glad welcome to Bob Acres with 'his courage oozing out at his finger ends,' or to dear old Rip and 'Here's to yourself and to your family. Jus' one more; *this one won't count!*'

"The superb acting of Irving in Louis the Eleventh; the grandeur of Forrest with 'Othello's occupation gone'; of McCullough in Macbeth, 'supped full with horrors'; even of Booth with the ever-recurring 'To be, or not to be,' the eternal question, all pass with the occasion. But who can forget the gladsome hours of mingled pathos and mirth with glorious Joe Jefferson, the star! His life was hourly the illustration of the sublime truth:

'There is nothing so kingly as kindness.'

"Upon his tablet might truly be written:

'He never made a brow look dark,
Nor caused a tear but when he died.'

"It is ever an ungracious task to speak in terms of disparagement of a lady. There is one, however, of whom, even in this gracious presence, I am constrained to speak without restraint. To the splendid assemblage before me she was unknown; possibly, however, some veteran upon this platform may have enjoyed her personal acquaintance. I refer to the late Mrs. Macbeth. I would not be misunderstood. My criticism of the conduct of this lady has no reference to her share in the 'taking off' of the venerable Duncan. Even barring her gentle interposition, he would long ere this have 'paid his breath to time and mortal custom.' My cause of complaint is more serious and far-reaching. It will be remembered that her high-placed husband upon a time was the victim of insomnia. In his wakeful hours, as he tossed upon his couch, he even made the confession, now of record, that

'Glamis hath murdered sleep.'

"He apparently drew no comfort from the reflection that his late benefactor, the murdered king,

'After life's fitful fever he sleeps well.'

"Burdened with thoughts beyond the reaches of our souls, the sometimes Thane of Cawdor indulged in an apostrophe to 'the dull god' which has enduring place in all language:

'Sleep, that knits up the ravell'd sleave of care
The death of each day's life, sore labour's bath,
Balm of hurt minds, great nature's second course,
Chief nourisher in Life's feast, ——'

"At this crucial moment, came the untimely interruption of Mrs. Macbeth, demanding of her husband, *'What do you mean?'*

"The spell was broken, and for all time the sublime apostrophe to sleep unfinished. What he might next have said, whose lips can tell? Words possibly to be spoken by every tongue, to be crystallized into every language. Her ill-fated interruption can never be forgiven. The practical lesson to be drawn, one for all the ages, is the peril involved in a wife's *untimely interruption* of the wise observations and sage reflections of her husband.

"This coming together to-night may justify the remark that satire upon the proverbial caution of candidates in expressing an opinion *upon any subject* was perhaps never better illustrated than in the incident now to be related. Upon a time many years ago, when approaching the Capitol from Pennsylvania Avenue in company with my friend Proctor Knott, a tall, solemn-appearing individual addressed the latter as follows; 'Mr. Knott, I would like to have your opinion as to which is the best play, "Hamlet" or "Macbeth."' With a characteristic expression of countenance, Knott, with deprecatory gesture, slowly replied:

"'My friend, don't ask me that question; I am a politician, a candidate for Congress, and my district is about equally divided; Hamlet has his friends down there, and Macbeth has his, and *I will take no part between them.'*

"This observation recalls an incident of recent occurrence in a neighboring city. A friend of mine, a minister of the Gospel—you will bear in mind that my friends are not *all* actors—and this recalls the dilemma of a candidate who, upon inquiry as to the comparative merits of heaven and its antipode, cautiously declined to express an opinion, on the ground that *he had friends in both places*—this minister, upon being installed in a new pastorate, was almost immediately requested to preach at the funeral of a prominent member of his congregation. Unacquainted as he was with the life of the deceased, he made inquiry as to his last utterances.

"He recalled the last words of Webster, 'I am content'; of John Quincy Adams, 'This is the last of earth'; and even the cheerless exclamation of Mirabeau, 'Let my ears be filled with martial music, crown me with flowers, and thus shall I enter on my eternal sleep.' Charged with these reflections, and hoping to find the nucleus of a funeral sermon, the minister made inquiry of the son of the deceased parishioner, 'What were the last words of your father?' The unexpected reply was 'Pap he didn't have *no last words;* mother she just stayed by him till he died.'

"And now, my friends, as the curtain falls, my last words to you:

'Say not Good-night,
But in some brighter clime
Bid me Good-morning!'"

XXIX THE LOST ART OF ORATORY

DANIEL WEBSTER'S SPEECHES—HIS PATRIOTIC SERVICE
IN FORMULATING THE ASHBURTON TREATY—
PRENTISS'S DEFENCE OF THE RIGHT OF MISSISSIPPI TO
REPRESENTATION—THE EFFECT OF HIS ELOQUENCE
ON A MURDERER—HIS PLEA FOR MERCY TO A CLIENT—
WEBSTER WINS AN APPARENTLY HOPELESS CASE—
INGERSOLL'S REVIEW OF THE CAREER OF NAPOLEON—
HON. ISAAC N. PHILLIPS'S EULOGY UPON ABRAHAM
LINCOLN—SENATOR INGALLS'S TRIBUTE TO A
COLLEAGUE—A SINGLE ELOQUENT SENTENCE FROM
EDWARD EVERETT— SPEECH OF NOMINATION FOR
WILLIAM J. BRYAN—MR. BRYAN'S ELOQUENCE —CLOSING
SENTENCES OF HIS "PRINCE OF PEACE."

One of the must cultured and entertaining gentlemen I have ever known was the late Gardner Hubbard. His last years were spent quietly in Washington, but earlier in life he was an active member of the Massachusetts bar.

In my conversations with him he related many interesting incidents of Daniel Webster, with whom he was well acquainted. In the early professional life of Hubbard, Mr. Webster was still at the bar; his speech for the prosecution in the memorable Knapp murder trial has been read with profound interest by three generations of lawyers. As a powerful and eloquent discussion of circumstantial evidence, in all its phases, it scarcely has a parallel; quotations from it have found their way into all languages. How startling his description of the stealthy tread of the assassin upon his victim! We seem to stand in the very presence of murder itself:

"Deep sleep had fallen on the destined victim and on all beneath his roof. A healthful old man, to whom sleep was sweet, and the first sound slumbers of the night held him in their soft but strong embrace. The assassin enters through the window, already prepared, into an unoccupied apartment. With noiseless foot he paces the lonely hall, half lighted by the moon; he winds up the ascent of the stairs, and reaches to door of the chamber .... The face of the innocent sleeper is turned from the murderer, and the beams of the moon, resting on the gray locks of his aged temple, show him where to strike. The fatal blow is given, and the victim passes, without a struggle, from the repose of sleep to the repose of death. The deed is done. He retreats, retraces his steps to the window, passes out through it as he came in, and escapes. He has done the murder. No eye has seen him, no ear has heard him. The secret is his own, and it is safe."

The speech throughout shows Webster to have been the perfect master of the human heart,—of its manifold and mysterious workings. What picture could be more vivid than this?

"Such a secret can be safe nowhere. The whole creation of God has neither nook nor corner where the guilty can bestow it and say it is safe. Not to speak of that eye which pierces through all disguises and beholds everything as in the splendor of noon, such secrets of guilt are never safe from detection even by men. True it is, generally speaking, that murder will out. True it is, that Providence hath so ordained, and doth so govern things, that those who break the great law of Heaven by shedding man's blood seldom succeed in avoiding discovery. Meantime the guilty soul cannot keep its own secret. It is false to itself; or rather, it feels an irresistible impulse of conscience to be true to itself. It labors under its guilty possession, and knows not what to do with it. The human heart was not made for the residence of such an inhabitant."

The closing sentences of the speech—which resulted in the conviction and execution of the prisoner—will endure in our literature unsurpassed as an inspiration to duty:

"There is no evil that we cannot either face or fly from but the consciousness of duty disregarded. A sense of duty pursues us ever. It is omnipresent like the Deity. If we take to ourselves the wings of the morning and dwell in the uttermost parts of the sea, duty performed, or duty violated, is still with us, for our happiness or our misery. If we say, 'the darkness shall cover us,' in the darkness as in the light our obligations are yet with us. We cannot escape their power, nor fly from their presence. They are with us in this life, will be with us at its close; and in that scene of inconceivable solemnity which lies yet farther onward, we shall still find ourselves surrounded by the consciousness of duty, to pain us wherever it has been violated, and to console us so far as God may have given us grace to perform it."

Upon one occasion, when in Boston, Mr. Hubbard and I visited together Faneuil Hall. He pointed out the exact place upon the platform where he saw Mr. Webster stand when he delivered his speech in vindication of his course in remaining in the Cabinet of President Tyler after all his Whig colleagues had resigned. The schism in the Whig ranks, occasioned by the veto of party measures, paramount in the Presidential contest of 1840, and the bitter antagonism thereby engendered between Henry Clay and President Tyler, will readily be recalled. The rupture mentioned occasioned the retirement of the entire Cabinet appointed by the late President

Harrison, except Mr. Webster, the Secretary of State. His reasons for remaining were in the highest degree patriotic, and his speech in Faneuil Hall a triumphant vindication. The enduring public service he rendered while in a Cabinet with which he had not partisan affiliation was formulating, in conjunction with the British Minister, the Ashburton treaty. If Mr. Webster had rendered no other public service, this alone would have entitled him to the gratitude of the country. This treaty, advantageous from so many points of view to the United States, adjusted amicably the protracted and perilous controversy—unsettled by the convention at Ghent—of our northeastern boundary, and possibly prevented a third war between the two great English-speaking nations. The words once uttered of Burke could never with truth be spoken of Webster: "He gave to party that which was intended for his country."

Mr. Hubbard insisted that the speech mentioned stood unrivalled in the realm of sublime oratory. He declared that the intervening years had not dimmed his recollection of the appearance of "the God-like Webster" when he exclaimed "The Whig party die! The Whig party die! Then, Mr. President, *where shall I go?"*

Some years before, I heard Wendell Phillips allude to the above speech in his celebrated lecture upon Daniel O'Connell. He said, when the startling words, "Then, Mr. President, where shall I go?" fell from the lips of the mighty orator, a feeling of awe pervaded the vast assemblage; something akin to an awful foreboding that the world would surely come to an end when there was no place in it for Daniel Webster.

This seems a fitting place to allude to possibly the highest tribute ever paid by one great orator to another—in the loftiest sense, a tribute of genius to genius. Mr. Hubbard told me he was one of the immense audience gathered in Faneuil Hall to ratify the nomination of Harrison and Tyler soon after the adjournment of the Whig National Convention in 1840. Edward Everett presided; and among the speakers were Winthrop, Choate, Webster, and the gifted Sargent S. Prentiss of Mississippi. The eloquence of the last named was a proverb in his day. He had but recently delivered a speech in the House, vindicating his right to his seat as a Representative from Mississippi, which cast a spell over all who heard it, and which has come down to the present generation as one of the masterpieces of oratory. The closing sentence of this wondrous speech—a thousand times quoted—was: "Deny her representation upon this floor; then, Mr. Speaker, strike from yonder escutcheon the star that glitters to the name of Mississippi—and leave only the stripe, fit emblem of her degradation!"

Upon the conclusion of Prentiss's Faneuil Hall speech, just mentioned, amidst a tumult of applause such as even Faneuil Hall had rarely witnessed,

Mr. Everett, turning to Mr. Webster, inquired: "Did you ever hear the equal of that speech?" "Never but once," was the deep-toned reply, "and then from Prentiss himself."

Judge Baldwin, his long-time associate at the bar of Mississippi, has given a vivid description of the effect of the power of Mr. Prentiss before the jury in the prosecution of a noted highwayman and murderer in that State:

"Phelps was one of the most daring and desperate of ruffians. He fronted his prosecutor and the court not only with composure, but with scornful and malignant defiance. When Prentiss arose to speak, and for some time afterwards, the criminal scowled upon him a look of hate and insolence. But when the orator, kindling with his subject, turned upon him and poured down a stream of burning invective like lava upon his head; when he depicted the villainy and barbarity of his bold atrocities; when he pictured, in dark and dismal colors, the fate which awaited him, and the awful judgment to be pronounced at another Bar upon his crimes when his soul be confronted with his innocent victims; when he fixed his gaze of concentrated power upon him, the strong man's face relaxed; his eyes faltered and fell; until, at length, unable to bear up under self-conviction, he hid his head beneath the bar, and exhibited a picture of ruffianly audacity cowed beneath the spell of true courage and triumphant genius."

In his early practice in Mississippi, in closing a touching and eloquent appeal to the jury on behalf of a client whose life was trembling in the balance, Prentiss said:

"I have somewhere read that when God in His eternal councils conceived the thought of man's creation, he called to him the three ministers who wait constantly upon the throne, Justice, Truth, and Mercy, and thus addressed them:

"'Shall we make man?'

"Then said Justice, 'O God, make him not, for he will trample upon Thy laws.'

"Truth made answer also, 'O God, make him not, for he will pollute Thy sanctuaries.'

"Then Mercy, dropping upon her knees and looking up through her tears, exclaimed, 'O God, make him. I will watch over him through all the dark paths he may have to tread.'

"Then God made man and said to him: 'Thou art the child of Mercy; *go and deal in mercy with thy brother.*'"

In speaking of Mr. Webster's marvellous power over a jury, Mr. Hubbard told me that he was present during the trial of a once celebrated divorce case in one of the courts of Boston. The husband was the complainant, and the alleged ground the one of recognized sufficiency in all countries. Mr. Webster was the counsel for the husband; Rufus Choate for the wife. As an advocate, the latter has had few equals, no superiors, at the American bar. In the case mentioned, with a distressed woman for a client, what was dearer than life, her reputation, in the balance, it may well be believed that the wondrous powers of the advocate were in requisition to the utmost.

At the conclusion of Choate's speech, as Mr. Hubbard assured me, the case of the injured husband appeared hopeless. It seemed impossible that such a speech could be successfully answered.

The opening sentence, in deep and measured tones, of Webster in reply, the prelude to an unrivalled argument and to victory, was:

"Saint Paul in the twenty-fourth verse of the seventh chapter of his wondrous Epistle to the Romans says: 'O wretched man that I am! who shall deliver me from the body of this death?' You alone, gentlemen, can deliver this wretched man *from the body of this dead woman!*"

What in word-painting can exceed the following from an address by Robert G. Ingersoll?

"A little while ago, I stood by the grave of the old Napoleon—a magnificent tomb of gilt and gold, almost fit for a dead deity— and gazed upon the sarcophagus of black Egyptian marble where rest the ashes of that restless man. I leaned over the balustrade and thought about the career of the greatest soldier of the modern world.

"I saw him walking upon the banks of the Seine contemplating suicide. I saw him at Toulon; I saw him putting down the mob in the streets of Paris; I saw him at the head of the army in Italy; I saw him crossing the bridge at Lodi with the tricolor in his hand; I saw him in Egypt in the shadow of the Pyramids; I saw him conquer the Alps and mingle the eagles of France with the eagles of the crags; I saw him at Marengo, at Ulm, and at Austerlitz; I saw him in Russia, where the infantry of the snow and the cavalry of the wild blast scattered his legions like winter's withered leaves; I saw him at Leipsic in defeat and disaster—driven by a million bayonets back upon Paris—clutched like a wild beast—banished to Elba. I saw him escape and retake an empire by the force of his genius. I saw him upon the frightful field of Waterloo, where Chance and Fortune combined to wreck the fortunes of their former king, and I saw him at St. Helena, with his hands crossed behind him, gazing out upon the sad and solemn sea.

"I thought of the orphans and widows he had made, of the tears that had been shed for his glory, and of the only woman who ever loved him, pushed from his heart by the cold hand of ambition; and I said I would rather have been a French peasant and worn wooden shoes; I would rather have lived in a hut with a vine growing over the door, and the grapes growing purple in the rays of the autumn sun; I would rather have been that poor peasant with my loving wife by my side, knitting as the day died out of the sky, with my children about my knee and their arms about me; I would rather have been that man and gone down to the tongueless silence of the dreamless dust, than have been that imperial impersonation of force and murder."

In his eloquent eulogy upon Abraham Lincoln, my neighbor and friend, Hon. Isaac N. Phillips, said:

"He lived with Nature and learned of her. He toiled, but his toil was never hopeless and degrading. His feet were upon the earth but the stars shining in perennial beauty were ever above him to inspire contemplation. He heard the song of the thrush, and the carol of the lark. He watched the sun in its course. He knew the dim paths of the forest, and his soul was awed by the power of the storm."

The closing sentences of Senator Ingalls's tribute to a departed colleague were sombre indeed:

"In the democracy of Death all men are equal. There is neither rank, nor station, nor prerogative, in the republic of the grave. At that fatal threshold the philosopher ceases to be wise, and the song of the poet is silent. There Dives relinquished his riches and Lazarus his rags; the creditor loses his usury, and the debtor is acquitted of his obligation; the proud man surrenders his dignity, the politician his honors, the worldling his pleasures. Here the invalid needs no physician, and the laborer rests from unrequited toil. Here at last is Nature's final decree of equity. The wrongs of time are redressed, and injustice is expiated. The unequal distribution of wealth and honor, capacity, pleasure, and opportunity, which makes life so cruel and inexplicable a tragedy, ceases in the realms of Death. The strongest has there no supremacy, and the weakest needs no defence. The mightiest captain succumbs to the invincible adversary who disarms alike the victor and the vanquished."

In his day Edward Everett was the most gifted of American orators. His style, however, to readers in "these piping times of peace," seems a trifle stilted. What orator of the twentieth century would attempt such a sentence as the following from Everett's celebrated eulogy upon Washington:

"Let us make a national festival and holiday of his birthday; and ever, as the twenty-second of February returns, let us remember that, while with these solemn and joyous rites of observance we celebrate the great anniversary, our fellow-citizens on the Hudson, on the Potomac, from the Southern plains to the Western lakes, are engaged in the same offices of gratitude and love. Nor we, nor they alone; beyond the Ohio, beyond the Mississippi, along that stupendous trail of immigration from the East to the West, which, bursting into States as it moves westward, is already threading the Western prairies, swarming through the portals of the Rocky Mountains and winding down their slopes, the name and the memory of Washington on that gracious night will travel with the silver queen of heaven through sixty degrees of longitude, nor part company with her till she walks in her brightness through the Golden Gate of California, and passes serenely to hold midnight court with her Australian stars. There and there only in barbarous archipelagos, as yet untrodden by civilized man, the name of Washington is unknown; and there, too, when they swarm with enlightened millions, new honors shall be paid with ours to his memory."

In my judgment the greatest living orator is William J. Bryan. I have never known a more gifted man. A thorough scholar—having like Lord Bacon taken all knowledge for his province—a fearless champion of what he deems the right, he is in the loftiest sense "without fear and without reproach."

In introducing him to an immense audience in Bloomington when he was first a candidate for the Presidency, I said:

"The National Democracy in the Chicago convention selected for the Presidency a distinguished statesman of the great Northwest. For the first time in more than one hundred years of our history, a candidate for the great office has been taken from a State lying west of the Mississippi.

"In the nomination of our standard-bearer, the convention builded better than it knew. Each passing hour has but emphasized the wisdom of its choice. Truly it has been said: 'When the times demand the man, the man appears.' The times demanded a great leader—the great leader has appeared! His campaign is the marvel of the age. From the Atlantic seaboard, two thousand miles to the westward, his eloquent words have cheered the despondent, given new hopes and aspirations to the people, touched the hearts of millions of his countrymen. In advocating his election we have kept the faith. We have not departed from the teachings of our fathers. We sacredly preserve the ancient landmarks—the landmarks of all previous Democratic conventions."

Rarely has a speech been uttered so effective in its immediate results as that of Mr. Bryan in the Democratic National Convention of 1896. The occasion was one never to be forgotten. When Mr. Bryan began his speech he had not been mentioned as a candidate for the Presidency; at its close there was no other candidate. The closing sentences of the memorable speech were:

"Our ancestors, when but three millions in number, had the courage to declare their political independence of every other nation; shall we, their descendants, when we have grown to seventy millions, declare that we are less independent than our forefathers? No, my friends, that will never be the verdict of our people. Therefore, we care not upon what lines the battle is fought. If they say bimetallism is good, but that we cannot have it until other nations help us, we reply that, instead of having a gold standard because England has, we will restore bimetallism, and then let England have bimetallism because the United States has it. If they dare to come out in the open field and defend the gold standard as a good thing, we will fight them to the uttermost. Having behind us the productive masses of this nation and the world, supported by the commercial interests, the laboring interests, and the toilers everywhere, we will answer their demand for a gold standard by saying to them: 'You shall not press down upon the brow of labor this crown of thorns, you shall not crucify mankind upon a cross of gold.'"

The closing sentences of his "Prince of Peace" have been read in all languages:

"But this Prince of Peace promises not only peace but strength. Some have thought His teachings fit only for the weak and the timid and unsuited to men of vigor, energy, and ambition. Nothing could be farther from the truth. Only the man of faith can be courageous. Confident that he fights on the side of Jehovah, he doubts not the success of his cause. What matters it whether he shares in the shouts of triumph? If every word spoken in behalf of truth has its influence and every deed done for the right weighs in the final account, it is immaterial to the Christian whether his eyes behold victory or whether he dies in the midst of the conflict.

'Yea, though thou lie upon the dust,
When they who helped thee flee in fear,
Die full of hope and manly trust,
Like those who fell in battle here.
Another hand thy sword shall wield,
Another hand the standard wave,
Till from the trumpet's mouth is pealed
The blast of triumph o'er thy grave.'

"Only those who believe attempt the seemingly impossible and, by attempting, prove that one with God can chase a thousand and two can put ten thousand to flight. I can imagine that the early Christians who were carried into the arena to make a spectacle for those more savage than the beasts, were entreated by their doubting companions not to endanger their lives. But, kneeling in the centre of the arena, they prayed and sang until they were devoured. How helpless they seemed and, measured by every human rule, how hopeless was their cause! And yet within a few decades the power which they invoked proved mightier than the legions of the emperor, and the faith in which they died was triumphant o'er all that land. It is said that those who went to mock at their sufferings returned asking themselves, 'What is it that can enter into the heart of man and make him die as these die?' They were greater conquerors in their death than they could have been had they purchased life by a surrender of their faith.

"What would have been the fate of the Church if the early Christians had had as little faith as many of our Christians now have? And, on the other hand, if the Christians of to-day had the faith of the martyrs, how long would it be before the fulfilment of the prophecy that every knee shall bow and every tongue confess?

"Our faith should be even stronger than the faith of those who lived two thousand years ago, for we see our religion spreading and supplanting the philosophies and creeds of the Orient.

"As the Christian grows older he appreciates more and more the completeness with which Christ fills the requirements of the heart and, grateful for the peace which he enjoys and for the strength which he has received, he repeats the words of the great scholar, Sir William Jones:

'Before thy mystic altar, heavenly truth,
I kneel in manhood, as I knelt in youth.
Thus let me kneel, till this dull form decay,
And life's last shade be brightened by thy ray.'"

XXX THE COLONELS

A CONVIVIAL MEETING OF LAWYERS—HILARITY SMOTHERED BY THE MAINE LAW—A FAINTING WAYFARER IS REFUSED A DRINK IN A MAINE VILLAGE— THE APOTHECARY DEMANDS A PHYSICIAN'S PRESCRIPTION—SNAKE-BITES IN GREAT DEMAND.

Some years ago, I spent a few weeks of inclement weather in a beautiful village in southern Georgia. Upon calling at his office to renew my acquaintance with a well-known lawyer, he soon invited in the remaining members of the local bar. Everything was propitious, and the conversation never for a moment flagged, many experiences of the legal practitioners of the South and of the North being related with happy effect.

I at length remarked that since my arrival, I had, somewhat to my surprise, learned that "local option" had been adopted in their county. An aged brother, in a tone by no means exultant, assured me that such was the fact. I then observed that I was not a hard drinker, but being a total stranger and liable to sudden sickness, I asked what I would do under such circumstances.

An equally venerable brother, who bore the unique title of "Colonel," slowly responded, "Have to do without, sir, *have to do without;* not a drop to be had in the county, absolutely not a drop, sir."

The brief silence which followed this announcement was broken by the corroborative testimony of a more youthful associate of similar official distinction, and a genial and hospitable expression of countenance, somehow suggesting memories of old cognac.

"Yes, sir, the use of spirituous liquors is now only a tradition with us; but I have heard my father say, that before the war, the indulgence in such hospitality was not uncommon among gentlemen."

At the conclusion of still further cumulative testimony of the same tenor, I remarked that something about the general situation reminded me of an incident that occurred in a State far to the north while the "Maine Law" was in operation.

A dilapidated-looking pedestrian, with a pack on his back, early one afternoon of a hot July day pulled up in front of the post-office in a small village in the interior of Maine. Humbly addressing a citizen who was just coming out with his copy of the *Weekly Tribune* in hand, he inquired,

"Where can I get a drink?"

"The Maine Law is in force," was the reply, "and it is impossible for you to get a drink in the State."

The heart of the wayfarer sank within him.

"Would you let a man die right here on your streets, for lack of a drink?"

The "better angel" of the citizen being touched thereat, he replied,

"My friend, I am very sorry for you, but no liquor is ever sold here, except by the apothecary, and then only as a medicine."

Upon further inquiry, the important fact was disclosed that the shop of the apothecary was three-quarters of a mile away, on the left-hand side of the road. With an alacrity indicating something of hope, the pedestrian immediately gathered up his pack, and through the dust and heat at length reached the designated place. Sinking apparently exhausted upon the door-step, he feebly requested the man behind the counter to let him have something to drink. The immediate reply of the apothecary was that the Maine Law was in force, and no spirituous liquors could be sold except upon the prescription of a physician. After earnest inquiry, it was ascertained that the nearest doctor's office was one mile away, and the man with the pack again betook himself to the weary highway. Returning an hour later, in tone more pitiful than before, he begged the apothecary, as he hoped for mercy himself, to let him have a drink. Upon inquiry as to whether he had procured the required certificate, he said, "No, the doctor wouldn't give me any."

The assurance of the apothecary that the case appeared hopeless only added to the distress of the poor man, whose sands seemed now indeed to be running low.

Stirred to the depths by the agony of his visitor, the apothecary at length said,

"My friend, I would be glad to help you, but it is impossible for me to let you have a drink of spirituous liquor unless you have a doctor's certificate *or have been snake-bit.*"

At the last-mentioned suggestion, the face of the man of repeated disappointments measurably brightened, and he eagerly inquired where he could find a snake. The now sympathetic man of bottles told him to follow the main road three miles to the forks, and then a few hundred yards to the west, and he would find a small grove of decayed tress, where there still lingered a few snakes, and by the exercise of a reasonable degree of diligence he might manage *to get bit,* and thereby lay the foundation for the desired relief. With bundle again in place, and evincing a buoyancy of manner to which he had been a stranger for many hours, the traveller resumed the quest.

Hours later, when the shadows had lengthened, and the fire-flies were glistening in the distance,

"With a look so piteous in purport,
As if he had been loosed out of hell
To speak of horrors,"

he re-entered the apothecary's shop, threw down his bundle, and in tones suggestive of the agony of lost souls, again begged for a drink.

"Did you get snake-bit?" was the feeling inquiry of the man at the helm.

"No," was the heart-rending reply, *every snake I met had engagements six months ahead, for all the bites he could furnish!*"

XXXI REMINISCENCES

A BARBECUE AT THE BLUE SPRING, KY.—NOTABLE
NATIVES OF THE NEIGHBORHOOD —THE
SCHOOLHOUSE CHURCH—SOME OF THE PREACHERS—
THE TEACHER OF SINGING—HOW THE SCHOOLMASTER
WAS PAID—MANNERS AND DISCIPLINE—THE DEBATING
SOCIETY—THE WRITER'S SPEECH TO HIS OLD
NEIGHBORS—SOME BOYHOOD FRIENDS.

Soon after my nomination for the Vice-Presidency, in 1892, I attended a barbecue at the Blue Spring, a stone's throw from my father's old home in Kentucky. This was in the county of Christian, in the southwestern part of the State. It is a large and wealthy county, its tobacco product probably exceeding that of any other county in the United States.

Christian County was the early home of men distinguished in the field, at the bar, and in the State and National councils. Hopkinsville, the county-seat, had been the home of Stites, the learned Chief Justice of the Court of Appeals; of Jackson, who fell while gallantly leading his command at the battle of Perryville; of Morehead, an early and distinguished Governor of the Commonwealth; of Sharp, whose legal acumen would have secured him distinction at any bar; of McKenzie, whose wit and eloquence made him the long-time idol and the Representative in Congress, of the famed "Pennyrile" district; of Bristow, the accomplished Secretary of the Treasury during the administration of President Grant; of the Henry brothers, three of whom, from different States, were at a later day Representatives in Congress, and one the Whig candidate against Andrew Johnson for Governor of Tennessee.

Hon. Gustavus A. Henry, well known as the "Eagle Orator of Tennessee," was the Whig candidate for Governor of the State in opposition to Andrew Johnson, at a later day President of the United States. The latter was at the time an old-fashioned, steady-going mountain orator with none of the brilliancy of his gifted antagonist. At the close of a series of joint debates Johnson said: "This speech terminates our joint debates. I have now encountered the 'Eagle Orator' upon every stump in the State, and come out of the contest with no flesh of mine in his claws—no blood of mine upon his beak." To which Henry instantly replied: "The eagle—the proud bird of freedom—never wars upon a corpse!"

A few miles from the Blue Spring, in the same county, were the early homes of Senator Roger Q. Mills of Texas, Governor John M. Palmer of

Illinois, and Jefferson Davis of the Southern Confederacy. Less than a score of miles to the southward, upon the banks of the Cumberland in Tennessee, stood historic Fort Donelson; while a few hours' journey to the northward stands the monument which marks the birthplace of Abraham Lincoln.

Following the earliest westward trail from Iredell County, North Carolina, across the Blue Ridge Mountains, for a great distance along the banks of the romantic French Broad my grandfathers, "Scotch-Irish Presbyterians," James Stevenson and Adlai Ewing, with their immediate families and others of their kindred, had in the early days of the century, after a long and perilous journey, finally reached the famous Spring already mentioned. Near by, their tents were pitched, and in time permanent homes established in the then wilderness of southwestern Kentucky.

The first public building constructed was of logs, with puncheon floor, and set apart to the double purpose of school-house and church for the use of all denominations. Its site was near the spot where the speaker's stand was now erected for the barbecue which I have mentioned.

From the pulpit of this rude building, the early settlers had more
than once listened spell-bound to the eloquence of Peter Cartwright,
Henry B. Bascom, Nathan L. Rice, Finis Ewing, and Alexander
Campbell.

In this old church the time-honored custom was for some one of its officers to line out the hymn, two lines at a time, and then lead the singing, in which the congregation joined. Among my earliest recollections is that of my uncle, Squire McKenzie, one of the best of men, standing immediately in front of the pulpit, and faithfully discharging this important duty after the hymn had been read in full by the minister. I distinctly recall the solemn tones in which, upon communion occasions, he lined out, in measured and mellow cadence, the good old hymn beginning:

"'T was on that dark, that doleful night,
When powers of earth and hell arose."

Mr. Sawyer, too, the old-time singing-school teacher, has honored place in my memory. Once a month, in the old church, the singing-school class of which we were all members regularly assembled. The school was in four divisions, Bass, Tenor, Counter, and Treble; each member was provided with a copy of the "Missouri Harmony," with "fa," "sol," "la," "mi," appearing in mysterious characters upon every page; the master, magnifying his office, as with tuning-fork in hand he stood proudly in the midst, raised the tune, and as it progressed smiled or deeply frowned upon each of the divisions as occasion seemed to require. His voice has long been hushed, but I seem again to hear his cheery command, "Attention, class! Utopia, page one hundred!"

Looking back through the long vista of years, it is my honest belief that such singing as his, at home or abroad, I have never heard. Upon his tablet might appropriately have been inscribed:

"Sleep undisturbed within this sacred shrine,
Till angels wake thee with notes like thine."

To this old field school came in the early time the "scholars" for many miles around. It was in very truth the only Alma Mater, for that generation, of almost the entire southern portion of the county. My father in his boyhood attended this school, as did his kinsmen, John W. and Fielding N. Ewing; the last named of whom was, at a much later period, the pastor of the First Presbyterian Church of Bloomington, Illinois, and his elder brother was the Mayor of that city.

At that early day, and later when I attended the same school, there were no salaries provided for the teachers, The schoolmaster visited the families within reasonable distance of the schoolhouse with his subscription paper, and the school was duly opened when a sufficient number of pupils had subscribed.

The ways of the old field school and the methods of the old-time teachers belong now to the past. Once experienced, however, they have an abiding place in the memory. The master, upon his accustomed perch near the spacious fire-place, with his ever-present symbol of authority, the rod—which even Solomon would have considered fully up to the orthodox standard—in alarming proximity; the boys "making their manners" by scraping the right foot upon the floor and bowing low as they entered the school-room; the girls upon like occasions equally faithful in the practice of a bewitching little "curtsey" which only added to their charms; the "studying aloud," the hum of the school-room being thereby easily heard a mile or two away; the timid approach to the dreaded master with the humble request that he would "mend a pen," "parse a verb," or "do a sum."

An hour, called recess, was given for the dinner from the baskets brought from home, and then the glorious old games, marbles, town-ball, and "bull pen," to the heart's content! At the sound of the ominous command, "Books!" each scholar promptly resumed his seat, the merry shout of the playground at once giving way to the serious business of "saying lessons." In those good old days, the slightest act of omission or commission upon the part of the pupil was confronted with a terrible condition instead of a harmless theory. In very truth the uncomfortable effect of the punishment unfailingly administered—"doing his duty to your parents," as the petty school-room tyrant was wont to observe—was in small degree lessened by the comforting assurance that the victim "would thank him for it the longest day he lived!"

Then, to crown all, came the debating society, with the schoolmaster presiding, and the entire neighborhood, sweethearts and all, in attendance, and the boys for the first time testing their oratorical powers. Vigilant preparations having been made for the discussion of such momentous questions as: "Which deserves the most credit, Columbus for discovering America, or Washington for defending it?" or "Which brings the greatest happiness to mankind, pursuit or possession?"

In "Georgia Scenes" is an amusing account of a debate in a backwoods "Academy" nearly a century ago. The two brightest boys, after anxious preparation, succeeded in formulating for debate a question utterly meaningless, but which appeared upon hurried reading to touch the very bed-rock of human government. The "conspirators" mentioned were the respective leaders in the debate which closed the public exercises of the annual "Exhibition" of the Academy. The leaders had made careful preparation for the contest, and appeared fully to understand the question, and each in turn highly complimented the able argument of his rival. Much amusement was caused by the remaining speakers, when called in order, who candidly admitted that they didn't understand the question, and patiently submitted to the fine imposed by the rules of the Society. That a boy of but mediocre talents should have failed to participate in the debate, will not be considered remarkable when the question is stated: "Whether, in public elections, the vote of faction should prevail by internal suggestions, *or the bias of jurisprudence?"*

The late General Gordon related to me the above incident, and added that the leaders mentioned were at a later day well known to the country, one the learned Bishop Longstreet of Georgia, the other the eloquent Senator McDuffie of South Carolina.

Events almost forgotten, forms long since vanished, were vividly recalled as, after long absence, I revisited the spot inseparably blended with the joyous associations of childhood. The platform from which I was to speak had been erected near the ruins of the old church above mentioned, of which my grandfather had been a ruling elder, my father, mother, and other kindred the earliest members.

Upon my introduction to the vast assemblage—the good things suggested by "barbecue" having meanwhile given to all an abundant feeling of contentment—I began by brief reference to the pleasure I experienced in again visiting, after the passing of the years which separated childhood from middle age, scenes once so familiar, and meeting face to face so many of my early associates and friends, and remarked, that in the early days in Illinois the not unusual reply of the Kentucky emigrant, when asked what part of the Old Commonwealth he came from was, "From the Blue Grass," or "From near Lexington," but that my invariable answer to that inquiry had even been, "From the Pennyrile!"

Some mention I made of Mr. Caskie, the dreaded school-master of the long ago, caused a momentary commotion in the audience, and immediately a man of white hairs and bowed by the weight of more than fourscore years, was lifted to the front of the platform. With arm about my neck, he earnestly inquired: "Adlai, I came twenty miles to hear you speak; don't you remember me?" The audience apparently appreciated the instant reply: "Yes, Mr. Caskie, *I still have a few marks left to remember you by!*"

The venerable and long ago forgiven schoolmaster was fearfully deaf, and to prevent the possibility of a single word escaping him, he stood close beside me, and with his hand behind his ear and the other resting tenderly on my shoulder, faithfully followed me in my journeyings to and fro across the stage during the two-hours' speech which followed.

My speech at length concluded, I was warmly greeted by scores of old neighbors and friends. Just forty years had passed since my father had removed his family to Illinois, and it may well be believed that it was difficult to recall promptly all the names and faces of those I had known in childhood. Even a candidate has, at such times, "some rights under the Constitution"; one of which, I honestly believe, is total exemption from the tormenting inquiries: "Do you know me? Well, what is my name?" The laurels, even of Job, had he ever been a candidate, would probably have turned to willows.

I am here reminded of an experience of one of my early competitors for Congress. It was his happy forte to remember instantly all his old acquaintances; not only that, but to know their full names. To call out in friendly and familiar tone, in and out of season, "Bill," "Dick," "Sam," "Bob," a hundred times a day, was as natural to him as to breathe.

Upon one occasion, however, the fates seemed slightly untoward. At the close of one of our joint debates, in the southern part of the district, he was greeted by a demure-looking individual with the salutation, "How are you, Judge?"

"My dear sir," exclaimed the regular candidate, grasping the interrogator warmly by the hand, "how are you, and how is the old lady?"

"I am not married, Judge," was the deliberate response, as of one assuming the entire responsibility.

"Certainly not, certainly not, my dear sir; I meant you mother. How is that excellent old lady?"

"My mother has been dead twenty years, Judge," was the mournful reply.

A trifle embarrassed, but not entirely off his base, the judge looked earnestly into the face of the bereaved, and said:

"My friend, excuse me, your countenance is perfectly familiar to me, but I do not at this moment remember exactly who you are."

The response was, "Judge, *I am an evangelist.*"

To which the candidate for Congress, now upon a firm footing, tapped the man of the sacred office familiarly upon the shoulder and cheerfully exclaimed, "Why, damn it, *Van*, I thought I ought to know you!"

Returning now for brief sojourn to the afore-mentioned barbecue, with a faithful kinsman as monitor, aided by a slight moiety of tact to be credited to personal account, I managed passably well to get through the trying ordeal. "The old gentleman with the long white beard, coming toward us," observed my monitor, "is Uncle Jake Anderson. He has a hat bet that you will know him." Thus advised, I was ready for trial, and warmly grasping the hand extended me, I earnestly inquired, "Uncle Jake, *how are you?*" "Do you know me, boy?" was the immediate response. "Know you?" I replied. "You and my father were near neighbors for years; how could I help knowing you?" "Yes, of course," he said, "but you being gone so long, and now running for President, I didn't know but what you had forgotten all about the old neighbors down on the Lick." Assuring him that I had forgotten none of them, and congratulating him upon the hat he had won, I passed on to the next.

The interview described was repeated with slight variations, many times, when my attendant remarked:

"That man leaning against the tree is John Dunloe; do you remember him?"

"Certainly," I replied, "I went to school with him."

Immediately approaching my early classmate I took him by the hand and said, "How are you, John?"

"Why, Adlai, do you know me?" was the prompt response.

"Know you," said I, "didn't we go to school together to Mr. Caskie right here at Blue Water, when we were boys?"

"Yas, of course we did," slowly answered by sometime school-fellow, "but you been 'sociatin' with them big fellows down about Washington so long, that I didn't know but what you had forgot us poor fellows down in the Pennyrile."

Assuring him that I never forgot my old friends, I inquired, "John, where is your brother Bill?"

"He's here," was the instant reply. "Me and Bill started before daylight to get to this barbecue in time. Bill 'lowed *he'd ruther go forty miles on foot to hear you make a speech, than go to a hangin'.*"

XXXII A TRIBUTE TO IRELAND*

[*Footnote: Speech delivered by Mr. Stevenson at a banquet of the United Irish Societies of Chicago, September, 1900.]

THE WRITER'S VISIT TO NOTABLE PLACES IN IRELAND— HIS TRIBUTE OF PRAISE TO HER GREAT MEN—AMERICA'S OBLIGATION TO IRISH SOLDIERS AND STATESMEN.

I accepted with pleasure the invitation to meet with you. For the courtesy so generously extended me I am profoundly grateful.

Within late years it has been my privilege to visit Ireland; and I can truly say that no country in Europe possessed for me a deeper interest than the little island about whose name clusters so much of romance and of enchantment. I saw Ireland in its beauty and its gloom; in its glory and in its desolation. I stood upon the Giant's Causeway, one of the grand masterpieces of the Almighty; I visited the historic parks and deserted legislative halls of venerated Dublin; threaded the streets and byways of the quaint old city of Cork; listened the bells of Shandon; sailed over the beautiful lakes of Killarney, and gazed upon the old castles of Muckross and of Blarney, whose ivy-covered ruins tell of the far-away centuries. What a wonderful island! The birthplace of wits, of warriors, of statesmen, of poets, and of orators. Of its people it has been truly said: "They have fought successfully the battles of every country but their own."

Upon occasion such as this, the Irishman—to whatever spot in this wide world he may have wandered—lives in the shadow of the past. In imagination he is once more under the ancestral roof; the vine-clad cottage is again a thing of reality. Again he wears the shamrock; again he hears the songs of his native land, while his heart is stirred by memories of her wrongs and of her glory.

What a splendid contribution Ireland has made to the world's galaxy of great men! In the realm of poetry, Goldsmith and Tom Moore; of oratory, Sheridan, Emmett, Grattan, O'Connell, Burke, and in later years Charles Stewart Parnell, whose thrilling words I heard a third of a century ago, pleading the cause of his oppressed countrymen.

The obligation of America to Ireland for men who have aided in fighting her battles and framing her laws cannot be measured by words. In the British possessions to the northward, in the old city of Quebec, there is one spot dear to the American heart—that where fell the brave Montgomery, fighting the battles of his adopted country. What schoolboy is not familiar with the story of gallant Phil Sheridan and "Winchester twenty miles away?" Illinoisans will never forget Shields, the hero of two wars, the senator from three States. It was an Irish-American poet of a neighboring State who wrote of our fallen soldiers words that will live while we have a country and a language:

"The muffled drum's sad roll has beat
The soldier's last tattoo;
No more of life's parade shall meet
That brave and fallen few."

The achievements of representatives of this race along every pathway of useful and honorable endeavor are a part of our own history. We honor to-day the far-away island, the deeds and sacrifices of whose sons have added so brilliant a chapter to American history. From the assembling of the First Continental Congress to the present hour, in every legislative hall the Irishman has been a factor. His bones have whitened every American battlefield from the first conflict with British regulars to the closing hour of our struggle with Spain.

The love of liberty is deeply ingrained into the very life of the Irishman. The history of his country is that of a gallant people struggling for a larger measure of freedom. His most precious heritage is the record of his countrymen, who upon the battlefield and upon the scaffold have sealed their devotion to liberty with their blood. With such men it was a living faith that—

"Whether on the scaffold high
Or in the battle's van
The fittest place for man to die
Is where he dies for man."

With a history reaching into the far past, every page of which tells of the struggle for liberty, it is not strange that the sympathies of the Irishman are with the oppressed everywhere on God's footstool. Irishmen, in common with liberty-loving men everywhere, looked with abhorrence upon the attempt of a great European power to establish monarchy upon the ruins of republics.

May we not confidently abide in the hope that brighter days are in waiting for the beautiful island and her gallant people? I close with the words: "God bless old Ireland!"

XXXIII THE BLIND CHAPLAIN

DR. MILBURN'S SOLEMNITY IN PRAYER—HIS VENERABLE APPEARANCE—HIS CONVERSATIONAL POWERS—HIS CUSTOM OF PRAYING FOR SICK MEMBERS.

No Senator who ever sat under the ministrations of Dr. Milburn, the blind chaplain, can ever forget his earnest and solemn invocation. When rolling from his tongue, each word of the Lord's Prayer seemed to weigh a pound. His venerable appearance and sightless eyes gave a tinge of pathetic emphasis to his every utterance. He was a man of rare gifts; in early life, before the entire failure of his sight, he had known much of active service in his sacred calling upon the Western circuits. He had been the fellow-laborer of Cartwright, Bascom, and other eminent Methodist ministers of the early times.

Dr. Milburn was the Chaplain of the House during the Mexican War, and often a guest at the Executive Mansion when Mr. Polk was President. He knew well many of the leading statesmen of that period. He possessed rare conversational powers; and notwithstanding his blindness, poverty, and utter loneliness, he remained the pleasing, entertaining gentleman to the last.

It was the custom of the good Chaplain, with the aid of a faithful monitor, to keep thoroughly advised as to the health of the senators and their families. The bare mention, in the morning paper, of any ill having befallen any statesman of whom he was, for the time, the official spiritual shepherd, was the unfailing precursor of special and affectionate mention at the next convening of the Senate. Moreover, in the discharge of this sacred duty, his invariable habit was to designate the object of his special invocation as "the Senior Senator" or "Junior Senator," carefully giving the name of his State. It is within the realm of probability that since the first humble petition was breathed, there has never been an apparently more prompt answer to prayer than that now to be related.

The Morning Post contained an item to the effect that Senator Voorhees was ill. During the accustomed invocation which preceded the opening of the session, an earnest petition ascended for "the Senior Senator from Indiana," that he might "soon be restored to his wonted health, and permitted to return to the seat so long and so honorably occupied."

A moment later, the touching invocation being ended, and the Senate duly in session, the stately form of "the Senior Senator from Indiana" promptly emerged from the cloak-room, and quietly resumed the seat he had "so long and so honorably occupied."

XXXIV A MEMORABLE CENTENNIAL

GEORGE WASHINGTON LAYING THE CORNER-STONE OF
THE CAPITOL—PROGRESS OF THE REPUBLIC DURING
THE NINETEENTH CENTURY—NOTABLE MEN WHO
WERE CONSPICUOUS AT THE NATION'S BIRTH—
CONGRESS HELD AT VARIOUS PLACES BEFORE 1800—THE
DISTRICT OF COLUMBIA FORMED—NECESSITY FOR
ENLARGING THE CAPITOL AT WASHINGTON—A
DOCUMENT BY WEBSTER DEPOSITED BENEATH THE
CORNER-STONE OF THE ADDITIONS—HIGH DEBATES
HELD IN THE UNITED STATES SENATE—PRESENT
LOCATION OF THE SENATE CHAMBER—GREAT INCREASE
OF POPULATION, TERRITORY, AND COMMERCE—THE
TWO DIVISIONS OF CONGRESS.

On the eighteenth day of September, 1893, the first centennial of the laying of the corner-stone of the national Capitol was celebrated by appropriate ceremonies in Washington City.

President Cleveland presided, and seated upon the platform were the members of his Cabinet, the Senate, the House of Representatives, the Supreme Court of the United States, and the Foreign Ambassadors.

The oration was delivered by the Hon. William Wirt Henry, of Richmond, Virginia, grandson of Patrick Henry. The addresses which followed were by myself, representing the Senate; Speaker Crisp, representing the House; and Justice Brown, the Supreme Court. I spoke as follows:

"This day and this hour mark the close of a century of our national history. No ordinary event has called us together. Standing in the presence of this august assemblage of the people, upon the spot where Washington stood, we solemnly commemorate the one-hundredth anniversary of the laying of the corner-stone of the nation's Capitol.

"It is well that this day has been set apart as a national holiday, that all public business has been suspended, and that the President and his Cabinet, the members of the great Court, and of the Congress, unite with their countrymen in doing honor to the memory of the men who, one hundred years ago, at this hour, and upon this spot, put in place the corner-stone of the Capitol of the American Republic. The century rolls back, and we stand in the presence of the grandest and most imposing figure known to any age or country. Washington, as Grand Master of Free and Accepted Masons, clothed in the symbolic garments of that venerable Order, wearing the apron and the sash wrought by the hands of the wife of the beloved Lafayette, impressively and in accordance with the time-honored usages of that Order, is laying his hands upon the corner-stone of the future and permanent Capitol of his country. The solemn ceremonies of the hour were conducted by Washington, not only in his office of Grand Master of Free Masons, but in his yet more august office of President of the United States. Assisting him in the fitting observance of these impressive rites, were representatives of the Masonic Lodges of Virginia and Maryland, while around him stood men whose honored names live with his in history—the men who, on field and in council, had aided first in achieving independence, and then in the yet more difficult task of garnering, by wise legislation, the fruits of victory. Truly, the centennial of an event so fraught with interest should not pass unnoticed.

"History furnishes no parallel to the century whose close we now commemorate. Among all the centuries it stands alone. With hearts filled with gratitude to the God of our fathers, it is well that we recall something of the progress of the young Republic, since the masterful hour when Washington laid his hands upon the foundation-stone of yonder Capitol.

"The seven years of colonial struggle for liberty had terminated in glorious victory. Independence had been achieved. The Articles of Confederation, binding the Colonies together in a mere league of friendship, had given place to the Constitution of the United States—that wonderful instrument, so aptly declared by Mr. Gladstone to be 'the most wonderful work ever struck off at a given time by the brain and purpose of man.'

"Without a dissenting voice in the Electoral Colleges, Washington had been chosen President. At his council-table sat Jefferson, the author of the Declaration of Independence; Hamilton, of whom it has been said, 'He smote the rock of the national resources, and abundant streams of revenue gushed forth. He touched the dead corpse of the public credit, and it sprung upon its feet'; Knox, the brave and trusted friend of his chief during the colonial struggle; and Edmund Randolph, the impress of whose genius has been indelibly left upon the Federal Constitution. Vermont and Kentucky, as sovereign States—coequal with the original thirteen—had been admitted into the Union. The Supreme Court, consisting of six members, had been constituted, with the learned jurist John Jay as its Chief Justice. The popular branch of the Congress consisted of but one hundred and five members. Thirty members constituted the Senate, over whose deliberations presided the patriot statesman, John Adams. The population of the entire country was less than four millions. The village of Washington, the capital—and I trust for all coming ages the capital—contained but a few hundred inhabitants.

"After peace had been concluded with Great Britain, and while we were yet under the Articles of Confederation, the sessions of the Congress were held successively at Princeton, Annapolis, Trenton, and New York. In the presence of both houses of Congress, on the thirtieth day of April, 1789, in the city of New York, Washington had been inaugurated President. From that hour—the beginning of our Government under the Constitution—the Congress was held in New York, until 1790, then in Philadelphia until 1800, when, on November 17, it first convened in Washington. The necessity of selecting a suitable and central place for the permanent location of the seat of Government early engaged the thoughtful consideration of our fathers. It cannot be supposed that the question reached a final determination without great embarrassment, earnest discussion, and the manifestation of sectional jealousies. But, as has been well said, the good genius of our system finally prevailed, 'and a district of territory on the River Potomac, at some place between the mouths of the Eastern branch and the Conococheague,' was, by Act of Congress of June 28, 1790, 'accepted for the permanent seat of the Government of the United States.' From the seventeenth day of November, 1800, this city has been the capital. When that day came, Washington had gone to his grave, John Adams was President, and Jefferson the presiding officer of the Senate. It may be well to recall that upon the occasion of the assembling for the first time of the Congress in the Capitol, President Adams appeared before the Senate and the House, in joint session, and said:

"'It would be unbecoming the representatives of this nation to assemble for the first time in this solemn temple, without looking up to the Supreme Ruler of the Universe and imploring His blessing. You will consider it as the capital of a great nation, advancing with unexampled rapidity in arts, in commerce, in wealth, and population, and possessing within itself those resources which, if not thrown away or lamentably misdirected, will secure it a long course of prosperity and self-government.'

"To this address of President Adams the Senate made reply:

"'We meet you, sir, and the other branch of the national Legislature, in the city which is honored by the name of our late hero and sage, the illustrious Washington, with sensations and emotions which exceed our power of description.'

"From the date last given until the burning of the Capitol by the British, in 1814, in the room now occupied by the Supreme Court Library, in the north wing, were held the sessions of the Senate. That now almost forgotten apartment witnessed the assembling of Senators who, at an earlier period of our history, had been the associates of Washington and Franklin, and had themselves played no mean part in crystallizing into the great organic law, the deathless principles of the Declaration of Independence. From this chamber went forth the second Declaration of War against Great Britain; and here, before the Senate as a court of impeachment, was arraigned a Justice of the Supreme Court of the United States, to answer the charge of alleged high crimes and misdemeanors.

"With the rolling years and the rapid growth of the Republic, came the imperative necessity for enlarging its Capitol. The debates upon this subject culminated in the Act of Congress of September 30, 1850, providing for the erection of the north and south wings of the Capitol. Thomas U. Walter was the architect to whose hand was committed the great work. Yonder noble structure will stand for ages the silent witness of the fidelity with which the important trust was discharged.

"The corner-stone of the additions was laid by President Fillmore, on the fourth day of July, 1851. In honor of that event, and by request of the President, Mr. Webster pronounced an oration, and while we have a country and a language his words will touch a responsive chord in patriotic hearts. Beneath the corner-stone was then deposited a paper, in the handwriting of Mr. Webster, containing the following words:

"'If it shall be, hereafter, the will of God, that this structure shall fall from its base, that its foundation be upturned and this deposit brought to the eyes of men, be it then known that on this day the Union of the United States of America stands firm, that their Constitution still exists unimpaired, with all its original usefulness and glory, growing every day stronger and stronger in the affections of the great body of the American people, and attracting more and more the attention of the world. And all here assembled, whether belonging to public life or to private life, with hearts devoutly thankful to Almighty God for the preservation of the liberty and happiness of the country, unite in sincere and fervent prayers that this deposit, and the walls and arches, the domes and towers, the columns and entablatures now to be erected over it, may endure forever.'

"From the sixth day of December, 1819, until January 4, 1859, a period of thirty-nine years, the sessions of the Senate were held in the present Supreme Court room. This was, indeed, the arena of high debate. When, in any age, or in any country, has there been gathered, within so small compass, so much of human greatness? Even to suggest the great questions here discussed and determined, would be to write a history of that eventful period. It was, indeed, the coming together of the master spirits of the second generation of American statesmen. Here were Macon and Crawford, Benton, Randolph, Cass, Bell, Houston, Preston, Buchanan, Seward, Chase, Crittenden, Sumner, Choate, Everett, Breese, Trumbull, Fessenden, Douglas, Clay, Calhoun, Webster, and others scarcely less illustrious. Within the walls of that little chamber was heard the wondrous debate between Hayne and Webster. There began the fierce conflict of antagonistic ideas touching the respective powers of the State and of the Nation—a conflict which, transferred to a different theatre, found final solution only in the bloody arbitrament of arms.

"For more than a third of a century the sessions of the Senate have been held in the magnificent chamber of the north wing of the Capitol. Of the procession of sixty-two Senators that, preceded by the Vice-President, Mr. Breckenridge, entered the Chamber for the first time, on the fourth day of January, 1859, but four survive; not one remains in public life. It is, indeed, now a procession of shadows.

"When the foundation-stone of this Capitol was laid, our Republic was in its infancy, and self-government yet an untried experiment. It is a proud reflection to-day that time has proved the true arbiter, and that the capacity of a free and intelligent people to govern themselves by written constitution and laws, of their own making, is no longer an experiment. The crucial test of a century of unparalleled material prosperity has been safely endured.

"In 1793 there was no city west of the Alleghanies. To-day a single city on Lake Michigan contains a population of a little less than one-half of the Republic at the time of the first inauguration of Washington. States have been carved out of the wilderness, and our great rivers, whose silence met no break on their pathway to the sea, are now the arteries of our interior trade, and bear upon their bosoms a commerce which surpasses a hundred-fold that of the entire country a century ago.

"From fifteen States and four millions of people, we have grown to fifty States and Territories, and sixty-seven millions of people; from an area of eight hundred and five thousand, to an area of three million, six hundred thousand square miles; from a narrow strip along the Atlantic seaboard, to an unbroken possession from ocean to ocean. How marvellous the increase in our national wealth! In 1793, our imports amounted to thirty-one million, and our exports to twenty-six million dollars. Now our imports are eight hundred and forty-seven million, and our exports one billion and thirty million dollars. Thirty-three million tons of freight are carried on our Great Lakes, whose only burden then was the Indian's canoe. Then our national wealth was inconsiderable; now our assessed valuation amounts to the enormous sum of twenty-four billion, six hundred and fifty million dollars. Then trade and travel were dependent upon beasts of burden and on sailing vessels; now steam and electricity do our bidding, railroads cover the land, boats burden the waters, the telegraph reaches every city and hamlet; distance is annihilated, and

"'Civilization, on her luminous wings,
Soars, Phoenix-like, to Jove.'

"In the presence of this wondrous fulfillment of predicted greatness, prophecy looks out upon the future and stands dumb.

"When this corner-stone was laid, France, then in the throes of a revolution, had just declared war against Great Britain—a war in which all Europe eventually became involved. Within a century of that hour, in the capital of France, there convened an international court, its presiding officer an eminent citizen of the French Republic, its members representatives of sovereign European States, its object the peaceable adjustment of controversies between Great Britain and the United States.

"Was it Richelieu who said, 'Take away the sword; States can be saved without it'?

"In no part of our mechanism of government was the wisdom of our fathers more strikingly displayed than in the division of power into the three great departments—legislative, executive, and judicial. In an equal degree was that wisdom manifested by the division of Congress into a Senate and a House of Representatives. Upon the Senate the Constitution has devolved important functions other than those of a merely legislative character. Coequal with the House in matters of legislation, it is, in addition, the advisory body of the President in appointments to office, and in treating with foreign nations. The mode of election, together with the long term of service, unquestionably fosters a spirit of conservatism in the Senate. Always organized, it is the continuing body of our national legislature. Its members change, but the Senate continues —the same now as at the first hour of the Republic. Before no human tribunal come for determination issues of weightier moment. It were idle to doubt that problems yet lie in our pathway as a nation, as difficult of solution as any that in times past have tried the courage or tested the wisdom of our fathers. Yet, may we not confidently abide in the faith that in the keeping of those who succeed the illustrious sages I have named, the dearest interest of our country will be faithfully conserved, and in the words of an eminent predecessor, 'though these marble walls moulder into ruin, the Senate, in another age, may bear into a new and large chamber the Constitution, vigorous and inviolate, and that the last generation of posterity shall witness the deliberations of the representatives of American States, still united, prosperous, and free'?

"And may our fathers' God, 'from out of whose hand the centuries fall like grains of sand,' continue to the American people, throughout all the ages, the prosperity and blessings which He has given to us in the past."

XXXV COLUMBUS MONUMENT IN CENTRAL PARK

FITNESS OF NEW YORK AS THE SITE FOR THE STATUE— VAST IMPORTANCE OF THE DISCOVERY OF AMERICA— COLUMBUS'S HUMILITY AND HIS TRUST IN GOD —THE STATUE UNVEILED—CONCLUDING WORDS OF MR. DEPEW'S ORATION.

Facing the statue of Shakespeare in Central Park, New York, is that of Christopher Columbus. It was unveiled with appropriate ceremonies. General James Grant Wilson presided; Mrs. Julia Ward Howe read her beautiful poem, "The Mariner's Dream," and the oration was delivered by the Hon. Chauncey Depew. Upon this occasion I spoke as follows:

"This hour will live in history. Central Park, beautiful and magnificent, is the fitting place for the statue of Columbus. It is well that to the City of New York, the metropolis of the continent, should have fallen the grateful task of portraying to the millions of all the coming ages the features of the man who, despite obstacles and dangers, marked out the pathway to the New World.

"The name and fame of Columbus belong exclusively to no age or country. They are the enduring heritage of all people. Your President has truly said: 'In all the transactions of history, there is no act which, for vastness and performance, can be compared to the discovery of the continent of America.' In the modest words of the great navigator, he 'only opened the gates'; and lo! there came in the builders of a new and mighty nation.

"It is said that in Venice there is sacredly preserved a letter written by Columbus a few hours before he sailed from Palos. With reverent expression of trust in God, humbly, but with unfaltering faith, he spoke of his proposed voyage to that famous land. He builded better than he knew. His dream, while a suppliant in the outer chambers of kings, and while keeping lonely vigil on the deep, was the discovery of a new pathway to the Indies. Yet who can doubt that to his prophetic soul was then foreshadowed something of that famous land with the warp and woof of whose history, tradition, and song, his name and fame are linked for all time? Was it Mr. Winthrop who said of Columbus and his compeers: 'They were the pioneers in the march to independence; the precursors in the only progress of freedom which was to have no backward steps.'

"Is it too much to say of this man that among the world's benefactors a greater than he hath not appeared? What page in our history tells of deeds so fraught with blessings to the generations of men as the discovery of America? Columbus added a continent to the map of the world.

"I will detain you no longer. Your eyes will now behold this splendid work of art. It is well that its approaches are firm and broad, for along this pathway, with the rolling centuries, will come, as pilgrims to a shrine, the myriads of all lands to behold this statue of Columbus, this enduring monument of the gratitude of a great city, of a great nation."

As the last words were spoken, I leaned over and grasped the rope fastened to the flag that enveloped the statue. The flag parted on either side and was removed by the attendants. The statue stood revealed in all its beauty under the shade of the great elms of the Mall.

Mr. Depew concluded his eloquent oration with the following words:

"We are here to erect this statue to his memory because of the unnumbered blessings to America and to the people of every race and clime which have followed his discovery. His genius and faith gave succeeding generations the opportunity for life and liberty. We, the heirs of all the ages, in the plenitude of our enjoyments, and the prodigality of the favors showered upon us, hail Columbus our benefactor."

XXXVI A PLATFORM NOT DANGEROUS TO STAND UPON

A CITIZEN WHO LONGED TO BE A MEMBER OF THE MISSOURI LEGISLATURE—A COMMITTEE APPOINTED BY A MEETING OF HIS FRIENDS—DIFFICULTY IN ARRANGING THE PLATFORM—THE RESOLUTIONS ADOPTED UNANIMOUSLY.

The builders of political platforms, which uniformly "point with pride" and "view with alarm," may possibly glean a valuable suggestion from the following incident related by Governor Knott. In the county in the good State of Missouri in which his fortune was cast for a while, there lived and flourished, in the ante-bellum days, one Solomon P. Rodes, whose earnest and long-continued yearning was to be a member of the State Legislature. So intense, indeed, had this feeling become in the mind of Solomon, that he at length openly declared that he "would rather go to the Missouri Legislater, than to be the Czar of Roosky." And in passing, it may here be safely admitted that even a wiser man than Solomon might make this declaration in these early years of the twentieth century.

Following the example of greater men than himself when aspiring to public office, Mr. Rodes called a meeting of his party friends in his precinct, to the end that his modest "boom" might be successfully launched. After the accustomed organization had been effected, a committee of five, of which our aspirant was chairman, was duly appointed to prepare and present appropriate resolutions. The committee at once retired for consultation, to a log in the rear of the schoolhouse, leaving the convention in session. No rattling orator being present to arouse the enthusiasm so essential to patient waiting, the little assemblage, wearied by the delay, at length despatched a messenger to expedite, if possible, the labors of the committee. The messenger found the committee in a condition far otherwise than encouraging. The resolutions had failed to materialize, and the chairman, seated upon the log, with pencil in hand, and gazing pensively upon a blank leaf before him, seemed the very picture of despair. Upon a second admonition from the unreasonably impatient meeting, that adjournment would immediately take place unless the resolutions were reported, the committee hastily concluded its labors and, preceded by the chairman with document in hand, solemnly returned to the place of assembly.

The resolutions, two in number, and unanimously and with great enthusiasm promptly adopted, were in words and figures as follows, to-wit:

"(1) Resolv that in the declaration of independence and likewise also in the constitution of the united states, we recognize *a able and well ritten document,* and that we are tetotually oppose to the repeal of airy one of the aforesaid instruments of riting. Resolv:

"(2) that in our fellow-townsman, Solomon P. Rodes, we view a onest man and *hereby annominate him for the legislater."*

XXXVII ANECDOTES OF GOVERNOR OGLESBY

OGLESBY'S GREATNESS IN DISCUSSING QUESTIONS CONNECTED WITH THE REBELLION—HIS WORK IN THE MEXICAN AND CIVIL WARS—HE VISITS THE ORIENT— FAILS TO FIND OUT WHO BUILT THE PYRAMIDS.

Few men have enjoyed a greater degree of popularity than did the late Governor Oglesby of Illinois. He was whole-souled, genial, and at all times the most delightful of companions. He stood in the front rank of campaign orators when slavery, rebellion, war, and reconstruction were the stirring questions of the hour. In the discussion of these once vital issues, with the entire State for an audience, he was without a peer. But when they were relegated to the domain of history and succeeded by tariff, finance, and other commonplace, everyday questions, the Governor felt greatly hampered. In a large degree Othello's occupation was gone. Cold facts, statistics, figures running up into the millions, gave little opportunity for the play of his wonderful imagination.

In his second race for Governor, in a speech at Bloomington, he said, in a deprecatory tone: "These Democrats undertake to discuss the financial question. They oughtn't to do that. They can't possibly understand it. The Lord's truth is, fellow-citizens, *it is about all we Republicans can do to understand that question!"*

He was a gallant soldier in the Mexican and in the great Civil War, and in the latter achieved distinction as a commanding officer. With Weldon, Ewing, McNulta, Fifer, Rowell, and others as listeners, he once graphically described the first battle in which he was engaged. Turning to his old-time comrade, McNulta, he said: "There is one supreme moment in the experience of a soldier that is absolutely ecstatic!" "That," quickly replied McNulta, "is the very moment when he gets into battle."

"No, damn it," said Oglesby, *"it is the very moment he gets out!"*

In his early manhood, Oglesby spent some years abroad. His pilgrimage extended even to Egypt, up the Nile, and to the Holy Land.

Few persons at the time having visited the Orient, Oglesby's descriptions of the wonders of the far-off countries were listened to with the deepest interest. With both memory and imagination in their prime, it can easily be believed that those wonders of the Orient lost nothing by his description. Soon after his return he lectured in Bloomington. The audience were delighted, especially with his description of the Pyramids.

None of us had ever before seen or heard a man who had actually, with his own eyes, beheld these wonders of the ages. Near the close of his lecture, and just after he had suggested the probability of Abraham and Sarah having taken in the Pyramids on their wedding trip, some one in the audience inquired;

"Who built the Pyramids?"

"Oh, damn it," quickly replied the orator, "I don't know who built them; *I asked everybody I saw in Egypt and none of them knew!*"

For much that is of interest in the career of Governor Oglesby I am indebted to his honored successor in office, my neighbor and friend, Hon. Joseph W. Fifer—than whom the country has had no braver soldier and the State no abler Chief Executive.

XXXVIII THE ONE ENEMY

CALEB CUSHING'S POLITICAL CAREER—HIS GREAT AMBITION A SEAT UPON THE SUPREME BENCH—HIS APPOINTMENT THERETO—HIS ONE ENEMY DEFEATS HIS CONFIRMATION.

"He who has a thousand friends has not a friend to spare, And he who has one enemy will meet him everywhere."

The truth of the above couplet has rarely had more forcible illustration than in the case of the late Caleb Cushing of Massachusetts. In politics he was successively Whig, Democrat, and Republican. During his first political affiliation, he was a Representative in Congress; in the second a member of Pierce's Cabinet; and in the third a Minister abroad. He was an eminent lawyer, and for a term ably discharged the duties of Attorney-General of the United States. His one ambition was a seat upon the Supreme Bench.

This was at length gratified by his appointment as Chief Justice of the Great Court. Unfortunately he had, years before, given mortal offence to Aaron A. Sargent, then recently admitted to the bar. The latter soon after moved to California, and became in time a Senator from that State.

When the appointment of Cushing came before the Senate for confirmation, his *one enemy* was there. The appointee had long since forgotten the young lawyer he had once treated so rudely, but he had not been forgotten. The hour of revenge had now come. After a protracted and bitter struggle, Sargent, of the same political affiliation as Cushing, succeeded in defeating the confirmation by a single vote. The political sensation of the hour was the Senator's prompt message to his defeated enemy:

"Time at last sets all things even;
And if we do but watch the hour,
There never yet was human power
Which could evade, if unforgiven,
The patient search and vigil long,
Of him who treasures up a wrong."

XXXIX CONTRASTS OF TIMES

TRAVELLING IN 1845 COMPARED WITH THAT OF THE PRESENT DAY.

While I was Assistant Postmaster-General, Senator Whittihorne, of Tennessee, called at the Department to see me on official business. Seated at a window overlooking the Capitol, he remarked that the chords of memory were touched as he entered the room; that when barely of age, he occupied for a time a desk as a clerk just where he was seated.

He then told me that at the time of the Presidential election in 1844 he was a law student in the office of Mr. Polk, and by his invitation came on with him to Washington. The journey of the President-elect, from Nashville to Washington, was in February, 1845, just prior to his inauguration. He was accompanied by the members of his immediate family, his law student Mr. Whittihorne, and the Hon. Cave Johnson, who was soon to hold a position in his Cabinet. The journey to Washington, as Senator Whittihorne told me, was of two weeks' duration: first, by steamboat on the Cumberland and the Ohio to Pittsburg; thence by stage coach to the national Capitol.

At the time mentioned, railroads scarcely had an existence south of the Ohio and west of the Alleghanies; and save the single wire from Washington to Baltimore, no telegraph line had been constructed.

How striking the commentary, alike upon human accomplishment, and upon opportunity under our free institutions, is here presented! The wearisome and hazardous journey of half a month by steamboat and stage coach had been succeeded by one in palace car of a day and a night of comparative ease and safety, and the clerk had risen from a humble place in the Department to that of Senator from one of the great States in the Union.

XL ENDORSING THE ADMINISTRATION

DIFFICULTY EXPERIENCED BY DEMOCRATIC MEMBERS IN PROCURING APPOINTMENTS FOR THEIR CONSTITUENTS—A NEW MEMBER THREATENS TO FRAME RESOLUTIONS OF CONDEMNATION—HE DOES THE VERY OPPOSITE—AN EXPLANATORY ANECDOTE.

The Democratic members of the forty-ninth Congress who yet survive will probably recall something of the difficulty they experienced in procuring for aspiring constituents prompt appointments to positions of honor, trust, and profit, under the then lately inaugurated administration. An earnest desire was felt, and vehemently expressed at times, by those who had been long excluded from everything that savored of Federal recognition, for sweeping changes all along the line.

A new member of the House, from one of the border States, believing that his grievances were far too heavy to be meekly borne, made open declaration of war, and asserted with great confidence and with the free use of words nowhere to be found in "Little Helps to Youthful Beginners," that at the approaching Democratic convention of his State, resolutions of condemnation of no uncertain sound would be adopted. Some conciliatory observations, which I ventured to offer, were treated with scorn, and the irate member, still breathing out threatenings, hastily turned his footsteps homeward.

A few mornings later, I was agreeably surprised to find in *The Post* a telegram to the effect that upon the assembling of the convention aforementioned, the honorable gentleman above designated, securing prompt recognition from the chair, had, under a suspension of the rules, secured the unanimous adoption of a resolution enthusiastically and unconditionally endorsing every act, past, present, and to come, of the national Democratic administration.

Upon the return of the member to Washington, I expressed to him my surprise at a conversion which, in suddenness and power, had possibly but one parallel in either sacred or profane history. Closing his near eye, he said:

"Look here! I can illustrate my position about this matter by relating a little incident I witnessed near the close of the war. Just as I was leaving an old ferry-boat in which I had crossed the Tennessee River, my attention was attracted to a canoe near by in which were seated two fishermen, both negroes, one a very old man and the other a small boy. Suddenly the canoe capsized and they were both dumped in the deep water. The boy was an expert swimmer and was in no danger. Not so with the old man; he sank immediately, and it certainly seemed that his fishing days were over. The boy, however, with a pluck and skill that did him great credit, instantly dived to the bottom of the river, and with great difficulty and much personal peril finally succeeded in landing the old man upon the shore.

"Approaching the heroic youth, as he was wringing the water from his own garments, I inquired,

"'Your father, is he?'

"'No, sir,' was the quick reply, 'he ain't my father.'

"'Your grandfather, then?'

"'No, sir, he ain't my grandfather nuther, he ain't no kin to me, I tell you.'

"'Earnestly expressing my surprise at his having imperilled his own life to save a man who was no kin to him, the boy replied,'

"'You see, dis was de way of it boss; *de ole man, he had de bait!*"

XLI ANECDOTES ABOUT LINCOLN

LINCOLN'S TROUBLE WITH THREE EMANCIPATION ENTHUSIASTS—A SCHOOLBOY'S TROUBLE WITH SHADRACH, MESHACH, AND ABEDNEGO—PRETTY WELL OFF WITH A FORTUNE OF FIFTEEN THOUSAND DOLLARS—LINCOLN REBUKES SOME RICH MEN WHO DEMAND A GUNBOAT FOR THE PROTECTION OF NEW YORK.

The Hon. John B. Henderson, now of Washington City, but during the war and the early reconstruction period a distinguished Union Senator from Missouri, relates the following incident of Mr. Lincoln. During the gloomy period of 1862, late one Sunday afternoon he called upon the President and found his alone in his library. After some moments Mr. Lincoln, apparently much depressed, stated in substance: "They are making every effort, Henderson, to induce me to issue a Proclamation of Emancipation. Sumner and Wilson and Stevens are constantly urging me, but I don't think it best now; do *you* think so, Henderson?" To which the latter promptly replied that he did not think so; that such a measure, under existing conditions, would, in his judgment, be ill-advised and possibly disastrous. "Just what I think," said the President, "but they are constantly coming and urging me, sometimes alone, sometimes in couples, and sometimes *all three together*, but constantly pressing me." With that he walked across the room to a window and looked out upon the Avenue. Sure enough, Wilson, Stevens, and Sumner were seen approaching the Executive Mansion. Calling his visitor to the window and pointing to the approaching figures, in a tone expressing something of that wondrous sense of humor that no burden or disaster could wholly dispel, he said, "Henderson, did you ever attend an old field school?" Henderson replied that he did.

"So did I," said the President; "what little education I ever got in early life was in that way. I attended an old field school in Indiana, where our only reading-book was the Bible. One day we were standing up reading the account of the three Hebrew children in the fiery furnace. A little tow-headed fellow who stood beside me had the verse with the unpronounceable names; he mangled up Shadrach and Meshach woefully, and finally went all to pieces on Abednego. Smarting under the blows which, in accordance with the old-time custom, promptly followed his delinquency, the little fellow sobbed aloud. The reading, however, went round, each boy in the class reading his verse in turn. The sobbing at length ceased, and the tow-headed boy gazed intently upon the verses ahead.

"Suddenly he gave a pitiful yell, at which the school-master demanded:

"'What is the matter with you now?'

"'Look there,' said the boy, pointing to the next verse, 'there comes them same damn three fellows again!'"

As indicating the slight concern Mr. Lincoln had about money-making, as well as the significance of the expression "well-off" half a century or so ago, the following conversation, related by Judge Weldon, is in point.

At the opening of the De Witt Circuit Court in May, 1859, just a year before his first nomination for the Presidency, Mr. Lincoln was present, unattended for possibly the first time by his life-long friend, Major John T. Stuart. Upon inquiry from Weldon as to whether Stuart was coming, Lincoln replied, "No, Stuart told me that he would not be here this term."

Weldon then remarked, "I suppose the Major has gotten to be pretty well off and doesn't have to attend all the courts in the Circuit."

"Yes," replied Lincoln, "Stuart is pretty well to do, pretty well to do."

"How much is the Major probably worth, Mr. Lincoln?" asked Mr. Weldon.

"Well," replied the latter, after a moment's thought, "I don't know exactly; Stuart is pretty well off; *I suppose he must be worth about fifteen thousand dollars.*"

Another incident characteristic of Mr. Lincoln, was related by his friend Judge Weldon.

During the gloomiest period of the war, and while our seaboard cities were in constant apprehension of attack, a delegation of business men from New York visited Washington for the purpose of having a gunboat secured for the defence of their city. At their request, Judge Weldon accompanied them to the Executive Mansion and introduced them to the President. The spokesman of the delegation, after depicting at length and in somewhat pompous manner, the dangers that threatened the great metropolis, took occasion, in manner at once conclusive, to state that he spoke with authority, that the gentlemen represented property aggregating in value many hundreds of millions of dollars. At this, Mr. Lincoln interposing impatiently, and in a manner never to be forgotten, said:

"It seems to me, gentlemen, that if I were as rich as you *say* you are, and as badly *scared* as you *appear* to be, I would, in this hour of my country's distress, *just buy that gunboat myself!*"

XLII THE FIRST LEGISLATIVE ASSEMBLY IN AMERICA

FAR-REACHING EFFECTS OF THE FOUNDING OF THE VIRGINIA HOUSE OF BURGESSES—VIRGINIA'S GIFT OF TERRITORY TO THE GOVERNMENT—KASKASKIA CAPTURED FROM THE BRITISH—JAMESTOWN THE SCENE OF THE FIRST BRITISH COLONY—THE BEGINNINGS OF COLONIAL SELF-GOVERNMENT— SALUTARY LAWS MADE—POCAHONTAS—GOVERNMENT BY CHARTER—DESPOTISM OF JAMES I—MACAULAY ON THE STUART DYNASTY—THE THIRTEEN ORIGINAL COLONIES— UNJUST TAXATION—PROGRESS OF REPUBLICAN PRINCIPLES—VIRGINIA NOTABLE FOR HER STATESMEN.

On the thirtieth of July, 1907, at the Jamestown Exposition, was celebrated the anniversary of the assembling of the House of Burgesses of Virginia, the first legislative body to assemble upon the Western continent. The meeting was presided over by the present Speaker of the Virginia House of Burgesses, and by invitation of the President of the Exposition addresses were made by ex-speakers Carlisle, Keifer, and myself.

My address was as follows:

"We have assembled upon historic ground. We celebrate to-day a masterful historic event. Other anniversaries, sacredly observed, have their deep meaning; no one, however, is fraught with profounder significance than this.

"The management of the great Exposition did well to set apart this thirtieth of July to commemorate the coming together at Jamestown of the first legislative assembly in the New World. The assembling of the representatives of the people upon the eventful day two hundred and eighty-six years ago—of which this is the anniversary —marked an epoch which, in far-reaching consequences, scarcely finds a parallel in history. It was the initial step in the series of stupendous events which found their culmination in the Bill of Rights, the Declaration of Independence, and the formulation of the Federal Constitution.

"From my home, a thousand miles to the westward, in the great valley of the Mississippi, I come at your bidding to bear part in the exercises of this day. Not as a stranger, an alien to your blood, but as your countryman, your fellow-citizen, I gladly lift my voice in this great assemblage. And when were the words, 'fellow-citizens,' of deeper significance as suggestive of a more glorious past then to-day, as we gather upon this hallowed spot to commemorate one of the grandest events of which history has any record?

"The magical words, 'fellow-citizens,' never fail to touch a responsive chord in the patriotic heart. Was it the gifted Prentiss who at a critical moment of our history exclaimed, 'For whether upon the Sabine or the St. Johns; standing in the shadow of Bunker Hill, or amid the ruins of Jamestown; near the great northern chain of lakes, or within the sound of the Father of Waters, flowing unvexed to the sea; in the crowded mart of the great metropolis, or upon the western verge of the continent, where the restless tide of emigration is stayed only by the ocean—everywhere upon this broad domain, thank God, I can still say, "fellow-citizens"'?

"And truly, an Illinoisan is no stranger within the confines of 'the Old Dominion.' You have not forgotten, we cannot forget, that the territory now embraced in five magnificent commonwealths bordering upon the Ohio and the Mississippi, was at a crucial period of our history the generous gift of Virginia to the general Government,—a gift that in splendid statesmanship and in far-reaching consequence has no counterpart; one which at the pivotal moment made possible the ratification of the Articles of Confederation—the sure forecast of 'the more perfect Union' yet to follow. Illinois, the greatest of the commonwealths to which I have alluded, can never forget that it was a Virginian, George Rogers Clark, who, in the darkest days of the Revolution, led the expedition—'worthy of mention,' as was said by John Randolph, 'with that of Hannibal in Italy,'—by which the ancient capital, Kaskaskia, was captured, the British flag deposed, and Illinois taken possession of in the name of the commonwealth whose Governor, Patrick Henry, had authorized the masterful conquest. Nor can it be forgotten that the deed of cession by which Illinois became part and parcel of the general Government, bears—as commissioners upon the part of Virginia—the honored names of Arthur Lee, James Monroe, and Thomas Jefferson. Is it to be wondered at, that a magnificent Illinois building adorns the grounds of the Jamestown Exposition,—and that Illinois hearts everywhere beat in unison with yours in the celebration of one of the epoch-marking days of all the ages?

"The time is propitious for setting history aright. This exposition will not have been in vain if the fact be crystallized into history yet to be written, that the first settlement by English-speaking people—just three centuries ago—upon this continent, was at Jamestown. And that here self-government—in its crude form but none the less self-government—had its historical beginning. Truly has it been said by an eminent writer of your own State, that prior to December, 1620, 'the colony of Virginia had become so firmly established and self-government in precisely the same form which existed up to the Revolution throughout the English colonies had taken such firm root thereon, that it was beginning to affect not only the people but the Government of Great Britain.' In the old church at Jamestown, on July 30, 1619, was held the first legislative assembly of the New World—the historical House of Burgesses. It consisted of twenty-two members, and its constituencies were the several plantations of the colony. A speaker was elected, the session opened with prayer, and the oath of supremacy duly taken. The Governor and Council occupied the front seats, and the members of the body, in accordance with the custom of the British Parliament, wore their hats during the session.

"This General Assembly convened in response to a summons issued by Sir George Yeardley, the recently appointed Governor of the colony. Hitherto the colony had been governed by the London Council; the real life of Virginia dates from the arrival of Yeardley, bringing with him from England 'commissions and instructions for the better establishing of a commonwealth.'

"The centuries roll back, and before us, in solemn session, is the first assembly upon this continent of the chosen representatives of the people. It were impossible to overstate its deep import to the struggling colony, or its far-reaching consequence to States yet unborn. In this little assemblage of twenty-two burgesses, the Legislatures of nearly fifty commonwealths to-day and of the Congress with its representatives from all the States of 'an indestructible union' find their historical beginning. The words of Bancroft in this connection are worthy of remembrance: 'A perpetual interest attaches to this first elective body that ever assembled in the Western world, representing the people of Virginia and making laws for their government more than a year before the *Mayflower* with the Pilgrims left the harbor of Southampton, and while Virginia was still the only British colony on the continent of America.'

"It is to us to-day a matter of profound gratitude that these the earliest American lawgivers were eminently worthy their high vocation. While confounding, in some degree, the separate functions of government, as abstractly defined at a later day by Montesquieu, and eventually put in concrete form in our fundamental laws, State and Federal—it is none the less true that these first legislators clearly discerned their inherent rights as a part of the English-speaking race. More important still, a perusal of the brief records they have left, impresses the conviction that they were no strangers to the underlying fact that the people are the true source of political power, the evidence whereof is to be found in the scant records of their proceedings—a priceless heritage of all future generations. And first—

and fundamental in all legislative assemblies—they asserted the absolute right to determine as to the election and qualification of members. Grants of land were asked, not only for the planters, but for their wives, 'as equally important parts of the colony.' It was wisely provided that of the natives 'the most towardly boys in wit and the graces' should be educated and set apart to the work of converting the Indians to the Christian religion; stringent penalties were attached to idleness, gambling, and drunkenness; excess in apparel was prohibited by heavy taxation; encouragement was given to agriculture in all its known forms; while conceding 'the commission of privileges' brought over by the new Governor as their fundamental law, yet with the liberty-guarding instinct of their race they kept the way open for seeking redress, 'in case they should find aught not perfectly squaring with the state of the colony.' No less important were the enactments regulating the dealings of the colonists with the Indians. Yet to be mentioned, and of transcendent importance, was the claim of the burgesses 'to allow or disallow,' at their own good pleasure, all orders of the court of the London Company. And deeply significant was the declaration of these representatives of three centuries ago, that their enactments were instantly to be put in force, without waiting for their ratification in England. And not to be forgotten is the stupendous fact that while the battle with the untamed forces of nature was yet waging, and conflict with savage foe of constant recurrence, these legislators provided for the maintenance of public worship, and took the initial steps for the establishment of an institution of learning. It is not too much to say that the hour that witnessed these enactments witnessed the triumph of the popular over the court party; in no unimportant sense, the first triumph of the American colonists over kingly prerogative. Looking through the mists of the mighty past, Mr. Speaker, to the House of Burgesses, over which your first predecessor presided, would it be out of place to apply to that assemblage the historic words spoken of one of a later period: 'Nobles by the right of an earlier creation, and priests by the imposition of a mightier hand'?

"Did the occasion permit, it would be of wondrous interest to linger for a time with these, the earliest colonies in this, the cradle of American civilization; to know something of their daily life, their hopes and ambitions, their struggles and triumphs; something of their ceaseless vigil and of the perils that environed them; to recall stirring incidents and heroic achievements; to catch a gleam of a spirit of self-sacrifice and devotion which in all the annals of men scarcely finds a parallel. It would be of curious interest to watch the parade and pomp of governors and councils of royal appointment in attempted representation of a pageantry familiar to the Old World, but which was to have no permanent abiding place in the New. Governors and their subordinates—though bearing the royal commission, yet in rare instances to be classed only as bad or indifferent—

pass in long procession before us into the dim shadows. But out of the mists of this long past, two figures emerge that have for us an abiding interest, John Smith and Pocahontas—names that have place not alone in romance and song, but upon the pages of veritable history.

"Colonial governors strutted their brief hour upon the stage and have long passed to oblivion; but Smith, the intrepid soldier, the ever-present friend and counsellor of the early colonists, their stalwart protector—alike against the bullet of the savage and the mandate of official power—will not pass from remembrance so long as heroic deeds are counted worthy of enduring record among men.

"With dark background of rude cabin and wigwam, of scantily appointed plantation, and of far-stretching forest—with its mysterious voices and manifold perils—there passes before us the lovely form of the beautiful Indian maiden, the daughter and pride of the renowned native chieftain. So long as courage and fidelity arouse sympathy and admiration, so long will the thrilling legend of Pocahontas touch responsive chords in human hearts. Its glamour is upon the early pages of colonial history; her witchery lingers upon stream and forest, and the firm earth upon which we tread seems to have been hallowed by her footsteps.

"A name that sheds lustre upon the earliest pages of our Colonial history is that of Sir Edwin Sandys. Under his courageous leadership, what was known as the Virginia or Liberal party in the London Company obtained a signal triumph over that of the court. The result was the formal grant to the colony guaranteeing free government by written charter. Its declared purpose was to secure 'the greatest comfort and benefit to the people and the prevention of injustice, grievances, and oppression.' It provided for full legislative authority in the Assembly, and was with some modifications the model of the systems subsequently introduced into the other English colonies.

"By this charter, representative government and trial by jury became recognized rights in the New World. Upon this charter, as has been truly said, 'Virginia erected the superstructure of her liberties.'

"The coming of this charter marked an epoch in the history of the Jamestown colony, and set the pace for English-speaking settlements yet in the future.

"It was in very truth the first step in the direction of the establishment of the great Republic which was to be the enduring beacon-light of self-governing people in all future ages.

"To a full appreciation of the supreme significance of the mighty event we to-day celebrate and its results—now constituting so inspiring a chapter of history—some account must be taken of conditions then existing in the mother country. While obtaining the guarantee of a large measure of self-government for the New World, Sir Edwin Sandys and his co-patriots were unable to secure that which even savored of liberal administration in the Old. James—the first of the Stuart Dynasty—was upon the English throne. In narrow, selfish state-craft his is possibly in the long list of sovereigns without a rival. The exercise and maintenance of royal prerogative was with him the 'be all and end all' of government, and, abetted by the sycophants about him, he unwittingly laid the train of inexorable events that were to culminate in the execution of one and the banishment of another of his line. His claim was that of absolute power, and during a reign of twenty-two years—extending from the death of Queen Elizabeth to the year 1625—he was the unrelenting foe of whatever pertained to freedom in religion or in government. His apparent indifference to the execution of his mother—the ill-fated Mary, Queen of Scots—and his condemnation of the illustrious Sir Walter Raleigh to the scaffold, are alone sufficient to render the memory of this monarch forever infamous. It is a marvel, indeed, that with James the First upon the throne, and popular freedom in such a low state throughout his immediate realm, that so large a measure of liberty should have been conceded to the distant colony. The achievement is the enduring evidence of unsurpassed courage in the men in whose immediate keeping were the early fortunes of the Virginia colony, and sheds unfading lustre upon their memories.

"Nor can it be forgotten that from the masterful hour that witnessed the assembling of the first House of Burgesses until the abdication of James the Second, the welfare of the Virginia colony was in large measure in the iron grasp of stern antagonists to all that pertained to liberty of conscience and to popular rule. Whatever there was of progress during the seventy years—barring the brief period of the Commonwealth—that immediately preceded the historic English Revolution, and the crowning of William and Mary, was despite the untiring hostility of the Stuart Dynasty. During this period the lives of Englishmen at home were as the dust in the balance. It witnessed the very heyday of the infamous Star Chamber. It was of Strafford, the bloody instrument (though wearing judicial ermine) of Charles the First, that Macaulay said: 'If justice, in the whole range of its wide armory, contained one weapon which could pierce him, that weapon his pursuers were bound, before God and man, to employ.'

"And for all time, the Stuart Dynasty itself remains impaled by the pen of the same master:

"'Then came those days never to be recalled without a blush—the days of servitude without loyalty, and sensuality without love, of dwarfish talents and gigantic vices, the paradise of cold hearts and narrow minds, the golden age of the coward, the bigot, and the slave. The principles of liberty were the scoff of every grinning courtier, and the *anathema maranatha* of every fawning dean. In every high place worship was paid to Charles and James— Belial and Moloch,—and England propitiated those obscene and cruel idols with the blood of her best and bravest children. Crime succeeded to crime and disgrace to disgrace, until the race, accursed of God and man, was a second time driven forth to wander on the face of the earth, and to be a byword and a shaking of the head to the nations.'

"It is our pleasing task to turn now from the dark annals of our English forebears to the stupendous events of which that we to-day celebrate in the historical forecast. With the passing years, a continuing tide of emigration was setting in from the Old to the New World. Additional settlements had sprung into being, and the Plantation in its distinctive sense had given way to the Colony, to be succeeded yet later by the State. The glory of Jamestown had measurably departed, and to Williamsburg, and yet later to the now splendid city upon the James, had been transferred the seat of Virginia authority. New England, despite natural obstacles and constant peril, was surely working out her large place in history. Puritan, Quaker, Dutchman, Cavalier, Scotch-Irish, and Huguenot —'building better than they knew'—had established permanent habitations from Plymouth Rock to Savannah. Brave men from the early fringe of settlements upon the Atlantic—regardless of obstacle and danger—had pushed their way westward, and laid the sure foundations of future commonwealths. From New Hampshire to Georgia, thirteen English-speaking colonies, with a population aggregating near two millions, had attained to a large measure of the dignity of distinctive States. Their allegiance, meanwhile, to the mother country had been unfaltering, and in her fierce struggle with France for the mastery of the continent, America had sealed her loyalty with the best blood of her sons.

"The successors to the first House of Burgesses had learned well the lessons gleaned from the scant pages of their earliest history. Attempts to tax the unrepresented colonies soon encountered concerted hostility. 'No taxation without representation' became the universal slogan. The words spoken in the British Parliament by Barre—worthy comrade of the gallant Wolfe on the Heights of Abraham—near a century and a half after the event we now celebrate, will quicken the pulse of all coming generations of American patriots. Said he:

"'Your oppressions planted them in America. They fled from your tyranny to a then uncultivated, unhospitable country where they exposed themselves to almost all the hardships to which human nature is liable, among others to the cruelties of a savage foe; they grew by your neglect of them. As soon as you began to care for them, that care was exercised in sending persons to rule them, to spy out their liberties, to misrepresent their actions and to prey upon them; men whose behavior on many occasions has caused the blood of those sons of liberty to recoil within them; men promoted to the highest seats of justice, some who, to my knowledge, were glad, by going to a foreign country, to escape being brought to the bar of a court of justice in their own. The colonists have nobly taken up arms in your defence; have asserted a valor amid their constant and laborious industry for the defence of a country whose frontier was drenched in blood. And, believe me—remember, I warn you—the same spirit of freedom which actuated that people at first will accompany them still.'

"And how prophetic now seem the words of Burke in the same great debate:

"'There is America, which at this day serves for little more than to amuse you with stories of savage men and uncouth manners, yet shall, before you taste of death, show itself equal to the whole of that commerce which now attracts the envy of the world.'

"Standing at his hour almost within hailing distance of the spot that witnessed the surrender of Cornwallis and the termination of the War of the Revolution, it would be passing strange if we should fail to catch something of the inspiration of the impassioned words of Barre and of Burke, and their wondrous associations.

"It is said that in Venice there is sacredly preserved a letter written by Columbus a few hours before he sailed from Palos. With reverent expression of trust in God—humbly but with unfaltering faith—he spoke of his past voyage to 'that famous land.' His dream while a suppliant in the outer chambers of kings, and while keeping lonely vigil upon the deep, was the discovery of a new pathway to the Indies. Yet who can doubt that to his prophetic soul was even then fore-shadowed something of 'that famous land' with the warp and woof of whose history, tradition, and song his name and fame are linked for all time. Can it not truly be said of the members of the first House of Burgesses, as was said of Columbus and his compeers, 'They were pioneers in the march to independence—precursors in the only progress of freedom which was to have no backward steps?' They only 'opened the gates' and lo! there came in the builders of a new and mighty nation.

"Had it been given to the Virginia—the American—legislators whose memories we honor this day, 'to look into the seeds of time,' what mighty events, with the rolling years and centuries, would have passed before their visions. They would have seen the colony they had planted in the wilderness, day by day strengthening its cords, enlarging its borders, and with firm tread advancing steadily to recognized place among the nations.

They would have beheld the savage foe—giving way before the inexorable advance of the hated 'pale face'—sadly retreating toward the ever-receding western verge of civilization. It would have been theirs to witness the symbols of French and Spanish authority disappear forever from mainland and island of the New World. Following the sun a thousand miles toward his setting, their eyes would have been gladdened by the great river flowing unvexed from northern lake to southern sea through a mighty realm that knew no allegiance other than to the government that here had its feeble beginning. They would—near a century and a half later than the meeting of the first House of Burgesses—have beheld their descendants listening in rapt attention to the impassioned denunciation by Patrick Henry of the tyranny of the royal successor of James the First; the thirteen colonies arming for the seven years' struggle with the most powerful of nations; the presentation, by a Virginian, in the wondrous assemblage at Philadelphia of the Declaration of Independence; under the matchless leadership of a Virginian yet more illustrious than Jefferson, the Colonial army, with decimated ranks and tattered standards, would have passed in review—all past suffering, sacrifice, humiliation, and defeat forgotten in the hour of splendid triumph. Yet later, and in the great convention over which Washington presided, and in which Madison was the chief factor, they would have witnessed the deathless principles of the historic Declaration crystallized into the Federal compact, which was destined forever to hold States and people in fraternal union. They would have seen a gallant people of the Old World—catching inspiration from the New—casting off the oppression of centuries and, through baptism of blood, fashioning a Republic upon that whose liberties they had so signally aided to establish. Yet later, and not France alone, but Mexico and States extending far to the southward, substituting for monarchical rule that of the people under written Constitutions modeled after that of the great American Republic. And yet more marvellous, in Great Britain the divine right of kings an exploded dogma; the royal successor to the Stuarts and George the Third only a ceremonial figurehead in government; the House of Lords in its death struggle; all real political power centred in the Commons, and England—though still under the guise of monarchy—essentially a republic.

"And what a grand factor Virginia has been in all that pertains to human government in this Western world during the past three centuries. From the pen of one of her illustrious sons, George Mason, came the 'Bill of Rights'—now in its essentials embedded by the early amendments into our Federal Constitution; from that of another, not alone the great Declaration, but the statutes securing for his own State religious freedom, and the abolition of primogeniture—the detested legacy of British ancestors. His sword returned to its scabbard with the achievement of the independence of the colonies, and the mission of Washington was yet but half accomplished. To garner up the fruits of successful revolution by ensuring stable government was the task demanding the loftiest statesmanship. The five years immediately succeeding our first treaty of peace with Great Britain have been truly defined, 'our period of greatest peril.' It was fortunate, indeed, that Washington was called to preside over the historic convention of '87, and that his spirit—a yearning for an indissoluble union of the States— permeated all its deliberations. Fortunate, indeed, that in its councils was his colleague and friend, the constructive statesman, James Madison. Inseparably associated for all time with the formulation and interpretation of the great covenant are the names of two illustrious Virginians—for all the ages illustrious Americans —Madison, the father, and Marshall, the expounder of the Constitution.

"It remained to another son of this first commonwealth, from the high place to which he had been chosen, to enunciate in trenchant words, at a crucial moment, a national policy which, under the designation of 'the Monroe doctrine,' has been the common faith of three generations of his countrymen and is to remain the enduring bar to the establishment of monarchial government upon this western hemisphere.

"Four decades later, at the striking of the hour that noted the inevitable 'breaking with the past,' it remained to still another illustrious successor of Jefferson—alike of Virginian ancestry, and born within her original domain—by authoritative proclamation to liberate a race, and thereby, for all time, to give enlarged and grander meaning to our imperishable declaration of human rights.

"My countrymen, the little settlement planted just three centuries ago near the spot upon which we have to-day assembled has under divine guidance grown into a mighty nation. Eighty millions of people, proud of local traditions and achievements, yet looking beyond the mere confines of their distinctive commonwealths, find their chief glory in being citizens of the great Republic. The mantle of peace is over our own land, and our accredited representatives in the world's conference, at this auspicious hour, are outlining a policy that looks to the establishment of enduring peace among all the nations. To-day, inspired by the sublime lessons of the event we celebrate and with hearts of gratitude to God for all he hath vouchsafed to our fathers and to us in the past, let us take courage, and turn our faces hopefully, reverently, trustingly to the future."

XLIII A NEW DAY ADDED TO THE CALENDAR

THE HIGH CHARACTER OF STERLING MORTON AS A MAN AND A PUBLIC SERVANT —HONORED BY CLEVELAND— ORIGINATOR OF ARBOR DAY.

I recall with pleasure years of close personal friendship with J. Sterling Morton. He was a gentleman of lofty character and recognized ability. Much of his life was given to the public service. As Secretary of Agriculture he was in close touch with President Cleveland during his last official term.

At the dedication of the monument erected to his memory at his home, Nebraska City, October 28, 1905, I spoke as follows:

"I count it high privilege to speak a few words upon an occasion so fraught with interest to this State, and to the entire country. I gladly bear my humble tribute to the man whom I honored in life, and whose memory I cherish. A manlier man than Sterling Morton, one more thoughtful, kind, considerate, self-reliant, hopeful, I have not known. Truly—

'A man he seemed, of cheerful yesterdays,
And confident to-morrows.'

Of few men could it more truly be said, 'He took counsel ever of his courage—never of his fears.' With firm convictions upon pending vital issues, he did not shrink from the conflict. His antagonist he met in the open. In the words of Lord Brougham, 'His weapons were ever those of the warrior—never of the assassin.'

"This, is indeed no ordinary occasion. Here and now, we unveil a monument erected in honor of the memory of one who, alike in private life and in public station, illustrated the noblest characteristics of the American citizen. Something of his life and achievements we have heard with profound interest from the lips of the chosen orator of this great occasion, ex-President Cleveland —one indeed eminently fitted for the task. The orator was worthy the subject; the subject—honoring the memory of one of the benefactors of his age—worthy the orator.

"In all the relations of life, the man whose memory we honor this day was worthy the emulation of the young men who succeed him upon the stage of the world. With clear brain and clean hands he ably and faithfully administered high public trusts. He was in the loftiest sense worthy the personal and official association of the eminent Chief Magistrate at whose Council Board he sat, and whose confidence he fully shared.

"Fortune, indeed, came with both hands full to Nebraska, when J. Sterling Morton, in early manhood, selected this struggling frontier State for his home. How well, and with what large interest, he repaid Nebraska for a confidence that knew no abatement, this noble monument is the enduring witness.

"Under his guiding hand, a new day was added to the calendar. The glory is his of having called Arbor Day into being. Touched by his magic wand, millions of trees now beautify and adorn this magnificent State. It is no mere figure of speech to say that the wilderness—by transition almost miraculous—has become a garden, the desolate places been made to blossom as the rose. 'Tree-planting day' is now one of the sacred days of this commonwealth. Henceforth, upon its annual recurrence, ordinary avocations are to be suspended, and this day wholly set apart to pursuits which tend to beautify the home, make glorious the landscape, and gladden the hearts of all the people. Inseparably associated in all the coming years with this day and its memories will be the name of J. Sterling Morton. That he was its inspiration, is his abiding fame.

"In other times, monuments have been erected to men whose chief distinction was, that desolation and human slaughter had marked their pathways. The hour has struck, and a new era dawned. The monument we now unveil is to one whose name brings no thoughts of decimated ranks, or of desolated provinces, no memories of beleaguered cities, of starving peoples, or of orphans' tears. In all the years, it will be associated with glorious peace. Peace, 'that hath her victories no less renowned than war'; peace, in whose train are happy homes, songs of rejoicing, the glad laughter of children, the planting of trees, and the golden harvest.

'Soft peace she brings; wherever she arrives,
She builds our quiet as she forms our lives;
Lays the rough paths of peevish nature even,
And opens in each heart a little heaven.'"

XLIV A MOUNTAIN COLLEGE

SUCH INSTITUTIONS VALUABLE FOR MOULDING CHARACTER—MR. SCOTT BOTH HONORABLE AND PRUDENT IN BUSINESS—HIS GREATNESS AS AN AGRICULTURIST—HIS AVOIDANCE OF PUBLIC LIFE—HIS SOCIAL AND DOMESTIC VIRTUES—DEPENDENCE OF THE NATION ON THE CHARACTER OF ITS LITERARY INSTITUTIONS.

In 1895, Mrs. Julia Green Scott, of Bloomington, Illinois, established a college in the mountains of Kentucky in honor of the memory of her husband. He was a native of Kentucky, and the institution bears his honored name.

Upon the occasion of the dedication I spoke as follows:

"The dedication of the Matthew T. Scott, Jr., Collegiate Institute marks an important epoch in the history of central eastern Kentucky. It cannot be doubted that this institution will be potent for good in moulding the character and fitting the youth of this and succeeding generations for the important duties that pertain to citizenship in a great Republic. Is it too much to believe that this may be reckoned as one of the many agencies in this land, that in the outstretched years will inspire our youth with yet higher ideals of duties that await them in life? Would that the words I now repeat of one of England's great statesmen could be indelibly impressed upon the memory of all who may hereafter pass out from these walls: 'Be inspired with the belief that life is a great and noble calling; not a mean and grovelling thing that we are to shuffle through as we can, but an elevated and lofty destiny.'

"It is eminently fitting to this occasion, that I recall something of the man whose honored name has been appropriately given to this institution. And yet, I am not unmindful of the fact that if in life he would shrink from public mention of his name, or of aught associated with it in the way of benefactions. He was a native of Kentucky—born in Fayette County, February 4, 1828. His father, of the same name, was an honored citizen of Lexington, and for many years the leading banker of the State. The son inherited the high sense of personal honor, and the splendid capacity for business, that for a lifetime so eminently characterized his father. A graduate of Centre College at the age of eighteen, his fortunes were soon cast in Central Illinois, where his remaining years were spent, and where his ashes now repose. During his early residence in Illinois Mr. Scott realized—

as few men did fully at that day —the marvellous prosperity that surely awaited the development of the resources of that great State. It was the day of golden opportunity for the man of wise forecast. His investments were timely; his business methods all upon the highest plane. He became in time a large landed proprietor, and stood in the van of the advanced agriculturists of his day. He formulated enduring systems of tilling the soil, and making sure the munificent reward of labor wisely bestowed upon this, the primal calling of man. His methods were in large measure adopted by others, and have proved no unimportant factor in the development and prosperity of the great agricultural interests of the State.

"Mr. Scott was in the largest sense a man of affairs. He was ever the safe counsellor in the many business enterprises of which he was the founder. It were scant praise to say he was possessed of the highest integrity. His was indeed an integrity that could know no temptation. Faithful to every obligation, he was incapable of an ignoble act. He was eminently a just man, possessing in a marked degree the sturdy characteristics of his Scotch-Irish ancestors. His principle in action was:

'For justice all place a temple,
And all season Summer.'

"He was in no sense a self-seeker. Deeply interested in public affairs, and having the courage of his convictions upon the exciting questions of the day, he was never a candidate for public office. Declining the nomination tendered him by his party for Congress, he chose the quiet of home rather than the turmoil of public life. In the advocacy, however, of what he believed to be for the public weal, 'he took counsel ever of his courage, never of his fears.' That he possessed the ability to have acquitted himself with honor in responsible positions of public trust, no one who knew him could doubt.

"Courteous to all with whom he came in contact, he was the highest type of the old-school gentleman. He exemplified in his daily life the truth of the poet's words:

'That best portion of a good man's life,
His little, nameless, unremembered acts
Of kindness and of love.'

"No man ever had a loftier appreciation of what was due to woman. There was in very truth a relish of old-time chivalry in his bearing in the presence of ladies. He was never happier than when surrounded by children, by whom he was ever trusted and loved.

"No higher tribute could be paid him than by the words spoken with equal truth of another: 'With him the assured guardian of my children, I could have pillowed my head in peace.'

"Holding steadily, and without reservation, to the Presbyterian faith of his fathers, he was none the less imbued with a true catholic spirit, and gave where needed, liberally of his abundance. He was deeply touched by every tale of human sorrow,

'His hand open as day to melting charity.'

"I may be pardoned for adding that Mr. Scott was supremely happy in his domestic ties. Blessed in all who gathered about his hearthstone, his cup of happiness was full to overflowing. All who crossed his threshold felt that they were indeed in the sunshine of the perfect home. He sleeps in the beautiful cemetery near the city he loved, his grave covered with flowers by those to whom in life he had been a benefactor and friend. To those to whom his toils and cares were given, to kindred and friends, his memory will ever be a precious heritage. Truly,

'the just Keeps something of his glory, in his dust.'

"I know of no words more fitting with which to close this poor tribute to the man I honored and loved, than those of Dr. Craig in his beautiful eulogy upon the Rev. Dr. Lewis W. Green, father of Mrs. Julia G. Scott, the noble and gifted woman whose generosity has made possible the founding of the Institution we now dedicate:

"'Society at large felt the impress of his noble character, his polished breeding, and his widespread beneficence. His determination to excel, and that by means of faithful diligence and laborious applications, should arouse our young men to like fidelity to their increasing opportunities. He was the most unselfish of men, the most affectionate of friends, the humblest of Christians. He owed much to the soil from which he sprang. He repaid that much, and with large interest.'

"The Institution we now dedicate is just upon the threshold of what we trust will prove an abundantly useful and honorable career. And while we may not 'look into the seeds of time and say which grain will grow and which will not,' yet we may well believe that under judicious management, already assured, this will prove a potent agency in the great work of education.

"In this connection the words of a former President of Transylvania University, and of Centre College, Dr. Green, possess to-day as deep significance as when uttered almost a half-century ago:

"'But it may be truly said, that no domestic instruction, however wise, no political institution, however free, no social organization, however perfect, no discoveries of science, however rapid or sublime, no activity of the press—pouring forth with prolific abundance its multitudinous publications—no accumulation of ancient learning in stately libraries, no one, nor all of these together, can supersede the education of the school; nay, all of them derive their noblest elements and highest life from the instruction of the living teacher. The intelligence of families, the wisdom of Governments, the freedom of nations, the progress of science itself, and of all our useful arts, is measured by the condition and character of our literary institutions. . . . It is from such as these, that the world's great men have sprung. It is from the deep, granite foundations of society that the materials are gathered to rear a superstructure of massive grandeur and enduring strength. The God of nature has scattered broadcast over all our land and our mountain heights, in our secluded valleys, and in many a forest home, the choicest elements of genius; invaluable means of intellectual wealth, the noblest treasures of the State.'

"The hour has struck, and the Matthew T. Scott, Jr., Collegiate Institution enters now upon its sacred mission.

"May we not believe that here will be realized in full fruition the fond hopes of those who have given it being? that as the years come and go, there will pass out from its walls those who by diligent application are fitted for the responsible duties that await them in life, well equipped, it may be, to acquit themselves with honor, in the high places of school, of church, or of State?"

XLV DEDICATION OF A NATIONAL PARK

CHICKAMAUGA NATIONAL PARK DEDICATED BY ACT OF CONGRESS—THE SURVIVORS OF THE GREAT BATTLE NOW BUT FEW—THE REAL CONSECRATION WAS ACCOMPLISHED BY THE HEROES OF THE FIGHT.

The Chickamauga National Park was by act of Congress dedicated September 19, 1895. Senators Palmer, of Illinois, and Gordon, of Georgia, were the orators of the occasion. The immense audience assembled included the Governors of twenty States and committees of both Houses of Congress. I presided on the occasion, and delivered the following address:

"I am honored by being called to preside over the ceremonies of this day. By solemn decree of the representatives of the American people, this magnificent Park, with its wondrous associations and memories, is now to be dedicated for all time to national and patriotic purposes.

"This is the fitting hour for the august ceremonies we now inaugurate. To-day, by act of the Congress of the United States, the Chickamauga and Chattanooga National Military Park is forever set apart from all common uses, solemnly dedicated for all the ages to all the American people.

"The day is auspicious. It notes the anniversary of one of the greatest battles known to history. Here, in the dread tribunal of last resort, valor contended against valor. Here brave men struggled and died for the right, 'as God gave them to see the right.'

"Thirty-two years have passed, and the few survivors of that masterful day—victors and vanquished alike—again meet upon this memorable field. Alas, the splendid armies which rendezvoused there are now little more than a procession of shadows.

"'On fame's eternal camping-ground,
Their silent tents are spread.'

"Our eyes now behold the sublime spectacle of the honored survivors of the great battle coming together upon these heights once more. They meet, not in deadly conflict, but as brothers, under one flag, fellow-citizens of a common country, all grateful to God, that in the supreme struggle, the Government of our fathers—our common heritage—was triumphant, and that to all the coming generations of our countrymen, it will remain 'an indivisible union of indestructible States.'

"Our dedication to-day is but a ceremony. In the words of the immortal Lincoln at Gettysburg: 'But in a larger sense, we cannot dedicate, we cannot consecrate, we cannot hallow this ground. The brave men living and dead, who struggled here, have consecrated it far above our power to add or detract.'

"I will detain you no longer from listening to the eloquent words of those who were participants in the bloody struggle—the sharers alike in its danger and its glory."

XLVI A BAR MEETING STILL IN SESSION

APPOINTMENT OF A COMMITTEE TO FORMULATE RULES FOR COURT PROCEDURE— SOME MEMBERS AGREE TO VOTE DOWN THE MOTION TO ADJOURN—THE MOTION REJECTED THREE TIMES—INDIGNATION OF THE PRESIDENT.

A Bar meeting recalled by the mention of Mr. Ingersoll would be worth while if it could only be described as it actually occurred.

At the opening of the December term of the Circuit Court in Woodford in the year of grace 'fifty-nine, John Clark, Esq., announced that a meeting of the Bar would be held at the courthouse at "early candle-lighting" on that very evening, for the purpose of formulating rules to be presented to the Court for its government during the term.

At the appointed hour, the lawyers, "home and foreign," being promptly in attendance and the court-room crowded, an organization was duly effected by the election of Colonel Shope, an able and dignified barrister of the old school, as President. As undisputed spokesman of the occasion, Mr. Clark, at once moved the appointment of a committee of five to prepare the aforementioned rules. The motion prevailing, *nem. con.*, in accordance with the time-honored usage, the mover of the resolution was duly appointed Chairman, with Ingersoll, Shaw, Ewing, and the chronicler of these important events as his coadjutors. Upon the retirement of the committee, the rules already prepared by Clark were read and promptly approved, and that gentleman instructed to present them to the Bar meeting —then in patient waiting.

As the recognized parliamentarian of the occasion—with the proposed rules in safe keeping—was in the van, upon the return to the court-room Ingersoll quietly proposed to his three untitled associates that, after the adoption of the resolutions, we should *vote down Clark's motion to adjourn* and thereby remain all night in session. In approved form, and with a dignity that would have done no discredit to a high-church bishop, the rules were read off by the Chairman and agreed to without a dissenting voice.

After a brief silence, Mr. Clark arose and said: "Mr. President, if there is no further business before this meeting, I move we do now adjourn." The motion was duly seconded by Welcome P. Brown, who had been Probate Judge of McLean County far back in the thirties, and postmaster of the struggling village of Bloomington when Jackson was President. President Shope promptly arose and in the blandest possible terms submitted:

"Gentlemen of the Bar, all who are in favor of the motion to adjourn will please say, Aye." Clark, Brown, and a half-a-dozen others at once voted, "Aye." "Those opposed to the motion to adjourn will please say, No," was the alternative then submitted by the impartial presiding officer. Ingersoll, his confederates, and a sufficient contingent won over quietly voted, "No." "The motion is lost," observed the President, resuming his seat. "What is the further pleasure of the meeting?" The silence of the grave for a time prevailed. Ingersoll and his followers deporting themselves with a solemnity well befitting an occasion for prayer. Again arising, the chairman of the committee—in a voice less rotund than before—said: "Well, Mr. President, if there is no *further* business before this meeting, I move we do now adjourn." Duly seconded, the motion was again put, Clark and half a dozen others voting as before. "Those opposed," remarked the President— in tones perceptibly less conciliatory than an hour earlier—"will say, No." The scarcely audible, but none the less effective "no" prevailed, the leader meanwhile giving no sign and apparently rapt as if unravelling the mysteries beyond the veil.

A silence that could be felt now in very truth fell upon the meeting in the old courthouse assembled. Even the bystanders seemed impressed that something far out of the ordinary was happening.

Receiving little in the way of encouragement, the Chairman of the late committee, as he dubiously looked around upon the forms of the silent majority—each of whom sat apparently buried in thought that touched the very depths,—again and for the last time addressed the presiding officer:

"Mr. President, I move *that we adjourn.*"

Conclusions being again tried in wonted parliamentary form between the opposing forces, with like result as before, the venerable president,—by way of prelude first giving full vent to an exclamation nowhere to be found in the Methodist "book of discipline,"—at once indignantly vacated the chair, and literally shook the dust of the court-room from his feet. The others "stood not upon the order of their going," and although fifty years have come and gone, that identical Bar meeting in the old courthouse at Metamora *is still in session,*—never having been officially adjourned even to this day.

XLVII THE HAYNE-WEBSTER DEBATE RECALLED

THE PUBLIC CAREER OF LYMAN TRUMBULL—HE HEARS CALHOUN MAKE A MASTERLY SPEECH IN HIS OWN DEFENCE—TARIFF LAW THE SUBJECT OF DISCUSSION — MR. HAYNE'S REPLY.

Ex-Senator Lyman Trumbull called upon me at the Vice-President's Chamber a few months before his death. It was upon the occasion of his last visit to Washington. He pointed out to me with much interest the seat he had occupied for many years in the Senate. The Senators to whom I introduced him had all come in since his day. His associates in that chamber, with three or four exceptions, had passed beyond the veil.

The public career of Mr. Trumbull began nearly two-thirds of a century ago. He was distinguished as a judge, and later as an able and active participant in exciting debates in the Senate, extending from the repeal of the Missouri Compromise to the impeachment of President Johnson. He was a member when the sessions of the Senate were held in the old chamber, and Cass, Crittenden, Douglas, Tombs, and Jefferson Davis were among his early official associates. As Chairman of the Judiciary Committee he had reported the Thirteenth and Fourteenth Amendments to the Constitution of the United States.

In the course of my conversation with him upon the occasion first mentioned, I inquired whether he had ever met either Webster, Clay, or Calhoun. He replied that it was a matter of deep regret to him that he had never seen either Clay or Webster, but that he had in his early manhood heard a masterful speech from Mr. Calhoun. Mr. Trumbull had then just been graduated from an eastern college; and on his way to Greenville, Georgia, to take charge of a school, he spent a few days in Charleston, South Carolina. This was in 1833, and the speech of Mr. Calhoun was in vindication of his course in the Senate in voting for the Compromise Bill of Mr. Clay, which provided for the gradual reduction of the tariff. The alleged injustice of the tariff law then in force had been the prime cause of the "nullification" excitement precipitated by South Carolina at that eventful period. The proclamation of President Jackson, it will be remembered, proved the death-blow, and the nullification excitement soon thereafter subsided. Mr. Trumbull told me that he distinctly recalled John C. Calhoun, his commanding presence and splendid argument, as he addressed the large assemblage. As a clear-brained logician—whose statement alone was almost unanswerable argument—he thought Mr. Calhoun unsurpassed by any statesman our country had known. Mr. Trumbull added that at the close of Mr. Calhoun's speech before mentioned, amid great enthusiasm, "Hayne! Hayne!" was heard from every part of the vast assemblage. For an hour or more he then listened spell-bound to Robert Y. Hayne, the formidable antagonist even of Webster in a debate now historic. Mr. Trumbull said that of the two generations of public men he had heard, he had never listened to one more eloquent than Hayne.

XLVIII IN THE HIGHLANDS

THE WRITER THE GUEST OF A GENTLEMAN IN THE SCOTTISH HIGHLANDS— DUNSTAFFNAGE CASTLE—IONA AND SAINT COLUMBA—SENATOR BECK AND MR. SMITH BOTH DEVOTEES OF BURNS.

During a sojourn of some weeks on the western coast of Scotland, I was the guest for a time of Mr. Stewart, the head of what remained of a once powerful clan in the Highlands. My host was a distinguished member of the London Bar, but spent his Summers at the home of his ancestors a few miles out from Alpin. Here, in as romantic a locality as is known even to the Highlands, with his kindred about him he enjoyed a full measure of repose from the distracting cares of the great metropolis. At the time of my visit his brother, an officer of the British army, just returned from India, was with him. Both gentlemen wore kilts for the time; and all the appointments of the house were reminders of bygone centuries when border warfare was in full flower, forays upon the Lowlands of constant occurrence, and the principle of the clans in action,

"Let him take who has the power
And let him hold who can."

At the bountifully furnished board of my Highland host there was much "upon the plain highway of talk" I will not soon forget. And then, with the gathering shadows in the ancestral hall, with the rude weapons of past generations hanging upon every wall, and the stirring strains of the bagpipe coming from the distance, it was worth while to listen to the Highland legends that had been handed down from sire to son.

Not far away was the old castle of Dunstaffnage, which in its prime had been the scene of innumerable tournaments and battles that have added many pages to Scottish annals. Within the enclosure of the old castle sleeps the dust of long ago kings—the veritable grave of Macbeth being readily pointed out to inquiring travellers.

The conversation around the hearthstone of my host turned to the famous island of the Inner Hebrides, Iona, with its wonderful history reaching back to the sixth century. The ruins of the old monastery, built fourteen hundred years ago by the fugitive Saint, Columba, are well worth visiting. The dust of the early kings of Norway, Ireland, and Scotland rest within these ancient walls, and it is gratifying to know that here even the ill-fated Duncan

"After life's fitful fever sleeps well."

It would have been passing strange, with host and guests all of Scottish lineage, if there had been no mention of Robbie Burns, for in old Scotia, whether in palace or hovel, the one subject that never tires is the "ploughman poet of Ayr." A little incident of slightly American relish which I related the evening of my departure needed no "surgical operation" to find appropriate lodgment.

Senator Beck of Kentucky was a Scotchman. He was in the highest sense a typical Scotchman—lacking nothing, either of the brawn, brain, or brogue, of the most gifted of that race. It is needless to say he was a lover of Burns. From "Tam O'Shanter" to "Mary in Heaven," all were safely garnered in his memory—to be rolled out in rich, melodious measure at the opportune moment. The close friend and associate of Senator Beck, when the cares of State were for a time in abeyance, and the fishing season at its best, was "old Smith," superintendent of the Botanical Gardens, also a Scotchman, and likewise in intense degree a devotee of Burns. The bond of union between the man of flowers and the Kentucky statesman was complete.

Now, it so fell out that a newly elected member of the House, from the Green River district, one day called upon his distinguished colleague of the Senate, and requested a note of introduction to the superintendent of the Botanical Gardens, as he wished to procure some flowers to send a lady constituent then in the city. "Certainly, certainly," replied the ever-obliging statesman: "I will give you a line to old Smith." Just as the delighted member was departing with the letter in hand, Senator Beck remarked, in his peculiarly snappy Scotch accent, "Now, Tom, if you will only tell old Smith that you are a great admirer of his countryman, Robbie Burns, he will give you all the flowers in the conservatory." The member, who knew as little of Burns as he did of the "thirty-nine articles," departed in high feather.

Almost immediately thereafter, presenting his letter, he was received with great cordiality by the superintendent and assured that any request of Senator Beck would be cheerfully granted. Just as he was reaching out for the fragrant bouquet the superintendent was graciously presenting, the closing words of the Senator were indistinctly recalled, and in a manner indicating no small measure of self-confidence, the member remarked, "By the way, Mr. Smith, I am a great admirer of your countryman, *Jimmy* Burns." "Jimmy Burns! Jimmy Burns! Jimmy Burns!" exclaimed the overwhelmingly indignant Scotchman, *"Jimmy* Burns! *Depart instantly, sir!"*

The member from Green River district *departed* as bidden, taking no thought of the flowers; delighted—as he often asserverated—to have escaped even with his life.

XLIX ANECDOTES OF LAWYERS

JUDGE BALDWIN'S BOOK, "THE FLUSH TIMES"—
DEFENDANT'S COUNSEL ASKS ONE QUESTION TOO
MANY—CIRCUMSTANTIAL EVIDENCE AGAINST A CARD-
PLAYER —JOHN RANDOLPH'S REVENGE—HORACE
GREELEY NOT A MINISTER OF THE GOSPEL—A
CANDIDATE'S QUALIFICATIONS FOR SCHOOL-
TEACHING—THE AUTHOR OF "DON'T YOU REMEMBER
SWEET ALICE, BEN BOLT?"—A CANDIDATE'S POSITION
WITH REGARD TO THE MAINE LAW—GOVERNOR
TILDEN'S POPULARITY —MR. TRAVERS MISSES A
PORTRAIT—A CANDIDATE FOR HOLY ORDERS TELLS A
BIBLE STORY.

No better place can be found for studying that most interesting of all subjects, Man, than in our courts of justice. Indeed, what a readable book that would be which related the best things which have occurred at the bar!

Judge Baldwin conferred an inestimable blessing upon our profession when he wrote "The Flush Times," a book that will hold a place in our literature as long as there is a lawyer left on earth. To two generations of our craft this book has furnished agreeable and delightful entertainment. To the practitioner "shattered with the contentions of the great hall," its pages have been as refreshing as the oasis to the travel-stained pilgrim.

The late Justice Field, long his associate upon the supreme bench of California, told me that Judge Baldwin was one of the most genial and delightful men he had ever known, and certainly he must have been to have written "Cave Burton," "My First Appearance at the Bar," "A Hung Court," and "Ovid Bolus, Esq., Attorney-at-law and Solicitor in Chancery."

Almost every Bar has some tradition or incident worth preserving — something in the way of brilliant witticisms or repartee that should not be wholly lost. Of the race of old-time lawyers—of which Mr. Lincoln was the splendid type—but few remain. Of the survivors, I know of no better representative than Proctor Knott of Kentucky. The possessor of ability of the highest order, and of splendid attainments as well, he is of all men the best story-teller this country of ours has known. Among his delighted auditors in and out of Congress have been men from every section and of exalted public station. For some of the incidents to be related I am indebted to Governor Knott. The obligation would be much greater if the stories could be retold in manner and form as in the days gone by, and upon occasions never to be forgotten when they fell from his own lips.

If, however, even fairly well I might garner up and hand down some of the experiences of the generation of lawyers now passing, I would feel that I had, in some humble measure, discharged that obligation that Lord Bacon says, "every man owes to his profession."

ONE QUESTION TOO MANY

What lawyer has not, at some time, in the trial of a case asked just *one question* too many? I know of nothing better along that line of inquiry than the following related by Governor Knott. He was attending the Circuit Court in one of the Green River counties in Kentucky, when the case of the "Commonwealth *versus* William Jenkins" was called for trial. The aforesaid William was under indictment for having bitten off the ear of the prosecuting witness. Fairly strong but by no means conclusive testimony against the defendant had been given when the State "rested."

A lawyer of the old school, who still carried his green bag into Court, and who never wearied of telling of his conflicts at the bar with Grundy, Holt, and Ben Hardin, in their palmiest days, was retained for the defence. His chief witness was Squire Barnhouse, who lived over on the "Rolling Fork." He was the magistrate for his precinct, deacon in the church, and the recognized oracle for the neighborhood. Upon direct examination, in the case *at bar,* he testified that "he knowed the defendant William Jenkins; had knowed him thirty year or more; knowed his father and mother afore him." Inquired of then as to the general reputation of the defendant, as to his being "a peaceable and law-abiding citizen," he was found to be all that could be reasonably desired.

Squire Barnhouse was then asked whether he was present at the Caney Fork muster, where it was alleged that the defendant had bitten off the ear of the prosecuting witness. It turned out that he was present. Further questioned as to whether he had paid particular attention to the fight, he replied that he did; that he "had never seed Billy in a fout before, and he had a kind of family pride in seein' how *he would handle himself."* Further questioned as to whether he saw the defendant bite off the ear of the prosecuting witness he replied, "No, sir, nothin' uv the kind, nothin' uv the kind." This was followed by the inquiry as to whether his opportunities were such that he would most probably have seen it, if it had occurred. "In course I would, in course I would," was the emphatic reply.

The witness was here turned over to the Commonwealth's attorney, who declined to cross-examine, and Squire Barnhouse was in the act of leaving the stand when in an evil hour it occurred to defendant's counsel to ask one question more.

"By the way, Squire, *just one more question,* just where you stand; now I understood you to say"—repeating the answers already given; "now just this question, did you see anything occur while the fight was going on, or after it was over, that would lead you to believe that this defendant had bitten off the ear of the prosecuting witness?"

The Squire, half down the witness stand, answered, "No, sir, nothing uv the kind," then, slowly and thoughtfully, "nothing uv the kind." A moment's pause. "Well, since you mention it, I do remember that just as Billy rizened up offen him the last time, I seed him spit out a piece of ear, *but whose ear it was,* I don't pertend to know."

CIRCUMSTANTIAL EVIDENCE

In the good County of Scotland, in the State of Missouri, back in the ante-bellum days there lived one Solomon Davis, whose chronic horror was card-playing. The evils of this life were in his judgment largely to be attributed to this terrible habit. It was his belief that if the Grand Jury would only take hold of the matter in the right spirit, a stop could be put to the "nefarious habit of *card-playing,* which was ruining the morals of so many young men in Scotland County." This was the burden of his discourse in and out of season. His ardent desire that he himself should be called on the Grand Jury to the accomplishment of the end mentioned was at length gratified. At a certain term of court he was not only summoned upon the Grand Jury, but duly appointed its foreman.

Upon the adjournment of court for dinner, immediately thereafter, one Ben Mason, the wit of the bar,—and not himself wholly *unacquainted* with the pastime that involved spades, kings, and even queens,— ardently congratulated the new foreman upon his appointment, assuring him that now his opportunity had come to put to an end, by the omnipotent power of the Grand Jury, "to the nefarious habit of card-playing which was ruining the morals of so many young men in Scotland County."

"And now, Squire," continued Ben, "I can give you the name of a gentleman who doesn't play himself, but is always around where playing is going on, and he can tell you who plays, where they play, how much is bet, and all about it."

Delighted at this apparently providential revelation, the Squire had a subpoena forthwith issued for the witness mentioned, one Ranzey Sniffle, a half-witted fellow who had never taken or expected to take a part in the game himself, but whose cup of happiness was full to the brim when, in return for punching up the fires, mixing the drinks, and snuffing the candle, he was permitted *to see the play actually going on.*

Trembling with apprehension at the dread summons to appear before the "Grand Inquest"—if it had been three centuries earlier at Saragossa it could scarcely have appeared more alarming—the witness was ushered into the immediate presence of the awful tribunal over which Squire Davis was now presiding. After taking the customary oath, and telling his name, age, and where he lived, Mr. Sniffle was questioned by the foreman as to his personal knowledge of any game or games of cards being played for money, or any valuable thing, within one year last past, within the said County of Scotland, and solemnly warned, if he had any such knowledge, to proceed in his own way, and tell all about it; to tell when and where it was, *who were present*, and what amount, if any, was bet.

Recovering himself a little by this time, the witness began:

"The last time I seed them playin', Squire, was at Levi Myers's sto'; they sot in about sundown last Saturday night, and never loosened their grip until Monday mornin' about daylight."

"Now, Mr. Sniffle," interrupted the Squire with great dignity, "will you proceed in your own way, to give to the gentlemen of this Grand Jury *the names* of the persons who were thus engaged not only in violating the statute law of Missouri, but in violating the law of God by desecrating the holy Sabbath?"

"Well, Squire," continued the witness, slowly counting off on his fingers, "thar was Levi Myers, Sammy Hocum, Moss Johnson, Josiah Davis,"—"Suspend, Mr. Sniffle, *suspend,*" commanded the Squire with great indignation, and turning to his official associates, he continued, "I am aware, gentlemen of the Grand Jury, that my son Josiah is sometimes present when cards are being played, but he assures me on his honor as a gentleman, that he never *takes part*, and doesn't even know one card from another. Now, Mr. Witness, do you undertake, under the solemn sanction of an oath, to say that my son Josiah was *engaged* in the game? By the way, Mr. Sniffle, do you understand the nature of an oath?"

"No, Squire," slowly replied the witness, "I dun know as I do."

"Don't you know *what will become of you*, Ranze, if you swear to a lie?" quickly asked a juryman from a back seat.

"Yas, in course, if I swar to a lie, they'll send me to the penitentiary, and then I'll go to hell afterwards," replied Mr. Sniffle.

The *competency* of the witness thus appearing, the foreman proceeded:

"Now, Mr. Sniffle, do you, under the solemn sanction of an oath, undertake to say that my son Josiah was *engaged* in that game?"

"I dun know as I adzackly understand the meanin' of bein' engaged in the game; but I seed Josiah a-dealin' the papes, when his time come to fling a card he flung it, and uv'ry now and then, *he rech out and drug in the chicerokum.* I dun know as I adzackly understand 'bout bein' engaged in the game, but if *that* were bein' engaged, then Josiah were *engaged!*"

JOHN RANDOLPH OF ROANOKE

Seldom have more significant words been uttered than those of John Randolph of Roanoke, when told that a certain man had been denouncing him. "Denouncing me," replied Randolph, with astonishment, "that is strange, *I never did him a favor.*"

The voice of but one John Randolph of Roanoke has mingled in the contentions of the Great Hall. That was no cause for regret, as for a lifetime he was the dread of political foes and friends alike.

A colleague from "the valley" probably remembered him well to the last. That colleague, recently elected to fill a vacancy caused by the death of a member of long service, signalized his entrance into the House by an unprovoked attack upon Mr. Randolph. The latter, from his seat near by, listened with apparent unconcern to the fierce personal assault. To the surprise of all, no immediate reply was made to the speech, and the new member flattered himself, no doubt, that the "grim sage" was for once completely unhorsed.

A few days later, however, Randolph, while discussing a bill of local importance, casually remarked: "This bill, Mr. Speaker, lost its ablest advocate in the death of my lamented colleague, *whose seat is still vacant!*"

HORACE GREELEY

It will be remembered that the will of Stephen Girard of Philadelphia, after a splendid bequest for the establishment of the great University which bears his name, provided that no minister of the Gospel should ever be permitted to enter the grounds of the institution.

It so happened upon a time, that Horace Greeley, wearing white hat and cravat, and with his ministerial cast of countenance well in evidence, sauntered up to the gate of the Girard institution and was about to enter. He was instantly stopped by the keeper, who bluntly told him that he could not enter.

"What the hell is the reason I can't?" demanded Greeley.

"Oh! I beg your pardon," apologized the astonished gate-keeper, *"walk right in, sir; you can."*

PATRIOTIC TO THE CORE

Judge Allen of southern Illinois, a leading member of Congress a half-century ago, during a recent address to the old settlers of McLean County related an incident of early days on the Wabash. Population was sparse, and the common school was yet far in the future. The teacher who could read, write, and "cipher" to the "single rule of three" was well equipped for his noble calling. Lamentable failures upon the part of aspirants to attain even the modest standard indicated, were by no means of rare occurrence.

Back in the thirties, an individual of by no means prepossessing appearance presented himself to Judge Allen's father, the Magistrate, Ruling Elder, and *ex-officio* school director for his precinct, and asked permission "to keep school." Being interrogated as to what branches he could teach, the three R's—readin', 'ritin', and 'rithmetic—were, with apparent confidence, at once put in nomination.

"Have you ever taught geography and English grammar?" was the next inquiry.

With a much less confident tone, as he had probably never heard of either, he replied:

"I have teached geography some, but as for English grammar, I wouldn't 'low one of 'em to come into my school-house. *'Merican grammar is good enough for me!"*

"SWEET ALICE, BEN BOLT"

A touching scene occurred in the House of Representatives a number of years ago, when an aged member from New Jersey arose, and for the first time addressed the Speaker. All eyes were turned in his direction as he stood calmly awaiting recognition. He was tall, spare, and erect. His venerable appearance and kindly expression, coupled with most courteous manners, at once commanded attention. As in husky tones he again said, "Mr. Speaker!" there came from the farthest end of the Great Hall in a whisper but distinctly heard by all, the word, "Sweet Alice, Ben Bolt." A moment later, and from the floor and gallery many voices blended in the familiar refrain, "Don't you remember sweet Alice Ben Bolt?"

The ovation which immediately followed was such as is rarely witnessed in the Great Hall. Business was suspended for the moment, and the hand of the new member warmly grasped by the chosen representatives of all parties and sections. It was an inspiring tribute, one worthily bestowed. The member was Thomas Dunn English, author of the little poem, sung in palace and cottage, which has found its way into all languages, and touched all hearts.

THE MAINE LAW

The mention of the "Maine Law" recalls a little episode that occurred in the early days in the good county of McLean. One Duncan—no kinsman to him who had been

"So clear in his great office"—

was again a candidate for the Legislature. The temperance question, in some of its many phases, was then giving much trouble to aspirants to public place. In the midst of his opening speech at the old courthouse, the candidate was interrupted by one of the inquisitive men who always appear when least wanted, with the question: "Mr. Duncan, are you *in favor* of the Maine Law?" "Yes, yes," quickly replied the candidate, "I am coming to that very soon." Shying off to the tariff, the improvement of Western rivers, and the necessity of rigid economy in all public expenditures, our candidate was about to close when the same troublesome inquiry, "Mr. Duncan, *are you in favor* of the Maine Law?" again greeted his unwilling ears. "Oh, yes," exclaimed the orator, in tone and manner indicating much thankfulness. "I am glad you called my attention to his subject; I was about to forget it. My fellow-citizens have a right to know my views upon all public questions, and I have nothing to conceal. I have no respect for candidates who attempt to dodge any of these great questions. I have given you fully, my views upon the tariff, upon a general system of internal improvements, and something of my own services in the past; and now thanking you for your attention, will ——" "Mr. Duncan, are you *in favor of the Maine Law?*" were the words that again escaped the lips of the importunate inquisitor.

Fully appreciating his dilemma—with constituents about equally divided upon the dangerous question—the candidate at once nerved himself for the answer upon which hung his hopes and fears and boldly replied; "Yes, sir, I am in favor of the law, but *everlastingly opposed to its enforcement!"*

HOW HE GOT HIS MAJORITY

One of the candidates upon the ticket with Mr. Tilden when he was elected Governor of New York, was the late William Dorshemer. Judge Maynard told me that he was present in the library of Mr. Tilden when Dorshemer called, immediately after the full election returns had been received. Tilden's popularity at the time was very great —growing out of his successful prosecution of the noted Canal ring,—and resulted in the triumph of the ticket of which he was the head. Mr. Dorshemer, the Lieutenant-Governor elect, was greatly delighted that his own majority exceeded that of the more distinguished candidate for the Chief Executive office. During the conversation, Dorshemer remarked to Tilden: "Your majority is only fifty thousand, while mine is fifty-one thousand, five hundred." "Yes, yes," quickly remarked Tilden; "you got the fifteen hundred; *I gave you the fifty thousand!*"

WILLIAM R. TRAVERS

The generation now passing has known no man of keener wit than the late William R. Travers, of New York. An impediment of speech not infrequently gave zest and vim to his words, when they finally found utterance. He was for a lifetime steeped in affairs of great concern and among his associates were prominent factors in the commercial and political world.

On his revisiting Baltimore some years after his removal to New York, an old acquaintance remarked, "You seem to stutter more in New York than you did here, Mr. Travers." To this the brief reply at length came, "Have to—*it's a bigger place.*"

Back in the days when Gould and Fisk were names to conjure with in the mart and on the board; when railroads and gold mines were but pawns upon the chessboard of "money changers and those who sold doves"; when "Black Friday" was still fresh in the memories of thousands, this incident is said to have occurred.

To weightier belongings, Gould and Fisk had added by way of pastime a splendid steamer to ply between Fall River and New York. Upon its trial voyage, Travers was the guest of its owners. The appointments of the vessel were gorgeous in the extreme, and in the large saloon were suspended life-size portraits of Gould and of Fisk. After a promenade of an hour in company with the originals, Travers suddenly paused in front of the portraits, gazed earnestly at each in turn, and then—with eyes fixed on the intervening space —slowly ejaculated: *"Where's Christ?"*

TOLD BY COLONEL W. D. HAYNIE

The following, told with happy effect by Colonel W. D. Haynie of the Chicago Bar, probably has no parallel in theological literature. A colored brother who felt called upon to preach, applied to the Bishop of his church for license to exercise the sacred office. The Bishop, far from being favorably impressed by the appearance of the candidate, earnestly inquired whether he had read the Bible, and was familiar with appropriate stories to relate, as occasion might require, to his Sunday school and congregation. The answer was, "Boss, I has read dat book from led to led." In response to the request of the good Bishop that he would repeat a Bible story, the applicant for Holy Orders began:

"One time dar wus a wicked ole King, an' his name was Ahab; an' he live in Babylon; an' he wus a mighty warrior; an' one day he wuz marchin' along at de head uv his army fru de streets of Babylon, an' he seed Bersheby standin' up on de house-top; an' he said to his soldiers, 'Bring me Bersheby fur my wife'; an' day brung him Bersheby fur his wife. An' ole Ahab he march a long ways off, and fit a big battle, an' tuk a hull lot of prisoners; an' cum a-marchin' back fru de streets of Babylon, wid de brass bans a-playin', and de stars an' stripes a-floatin'; an' Bersheby she wuz a-standin' on de house-top, and she holler out,

"'How did you cum out wid' em, old Ahab?'

"An' it make him powerful mad you know, an he say to his soldiers, 'Frow her down to me.' And dey frowd her down to him; and den he say, 'Frow her down to me *seven* times'; and dey frowd her down seven times; and den he say, 'Frow her down to me *seventy times seven times!'* and dey frowed her down to him seventy times seven times; an' po' ole Bersheby, she crawl away and lay down at de rich man's gate, and de dogs come and lick her wouns, and when dey gevered he up, dar was 'leven basketfuls left, an' *whose wife will she be in de resurrection?"*

L OUR NOBLE CALLING

THE LEGAL PROFESSION—TAKEN BY SURPRISE—MISSING THE POINT OF THE JOKE—A REMARKABLE INCIDENT—A JUDICIAL DECISION ON BAPTISM—A DOUBTFUL COMPLIMENT—STRONG PERSONAL ATTACHMENT— IRISH WIT—ENGLISH JOKES ABOUT LAWYERS— GREATNESS UNAPPRECIATED—ALL IN HIS WIFE'S NAME—A RETORT BY CURRAN—REMITTING A FINE—A CASE "ON ALL-FOURS"— "GOING OUT WITH THE TIDE."

As we well know, lawyers generally entertain an exceedingly exalted opinion of their profession. Textbooks, opinions of courts, addresses innumerable to graduating students, all bear witness to the fact that our noble profession is the most honorable of human callings, the safeguard of society, the palladium of our liberty.

True, some uncharitable layman has suggested: "Yes, all this, and more, has been said a thousand times, *but always by lawyers.*"

There are persons yet in life, who, practically at least, hold with Aaron Burr, that "law is that which is boldly asserted and plausibly maintained," and that lawyers, like the Roman augurs of old, always smile when they meet one another on the street. The by no means exalted opinion of two men as to "our noble profession" will appear from the following.

A few days after Knott was admitted to the bar, he was sitting alone in his office, waiting for clients, when a one-gallowsed, awkward-looking fellow from the "brush" walked in without ceremony, dropped into the only vacant chair, and inquired: "Air you a lawyer, mister?" Assuming the manner of one of the regulars, Knott unhesitatingly answered that he was. "Well," said the visitor, "I thought I would drap in and git you to fetch a few suits for me." Picking up his pen with the air of a man with whom suing people was an everyday, matter-of-course sort of affair, Knott said: "Who did you wish to sue?" To which—with a prolonged yawn—the prospective client drawled out: "I ain't particular, Mister, I jest thought I'd get you to pick out a few skerry fellows *that would complemise easy!*"

The remaining incident is an experience of my own, when, at the age of twenty-two, I had hung out my sign in the then county-seat of Old Woodford.

My first client had retained me to obtain a divorce because of abandonment during the two years last past by the sometime partner of his joys and sorrows. The bill for divorce was duly filed; but on "the coming in of the answer," a continuance of the suit, for cause shown, was granted to the defendant.

At an early hour on the morning thereafter, my client called, and I soon discovered he was in a frame of mind by no means joyous. The disappointment he expressed at the continuance of his suit was evidently sincere. My explanation of the impossibility of preventing it, and the confident hope I held out that he would certainly get his divorce at the next term, evidently gave him little relief. He at length intimated a desire to have a confidential talk with me. I took him into my "private office" (that has a professional sound, but as a matter of fact my office had but one room, and that was "open as day" to everybody) and assured him that whatever he said to me would be in the strictest confidence. Feeling that I was on safe ground, I now spoke in a lofty tone of the sacred relation existing between counsel and client, and that any communication he desired to make would be as safe as within his own bosom, "or words to that effect." Relieved, apparently, by the atmosphere of profound secrecy that now enveloped us, he "unfolded himself" to the effect that some years before he had been deeply in love with an excellent young lady in his neighborhood, but for some trifling cause he could now hardly explain, he had in a pique suddenly turned his attentions to another to whom he was soon united in the holy bonds that he was now so anxious to have sundered by the strong arm of the law.

A deeply drawn sigh was here the prelude to the startling revelation, that since his present sea of troubles had encompassed him about the old flame had been rekindled in his heart. I now candidly informed him that I was wholly inexperienced in such matters, but as his counsel I would take the liberty to advise him of the monstrous impropriety of any visible manifestation or expression of the newly revived attachment. This was followed by the comforting assurance upon my part, however, that when divorced, he would be lawfully entitled to re-enter the matrimonial lists in such direction, and at whatever gait seemed to him best. The sigh to which the above was the prelude, hardly prepared me for the startling revelation that another fellow was now actually keeping company with the young lady. My client's feelings here overcame him for a moment, and he complained bitterly of his hard fate in being "tied up," while the coast was clear to his competitor. After a moment of deep study, he expressed the opinion in substance, that if his rival could only be held in check until the divorce was granted, he was confident all would be well.

I here told him that this was all beyond my depth, and along a line where it would be impossible for me to render him any service. Hitching his chair up a little closer, and looking at me earnestly he said: "You are a good-looking young fellow, and rather a glib talker, and I will give you this hundred dollars if you will cut that fellow out until I get my divorce!" Declining with some show of indignation, as well as surprise—for I was *young* then in the practice—I assured him that his proposal was out of the domain of professional service, and could not be thought of for a moment. In a tone indicating deep astonishment, he said: "Why, I thought a lawyer would do anything for money!"

"Yes," I replied, "most anything, but this is the exception; and besides, if the young lady is as beautiful as you say she is, you would be *in greater danger from me* at the end of your probation than from the other fellow." "Oh, Lord, I hadn't thought of that," he exclaimed, as he pocketed his hundred dollars, picked up his hat, and left my office.

Near the close of the following term of court, as the decree was being signed granting the divorce aforementioned, I approached my client as he sat solitary in the rear of the court-room, and earnestly congratulated him upon the fact that he was now free and at liberty to fight his own battles. "Yes," he replied, with a groan that touched the heart of the tipstaff near by, "but it's too late now; *she married that other fellow last Thursday.*"

TAKEN BY SURPRISE

Upon a time, far back, Ballou, of happy memory, was Judge of the Woodford Circuit Court. A young lawyer, after diligent preparation and exhaustive argument, confidently submitted his first case to the tender mercies of the Court. To his utter dismay, His Honor promptly rendered a decision adverse to the contention of the youthful barrister. Deeply humiliated by his defeat, the latter exclaimed: "I am *astonished* at such a decision!" The admonition of a brother, to patience, failing to accomplish its charitable purpose, the irate attorney asserrated more excitedly than before, his astonishment at such a decision. Whereupon the judge ordered the clerk to enter up a fine of five dollars against the offending attorney for contempt of court. Silence now reigned supreme, and the victim of judicial wrath sank back into his seat, utterly dismayed. The strain of the situation was at length relieved in part by an old lawyer from the opposite side of the trial table, slowly arising and solemnly remarking: "Something might be said, Your Honor, in extenuation of the conduct of my young friend. It is his first case, one in which he felt the deepest interest, and upon the successful issue of which, he had founded his fondest hopes. I trust Your Honor, upon due reflection, will remit this fine. It is true, he has with much vehemence expressed his astonishment at the decision of the Court. But his youth and inexperience must surely be taken into account. Ah, Your

Honor, when our young brother has practised before this court as long as some of us have, *he will not be surprised at any decision Your Honor may make!*"

THE POINT OF THE JOKE

Sydney Smith is credited with saying that it required a surgical operation to get a joke into a Scotchman's head. And not a bad reply is that of the Scotchman: "Yes, an *English* joke."

It is unnecessary, however, to cross the Atlantic in order to find a few well authenticated cases where the surgical operation would have been required. The Hon. Samuel H. Treat, United States Judge of Southern Illinois, was one of the ablest and most upright of judges, and possibly—on or off the bench—the most solemn-appearing of all of the sons of men.

This little incident was related by Judge Weldon. Soon after the close of the War, he one day told Judge Treat a story he had heard upon a recent visit to Washington. McDougall, formerly of Illinois, but at that time a Senator from California, had become very dissipated near the close of his term. At a late hour one night a policeman on the Avenue found him in an utterly helpless condition—literally in the gutter. As the officer was making an ineffectual attempt to get the unfortunate statesman upon his feet, he inquired: "Who are you?" The reply was: "This morning I was Senator McDougall, but now I am *Sewered!*"

A few moments later Mr. Hay came into the office and Judge Treat said: "Hay, Weldon has just told me a good story about our old friend McDougall. Mac was in the gutter, and a policeman asked him who he was, and Mac told him, 'This morning I was Senator McDougall, but now I am the Hon. William H. Seward!'"

AN INCIDENT

Upon the occasion of the celebration of the fiftieth anniversary of the organization of the City of Bloomington, the oration was delivered by the Hon. James S. Ewing, late Minister to Belgium. In the course of his address, he related the following incident:

"In the early history of this county, two boys one day went into the old courthouse to hear a lawsuit tried. There were assembled eight young lawyers, not all of them engaged in the trial, but giving strict attention to the proceedings. It was not a suit of great importance.

"The Court was presided over by Samuel H. Treat, who afterwards became a United States District Judge and one of the most distinguished lawyers and jurists in the State.

"One of the lawyers was David Davis, first a noted lawyer, then a circuit judge, then a judge of the Supreme Court of the United States, then a United States Senator and acting President of the Senate; a citizen of State and national fame whom the people of Bloomington loved and delighted to honor.

"Another was John T. Stuart, a brilliant lawyer, several times a member of Congress, and one of the most lovable of men.

"Another one was David B. Campbell, then the prosecuting attorney and afterwards a prominent lawyer and citizen of Springfield.

"Another was Edward D. Baker, who was afterwards a United State Senator from Oregon; a famous orator who immortalized himself by his marvellous oration over Senator Broderick.

"Another was James A. McDougall, a brilliant Irishman, afterwards a United States Senator from the State of California.

"And Abraham Lincoln, who has passed beyond the domain of human praise into the pantheon of universal history.

"I might add that one of those boys afterwards became the Vice-President of the United States; and the other is your speaker.

"Speaking to any audience in America, I might say in the world, I doubt if such an incident could be truthfully related of any other gathering."

A JUDICIAL DECISION ON BAPTISM

It is rarely the case that a Court is called upon to decide questions of a purely theological character. Of necessity, however—property interests being involved,—controversies, measurably of a religious character, sometimes arise for judicial determination.

The case to be mentioned is probably the only one where "baptism"— the true mode and manner thereof—has ever come squarely before an American judge. A man under sentence of death for murder was awaiting execution in the jail of one of the counties in northern Kentucky. Under the ministrations of the pastor of the Baptist Church, the prisoner at length made "the good confession" and desired to be baptized. To this end, the faithful pastor applied to the circuit judge before whom the prisoner had been tried, for permission to have the rite observed in the Kentucky River near by. The judge—more deeply versed in "Blackstone" and "Ben Monroe" than in theological lore—declined to have the prisoner removed from the jail, but gave permission to have him baptized in the cell. The physical impossibility of the observance of the solemn rite in the prisoner's cell was at once explained. "Certainly," said the judge in reply, "I know there is no room in there to baptize him that way; but take a bowl of water and sprinkle him right where he is confined." "But," earnestly interposed the man of the sacred office, "our church does not recognize sprinkling as valid baptism. We hold *immersion* to be the only Scriptural method." "Is it possible?" exclaimed the judge, greatly surprised. "Well, this Court decides that sprinkling *is* valid baptism; and I tell you once for all, that that infernal scoundrel will be sprinkled, *or he will be hung without being baptized at all!*"

Inasmuch as this decision has never been *overruled* by a higher court, it stands as the only judicial determination of the long-controverted question.

A DOUBTFUL COMPLIMENT

Mr. Clark was the leader of the Metamora Bar when I located there— *and so continued.* My first case, and the compliment of somewhat doubtful significance bestowed upon its termination, came about in this wise. I was retained for the plaintiff before Squire Fairchild in a suit involving the ownership of a calf of the alleged value of seven dollars. It being my first case, and having the aforementioned leader as my professional antagonist— and what was of far greater consequence, a contingent fee of two dollars and a half trembling in the balance—it may well be supposed that no effort was spared upon my part. I won the case, of course—*what lawyer ever told about a case that he had not won?*

The same evening a little group in the village store were discussing the merits of the case, and comparing the forensic effort of the new lawyer with that of the old-time leader already mentioned. At length one Tobias Wilson, as he slid down from his accustomed perch upon the counter, significantly observed, "Men, you may say what you please, but for my part, I had ruther hear Stevenson speak *two* minutes *than to hear old Clark all day!*"

STRONG PERSONAL ATTACHMENT

Mr. Clark—whose early advantages had been none of the best—was once counsel for the proponent in a closely contested will case. The testator, passing by the next of kin, had left his entire estate to a personal friend, a man not of his own blood.

In attempting to impress upon the jury the reasonableness of this disposition, Clark said: "This, gentlemen of the jury, is another striking illustration of the power of human friendship. All history—sacred and profane—is full of instances of strong personal attachments. Who can ever forget the undying affection of David and Jonathan, of Damon and Pythias, *of Scylla and Charybdis?*"

- 326 -

IRISH WIT

Judge Baldwin has left of record the witty reply of Jo Heyfron, an Irish lawyer, to a Mississippi judge. The judge, having rendered a very ridiculous decision in a cause in which Heyfron was engaged, the latter slowly arose as if to address the Court. The judge, exceedingly pompous and a poor lawyer withal, in imperative tone said: "Take your seat, Mr. Heyfron; you have practised at this bar long enough to know that when this Court renders a decision, its wisdom can only be called in question in a higher Court."

"If Your Honor plase," replied Jo in deprecatory tone, "far be it from me to impugn in the slightest degray the wisdom of Your Honor's decision. I only designed to rade a few lines from the book I hold in my hand, in order that Your Honor might parsave *how profoundly aignorant Sir William Blackstone was upon this subject!*"

It is difficult, at this day, to realize that such scenes could ever have been enacted in an English Court, as were not infrequent during the era embracing the celebrated "State Trials." While one of these was in progress, and Curran in the midst of his argument, the judge contemptuously turned his back upon the advocate, and began fondling a favorite dog at his side. The argument was at once suspended. "Proceed, sir," were the words which at length broke the stillness that had fallen upon the vast assemblage. "Ah!" exclaimed Curran, "I was only waiting for Your Lordship *to conclude your consultation with your learned associate!*"

ENGLISH JOKES ABOUT LAWYERS

Possibly the most solemn book in the world, not excepting Burton's "Anatomy of Melancholy," or even "Fearne on Contingent Remainders," is an English publication of a half-century or so ago, entitled "Jokes about Great Lawyers."

Of several hundred alleged jokes, two or three will bear transplanting.

"My Lord," began a somewhat pompous barrister, "it is written the book of nature ——" "Be kind enough," interposed Lord Ellenborough, "to give me the *page* from which you quote."

To the opening remark of an equally pompous barrister:

"My Lord, the unfortunate client for whom I appear ——" "Proceed sir, proceed," hastily observed the judge, *"so far the court is with you!"*

Ellenborough, when at the bar, after protracting his argument to the hour of adjournment, said that he would conclude when it should suit His Lordship's *pleasure* to hear him.

The immediate reply was: "The Court will hear you, sir, to-morrow; but as to the pleasure, *that* had long been out of the question."

GREATNESS UNAPPRECIATED

Gibbon has somewhere said, that one of the liveliest pleasures which the pride of man can enjoy is to reappear in a more splendid condition among those who have known him in his obscurity.

A case in point is a lawyer of prominence in one of the Western States, who soon after his appointment to a seat in the Cabinet revisited his early home. Meeting an acquaintance upon his arrival at the railway station, the visitor, with emotions akin to those described by Gibbon, ventured to inquire what his old neighbors said when they heard of him being appointed to a place in the Cabinet.

The unexpected reply was: "Oh, they didn't say nothin'; *they just laughed!*"

ALL IN HIS WIFE'S NAME

The late Colonel Lynch was for many years the recognized wit of the Logan County Bar. His repeated efforts, upon a time, to collect a judgment against a somewhat slippery debtor, were unavailing; the claim of the wife of the debtor, to the property attached, in each instance proving successful. Immeasurably disgusted at the "unsatisfied" return of the third writ, the Colonel indignantly exclaimed: "Yes, and I suppose if he should get religion, he would hold *that, too,* in his wife's name!"

A RETORT BY CURRAN

The stinging retort of the Irish advocate Curran is recalled. At the close of his celebrated encounter with one of the most overbearing of English judges, the latter insultingly remarked to the somewhat diminutive advocate: "I could put you in my pocket, sir." To which, with the quickness of a lightning flash, Curran retorted: "If you did, Your Lordship would have more law in your pocket *than you ever had in your head!*"

Fiercely indignant, the judge replied: "Another word, and I will commit you, sir." To which Curran fearlessly retorted: "Do, and it will be the best thing Your Lordship *has committed this term!*"

REMITTING A FINE

About every courthouse in the "Blue Grass" still linger traditions of the late Thomas F. Marshall. For him Nature did well her part. He was a genius if one ever walked this earth. Tall, erect, handsome, of commanding presence, and with intellectual endowment such as is rarely vouchsafed to man, no place seemed beyond his reach. Having in addition the prestige of family, that counted for much, and being the possessor of inherited wealth, it indeed seemed that to one man "fortune had come with both of her hands full." The successor of Clay and Crittenden as Representative for the Ashland District, a peerless orator upon the hustings, at the bar, and in the Great Hall, his life went out in sorrow and disappointment.

"Of all sad words of tongue or pen
    The saddest are these, 'It might have been!'"

His eulogy upon the gifted and lamented Menifee, the tribute of genius to genius, belongs to the realm of the loftiest eloquence, and seldom have words of deeper pathos been written than his own obituary —"Poor Tom's a-cold"—by George D. Prentice.

As to why that which seemed so full of promise "turned to ashes upon the lips," the following will explain. Meeting his kinsman, the Rev. Dr. Breckenridge, he said: "Bob, when you and I graduated, you took to the pulpit and I to the bottle, and *I have stuck to my text a good deal closer than you have to yours!"*

Not inaptly has hell been described as "disqualification in the face of opportunity."

Bearing in mind Marshall's invariable habit of *not* paying his debts, the point of the closing remark of the judge in the incident to be related will appear. Marshall was engaged in the defence of a man charged with murder in a county some distance from his own home. Failing repeatedly in his attempt to introduce certain testimony excluded by the Court, he at length exclaimed:

"It was upon just such rulings as that that Jesus Christ was convicted."

"Mr. Clerk, enter up a fine of ten dollars against Mr. Marshall for contempt of court," was the prompt response of the judge.

"Well," said Marshall, "this is the first time in a Christian country I have ever heard of a *man being fined for abusing Pontius Pilate!"*

"Mr. Clerk," said the judge, with scarcely suppressed indignation, "enter up a fine of twenty-five dollars against Mr. Marshall for contempt of court, and the further order that he be imprisoned in the common jail of the county until the fine and costs are paid."

The death-like stillness that fell upon the assemblage was at length broken by Mr. Marshall arising and gravely addressing the Court.

"If Your Honor please, I am engaged in the trial of an important case, one where human life may depend upon my efforts. I have just been fined twenty-five dollars and ordered to be imprisoned until the fine is paid. Upon a careful examination of my pockets, I find that I have not that amount *nor any other amount* about my person. I am more than one hundred miles from home and among strangers. In looking over this audience, I find but one familiar face, that of Your Honor. I am therefore constrained to request Your Honor, as an old and cherished friend, *to lend me* the amount necessary to discharge this fine."

Instantly the judge exclaimed: "Remit that fine, Mr. Clerk; *the State is more able to lose it than I am."*

A CASE "ON ALL-FOURS"

Near two-thirds of a century ago, one of the best-known lawyers in Illinois was Justin Butterfield. He was one of the most eloquent of the gifted Whig leaders of the State when the list included such names as Lincoln, Stuart, Hardin, Browning, Baker, and Linder. He was the earnest champion of General Zachary Taylor for the Presidency in 1848, and his party devotion was rewarded by appointment to the commissionership of the General Land Office. The only appointment for which Mr. Lincoln was ever an applicant was that given to Butterfield soon after the inauguration of President Taylor.

Of few lawyers have brighter things ever been told than of Justin Butterfield. During the fierce anti-Mormon excitement— which resulted in the destruction of the Nauvoo Temple and the expulsion of the Mormons from the State—the "Prophet," Joseph Smith, was placed upon trial for an alleged felony. The Hon. Nathaniel Pope was the presiding judge, and Butterfield counsel for Smith. A large audience, including many elegantly dressed ladies, was in attendance.

When he arose to address the Court, Butterfield with great dignity began:

"I am profoundly impressed with the solemnity of the situation and the awful responsibility resting upon me. I stand in the presence of his Holiness the Pope, surrounded by angels, *to speak in defence of the Lord's anointed Prophet!"*

While in active practice, Butterfield was upon one occasion opposing counsel to the Hon. David A. Smith in the Supreme Court of the State. The latter had concluded his argument and with head resting upon the table in front, had fallen asleep while Butterfield was speaking. A gleam of sunlight which had found its way through the window opposite, had fallen upon the very bald head of Smith, causing it to shine with unwonted brilliancy.

Suddenly pausing and with arm extended toward his sleeping antagonist, Butterfield solemnly observed:

"The light shineth upon the darkness *and the darkness comprehendeth it not!*"

As the Old State Bank was about to expire by reason of limitation, the General Assembly passed a bill extending its corporate life fifteen years. In litigation in which Butterfield was counsel, the legal effect of the Act mentioned being involved, the opposing counsel insisted that the legal effect of said Act was the creation of a *new* bank. Butterfield in reply insisted that "a new bank had not been created, but simply the life of the old one prolonged. A case in point, your Honor, precisely 'on all-fours' with this, is the well-authenticated one of the good Hezekiah when the Lord lengthened out his life fifteen years for meritorious conduct. Now, sir, did he thereby make a *new* Hezekiah, *or did he leave him just the same old Hezekiah?"*

"GOING OUT WITH THE TIDE"

Soldier, lawyer, and wit was Colonel Phil Lee of Kentucky. When it is borne in mind that he was of exceedingly small stature the following incident— one he often related—will be appreciated.

Immediately upon attaining his majority he was a candidate for the Legislature. On election day he was quietly seated on a barrel in the room where the election for his precinct was being conducted, when an old Deacon from the Tan Bark settlement came in to vote. His choice for the State officers and for Sheriff was called out after some little parleying as to who were the *best men*, and the voter was about to retire, when one of the judges said,

"Deacon, ain't you going to vote for a candidate for the Legislature?"

"Yas, of course, I like to forgot all about that; who is running for the Legislature?"

At which Phil, hopping down from the barrel, said, "Deacon, I am a candidate."

"Who, *you?"* inquired the Deacon—with half contemptuous gaze at the diminutive-looking aspirant; then turning to the judge he said, *"Just put me down for the other fellow!"*

Admitted to the bar at Shepherdsville in his native county of Bullitt, when barely of age, his first appearance was as attorney for the plaintiff in a breach-of-promise case of much local celebrity. His speech held the jury and by-standers literally spellbound, and it was confidently asserted that the classic banks of Salt River will probably never witness such flights of eloquence again. At its close Phil was warmly congratulated by an old Squire from the "Rolling Fork."

"Phil, that was a mighty fine speech, a mighty fine speech, Phil, now mind, I tell you. That speech reminded me of Henry Clay."

At the first mention of *that* name, the Squire was promptly invited out to take a drink. The first round of hospitality happily concluded, Phil was in readiness for any additional observations from the Squire.

"Yes, Phil, when you kinder rared back and throwed your right hand straight up, thinks I, Henry Clay, Henry Clay!"

Whereupon the Squire was without unnecessary delay invited to take another drink. This accomplished, the Squire still held the floor.

"Yes, Phil, yes, Phil, todes the last when you made that big swoop with both arms and 'peared like you was gwyen right up to the rafters, thinks I, Shore 'nough, Henry Clay come back from his grave!"

As flesh and blood could not stand everything, the old Squire was promptly invited to take another drink. Number three being property placed to his credit, the Squire continued:

"Yes, Phil, you peared to me to be Henry Clay right over again *with jist one leetle difference.*"

At this Mr. Lee, curious to know what could be the *one* possible little difference, when there were so many points of resemblance between two such orators as himself and Henry Clay, ventured to inquire. "I think," said the Squire, "this, Phil,—*you peared to kinder lack his ideas!*"

And now comes the tragic ending of a brilliant career. Lee, while Commonwealth's attorney, was in the last stages of that dread disease, consumption. A murder case was on trial in which he felt a deep interest. The case was one of unusual atrocity, and the accused—a man of some local prominence—had been exceedingly defiant towards the wan and emaciated prosecuting attorney from its beginning. With much difficulty Colonel Lee succeeded in getting to the court-room in order to make the closing speech to the jury. Utterly exhausted,—after depicting the horrible crime in all its enormity and demanding the extreme penalty of the law upon its perpetrator,—at its close, in tones that touched the hearts of all who heard him, he exclaimed:

"Gentlemen of the jury, I have prosecuted the pleas of this Commonwealth until the blood has dried up in my veins, and the flesh has perished from my bones!"

These were his *last* words—and his life went out that same night just as the clock struck twelve. At the self-same hour the steps of the jury were heard slowly ascending to the court-room which had witnessed his last effort— their verdict, *"Guilty, the penalty, death!"*

LI THE "HOME-COMING" AT BLOOMINGTON

McLEAN COUNTY'S READINESS TO WELCOME HER
CHILDREN—HONOR TO THE
EARLY SETTLERS—BEAUTY OF THE COUNTY—ITS
PROGRESS—ITS ORGANIZATION
—PRAISE OF JOHN McLEAN—HIS CAREER IN CONGRESS, IN
THE ILLINOIS
LEGISLATURE, AND IN THE SENATE—McLEAN COUNTY'S
HEROISM—REMINISCENCES
OF THE OLD COURT-HOUSE—FRENCH EXPLORERS IN THE
ILLINOIS COUNTRY
—MARQUETTE AND JOLIET EXPLORE THE UPPER
MISSISSIPPI—LA SALLE
EXPLORES THE ST. LAWRENCE, THE OHIO, AND THE
MISSISSIPPI TO ITS
MOUTH—EXTENT OF FRANCE'S POSSESSIONS IN AMERICA—
THE STRUGGLE
BETWEEN FRANCE AND GREAT BRITAIN—GEORGE R. CLARK
CAPTURES KASKASKIA
FROM THE BRITISH—VIRGINIA CEDES TERRITORY,
INCLUDING ILLINOIS, TO
THE UNITED STATES—THE LOUISIANA PURCHASE—ILLINOIS
ORGANIZED—
SUMMARY OF SUCCEEDING EVENTS IN THE HISTORY OF
ILLINOIS.

The McLean County (Illinois) "Home-Coming" of June 15, 1907, was an event of deep significance to all Central Illinois. On that occasion I delivered the welcoming address, as follows:

"These rare days in July mark an memorable epoch in the history of this good county. The authoritative proclamation has gone forth that her house has been put in order, that the latch-string is out —all things in readiness— and that McLean County would welcome the return of all her children who have in days past gone out from her borders.

"In the same joyous and generous spirit in which the welcome was extended, it has been heeded, and from near and far, from the land of flowers and of frosts, from the valley of the Osage, the Colorado, and the Platte, from the golden shores of California, and 'where rolls the Oregon'— sons and daughters of this grand old county have gladly turned their footsteps homeward.

"'When they heart has grown weary and thy foot has grown sore,
Remember the pathway that leads to our door.'

"As in the ancient days all roads led to Rome, so in this year of grace, and in this glorious month of June, all roads lead back to the old home; to the hearthstones around which cling the tender memories of childhood, and of loved ones gone—to the little mounds where sleep the ashes of ancestral dead.

"The 'Home-coming' to which you have been invited will leave its lasting impress upon all your hearts. The kindly words that have been spoken, the cordial grasp of the hand, the unbidden tear, the hospitality extended, have all given assurance that you are welcome. Here, for the time, let dull care and the perplexities that environ this mortal life be laid aside, let whatever would in the slightest mar the delight of this joyous occasion be wholly forgotten; so that in the distant future, to those who return and to those who stay, the recollection of these days will be one of unalloyed pleasure; and so that, when in the years to come we tell over to our children of the return to the old home, this reunion will live in our memories as one that, like the old sun-dial, 'marked only the hours which shine.'

"No place so fitting for this home-coming could have been selected as this beautiful park, where the springing grass, transparent lake, and magnificent grove—'God's first temple'—seem all to join in welcoming your return. How, from a mere hamlet, a splendid city has sprung into being during the years of your absence! No longer a frontier village, off the great highway of travel, with the mail reaching it semi-weekly by stage-coach or upon horseback,—as our fathers and possibly some who now hear me may have known it,—it is now 'no mean city.' Its past is an inspiration; its future bright with promise. It is in very truth a delightful dwelling-place for mortals, and possibly not an unfit abiding-place for saints. Whoever has walked these streets, known kinship with this people, called this his home—wherever upon this old earth he may since have wandered—has in his better moments felt an unconquerable yearning that no distance or lapse of time could dispel, to retrace his footsteps and stand once more within the sacred precincts of his early home. Truly has it been said: 'No man can ever get wholly away from his ancestors.' Once a Bloomingtonian, and no art of the enchanter can dissolve the spell. 'Once in grace, always in grace,' whatever else may betide! Eulogy is exhausted when I say that this city is worthy to be the seat of justice of the grand old county of which it is a part.

"Upon occasion such as this, the spirit of the past comes over us with its mystic power. The years roll back, and splendid farms, stately homes, magnificent churches, and the marvellous appliances of modern life are for the moment lost to view. The blooming prairie, the log cabin nestling near the border-line of grove or forest, the old water-mill, the cross-roads store, the flintlock rifle, the mould-board plough, the dinner-horn,—with notes sweeter than lute or harp ever knew,—are once more in visible presence. At such an hour little stretch of the imagination is needed to recall from the shadows forms long since vanished. And what time more fitting can ever come in which to speak of those who have gone before,—of the early settlers of this good county?

"It was from the beginning the fit abode for men and women of God's highest type—and such, indeed, were the pioneers. Their early struggles, their sacrifices, all they suffered and endured, can never be fully disclosed. But to them this was truly 'the promised land'—a land they might not only view, but possess. From New England, Ohio, the 'Keystone,' and the 'Empire' State, from the beautiful valley of the Shenandoah and the Commonwealths lying westward and to the south, came the men and women whose early homes were near the banks of the little streams and nestled in the shades of the majestic groves. Here they suffered the hardships and endured the privations that only the frontiersman might know. Here beneath humble roofs, their children were born and reared, and here from hearts that knew no guile ascended the incense of thanksgiving and praise. The early settlers, the pioneers, the men who laid the foundations of what our eyes now behold, builded wisely and well. Their descendants to-day are in large measure the beneficiaries of all that they so wisely planned, so patiently endured. These names and something of what they achieved will go down in our annals to the after times. Peace to their ashes; to their memory all honor! They were the advance guard—The builders—and faithfully and well they served their race and time. Upon nobler men and women the sun in all his course hath nowhere looked down.

"And where upon God's footstool can domain more magnificent than this good county be found; one better adapted to the habitation of civilized man? The untrodden prairies of three-quarters of a century ago, as if touched by the wand of magic, have become splendid farms. And groves more beautiful the eye of man hath not seen.

"Containing a population of less than two thousand at the time of its organization, there are more than seventy thousand souls within the bounds of this good county to-day. The log cabin has given way to the comfortable home. The value of farm lands and their products have increased beyond human forecast or dream. As shown by the last Governmental report, McLean County contains four thousand eight hundred and seventy-three farms, aggregating seven hundred thirty-seven thousand five hundred and seventy-eight acres. The corn product for the year 1899 exceeded fifteen millions of bushels, being near one-twentieth of that of the entire State. In the value of its agricultural products it is third upon the list of counties in the United States.

"The life of the farmer is no longer one of drudgery and isolation. Modern conveniences and appliances have in large measure supplanted the hard labor of human hands, lessened the hours of daily toil, and brought the occupant of the farm into closer touch with the outer world. More than all this, our schoolhouses, universities, churches, and institutions for the relief of the unfortunate and dependent, all bear witness to the glad fact that in our material development the claims of education, of religion, of charity, have not been forgotten. It is our glory, that in all that tends to human progress, in all that ministers to human distress, in whatever appeals to and develops what is best in man, or brings contentment and happiness to the home—in a word, in the grand march of civilization—McLean County moves in the van.

"Possibly no occasion more fitting can arise in which briefly to speak of the organization of McLean County, and something of important events of its history. At the session of the Legislature at Vandalia in the winter of 1830-31, a petition—borne to the State capital by Thomas Orendorff and James Latta—was duly presented, praying for the organization of a new county to be taken from Tazewell and Vermilion. The territory embraced in the proposed county included the present limits of McLean and large portions of neighboring counties organized at a later day. In accordance with the petition, a bill was passed, and its approval by the Governor on the twenty-fifth day of December, 1830, marks the beginning of the history of this good county.

"The name of 'McLean' was adopted upon the motion of the Hon. William Lee D. Ewing, some of whose kindred have for many years been residents of this city. Mr. Ewing had been the close friend of the man whose name he thus honored, and was himself in later years a distinguished Senator in Congress.

"By the terms of the bill mentioned, the seat of justice of said county was to be 'called and known by the name of Bloomington.' It was further provided that until otherwise ordered the courts of said county should be held at the house of James Allen. The first term of the Circuit Court was held in April, 1831, at the place indicated, the historic 'Stipp House,' but recently standing, a pathetic reminder of by-gone days. The presiding judge of that court was the Hon. Samuel D. Lockwood, of Springfield—an able and eminent jurist of spotless record. By legislative enactment, five times since its organization, valuable portions of McLean—aggregating nearly four-sevenths of its original territory—have been carved in the formation of the counties of Logan, Livingston, Piatt, De Witt, and Woodford.

Notwithstanding all this, McLean County yet remains—and by constitutional inhibition and the wisdom of our people will for all time remain—the largest county in the State.

"A word now of the man whose name was upon every invitation to this home-coming, in honor of whom this county was named, John McLean, one of the ablest and most distinguished of the first generation of public men in Illinois. Born in North Carolina in 1791, his early years were spent in Kentucky. In the last-named State he studied law and was admitted to the Bar. He removed to Illinois in 1815 and located in Shawneetown upon the Ohio River for the practice of his profession. The county of Gallatin, his future home, was then one of the most populous in the Illinois Territory. In fact, at the time mentioned, and for some years after the organization of the State, there were few important settlements one hundred miles north of the Ohio River.

"In the largest degree Mr. McLean was gifted with the qualities essential to popular leadership in the new State. He was present at all public assemblages whether convened for business or pastime, and a leading spirit in all the amusements and sports of the hour. But 'men are as the time is.' At all events, if the testimony of his contemporaries is to be taken, his popularity knew no bounds. The late General McClernand, his fellow-townsman, said of Mr. McLean:

"'His personality interested and impressed me. The image of it still lingers in my memory. Physically, he was well developed, tall, strong, and stately. Socially, he was affable and genial, and his conversation sparkled with wit and humor.'

"The following words of another contemporary, Governor Reynolds, are of interest:

"'Mr. McLean was a man of gigantic mind, of noble and manly form, and of lofty, dignified bearing. His personality was large, and formed on that natural excellence which at all times attracted the attention and admiration of all beholders. The vigor and compass of his intellect was exceedingly great, and his eloquence flowed in torrents, deep, strong, and almost irresistible.'

"At the election immediately succeeding the adoption of the Constitution under which Illinois was admitted into the Union, Mr. McLean was chosen the Representative in Congress. Soon thereafter, he presented to the House of Representatives the State Constitution then recently adopted at Kaskaskia; and upon its formal acceptance by that body, Mr. McLean was duly admitted to his seat as the first Representative from Illinois in the Congress of the United States. He was defeated for re-election by the Hon.

Daniel P. Cook, one of the most gifted men Illinois has known at any period of her history.

"Rarely have men of greater eloquence than Cook and McLean been antagonists in debate either upon the hustings or in the halls of legislation. With the people of the entire State for an audience, the exciting issues of that eventful period were argued with an eloquence seldom heard in forensic discussion. In very truth, each was the worthy antagonist of the other. It is not too much to say that, with the single exception of the masterful intellectual combat more than a third of a century later between Lincoln and Douglas, Illinois has been the theatre of no greater debate.

"Upon his retirement from Congress, Mr. McLean was elected to the Lower House of the Illinois Legislature and subsequently chosen Speaker of that body. The valuable service he there rendered is an important part of the early history of the State. He resigned the speakership in order the more effectually to lead the opposition to a bill chartering a State bank. His predictions as to the evils to the state, of which the proposed legislation would be the sure forerunner, were more than verified by subsequent events. More than a decade had passed before the people were relieved of the financial ills which John McLean ineffectually sought to avert. No other evidence of his statesmanship is needed than his masterly speech in opposition to the ill-timed legislation I have indicated.

"Apart from the fact that his name is continually upon our lips, the career of Mr. McLean is well calculated to excite our profound interest. During the fifteen years of his residence in Illinois, he held the high position of Representative in Congress, Speaker of the popular branch of the State Legislature, and was twice elected to the Senate of the United States. At his last election he received every vote of the joint session of the General Assembly—an honor of which few even of the most eminent of our statesmen have been the recipients.

"His personal integrity was beyond question, and it may truly be said of him that he ably and faithfully discharged every public duty. He died at the early age of thirty-nine, the period when, to most public men, a career of usefulness and distinction has scarcely begun. Upon the occasion of the announcement of his death to the Senate his colleague, Senator Kane, paid an eloquent tribute to his lofty character, his ability, and his worth, and deplored the loss his State had sustained in his early death.

"He lies buried in the State that had so signally honored him, near the beautiful river upon whose banks he found a home when Illinois was yet a wilderness. Such, in brief, was the man McLean, whose honored name this good county will hand down to the after times. No higher tribute need be paid to his memory than to say, his name was worthy of this magnificent domain to which it was given.

"In no part of this broad land has there been more prompt response than in this to the authoritative call to arms. In the largest measure McLean County has met every requirement that patriotism could demand. Full and to overflowing has been her contribution of means and men.

"In almost the last struggle with the savage foe, as he burned his wigwam and disappeared before the inexorable advance of civilized men; in the War with Mexico, by which States were added to our national domain; in that of the great Rebellion, where the life of the nation was at stake, and in our recent conflict with Spain—four times during a history that spans but a single life, McLean County has sent her full quota of soldiers to the field. Few survive of the gallant band who stood with Bissell and Hardin at Buena Vista, or followed Shields and Baker through the burning sands from the Gulf to the City of Mexico. And at each successive reunion of comrades in the great civil strife, there are fewer, and yet fewer, responses to the solemn roll-call.

"'On Fame's eternal camping-ground,
Their silent tents are spread.'

"And what a record is that of this glorious county during the eventful years of '61-'65! With a population of but forty per cent of that of to-day, more than four thousand of her brave sons marched gallantly to the front. They gathered from farm, from shop, from mart and hall—to die, if need be, that their country might live. On many fields now historic, where brave men struggled and died, soldiers from this grand county were steadily in line. Along every pathway of danger and of glory they were to be found. In every grade of rank were heroes as knightly as ever fought beneath a plume. Even to name the heroes that old McLean equipped for the great conflict would be but to call over her muster rolls of officers and men.

"The chords of memory are touched as the vision of the Old Courthouse rises before us. Its walls were the silent witnesses of events that would make resplendent the pages of history. Here assembled lawyers, orators, statesmen, whose names have been given to the ages. Here, at a critical period in our history the great masters of debate discussed vital questions of state—questions that took hold of the life of the republic. Here, at times, debate touched the springs of political power. Here in the high place of authority sat one destined later to wear the ermine of the greatest court known to men. During his membership of that court in the eventful years immediately following the great conflict, questions novel and far-reaching pressed for determination; questions no less important than those which had in the infancy of the republic exhausted the learning of Marshall and its associates. It is our pride that our townsman, David Davis, was among the ablest of the great court, by whose adjudication renewed vigor was given to the Constitution, and enduring safeguards established for national life and individual liberty.

"To the Old Courthouse in the early days came the talented and genial James A. McDougall, then just upon the threshold of a brilliant career, which culminated in his election as a Senator from California; also John T. Stuart, the able lawyer and gentleman of the old school. He was a Representative in Congress more than two-thirds of a century ago, when his district embraced all Central and Northern Illinois—extending from a line fifty miles south of Springfield to Chicago and Galena. In Congress he was the political associate and friend of Webster, of Crittenden, and of Clay. Many years ago, upon the occasion of Mr. Stuart's last visit to Bloomington, he told me, as we stood by the old 'Stipp' home, that he there, in 1831, witnessed the beginning of the judicial history of McLean County, when Judge Lockwood opened its first court. With deep emotion he added that he was probably the last survivor of those then assembled, and that his own days were almost numbered. His words were prophetic, as but a few months elapsed before he, too, had passed beyond the veil. There came also Edward D. Baker, Representative from Illinois and Senator from Oregon. To him Nature had been lavish with her gifts. His eloquence cast a spell about all who heard him. As was said of the gifted Prentiss: 'the empyrean height into which he soared was his home, as the upper air the eagle's.' Our language contains few gems of eloquence comparable to this wondrous eulogy on the lamented Broderick. His own tragic death in one of the early battles of the great war cast a gloom over the nation.

"In his official capacity as prosecuting attorney came also to the Old Courthouse the youthful Stephen A. Douglas. A born leader of men, with a courage and eloquence rarely equalled, he was well equipped for the hurly-burly of our early political conflicts. Save only in his last great contest, he was a stranger to defeat. Public Prosecutor, Member of the Legislature, and at the age of twenty-eight Judge of the Supreme Court of the State; later a Representative, and at the age of thirty-three a Senator in Congress. Amid storms of passion such as, please God, we may not see again, he there held high debate with Seward, Chase, and Sumner; and measured swords with Tombs, Benjamin, and Jefferson Davis upon vital issues which, transferred later from forum and from Senate, were to find bloody arbitrament by arms. Beginning near the spot where we have to-day assembled, the career of Douglas was indeed marvellous. Defeated for the great office which had been the goal of his ambition; amid the war-clouds gathering over the nation, and the yet darker shadows falling about his couch, he aroused himself to the last supreme effort, and in words that touched millions of responsive chords, adjured all who had followed his political fortunes to know only their country in its hour of peril. With his pathetic words yet lingering, and 'before manhood's morning touched its noon,' Douglas passed to the great beyond.

"Out of the shadowy past another form is evoked, familiar once to some who hear me now. Another name, greater than any yet spoken, is upon our lips. Of Abraham Lincoln the words of the great orator, Bossuet, when he pronounced his matchless elegy upon the Prince of Conde, might truly be spoken:

"'At the moment I open my lips to celebrate the immortal glory of the Prince of Conde, I find myself equally overwhelmed by the greatness of the theme and the needlessness of the task. What part of the habitable globe has not heard of the wonders of his life? Everywhere they are rehearsed. His own countrymen, in extolling them, can give no information even to the stranger.'

"Of Lincoln no words can be uttered or withheld that could add to or detract from his imperishable fame. His name is the common heritage of all people and all times.

"When in the loom of time have such words been heard above the din of fierce conflict as his sublime utterances but a brief time before his tragic death?

"'With malice toward none, with charity for all, with firmness in the right, as God gives us to see the right, let us strive on to finish the work we are in; to bind up the nation's wounds; to care for him who shall have borne the battle, and for his widow, and his orphan—to do all which may achieve and cherish a just and lasting peace among ourselves, and with all nations.'

"The men who knew Abraham Lincoln, who saw him face to face, who met him upon our streets, and heard his voice in our public assemblages have, with few exceptions, passed to the grave. Another generation is upon the busy stage. The book has forever closed upon the dread pageant of civil strife. Sectional animosities, thank God, belong now only to the past. The mantle of peace is over our entire land, and prosperity within all our borders.

"'Till the war-drum throbs no longer,
And the battle-flags are furled
In the parliament of man,
The federation of the world.'

"Through the instrumentality in no small measure of the man personally known to some who hear me, the man McLean County delighted to honor, no less as a private citizen than as President, this Government, untouched by the finger of time, has descended to us. Let it never be forgotten that the responsibility of its preservation and transmission will rest upon the successive generations of his countrymen, as they shall come and go.

"Truly it has been said: 'To-day is the pupil of yesterday,' and also 'History is the great teacher of human nature by means of object-lessons drawn from the whole recorded life of human nature.' There is, then, no dead past. Every event is in a measure significant. The annals of the ambitions, the crimes, the miseries, the wrongs, the struggles, the achievements of men in the long past are fraught with lessons of deep import to all succeeding generations. Each age is the heir to that which preceded. We make progress in proportion as we wisely ponder significant events.

"McLean County had its historical beginning as a dependent but distinct political organization on the joyous Christmas Day of 1830. Stretching backward from that date, its history is bound up solely in that of Illinois, under its various organizations and names. A brief time upon occasion such as this given to a hurried review of the masterful epochs in the history of the great State of which our own county is so important a part, cannot be wholly misspent.

"Bearing in mind that 'that which comes after ever conforms to that which has gone before,' significant events of the past must be known, to the end that we intelligently comprehend the present, and are enabled, even in scant measure, to forecast the future.

"No State of the American union has a history of more intense interest than our own. Its early chapters, indeed, savor of the romantic rather than of the real. I do not speak of the long-ago time when Illinois forest and prairie were the house and hunting-ground of the red men, and his frail bark the only craft known to its rivers. That period belongs to the border-land age of tradition rather than of veritable history. It is of Illinois under the domination of civilized men I would speak.

"For near a century preceding the Treaty of Paris in 1763, 'the Illinois country' was a part of the French domain. Inseparably linked with that portion of its history are names that will live with those of the Cabots and Columbus. The great navigator in his lonely search for a new pathway to the Indies was buoyed by a courage, a yearning for discovery, scarce greater than that which in the heart of the new continent sustained the later voyagers and discoverers, Marquette, Joliet, Hennepin, and La Salle.

"America's obligation to France is enduring—for explorers in the seventeenth century no less than for defenders in that which immediately followed. The historic page which tells of the lofty heroism of Lafayette has for us no deeper interest than that which records the daring achievements of the early French pathfinders and voyagers. Two centuries and a half ago Marquette and Joliet, bearing the commission of the French Governor of Quebec, embarked upon their expedition for the discovery of new countries to the southward. Animated by the earnest desire of extending the blessings of religion no less than that of adding to the domain of their imperial master, they set out upon an expedition which has become historic. The bare recital of what befell them would fill volumes. Now meeting with the scattered tribes of Indians, bestowing presents and in turn sharing the hospitality offered; now speaking words of admonition and of instruction; now gathering up the crude materials for history; now reverently setting up the cross in the wilderness; again threading the pathless forests, or in frail barks sailing unknown waters, they pursued their perilous journey.

"In time, after looking out upon the waters of Lake Michigan, crossing Lake Winnebago, visiting the ancient villages of the Kickapoos, 'with joy indescribable,' as Marquette declared, they for the first time beheld the Mississippi. In June, 1673, upon the east bank of the great river, they landed upon the soil of what is now the State of Illinois. At the little village they first visited they received hospitable treatment. Its inmates are known in our early history as 'the Illini'—a word signifying *men*. The euphonic termination added by the Frenchmen gives us the name Illinois. It is related that, upon the first appearance of Marquette and Joliet at the door of the principal wigwam of the village, they were greeted by an aged native with the words: 'The sun is beautiful, Frenchmen, when you come to visit us; you shall enter in peace into all our cabins; it is well, my brothers, you come.' In the light of the marvellous results of the visit, the words of the aged chieftain seem prophetic. We, too, may say it was well they came.

"The glory of having discovered the upper Mississippi and the valley which bears its name belongs to Marquette and Joliet. It was theirs to add the vast domain under the name 'New France' to the empire of *le Grand Monarque*. In very truth a princely gift. But no history of the great valley and the majestic river would be complete which failed to tell something of the priest and historian, Hennepin, and of the knightly adventures of the Chevalier La Salle.

"Much, indeed, that is romantic surrounds the entire career of La Salle. Severing his connection with a theological school in France, his fortunes were early cast in the New World. From Quebec, the ancient French capital of this continent, he projected an expedition which was to add empire to his own country and to cast a glamour about his own name. It has been said that his dream was of a western waterway to the Pacific Ocean. In 1669, with an outfit that had cost him his entire fortune, with a small party he ascended in canoes the St. Lawrence, and a few weeks later was upon the broad Ontario. Out of the mists and shadows that enveloped much of his subsequent career, it were impossible at all times to gather that which is authentic. It is enough that, with Hennepin as one of his fellow-voyagers, he reached the Ohio and in due time navigated the Illinois, meantime visiting many of the ancient villages.

"But his great achievement—and that with which abides his imperishable fame—was his perilous descent of the Mississippi from the Falls of St. Anthony to the Gulf of Mexico. On the sixth day of April, 1682, upon the east bank of the lower Mississippi, with due form and ceremony and amid the solemn chanting of the *Te Deum* and the plaudits of his comrades, La Salle took formal possession of the Louisiana country in the name of his royal master, Louis the Fourteenth of France.

"For the period of ninety-two years, beginning with the discoveries of Marquette and Joliet, the Illinois country was a part of the French possessions. Sovereignty over the vast domain of which it was a part was exercised by the French King through his commandant at Quebec. But as has been truly said, 'The French sought and claimed more than they had the ability to hold or possess. Their line of domain extended from the St. Lawrence around the Great Lakes and through the valley of the Mississippi to the Gulf of Mexico, a distance of over three thousand miles.' Truly a magnificent domain, but one destined soon to pass forever from the possession of the French monarch and his line.

"The hour had struck, and upon the North American continent the ancient struggle for supremacy between France and her traditional enemy was to find bloody arbitrament. Great Britain claimed as a part of her colonial possessions in the New World the territory bordering upon the Great Lakes and the rich lands of the Ohio and Mississippi valleys. As to the merits of the French and English contention as to superior right by discovery or conquest, it were idle now to argue. Our concern is with the marvellous results of the long-continued struggle which for all time determined the question of race supremacy upon this continent.

"Passing rapidly the minor incidents of the varying fortunes of the stupendous struggle which had been transferred for the time from the Old World to the New, we reach the hour which was to mark an epoch in history. The time, the thirteenth of September, 1759; the place, the Heights of Abraham at Quebec. There and then was fought out one of the pivotal battles of the ages. It was the closing act in a great drama. The question to be determined: Whether the English-speaking race or its hereditary foe was to be master of the continent. It was in reality a struggle for empire —the magnificent domain stretching from the St. Lawrence to the Gulf of

Mexico. The incidents of the battle need not now be told. Never were English or French soldiery led by more knightly captains. The passing years have not dispelled the romance or dimmed the glory that gathered about the name of Wolfe and Montcalm. Dying at the self-same moment—one amid the victors, the other amid the vanquished—their names live together in history.

"By the treaty of Paris which followed, France surrendered to her successful rival all claim to the domain east of the Mississippi River. In accordance with the terms of the treaty, Gage, the commander of the British forces in America, took formal possession of the recently conquered territory. Proclamation of this fact was made to the inhabitants of the Illinois country in 1764, and a garrison soon thereafter established at Kaskaskia. Here the rule of the British was for the time undisputed. British domination in the Mississippi Valley was, however, to be of short duration. Soon the events were hastening, the forces gathering, which were in turn to wrest from the crown no small part of the splendid domain won by Wolfe's brilliant victory at Quebec.

"In this hurried review I reach now an event of transcendent interest and one far-reaching in its consequences. While our Revolutionary War was in progress, and its glorious termination yet but dimly foreshadowed, General George Rogers Clark planned an expedition whose successful termination has given his name to the list of great conquerors. Bearing the commission of Patrick Henry, Governor of Virginia, the heroic Clark crossed the Ohio and began his perilous march. After enduring untold hardships, the undaunted leader and his little band reached Kaskaskia. The British commander and his garrison were surprised and quickly captured. The British flag was lowered, and on the fourth day of July, 1778, the Illinois country was taken possession of in the name of the Commonwealth whose Governor had authorized the expedition.

"Five years later occurred an event of mighty significance, and of far-reaching consequence—one that in very truth marks the genesis of Illinois history. I refer to the cession by Virginia of the vast area stretching to the Mississippi—of which the spot upon which we are now assembled is a part—to the general Government. To the deed of cession, by which Illinois became a part of the United States, as commissioners upon the part of Virginia, were signed the now historic names of Arthur Lee, James Monroe, and Thomas Jefferson.

"The next milestone of Illinois upon the pathway to statehood was what is so well known in our political history as the Ordinance of 1787. Not inaptly has it been called 'the second Magna Charta,' 'a pillar of cloud by day and of fire by night,' in the settlement and government of the Northwestern States.

Two provisions of the great ordinance possessed a value that cannot be measured by words: One, that the States to be formed out of said territory were to remain forever parts of the United States of America; the other, that neither slavery nor involuntary servitude should exist therein, otherwise than for crime whereof the party should have been duly convicted.

"The value of the great Ordinance to millions who have since found homes within the limits of the vast area embraced within its provision cannot be overstated. Our eyes behold to-day the marvellous results of the far-seeing statesmanship in which it was conceived.

"Momentous events now followed in rapid succession: the disastrous defeat of General St. Clair, first Governor of the Northwest Territory, near the old Miami village; the appointment of General Wayne, hero of Stony Point, to the command of the Western army; his crushing defeat of the Indian foe at the Maumee Rapids, and the treaty of Greenville, which for the time gave protection to the frontiersmen against the savage; the attempt of the French minister, Genet, to create discord in the western country, and in fact to establish a Government in the Mississippi Valley, independent of that of the United States; and the threatened conflict with Spain regarding the free navigation of the Mississippi—all possess an interest to Illinoisans which time cannot abate.

"All apprehension, however, was for the time removed by the treaty between our Government and Spain, by which it was provided that the middle of the Mississippi should be our western border and that the navigation of the entire river to the Gulf should be free to all the people of the United States. Passing over the later faithless attempt of Spain to abrogate this salient provision of the treaty, it is enough that the question was forever put at rest by the purchase by our Government in 1803, for fifteen millions of dollars, from the great Napoleon, of the entire Louisiana country, stretching from the Gulf to the domain of Canada—out of which have been carved sixteen magnificent States, destined to abide and remain forever sovereign parts of our federal Union.

"And while Spain has sustained crushing and retributive defeat and her flag has disappeared forever from mainland and island of the western world, the great river, gathering its tributaries from northern lake to southern sea, flows unvexed through a mighty realm that knows no symbol of authority save only our own Stars and Stripes.

"Illinois was represented for the first time in a legislative chamber in the general assembly of the Northwest Territory, which convened in Cincinnati in 1799. By act of Congress in May, 1800, a new territorial organization was created, by which the territory now embraced in the States of Indiana and Illinois was formed, to be known as 'Indiana Territory,' and the capital located at Vincennes. In February, 1809, by act of Congress, the 'Territory of Illinois' was duly organized, its seat of government established at Kaskaskia. Nine years later—December, 1818—with a population scarcely one-half that of McLean County to-day, it was duly admitted a State of the federal Union.

"Beginning with Illinois at the coming of Joliet and Marquette in the seventeenth century, we have rapidly followed its thread of history for a century and a half, until it became a State of the American Union. We have seen it under the rule of the Frenchman, the Briton, the Virginian, under its various territorial organizations, until eighty-nine years ago it reached the dignity of statehood. We have seen its seat of authority at Quebec, at New Orleans, at Cincinnati, at Vincennes, and finally at Kaskaskia. We have noted something of its marvellous development, of its wonderful increase in population.

"Just one hundred and seven years ago, when by act of Congress Illinois became part of the Indiana Territory, it contained a population of less than two thousand white persons, only eight hundred of whom were of the English-speaking race. Less than two decades later, with a population of less then forty thousand, and an area greater, with a single exception, than any of the original States, we have witnessed its admission to the Union. How marvellous the retrospect at this hour! And yet, 'the pendulum of history swings in centuries in the slow but sure progress of the human race to a higher and nobler civilization.'

"Events of thrilling interest and of scarce less consequence than those already mentioned followed the admission of the State into the Union. In brief summary: The unsuccessful attempt to introduce slavery; the fatal duel between Stewart and Bennet and the trial and execution of the survivor for murder, thereby placing the ban of judicial condemnation upon the barbarous practice; the visit of Lafayette to Illinois and his brilliant entertainment by the Governor and Legislature at the old executive mansion; the removal of the State capital from the ancient French village of Kaskaskia to Vandalia, and near two decades later to Springfield; the memorable contest for Congress between Cook and McLean, each possessing in large measure the rare gift of eloquence, and both dying lamented in early manhood; the organization of two splendid counties that will keep the honored names of Cook and McLean in the memories of men to the latest posterity; the Black Hawk War and the final treaty of peace which followed the defeat and capture of the renowned Sac chief; the riots at Alton and the assassination of the heroic Lovejoy while defending the right of free speech and of a free press; the advent of the prophet Joseph Smith, the rapid growth of the Mormon Church, its power as a political factor in the State, the building of the million-dollar temple at Nauvoo, the murder of the Mormon prophet, and the final exodus of his adherents to the valley of the Wasatch and the Great Salt Lake; the construction of the Illinois and Michigan Canal, the precursor of grander material achievements soon to follow; the bravery of the Illinois troops during the war with Mexico; the wonderful tide of immigration flowing in from the older States and from Europe; the invaluable services of Senator Douglas in securing the celebrated land grant under which the Illinois Central Railroad was constructed, and Chicago brought into commercial touch with the River Ohio and the States to the southward; the dawn of the era of stupendous agricultural development, and of marvellous activity on all lines and through all channels of trade; the wonderful growth of Chicago, springing with giant bound, within the span of a single life, from a mere hamlet to be the second city upon the continent; the unparalleled railroad construction, giving Illinois a greater mileage than any one of her sister States; the immense development of its untold mineral resources, and the advance by leaps and bounds along all lines of manufacturing; the impetus given to the higher conception and purpose of human life by the creation of a splendid system of public schools and universities; the establishment of institutions and asylums for the considerate care and relief of the unfortunate and afflicted of our kind; the building of homes 'for him who hath borne the battle and for his orphan'; the masterful debates between Lincoln and Douglas, the prelude to events destined to give pause to the world, and to change the trend of history. And, to crown all, how, when the nation's life was in peril, Illinois, true to her covenant under the great Ordinance that had given her being, gave one illustrious son to the chief magistracy of his country, another to the captaincy of its armies, and sent her soldier heroes by myriads along every pathway of danger and of glory.

"As one standing, alas, 'upon the western slope,' let me adjure the young men of this magnificent county—my home for more than half a century—to study thoroughly the history of our own State, and of the grand republic of which it is a part. Illinois, in all that constitutes true grandeur in a people, knows no superior among the great sisterhood of States. Her pathway from the beginning has been luminous with noble achievement. It is high privilege and high honor to be a citizen of this grand republic. It is in very truth a government of the people, in an important sense a government standing separate and apart; its foundations the morality, the intelligence, the patriotism of the people. Never forget that citizenship in such a government carries with it tremendous responsibility, a responsibility that we cannot evade.

Study thoroughly how our liberties were achieved, and the benefits of stable government secured by the great compact which for more than a century, in peace and during the storm and stress of war, has held States and people in indissoluble union; and how, during the great civil conflict—the most stupendous the world has known—human liberty, through baptism of blood, obtained a new and grander meaning, and the Union established by our fathers was made, as we humbly trust in God, enduring for all time."